Determinants of Economic Growth in Africa

Almas Heshmati
Editor

Determinants of Economic Growth in Africa

Editor
Almas Heshmati
Department of Economics, Jönköping
 International Business School
Jönköping University
Jönköping, Sweden

and

Department of Economics
Sogang University
Seoul, Korea

ISBN 978-3-319-76492-4   ISBN 978-3-319-76493-1 (eBook)
https://doi.org/10.1007/978-3-319-76493-1

Library of Congress Control Number: 2018933059

© The Editor(s) (if applicable) and The Author(s) 2018
This work is subject to copyright. All rights are solely and exclusively licensed by the Publisher, whether the whole or part of the material is concerned, specifically the rights of translation, reprinting, reuse of illustrations, recitation, broadcasting, reproduction on microfilms or in any other physical way, and transmission or information storage and retrieval, electronic adaptation, computer software, or by similar or dissimilar methodology now known or hereafter developed.
The use of general descriptive names, registered names, trademarks, service marks, etc. in this publication does not imply, even in the absence of a specific statement, that such names are exempt from the relevant protective laws and regulations and therefore free for general use.
The publisher, the authors and the editors are safe to assume that the advice and information in this book are believed to be true and accurate at the date of publication. Neither the publisher nor the authors or the editors give a warranty, express or implied, with respect to the material contained herein or for any errors or omissions that may have been made. The publisher remains neutral with regard to jurisdictional claims in published maps and institutional affiliations.

Cover credit: Eshma/Alamy Stock Photo

Printed on acid-free paper

This Palgrave Macmillan imprint is published by the registered company Springer International Publishing AG part of Springer Nature
The registered company address is: Gewerbestrasse 11, 6330 Cham, Switzerland

Contents

1 Introduction to Determinants of Economic Growth in Africa and Summary of the Contributions 1
Almas Heshmati

Part I Financing Growth

2 The FDI and Economic Growth Controversy in Sub-Saharan Africa 17
Yemane Michael

3 Determinants of Foreign Direct Investment Inflows to Africa 55
Alemayehu Geda and Addis Yimer

4 Impact of Foreign Direct Investment on Economic Growth in Eastern Africa 95
Biratu Bekere and Mekonnen Bersisa

5 The Role of Remittances, FDI and Foreign
   Aid in Economic Growth in Low and Middle
   Income African Countries   125
   Gutu Gutema

6 The Role of Financial Development
   and Institutional Quality in Economic Growth
   in Africa in the Era of Globalization   149
   Kahsay Berhane

Part II Sources of Productivity Growth

7 The Determinants of the Level and Growth
   of Total Factor Productivity in Sub-Saharan Africa   199
   Yemane Michael

8 Human Capital and Economic Growth
   in Developing Countries: Evidences from Low
   and Middle Income African Countries   237
   Jonse Bane

9 Labour Productivity in Kenyan Manufacturing
   and Service Industries   259
   Almas Heshmati and Masoomeh Rashidghalam

Part III Macroeconomic Determinants of Growth

10 Inferences on the Relationship Between Economic
   Growth and the Real Exchange Rate: A Meta-Analysis   289
   Fentahun Baylie

11	The Balance of Trade-Economic Growth Nexus in a Panel of Member Countries of the East African Community *Ferdinand Nkikabahizi, Theogene Rizinde and Mathias Karangwa*	319
12	Modeling the Effect of Food Price Volatility and Transmission to Market Efficiency and Welfare in the East African Community *Jean Baptiste Habyarimana and Tharcisse Nkunzimana*	345

Author Index — 373

Subject Index — 385

Contributors

Jonse Bane Department of Economics, Addis Ababa University, Addis Ababa, Ethiopia

Fentahun Baylie Department of Economics, Addis Ababa University, Addis Ababa, Ethiopia

Biratu Bekere Department of Development Economics, Bole Campus, Rift Valley University, Addis Ababa, Ethiopia

Kahsay Berhane Department of Economics, Addis Ababa University, Addis Ababa, Ethiopia

Mekonnen Bersisa Department of Economics, Addis Ababa University, Addis Ababa, Ethiopia

Alemayehu Geda Department of Economics, College of Business and Economics, Addis Ababa University, Addis Ababa, Ethiopia

Gutu Gutema Department of Economics, Addis Ababa University, Addis Ababa, Ethiopia

Jean Baptiste Habyarimana Department of Economics, University of Rwanda, Kigali, Rwanda

Almas Heshmati Department of Economics, Sogang University, Seoul, Korea; Jönköping International Business School, Jönköping University, Jönköping, Sweden

Mathias Karangwa National Bank of Rwanda, Kigali, Rwanda

Yemane Michael Department of Economics, College of Business and Economics, Addis Ababa University, Addis Ababa, Ethiopia; University of Gondar, Gondar, Ethiopia

Ferdinand Nkikabahizi School of Economics, University of Rwanda, College of Business and Economics, Butare, Rwanda

Tharcisse Nkunzimana Joint Research Centre (JRC/European Commission), Ispra, Italy

Masoomeh Rashidghalam Department of Agricultural Economics, University of Tabriz, Tabriz, Iran

Theogene Rizinde School of Economics, Department of Statistics, University of Rwanda, College of Business and Economics, Butare, Rwanda

Addis Yimer Department of Economics, College of Business and Economics, Addis Ababa University, Addis Ababa, Ethiopia

Abbreviations

2SLS	Two-Stage Least Square
3SLS	Three Stage Least Squares
ADB	African Development Bank
AERC	African Economic Research Consortium
AIC	Akaike Information Criterion
AR	Autocorrelation
AR	Adverse Redistribution
ARDL	Autoregressive Distributed Lag
BMI	Broad Market Index
CADF	Cross-Sectional Augmented Dickey-Fuller
CCE	Common Correlated Effects
CES	Constant Elasticity of Substitution
CMA	Comprehensive Meta-Analysis
CRS	Constant Returns to Scale
DEA	Data Envelopment Analysis
EAC	East African Community
ECT	Error Correction Term
ES	Enterprise Survey
FAO	Food and Agriculture Organization
FD-GMM	First Difference Generalized Method of Moment
FDI	Foreign Direct Investment

FE	Fixed Effects
FEM	Fixed Effects Model
GCF	Gross Capital Formation
GDP	Gross Domestic Production
GFCF	Gross Fixed Capital Formation
GLS	Generalized Least Square
GMM	Generalized Method of Moments
HC	Human Capital
ICT	Information and Communication Technology
IMF	International Monetary Fund
LDC	Least Developed Countries
LM	Lagrange-Multiplier
MENA	Middle East and North America
MIS	Market Information Services
MNC	Multinational Corporations
MNE	Multinational Enterprises
MSE	Mean Squared Error
NGO	Non-Governmental Organization
ODA-to-GDP	Official Development Assistance-to-GDP
OECD	Organization for Economic Co-operation and Development
OLS	Ordinary Least Squares
PCA	Principal Component Analysis
PMG	Pooled Mean Group
PMG-CCE	PMG estimator with a Common Correlated Effects Correction
PPP	Purchasing Power Parity
PRS	Country Risk Guide
PVAR	Panel Vector Autoregressive
R&D	Research and Development
S&P	Standard and Poor
SACU	Southern Africa Custom Union
SDG	Sustainable Development Goal
SF	Syndrome-Free
SPVAR	Spatial Panel Vector Autoregressive
SSA	Sub-Saharan African
TFP	Total Factor Productivity
UNDP	United Nations Development Program

VECM	Vector Error Correction Model
WDI	World Development Indicator
WGI	Worldwide Governance Indicator

List of Figures

Chapter 2
Fig. 1   Net FDI inflows as a percentage of GDP to various regions in the world (*Source* Based on the WDI database)   22

Chapter 3
Fig. 1   Summary of literature on an analytical basis for classifications   70

Chapter 4
Fig. 1   Net inflows of foreign direct investment (1996–2015)   114

Chapter 6
Fig. 1   Financial development indicators by income group for 40 African countries (*Source* Author's calculation based on the International Monetary Fund (IMF))   160
Fig. 2   World governance indicators by income group for 40 African countries (1996–2014) (*Source* Author's calculations based on the WGI dataset obtained from the World Bank—control of corruption, political stability

and absence of violence/terrorism, rule of law, government effectiveness, regulatory quality and voice and accountability) ... 161

Chapter 10
Fig. 1 Funnel plot of 45 sample studies (*Source* Author's computation) ... 306
Fig. 2 Funnel plot of sample studies including missing studies (*Source* Author's computation) ... 307

Chapter 12
Fig. 1 Cereal production versus population (*Source* Own computation from data sourced from the FAO database) ... 347
Fig. 2 Average yield and area harvested (*Source* Own computation from data sourced from the FAO database) ... 348
Fig. 3 EAC production of the total world (*Source* Own computation from data sourced from the FAO database) ... 348
Fig. 4 Use of cereals (*Source* Own computation from data sourced from the FAO database) ... 349
Fig. 5 Supply of cereals in EAC (*Source* Own computation from data sourced from the FAO database) ... 349
Fig. 6 Trends in food price and indices (*Source* Own computation from data sourced from the FAO database) ... 350
Fig. 7 Without spatial effects ... 360
Fig. 8 With spatial effects ... 360
Fig. 9 Without spatial effects ... 360
Fig. 10 With spatial effects ... 361
Fig. 11 Without spatial effects ... 361
Fig. 12 With spatial effects ... 362
Fig. 13 Without spatial effects ... 362
Fig. 14 With spatial effects ... 363
Fig. 15 Without spatial effects ... 363
Fig. 16 With spatial effects ... 364

List of Tables

Chapter 2

Table 1	Net FDI inflows as a percentage of GDP in various regions of the world (*Source* Author's calculations based on the World Development Indicators (2016) database)	22
Table 2	Two-sample *t*-test of GDP per capita growth of resource-rich and resource-poor countries with unequal variance	31
Table 3	Two-sample *t*-test of FDI inflow to resource-poor and resource-rich countries with unequal variance	31
Table 4	Estimating the GDP growth rate per capita using various forms of difference GMM	34
Table 5	Estimation of the GDP growth rate per capita using various forms of system GMM	36
Table 6	Estimating the GDP growth rate per capita for SSA using different methods (2001–2015)	42
Table 7	'Three-Year Average' Estimation results of GDP growth rate per capita using various forms of static panel data models	45

Chapter 3

Table 1	FDI flows by region in 2011–2014 (US$ billion) (*Source* UNCTAD (2014))	56
Table 2	Result of recent empirical studies on major determinants of FDI flows to Africa (and other developing countries)	64
Table 3	Results of the FDI model	83
Table 4	An alternative proposed country classification of African Economies	87
Table 5	Final analytical country classification for the model	88

Chapter 4

Table 1	Summary statistics of share of FDI in GDP by country (*Source* Authors' computation using Stata 13)	113
Table 2	Panel unit root test for all variables (*Source* Authors' computation using Stata 13)	114
Table 3	Autocorrelation test of variables	115
Table 4	Cross-sectional dependence test (*Source* Authors' computation using Stata 13)	116
Table 5	Cointegration test of FDI and GDPGR (*Source* Authors' computation using Stata 13)	116
Table 6	Long run causal relationship between FDI and GDPGR (*Source* Authors' computation using Stata 13. Eview 9)	116
Table 7	Effects of independent variables on GDP growth rate (*Source* Authors' computation using Stata 13)	117
Table 8	Relationships between FDI and its determinants (*Source* Authors' computation using Stata 13)	119

Chapter 5

Table 1	Descriptive statistics for African countries	134
Table 2	Growth regression using the system GMM	136
Table 3	Foreign direct investment regression using the system GMM	138
Table 4	Official development assistance regression using the system GMM	140
Table 5	Official development assistance regression using the system GMM	141
Table 6	Low and middle income African countries	145

Chapter 6

Table 1	Description of symbols, definitions of variables and data source	157
Table 2	Pair-wise correlation of important variables for the all 40 African countries	159
Table 3	Results of Pesaran's (2004) cross-sectional dependence test by income category	174
Table 4	Pesaran's (2007) Panel Unit Root test results for the full sample of countries	176
Table 5	Co-integration tests by income category	178
Table 6	Long run and short run estimation following the error correction model	179
Table 7	Estimates of pooled mean group model with common correlated effects correction, for entire sample of 40 African countries	181
Table 8	Estimates of dynamic common correlated effects by income level	182
Table 9	List of countries	187
Table 10	Hausman test on the MG and PMG models	188

Chapter 7

Table 1	Estimation results of the level of TFP using various forms of system GMM	217
Table 2	Estimation of TFP growth using a GMM model with various lags of the dependent and explanatory variables as internal instruments (dependent variable: TFP growth)	219
Table 3	Robustness check of the TFP level using deeper lags of the dependent and explanatory variables as internal instruments (dependent variable: TFP level)	220
Table 4	Robustness check of TFP growth using deeper lags of the dependent and explanatory variables as internal instruments (dependent variable: TFP growth)	221
Table 5	Estimation results of the level of TFP using various methods (2001–2015)	222

Chapter 8

Table 1	Definitions and descriptive statistics of variables used in regression analyses (1985–2015) (*Source* Author's computation based on the WDI database)	246

Table 2	Role of human capital in economic growth (Dependent variable—log of GDP)	249
Table 3	Determinants of health human capital (Dependent variable—log of health expenditure)	252
Table 4	Determinants of education human capital (Dependent variable—log of education expenditure)	254

Chapter 9

Table 1	Summary statistics of key variables in the Kenyan manufacturing and services enterprise data (2013), $N = 670$	272
Table 2	Summary statistics by firm characteristics and infrastructure in Kenyan manufacturing and services enterprise data (2013), $N = 670$	273
Table 3	Correlation matrix of the variables, $N = 670$	276
Table 4	Ordinary least squares parameter estimates (with robust standard errors) of labour productivity, $N = 670$	278
Table 5	F-tests for alternative model specifications	280

Chapter 10

Table 1	List of proposed moderators by different criteria (*Source* DeCoster 2004)	302
Table 2	Test of inclusion for categorical and continuous moderators (*Source* Author's computation)	303
Table 3	Summary statistics of sample studies (45) (*Source* Author's computation)	303
Table 4	Descriptive statistics of effect sizes (*Source* Author's own computation)	304
Table 5	Meta-regression results (excluding irrelevant moderators) (*Source* Author's computation)	305
Table 6	Meta-regression results (excluding insignificant moderators) (*Source* Author's computation)	305
Table 7	Point estimates adjusted for publication bias	308
Table 8	Correlation coefficients of relevant moderators	310
Table 9	Regression results (including all moderators)	310
Table 10	Joint test of publication bias	311
Table 11	Tests of publication bias	311

Chapter 11
Table 1	Panel unit root tests	335
Table 2	Estimation results for all models including all variables	337
Table 3	Correlation matrix of residuals	338

Chapter 12
Table 1	Descriptive statistics	353
Table 2	Pearson product-moment correlation coefficients	354
Table 3	Pesaran (2007) Panel unit root test (CIPS)	354
Table 4	Estimation results of PVAR and SPVAR	358
Table 5	Variance decomposition	364

1

Introduction to Determinants of Economic Growth in Africa and Summary of the Contributions

Almas Heshmati

1 Background and Motivation

A major policy challenge facing African countries is how to achieve and sustain a higher rate of economic growth that will help them reduce poverty while also being both socially inclusive and environmentally sustainable (Acemoglu 2009; Barro 1997; Barro and Sala-i-Martin 2004; Heshmati et al. 2015; Kim and Heshmati 2014; Tausch and Heshmati 2012; and others). The other challenges facing the continent include the rapidly increasing population and its ageing, rapid urbanization, increasing need for construction of urban infrastructure, providing services, recovering from the recent global economic crisis, corruption and inefficiency of governance and urgency in responding to climate

---

A. Heshmati (✉)
Department of Economics, Sogang University, Seoul, Korea

A. Heshmati
Jönköping International Business School, Jönköping University, Jönköping, Sweden

© The Author(s) 2018
A. Heshmati (ed.), *Determinants of Economic Growth in Africa*,
https://doi.org/10.1007/978-3-319-76493-1_1

change (AfDB 2016 and 2017; Belshaw and Livingstone 2002; Binns et al. 2012; Chitonge 2014; Johnson 2016; Ndudu et al. 2008; Robson and Lury 2011).

Against this background, the Jönköping International Business School in cooperation with some African national universities like the University of Rwanda and Addis Ababa University organize yearly conferences on economic development in the region. This volume is a collection of selected empirical studies on determinants of economic growth in Africa. Several of its papers were selected from those presented at a conference on *Recent Trends in Economic Development, Finance and Management Research in Eastern Africa* held at Kigali, Rwanda, on 14–16 June 2017. These selected papers are further complemented by other invited studies. Following the review process and revisions, 11 papers were finally accepted for publication in this edited volume.

The core argument for compiling this book is providing an up-to-date picture of the state and pattern of economic growth and development in Africa; the focus of attention is on the periods both before and after the global economic crisis. A main contribution of this volume is identifying important determinants of growth and development on the continent and estimating their effects using up-to-date standardized data, modelling and estimation methods. The studies jointly provide a comprehensive picture of the state of economic growth, its measurement, the causal relationships between the key determinants and efficient policies and practices for achieving progress on the African continent as a whole and also in selected groups of developing countries.

Growth rates vary in these countries and the low rates in some of them represent major challenges to governments and organizations whose aim is achieving higher growth and alleviating deep rooted chronic poverty in certain countries and regions.

This volume has contributions from 16 authors. The studies are grouped into three domains that influence financial sources and economic growth; sources of productivity growth; and the relationships of prices, exchange rates and trade with growth in regions in Africa or on the continent as a whole. The studies provide a comprehensive picture of the state of growth, its measurement and causal factors. They investigate heterogeneity by individual countries and efficient policies and practices in growth and poverty reduction on the African continent as a whole and also in selected countries. Variations in growth rates are high in these countries which pose major challenges for governments and international organizations whose aim is achieving economic growth and alleviating poverty. The results can have strong implications for economic growth and poverty reduction policies.

For several decades Swedish International Development Cooperation Agency (SIDA) has contributed to higher education and research in Africa. This volume is an addition to books edited in recent years on the subject as a part of the series. These books are the output of recent years of financial support from SIDA to collaborative higher educational programs and research capacity building in a number of African countries. This support has resulted in the publication of a number of academic books related to poverty and well-being (Heshmati 2016a), entrepreneurship and SME management (Achtenhagen and Brundin 2016), economic integration and currency (Heshmati 2016b), economic growth and development (Heshmati 2017a), poverty reduction (Heshmati 2017b), management challenges in different types of firms (Achtenhagen and Brundin 2017) and entrepreneurship in developing countries (Ramirez-Pacillias et al. 2017). Altogether, these studies have improved our understanding of the process of economic development and growth and the challenges facing African countries.

2   Summary of Individual Studies on Economic Growth in Africa

This volume is a collection of selected empirical studies on determinants of economic growth and development in Africa. The volume has 12 chapters (one introduction/summary and 11 contributory chapters) contributed by 16 experts specializing in the fields of growth and development. The studies are grouped into three domains that influence financing growth; sources of productivity growth; and macroeconomic determinants of growth with growth in regions in Africa or on the continent as a whole.

2.1 Part I: Financing Growth

This first part of this edited volume has 5 chapters on foreign direct investment (FDI), remittances, foreign aid inflows, the role of financial development and institutional quality and their impact on economic growth in Africa.

The first study (Chapter 2) by Yemane Michael, *The FDI and economic growth controversy in sub-Saharan Africa*, analyzes the impact of FDI on economic growth in 43 sub-Saharan African (SSA) countries for the period 2001–2015. It develops a dynamic system generalized method of moment (GMM) model to capture the impact of FDI on economic growth. The method takes care of endogeneity problems and it alleviates possible biases in estimation and accounts for time-invariant individual country heterogeneity. The study finds that there was no meaningful difference in the growth of per capita gross domestic product (GDP) and also in its ability to attract FDI inflows. The findings indicate that FDI had a negative and statistically significant effect on the growth rate of per capita GDP in SSA for the period under consideration.

The second study (Chapter 3) by Alemayehu Geda and Addis Yimer, *Determinants of FDI inflows to Africa*, identifies the main determinants of FDI inflows to Africa. Using a panel cointegration approach for the period 1996–2012 it finds that market size, availability of natural resources, openness to trade, a stable macroeconomic environment, better infrastructure and an effective bureaucracy had a strong positive impact on attracting FDI to Africa while political and macroeconomic instability and high financial and transfer risks had a negative effect on attracting FDI to the continent. The effects of these factors varied across the newly developed analytical country classification. Hence, the new classification scheme could be an important guide in the working of continental organizations.

The third study (Chapter 4) by Biratu Bekere and Mekonnen Bersisa, *Impact of FDI on economic growth in Eastern Africa*, indicates that the FDI and economic growth nexus is an intensely debated issue in developing countries. For East Africa a fundamental challenge is how to achieve a sustainable increase in output over time. The countries in this part of the continent have been attracting FDI to bridge the gaps between domestic savings and investment demands; generating foreign exchange; transferring technology; and enhancing job creation and human capital skills to achieve sustainable economic growth and development. The study examines the impact of FDI on economic growth and its determinants in 14 sub-Saharan African countries over 20 years. It employs the dynamic GMM estimator for the data analysis. Empirical evidence reveals that FDI had a positive effect on economic growth in the region. However, while attracting FDI the countries need to take care of its nature and composition.

The fourth study (Chapter 5) by Gutu Gutema, *The role of remittances, FDI and foreign aid on economic growth of low- and middle-income African countries*, investigates the relative contribution of FDI, net official development aid (ODA) and personal remittances to economic growth in 50 African countries during 1985–2015. It uses the system GMM approach and analyzes the effect of these three external factors by categorizing African countries into low- and middle-income countries. The results show that the three factors had a positive impact on the economic growth of low-income countries but none of them were significant determinants of economic growth in middle-income countries. Gross capital formation had a positive and significant effect on both country groups. Financial depth, expenditure on education and population growth had a positive effect on economic growth in middle-income countries. Openness positively affected economic growth while the inflation rate negatively affected economic growth in low-income countries. The findings suggest the need for promoting policies that encourage remittances, foreign aid and FDI for enhancing economic growth in low-income countries.

The fifth study (Chapter 6) by Kahsay Berhane, *The role of financial development and institutional quality on economic growth in Africa in the era of globalization*, examines the short- and long-run impact of financial development, institutional quality and globalization on economic growth for a sample of 40 African countries. It examines whether the relationships differed across the sub-groups of low-income, lower-middle-income and upper-middle-income countries over the period 1980–2014. It uses a new technique in macro-econometrics panel estimation to control for dynamic heterogeneity and cross-sectional dependence. The findings show that the presence of cross-sectional dependence, non-stationarity and cointegration had a long-run relationship with the variables. The results also show that financial development, institutional quality and globalization had positive effects on long-run economic growth for the entire sample of countries.

The findings of most of these studies imply that African countries need to reform their macroeconomic policies to attain improved macroeconomic performance and for strengthening their macroeconomic stability. Moreover, African countries should not only focus on investments in physical capital but also make efforts to put in place a framework that enables them to achieve high-quality growth enhancing investments.

2.2 Part II: Sources of Productivity Growth

Part II contains 3 chapters which analyze the sources of productivity growth. The studies cover human capital, growth of total factor productivity in Africa and single labor factor productivity in Kenya.

The first study in this part (Chapter 7) by Yemane Michael, *The determinants of the level and growth of TFP in SSA*, investigates the determinants of total factor productivity (TFP) in 43 sub-Saharan African countries for the period 2001–2015. The study looks at past literature to explain SSA's growth slumber and conundrum. It uses the system GMM's linear dynamic panel data model to estimate the model. The empirical findings show that the lagged value of TFP, gross capital formation and macroeconomic stability positively and significantly affected TFP while FDI and imports had no effect on TFP. The study also incorporates other variables of growth determinants in the models with varying effects and signs. Its results show that an improvement in TFP will put SSA on a trajectory of sustained growth.

The next study (Chapter 8) by Jonse Bane, *Human capital and economic growth in developing countries: Evidence from low- and middle-income African countries*, examines the impact of flow and stock of human capital measured in terms of education and health on economic growth in 52 low- and middle-income African countries using dynamic GMM estimation techniques. The study uses panel data over the period 1985–2015. The findings reveal that investments in education and health human capital positively and significantly affected economic growth in low- and middle-income countries where health investments had stronger effects in both the country groups. Similarly, in low-income countries the stock of human capital measured by life expectancy positively affected income growth, which is in line with previous findings in Asia. However, stock of health and human capital had no significant effect on economic growth in middle-income countries. Other control variables like net FDI inflows, openness, inflation and domestic credit affected income growth in low-income countries while in middle-income countries only inflation and domestic credit affected income growth.

The third study in this part (Chapter 9) by Almas Heshmati and Masoomeh Rashidghalam, *Labor productivity in Kenyan manufacturing and service industries*, analyzes single factor labor productivity which reflects a firm's ability to generate higher production or value-added. The study analyzes labor productivity and its determinants in the manufacturing and service sectors in Kenya. Using the World Bank's Enterprise Survey database for 2013, it finds that capital intensity and wage positively affected labor productivity. A higher share of women in the labor force reduced labor productivity. The study also finds that training and education were associated with higher labor productivity. Reliance on modern communication technologies had a positive but insignificant impact on firms' labor productivity. On the basis of these observations the study makes a number of recommendations to promote higher productivity of labor.

2.3 Part III: Macroeconomic Determinants of Growth

Part III has 3 chapters that analyze the relationship between economic growth and real exchange rate, balance of trade and economic growth and the effects of food price volatility and transmission on market efficiency and welfare in East Africa.

The first study in this part (Chapter 10) by Fentahun Baylie, *Inferences on the relationship between economic growth and the real exchange rate: A meta-analysis*, looks for empirical evidence on the Balassa effect. The Balassa effect represents the coefficient of the productivity growth variable in a relationship between productivity growth and the real exchange rate. A meta-analysis of 45 previous studies shows a large significant magnitude of the Balassa effect under a random-effects model after correction for publication bias. The results show that 79 percent of the effect of change in productivity growth was directly transmitted to the real exchange rate. About 64 percent of the variations in effect size were accounted for by differences in sample size, parameters and the estimation method. Policymakers should be aware of the impact of productivity growth on the real exchange rate while promoting a policy of rapid economic growth.

The next study (Chapter 11) by Ferdinand Nkikabahizi, Theogene Rizinde and Mathias Karangwa, *Balance of trade-economic growth nexus in a panel of East Africa community countries*, examines the relationship between balance of trade and economic growth in the countries in the East African Community (EAC) for the period 1991–2015. It obtains data on GDP growth, exports, imports, balance of trade, gross capital formation, FDI, exchange rate and labor force participation rates from the World Bank's World Development Indicators dataset. The results of the Hausman test indicate that there was no systematic difference between both fixed and random effects models. Further, exports, labor force, capital formation and FDI were positively associated with real GDP in the five EAC countries. In short, they were key pillars of a growing economy in the region under study which means that an increase in these variables led to an increase in real GDP. Similarly, an increase in the remaining variables (imports, balance of trade and exchange rate) led to a decrease in real GDP.

The third study in this part (Chapter 12) by Jean-Baptiste Habyarimana and Tharcisse Nkunzimana, *Modeling the effect of food price volatility and transmission on market efficiency and welfare in the East African Community*, investigates the effect of food price volatility and transmission on welfare and efficiency in EAC. The results show that it takes time for spatial effects to influence market prices. They also show that price volatility and transmission are more predictable in models accounting for spatial effects. The results of the variance decomposition analysis show that variations caused by a one-unit shock in the price of cereals in one market created strong variations in the prices of cereals in the other markets across EAC. The study suggests that agricultural policies should focus on ensuring crop yield stability and enhancing regional food distribution systems for stabilizing food prices and reducing food market inefficiencies across EAC. Trade policies should be formulated considering the gains of trading with near-neighboring markets to avoid delayed spatial effects on price volatility and transmission.

3 Result Divergence and Growth Controversy

The anonymous review of the manuscript led to suggestions in four key areas: First, Chapters 11 and 12 do not seem to fit into the structure and hence the reviewers asked for explanations in this chapter. Second, they suggest that the introduction needs to clearly explain growth theory in the context of the book and to outline why these given studies have been chosen. Third, they suggest that at some point in the book an up-to-date picture of growth and development in Africa relating to both the pre- and post-financial crisis periods, needs to be presented. Fourth, the book needs to say why certain determinants that are important for growth elsewhere or that should be important for growth in Africa have not been very important in Africa. Responses to these suggestions are now provided.

As mentioned previously, the main objective of the book is addressing the question: what is the significance of certain factors/variables which have been found to be important in the economic growth of countries worldwide in determining economic growth in African countries? In addressing this question, the main factors/variables selected by the authors of the book are: foreign direct investments, remittances, foreign aid, financial development, institutional quality, human capital and the real exchange rate. Given its objective, the book helps provide a picture of growth conditions and its determinant factors in Africa. In sum, the different studies suggest positive and relatively high growth rate in recent years. However, the growth is not inclusive and its distribution is unequal across countries and among urban-rural and regional dimensions. A major contribution of the book is the use of consistent data as well as current analytical tools. This will make the text attractive to students, researchers and policymakers.

The first key area is related to the relevance and fit of Chapters 11 and 12 in the structure of the book. Chapter 11 looks at trade and growth, which have implications for the analyses in earlier chapters. Similarities and differences can be accounted for by cross-referencing. However, this was not possible prior to the chapter submissions. Chapter 12 responds to some of the issues raised earlier—the welfare impacts of growth. It is acknowledged that growth does not enhance social welfare, especially of the poor majority and as such is not sustainable. In sum, both chapters are important determinants of economic growth. Their inclusion is justified by the welfare effects of inclusive and sustainable growth.

With regard to the second key issue the reviewers suggest that the introduction needs to clearly explain growth theory in the context of the book and in familiar terms, and to outline why the studies included in the book were chosen. Several chapters in the book are from papers presented at international conference at the University of Rwanda International Scientific Conference Week, 14–16 June 2017 while the remaining are invited papers to form a suitable and comprehensive book manuscript. The issue of growth theory, models and estimation are determined by individual authors.

Third, they suggest that at some point in the book the up-to-date picture of growth and development in Africa relating to both the pre- and post-financial crisis periods needs to be presented. The introduction provides a summary of the different contributions and their complementary relationships. Explanations for the growth theory, the sources of the research, motivations for the choices and growth and development in Africa are provided in individual chapters. Several of the studies attempt to explain growth by its determinants including institutions, governance and regulation effects.

Fourth, it is suggested that the book needs to say why certain determinants that are important for growth elsewhere or that should be important for growth in Africa have not been very important in Africa. As an example, Chapter 2 refers to results that FDI had a negative and significant impact on growth which is a controversial result. It is suggested that the authors must look at studies pointing in the opposite direction and try to explain this divergence. It is true that the finding of a negative relationship between FDI and growth in Chapter 2 may sound controversial. However, such controversies are not new in growth literature. A well-known example is the general switching from commonly employed import substitution policies to trade liberalization.

This book manuscript tries to provide sound explanations for the possible divergences. The results of Chapter 4 on East Africa show that FDI was positive for growth which is contradicts the results of Chapter 2. The two opposing results can be explained by an East African dummy because the region is more integrated than others. However, it will not be possible to combine the two chapters, and neither will it be correct to drop the one with diverging results. The divergence in the effects of FDI on economic growth can be attributed to factors like data and definitions, model specification and estimation methods.

The anonymous reviewers' critical observations and their recommendations are highly appreciated. I and the authors have done our outmost to explain discrepancies from expected effects. The sources of such deviations from expected results may be found in factors including data, modelling, estimation methods and analyses of the results. Special care was taken in the analyses of the results. Again, unexpected results will lead to new research which will reconfirm or reject the unexpected results leading to improvements in our analyses and understandings of economic growth and its determinants in Africa.

4 Final Words and Recommendations

This edited volume adds value to the growing literature on economic growth in Africa. The primary market for this volume is wide and includes undergraduate and graduate students, lecturers, researchers, public and private institutions, NGOs, international aid agencies and national and regional decision makers. The book can serve as complementary reading to texts on economic growth, development, investment, welfare and poverty in Africa. The organizers of the annual conference on economic development in East Africa will market the book at their annual East Africa conferences.

There are several books on development and growth in Africa which were mostly published in earlier years and were written by non-Africans. The novelty of this volume is that it is an up-to-date study of the African economy which is written exclusively by African researchers. Hence, this volume will be an updated addition to existing literature on the African economy.

This edited book is authored by African experts in the field who employ diverse up-to-date data and methods to provide robust empirical results based on representative firms, household surveys and secondary country level data covering individuals or multiple countries on the continent. It contains a wealth of empirical evidence, deep analyses and sound recommendations for policymakers and researchers for designing and implementing effective social and national policies and strategies to prevent and to reduce poverty and its negative effects on poor households and in poor regions. The volume will be a useful resource for policymakers and researchers involved in promoting economic growth and fighting poverty. It will also appeal to a broader audience interested in economic development, resource economics, policies, economic welfare and inclusive growth.

The Editor of the volume is grateful to a host of dedicated authors, rigorous referees and conference participants who helped in assessing the submitted papers. Many were presenters at the 2017 conference at the University of Rwanda. Special thanks go to Bideri Ishuheri Nyamulinda, Rama Rao and Lars Hartvigson for their efforts in organizing the conference. The Editor would also like to thank Rachel Sangster, Palgrave Macmillan Head of Economics and Finance, for guidance and assessing the manuscript for publication. Financial support by the Swedish International Development Cooperation Agency (SIDA) to organize the conference is gratefully acknowledged.

References

Acemoglu, D. (2009). *Introduction to Modern Economic Growth*. New Jersey: Princeton University Press.

Achtenhagen, L. and E. Brundin (eds.) (2016). *Entrepreneurship and SME Management Across Africa: Context, Challenges, Cases*. Singapore: Springer.

Achtenhagen, L. and E. Brundin (eds.) (2017). *Management Challenges in Different Types of African Firms: Processes, Practices and Performance*. Singapore: Springer.

AfDB (2016). *Africa Economic Outlook 2016: Sustainable Cities and Structural Transformation*. Abidjan: African Development Bank Group.

AfDB (2017). *Africa Economic Outlook 2017: Entrepreneurship and Industrialization*. Abidjan: African Development Bank Group.

Barro, R.J. (1997). *Determinants of Growth: A Cross Country Empirical Study*. Cambridge, MA: MIT Press.

Barro, R.J. and X. Sala-i-Martin (2004). *Economic Growth*. 2nd edition. Cambridge, MA: MIT Press.

Belshaw, D. and I. Livingstone (2002). *Renewing Development in Sub-Saharan Africa: Policy, Performance, and Prospects*. London: Routledge.

Binns, T., A. Dixon, and E. Nel (2012). *Africa: Diversity and Development*. London: Routledge.

Chitonge, H. (2014). *Economic Growth and Development in Africa: Understanding Trends and Prospects*. London: Routledge.

Heshmati, A. (ed.) (2016a). *Poverty and Well-Being in East Africa: A Multifaceted Economic Approach*. Singapore: Springer.

Heshmati, A. (ed.) (2016b). *Economic Integration, Currency Union, and Sustainable and Inclusive Growth in East Africa*. Singapore: Springer.

Heshmati, A. (ed.) (2017a). *Studies on Economic Development and Growth in Selected African Countries*. Singapore: Springer.

Heshmati, A. (ed.) (2017b). *Economic Transformation for Poverty Reduction in Africa: A Multidimensional Approach*. London: Routledge.

Heshmati, A., E. Maasoumi, and G. Wan (eds.) (2015). *Poverty Reduction Policies and Practices in Developing Asia*. Singapore: Springer.

Johnson, O.E.G. (2016). *Economic Diversification and Growth in Africa: Critical Policy Making Issues*. London: Palgrave Macmillan.

Kim, T.Y. and A. Heshmati (2014). *Economic Growth: The New Perspectives for Theory and Policy*. Singapore: Springer.

Ndudu, B.J., S.A. O'Connell, R.H. Bates, P. Collier, and C.C. Soludo (eds.) (2008). *Political Economy of Growth in Africa, 1960–2000*. Cambridge: Cambridge University Press.

Ramirez-Pacillias, M., E. Brundin, and M. Markowska (2017). *Contextualizing Entrepreneurship in Emerging Economies and Developing Countries*. London: Edward Elgar.

Robson, P. and D.A. Lury (2011). *The Economies of Africa*. London: Routledge.

Tausch, A. and A. Heshmati (2012). *Globalization, the Human Condition and Sustainable Development in the 21st Century: Cross-National Perspectives and European Implications*. London: Anthem Press.

Part I
Financing Growth

2

The FDI and Economic Growth Controversy in Sub-Saharan Africa

Yemane Michael

1 Introduction

There is no unanimity among scholars and academicians when it comes to defining foreign direct investment (FDI). Several studies define FDI as an investment made by a company or individual based in one country in business interests in another country in the form of either establishing business operations or acquiring business assets in the other country such as ownership or having a controlling interest in a foreign company. FDI is distinguished from portfolio investments in which an investor merely purchases equities of foreign-based companies. The key feature of FDI is that it is an investment that establishes either effective control of, or at least substantial influence over, the decision making of a foreign business.

Y. Michael (✉)
Department of Economics, College of Business and Economics,
Addis Ababa University, Addis Ababa, Ethiopia

Y. Michael
University of Gondar, Gondar, Ethiopia

UNCTAD (2014) in its World Investment Report defines FDI as the net inflow of investment to acquiring long lasting management interest in an enterprise operating in an economy other than that of the investor.

The World Development Report (2016) asserts that global FDI flows increased by about 40 percent to $1.8 trillion, the highest level since the global economic and financial crisis in 2008. However, this growth did not translate into an equivalent expansion in productive capacity in all the countries. The report goes on to say that such a scenario is troubling because of the huge investment requirements to meet the targets of the newly adopted sustainable development goals (SDGs) and the ambitious action envisaged in the landmark Paris Agreement on climate change. To this end, the Addis Ababa Action Agenda calls for reorienting the national and international investment regimes towards sustainable development.

The differences in findings regarding the impact of FDI on a host country's economy is due to estimation methods, types of data (cross-sectional, time series or panel) used in the analysis, the unit of analysis (country, industry or firm) and the explanatory variables used in the models. For example, most cross-sectional studies usually report a positive nexus between FDI and economic growth. They also find positive spillover effects of FDI on domestic firms. However, panel data studies that can account for cross-country differences in technology, institutions, geography, policies and other socioeconomic factors do not produce any robust evidence to support a positive relationship between FDI and growth. Nor do they find any strong evidence to justify any positive spillovers from FDI to firms.

Our study differs from other similar studies done in some important ways. First, it applies the dynamic panel system GMM to assess the effect of FDI on economic growth in SSA. The choice of the dynamic panel system GMM is not haphazard and is not without purpose. It is superior to other models in that it takes care of endogeneity, autocorrelation and heterogeneity problems and alleviates possible biases in estimation. Besides, it provides a solution to the problems associated with time-invariant individual heterogeneity among others.

Our study's contribution is two-fold. Methodologically, it employs the dynamic panel system GMM which has been rarely used in an analysis of the impact of FDI on economic growth. However, this does not mean that the author is a pioneer of the methodology. Practically, the research contributes to the small but burgeoning literature on FDI in economic growth in SSA.

The overarching objective of our paper is to empirically investigate the impact of FDI on economic growth in SSA countries for which relevant macroeconomic data is available for the period 2001–2015. Starting with 2001 is not arbitrary. Empirical evidence by Buckley (2003) and Kamara (2013) indicates that FDI inflows to SSA showed an upsurge from the turn of the new millennium. This tremendous increase was mainly because of the improved macroeconomic environment on the continent which boosted FDI inflows. The *Economist* that once dubbed Africa as a 'dark continent' has done a U-turn and in 2011 called it a 'rising continent.' The change in SSA's fortunes coincided with a surge in FDI.

It is difficult to make any robust conclusion on the impact of FDI on economic growth in SSA from existing studies. Specifically, our paper contributes to the current debate on FDI and economic growth.

2   Literature Review

FDI's role in economic growth is highly contentious and controversial when viewed from both flanks of theoretical and empirical literature. The differences between theoretical and empirical literature regarding FDI are blurred and murky. Thus, we only review empirical literature.

Theoretically, there is widespread consensus about FDI's positive contributions to economic growth. However, empirical findings on this issue are inconclusive and controversial. Some empirical evidence reveals that FDI is crucial for economic growth. Others argue that the effect of FDI depends on the degree of complementarity and substitutability between FDI and domestic investments, macroeconomic stability, the institutional and legal framework, knowledge and human capital, trade openness and other socioeconomic and demographic characteristics (Agrawal 2011, 2015; Alege and Ogundipe 2013; Beugelsdijk and Zwinkels 2008; Lamine 2010; Sala and Trivin 2014). Generally, the results of the empirical evidence contradict one another.

Suleiman et al. (2013) using dynamic ordinary least squares for the Southern Africa Custom Union (SACU) countries of Botswana, Lesotho, Namibia, South Africa and Swaziland found that FDI's impact on economic growth was positive and significant. Stoneman (1975) analyzed the power of FDI on economic growth in developing countries and found that foreign direct investments increased productivity levels due to higher capital stock and at the same time improved the balance of payments positions of the host countries.

On the basis of panel data and a time series regression analysis, De Mello (1997) found that the relationship between FDI and economic growth tended to be weak and was conditional on the host country's characteristics that were taken into account by a country-specific term incorporated in the panel data procedure.

Among many others, Acemoglu and Robinson (2006) stress that FDI is crucial for economic growth in developing countries because FDI has several positive spillover effects such as the transfer of technology, expertise and know-how, enhancing domestic production, reducing production costs, brining efficiency in management, restructuring domestic investments, increased competition through mergers and acquisitions and the creation of employment opportunities.

On the other hand, a research undertaken by Saqib et al. (2013) found that FDI had a negative impact on economic growth in Pakistan. They ascribe the reason for the negative relationship to the dependency theory. According to Osvaldo (1969) the dependency theory can be defined as 'economic development of a state in terms of the external influences—political, economic, and cultural on the national development policies.' In other words, the dependency theory is a notion that resources flow from the periphery of a poor and under-developed state to a core of wealthy states, enriching the core states at the expense of the periphery.

Empirical studies also find that export dependency and a strong FDI presence contribute to lower economic growth and worse quality of life including a lower food supply, higher infant mortality, higher inequalities, higher pollution and reduced access to clean potable water, doctors and education (Anderson 2006). Moreover, reliance on foreign capital from multinational corporations (MNCs) perpetuates the low status of developing countries in the world hierarchy (Bornschier and Chase-Dunn 1985).

Most authors who have undertaken research on the role of FDI in economic growth come to very cautious conclusions. Rather than making bold claims that FDI does not have any impact on economic growth, they allege that the effect of FDI on economic growth is conditional on the economic realities in the host country. One notable finding in this regard is that by Carkovic and Levine (2002) who claim that the exogenous component of FDI does not exert a robust, positive influence on economic growth.

FDI inflows into developing countries have grown tremendously in recent years. Developing countries attracted $334 billion in 2005, or to put it into perspective, more than 36 percent of all inward FDI flows (UNCTAD 2006). This figure had reached a new high of $778 billion or 54 percent of the global FDI flows by 2013. Moreover, the importance of FDI for the economies in developing countries had increased from an average of barely 1 percent of GDP in the 1970s to above 2 percent of GDP on average by 2006 (Table 1).

Though FDI as a percentage of GDP for SSA seems more or less on par with that in other developing countries, the share of global FDI inflows to developing countries is extremely low. North Africa saw its FDI flows decline by 15 percent to $11.5 billion. FDI fell overall in the region because of tensions and conflicts in some countries despite significant inflows to others. UNCTAD's (2015) World Investment Report shows that FDI into Egypt grew by 14 percent to $4.8 billion and flows to Morocco by 9 percent to $3.6 billion.

In sub-Saharan Africa, where investments from abroad increased by 5 percent, there is variance by sub-regions. FDI flows to West Africa declined by 10 percent to $12.8 billion as the Ebola outbreak, security issues and falling commodity prices negatively affected several countries. East Africa saw its FDI flows increasing by 11 percent to $6.8 billion. FDI rose in the gas sector in the United Republic of Tanzania and Ethiopia is becoming a hub of multinational enterprises producing garments and textiles.

Figure 1 depicts FDI inflows into different territories and shows that there has been a deterioration following the 2008 financial crisis. Though there are signs of recovery the figures for most regions have not returned to the pre-crisis levels. There are indications that cautious

Table 1 Net FDI inflows as a percentage of GDP in various regions of the world (*Source* Author's calculations based on the World Development Indicators (2016) database)

Region	2006	2007	2008	2009	2010	2011	2012	2013	2014	2015
East Asia & Pacific	2.75	3.30	2.77	2.00	2.96	2.88	2.49	2.81	2.83	2.84
Latin America & Caribbean	2.91	3.45	3.30	2.21	3.35	3.56	3.48	3.22	3.49	3.78
Middle-East & North Africa	6.18	6.00	4.37	3.52	3.15	1.97	1.76	1.68	1.52	1.82
OECD members	4.03	5.35	3.57	1.78	2.22	2.79	2.45	2.28	1.69	2.63
South Asia	2.12	2.18	3.38	2.38	1.55	1.79	1.21	1.42	1.56	1.85
Sub-Saharan Africa	2.07	3.25	3.70	3.63	2.10	2.68	2.28	2.27	2.51	2.61
World	4.17	5.23	3.76	2.17	2.74	3.03	2.73	2.57	2.19	2.87

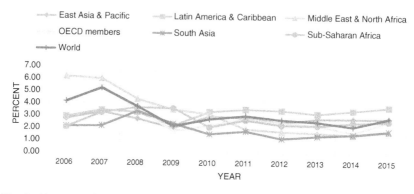

Fig. 1 Net FDI inflows as a percentage of GDP to various regions in the world (*Source* Based on the WDI database)

optimism is returning to global FDI. After the 2012 slump, global FDI started growing with inflows increasing to 9 percent in 2013, to $1.45 trillion.

FDI remained an essential stabilizer for emerging economies in the early stages of the crisis. Even though their net inflows of portfolio investments and bank lending were negative in 2008 (IMF 2009) their

FDI inflows increased, albeit at a slower pace than previous years and their outflows grew as well. However, as the credit crunch and recession spread more severely with deleterious repercussions for emerging markets in the second half of 2008, both FDI outflows and inflows started declining and in 2009 FDI recession became truly global in character. This decline was not limited to mergers and acquisitions (M&As) but was also reflected in greenfield investments which are more important sources of FDI in emerging markets than they are in developed economies. Greenfield investments dropped by 15 percent in emerging economies from 2008 to 2009. However FDI inflows have started recovering modestly, mainly driven by strong economic performance in Latin America, Asia and SSA.

3 Methodology

This paper used the Generalized Method of Moments (GMM) panel estimator popularized by Arellano and Bover (1995) and Blundell and Bond (1998) to extract consistent and efficient estimates of the impact of FDI on economic growth. Unlike other models, the GMM panel estimator exploits the time-series variations in the data, accounts for unobserved country-specific effects, allows for the inclusion of lagged dependent variables as regressors and controls for endogeneity of all the explanatory variables including international capital flows. In addition, the use of this dynamic panel model helps account for temporal serial correlations and minimizes the likelihood of estimating a spurious regression model.

Our study used the dynamic panel regression model in estimating the effect of FDI on economic growth in SSA. The predetermined variables in the model include lagged values of the dependent variable (GDP growth rate) and independent variables which comprise of FDI, inflation, trade openness, human capital (whose proxy variable is average years of schooling), capital stock, the institutional quality index and others. The lagged value of GDP is incorporated into the model to capture the persistence of the variable.

Following Fedderke and Romm (2006), Ramirez (2000), and De Mello (1997), and more recently the spirit of the Alege and Ogundipe (2013) model, the analytical framework that links FDI to economic growth can be analyzed using the augmented Cobb-Douglas production function as:

$$Y = f[L, K_p, K_f, E] = AL^\alpha K_p^\beta K_f^\gamma E^{(1-\alpha-\beta-\gamma)} \qquad (1)$$

where, Y is the real GDP, K_p is domestic capital, K_f is foreign capital, L is labor and E refers to the externality or spillover effect generated by additions to the FDI stock. α, β and γ are the shares of domestic labor, domestic capital and foreign capital respectively while 'A' captures the total factor productivity or efficiency of production. In our study, foreign capital is captured by FDI.

This empirical model is built based on Romer (1986) using the endogenous growth in a panel framework and thus postulates that the relationship between economic development and its various determinants is an implicit function of the form:

$$Y_{it} = f(Y_{i,t-1}, INV_{it}, L_{it}, FDI_{it}, X'_{it}) \qquad (2)$$

Where $(X_{it})' = (HC_{it}, Inf_{it}, EXP_{it}, M_{it}, GOVEXP_{it}, ODA_{it}, IQI_{it}, Ifs, dumres_i)$

$(X_{it})'$ consists of fundamental determinants of growth such as human capital (HC), macroeconomic stability (inf), external trade (that is export (EXP)) and financial development (M2) or broad money (which is a proxy for financial development), government expenditure (GOVEXP), official development assistance (ODA), infrastructure (ifs), the institutional quality index (IQI) and *dumres* which is a dummy variable for natural resource endowments. Y_{it-1} is the lagged value of output (GDP) which is likely to affect current output.

Assuming that the relationship between the dependent variable and the independent variables is non-linear, the function after adding an interaction term between human capital and FDI, and FDI and financial development (M2), can be written explicitly as:

2 The FDI and Economic Growth Controversy in Sub-Saharan Africa

$$Y_{it} = AY_{i,t-1}^{\beta_1} INV_{it}^{\beta_2} L_{it}^{\beta_3} FDI_{it}^{\beta_4} HC_{it}^{\beta_5} \inf_{it}^{\beta_6} (HC.FDI)_{it}^{\beta_7}$$
$$EXP_{IT}^{\beta_8} M_{it}^{\beta_9} (FDI_{it}.M_{it})^{\beta_{10}} GOVEXP_{it}^{\beta_{11}} ODA_{it}^{\beta_{12}} \quad (3)$$
$$IQI_{it}^{\beta_{13}} Ifs_{it}^{\beta_{14}} e^{\beta_{15} dumres}$$

Taking the natural logarithm of both sides of Eq. (3) yields:

$$\begin{aligned} \ln Y_{it} = & \ \beta_0 + \beta_1 Y_{i,t-1} + \beta_2 \ln INV_{it} + \beta_3 \ln L_{it} + \beta_4 FDI_{it} \\ & + \beta_5 \ln HC_{it} + \beta_6 \inf_{it} + \beta_7 \ln(HC_{it}.FDI_{it}) \\ & + \beta_8 EXP_{it} + \beta_9 M_{it} + \beta_{10} \ln(FDI_{it}.M_{it}) \quad (4) \\ & + \beta_{11} \ln GOVEXP_{it} + \beta_{12} ODA_{it} + \beta_{13} \ln IQI_{it} \\ & + \beta_{14} \ln Ifs_{it} + \beta_{15} dumres + \eta_i + \varepsilon_{it} \end{aligned}$$

Where, Y_{it} is the GDP of country i at time t, L_{it} is the labor force in country i at time t, FDI_{it} is the foreign direct investment in country i at time t, K_{it} is the stock of capital in country i at time t, HC_{it} is human capital of country i at time t measured in the average years of schooling, $\inf_{it}$ is the inflation rate in country i at time t which is used to measure macroeconomic stability, INV_{it} is domestic investments in country i at time t which is proxied by gross capital formation (GCF_{it}), EXP_{it} is exports of country i at time t, M is the stock of broad money (M2)[1] of country i at time t, $GOVEXP_{it}$ represents government expenditure of country i at time t, ODA_{it} is official development assistance[2] of country i at time t, while IQI stands for the institutional quality index which is constructed from the World Bank's Worldwide Governance Indicators (WGI). The six main indicators of governance are control of corruption, government effectiveness, political stability and absence of violence or terrorism, regulatory quality, rule of law and voice and accountability. Ifs_{it} stands for infrastructure of country i at time t which is proxied by the sum of fixed line and mobile subscribers out of 100 people

---

[1] In this study, broad money and M2 are used interchangeably.
[2] In this study, the terms official development assistance, foreign aid and aid are used interchangeably

and the dummy variable *dumres* stands for resource abundance. ε_{it} is an 'idiosyncratic' component and η_i is the 'unobserved heterogeneity' component.

While virtually all variables are transformed into logarithmic values, inflation and ODA are not. Inflation (inf) is given as the annual growth rate of the consumer price index whereas ODA is given as a percentage of GDP. For most SSA countries the percentage of ODA in the national income constitutes a very small fraction which falls below 1 and transforming that type of number will result in a negative value. Hence, ODA is simply given as a percentage of GDP and is not transformed into a logarithmic form.

The variable (HC.FDI) is an interaction term between human capital and FDI. In a panel data analysis of 84 countries over the period 1970–1999 Li and Liu (2005) found that FDI affected growth directly and indirectly through its interaction with human capital. Accounting for human capital is important because of the support in 'new growth' or 'endogenous growth' theories. Contrary to Solow (1956), average incomes in developing countries converge on those in the economically advanced nations only when human capital is considered. New growth theories reject two central assumptions of the older neo-classical model: (1) that technological change is exogenous, and (2) that the same technological opportunities are available to all countries (Barro and Lee 1994). Moreover, instead of diminishing returns to capital, new growth theorists expect constant returns to a broad range of investments including human capital and infrastructure (Lucas 1993; Romer 1986). The other interaction term incorporated in Eq. (4) is the one between FDI and financial development (proxied by M2, broad money). The presumption here is that lack of development of local financial markets can limit the economy's ability to take advantage of potential FDI spillovers.

The other interaction term between FDI and M (FDI.M) captures the impact of FDI and financial development on economic growth. FDI could affect economic growth through myriad channels one of which is financial development. The main point being highlighted is whether the level of financial development in the host country has

2 The FDI and Economic Growth Controversy in Sub-Saharan Africa

something to do with the impact of FDI on economic growth. To attain this goal, an interaction term between FDI and M2 (a proxy for financial development) is used. A positive sign on the coefficient implies that the impact of FDI on economic growth will be greater when it is complemented with a well-developed financial system.

Based on Eq. (4), the growth rate of per capita GDP can be written as:

$$\begin{aligned}\ln GDPPC_{it} =\ & \beta_0 + \beta_1 \ln Y_{it-1} + \beta_2 \ln GCFG_{it} + \beta_3 \ln L_{it} \\ &+ \beta_4 FDIG_{it} + \beta_5 \ln HC_{it} + \beta_6 \inf_{it} \\ &+ \beta_7 \ln(HC_{it}.FDIG_{it}) + \beta_8 \ln EXPG_{it} \\ &+ \beta_9 \ln MG_{it} + \beta_{10} \ln(FDIG_{it}.MG_{it}) \\ &+ \beta_{11} \ln GOVEXPG_{it} + \beta_{12} ODAG_{it} \\ &+ \beta_{13} \ln IQI_{it} + \beta_{14} \ln Ifs + \beta_{15} dumres + \mu_{it}\end{aligned} \quad (5)$$

where, GDPPC = GDP/N, per capita GDP, EXPG = EXP/GDP, the ratio of exports to GDP, GCFG = GCF/GDP, the ratio of gross capital formation to GDP, FDIG = FDI/GDP, the ratio of FDI to GDP, MG = M2/GDP, the ratio of M2 (broad money) to GDP, which is a measure of financial development or financial-deepening, GOVEXPG = GOVEXP/GDP, the ratio of government expenditure to GDP, ODAG = ODA/GDP, the ratio of ODA to GDP, and N = Population. The error term μ_{it} consists of two components, ε_{it} which is an 'idiosyncratic' component and an 'unobserved heterogeneity' component which is denoted by η_i (this is a time-invariant but individual-variant variable). The caveat one should be aware of here is that since Y stands for GDP, GDP/N yields GDPPC (GDP per capita).

Equation (5) can be more compactly written as:

$$\begin{aligned}\ln GDPPC_{it} =\ & \beta_0 + \beta_1 \ln Y_{it-1} + \beta_2 FDIG_{it} \\ &+ \beta_3 \ln FDIG_{it} * \ln HC_{it} \\ &+ \beta_4 \ln FDIG_{it} * \ln MG_{it} + \beta_5 X_{it} + \mu_{it}\end{aligned} \quad (5a)$$

Where, X_{it} includes all the other control variables from Eq. (5).

4 Data Sources and a Description of Variables

The data for this study is obtained from the World Bank's World Development Indicators (2016), International Financial Statistics and IMF's World Economic Outlook (2016) database. Data on FDI is from the United Nations Conference on Trade and Development (UNCTAD 2016) database. Sub-Saharan Africa comprises of 48 countries. However, due to data unavailability for some important variables for a certain number of countries, annual data for 43 SSA countries is used in this research.[3] The study covers a time period of 15 years (2001–2015). Due to lack of complete data for the stated variables for all the required time periods in executing the dynamic panel system GMM approach based regressions, some of the countries could not make it into the detailed econometric analyses of the FDI-growth nexus. Based on natural resource endowments the countries in the region are categorized into two—'resource-rich' and 'resource-poor.'

GDPPC:	Stands for GDP per capita and is used as a dependent variable. The growth of per capita GDP is explained as a function of other covariates.
Investment:	Shorthand for 'gross domestic investment' which measures the outlays on additions to the fixed assets of the economy plus net changes in the level of inventories. This variable is proxied by gross capital formation as a percentage of GDP.

---

[3] The SSA countries included in the study are Angola, Benin, Botswana, Burkina Faso, Burundi, Cameroon, Cape Verde, Central African Republic, Chad, Comoros, Congo (Brazzaville), Congo (Democratic Republic), Côte d'Ivoire, Equatorial Guinea, Ethiopia, Gabon, Gambia, Ghana, Guinea, Guinea-Bissau, Kenya, Liberia, Madagascar, Malawi, Mali, Mauritania, Mauritius, Mozambique, Namibia, Niger, Nigeria, Rwanda, Senegal, Seychelles, Sierra Leone, South Africa, Sudan, Swaziland, Tanzania, Togo, Uganda, Zambia and Zimbabwe.

Labor Force: Total labor force obtained from the World Bank's WDI (2016) database is used in our research.

FDI: Net FDI inflow as a percentage of GDP is the variable of interest here.

Human Capital: Seeks to investigate the role of human capital using average years of schooling as a proxy in the FDI-growth nexus in SSA.

Inflation: Inflation is taken as proxy to capture that level of economic stability. Inflation as measured by the consumer price index reflects the annual percentage change in the cost to the average consumer of acquiring a fixed basket of goods and services.

EXP: Is the export of goods and services as a ratio of GDP. Exports as a percentage of GDP are applied in the model of the FDI-growth nexus.

Financial Development: In this study, M2 (broad money) as a percentage of GDP is used as an indicator of financial development.

Government Expenditure: This represents the total expenditure of the central government as a share of GDP. It includes both current and capital (development) expenditure and excludes lending minus repayments. This variable too is taken as a percentage of GDP.

ODA: Official development assistance (ODA) as a percentage of GDP is used in the model.

Institutions: The institutional quality index is developed by calculating the average of the World Bank's six Worldwide Governance Indicators (WGIs, 2016 database): control of corruption, government effectiveness, political stability and absence of violence/terrorism, regulatory quality, rule of law and voice and accountability.

Infrastructure: Addison and Heshmati (2004), Heshmati and Davis (2007) and Gholami et al. (2006) found that infrastructure in its various forms, especially ICT, plays a vital role in attracting FDI and hence promoting economic growth. We use the number of mobile and fixed line subscribers per 100 people as a proxy for infrastructure.

dumres: This is a dummy variable for natural resource endowments. Countries that are resource endowed take a value of 1 and those that are not take a value of 0.

5 Model Estimation and Discussion of Findings

5.1 Descriptive Statistics

The important point that should be emphasized here is that the average growth rate of GDP and per capita GDP of 'resource-rich' countries is not much better than that of 'resource-poor' countries. The countries that are highly endowed with resources have not fared better than those that are resource constrained. As the results in Table 2 show the difference in the growth rate of per capita GDP between the two groups of countries is not statistically significant.

Contrary to the widely held view, average FDI inflows as a percentage of GDP for the resource-rich countries are not statistically different from their resource-poor counterparts. This contradicts the popular view that the FDI inflows into SSA are resource-seeking in nature. However, this result is in line with Chika (2014) who found that natural resource endowments are not significant determinants of FDI inflows. As opposed to this, Asiedu and Lien (2011) found that natural resources which are measured as the sum of minerals and oil in total merchandise exports have a negative impact on FDI (see Table 3).

Table 2 Two-sample t-test of GDP per capita growth of resource-rich and resource-poor countries with unequal variance

Group	Obs.	Mean	Std. Err.	Std. Dev.	[95% Conf. Interval]
0	345	2.028	0.211	3.923	1.613 2.444
1	300	2.484	0.398	6.894	1.700 3.267
combined	645	2.240	0.217	5.508	1.814 2.666
diff		−0.456	0.451		−1.34 0.430
Diff = mean(0)−mean(1)		t = −1.011	Satterthwaite's degrees of freedom = 459.458		
H_0:diff = 0	Ha:diff < 0	Ha:diff! = 0	Ha:diff > 0		
	Pr(T < t) = 0.156	Pr(|T| > |t|) = 0.312[a]	Pr(T > t) = 0.843		

[a] The decision rule is that if the p-value is less than the pre-specified alpha level (usually 0.05 or 0.01) we will conclude that the mean is statistically and significantly greater or less than the null hypothetical value

Note diff is the difference in mean between resource-poor countries represented by 0 and resource-rich countries represented by 1. H_0 stands for the null-hypothesis and Ha for the alternative hypothesis. Mean (0) refers to the mean growth rate of the resource-poor countries while mean (1) stands for that of the resource-rich countries. Obs. stands for observations, Std. Err. for standard errors and Std. Dev. for standard deviation

Table 3 Two-sample t-test of FDI inflow to resource-poor and resource-rich countries with unequal variance

Group	Obs.	Mean	Std. Err.	Std. Dev.	[95% Conf. Interval]
0	345	5.442	0.527	9.791	4.405 6.479
1	300	5.077	0.421	7.293	4.249 5.906
combined	645	5.272	0.343	8.714	4.599 5.946
diff		0.365	0.674		−0.960 1.689
Diff = mean(0)−mean(1)		t = 0.54	Satterthwaite's degrees of freedom = 628.602		
H_0:diff = 0	Ha:diff < 0	Ha:diff! = 0	Ha:diff > 0		
	Pr(T < t) = 0.705	Pr(|T| > |t|) = 0.589	Pr(T > t) = 0.294		

Note diff is the difference in mean between resource-poor countries represented by 0 and resource-rich countries represented by 1. H_0 stands for null-hypothesis and Ha for the alternative hypothesis. Mean (0) refers to the mean inflow of FDI as a percentage of GDP to the resource-poor countries while mean (1) stands for that of resource-rich countries. Obs. stands for observations, Std. Err. for standard errors and Std. Dev. for standard deviation

5.2 Estimation Results of the Econometric Model

We estimated the equation using the system GMM dynamic panel estimator (Blundell and Bond 1998). This method jointly estimates the equation in levels and in first difference, imposing the restriction that the coefficients in the level and differenced equation are equal. The instruments used in the level equation are the lagged first-differences of the variables. The GMM-type instruments for the differenced equation are the lagged levels of the variables. The equation in levels allows one to exploit large cross-country variations in the variables, whereas in the differenced equation the time-invariant and country-specific sources of heterogeneity are removed. In addition, the use of appropriate lags of right-hand side variables as instruments allows one to address problems of measurement errors, omitted variables and endogeneity (Dollar and Kraay 2004). The validity of the GMM instruments is tested using the Hansen-J statistic of over-identifying restrictions.

The system GMM performs better than difference GMM in estimating empirical growth models when the time dimension of the panel dataset is short and the outcome variable shows persistence (Roodman 2009a, b) which is the case in our empirical research. The difference GMM estimators are weak and may lead to problematic statistical inferences. Using lagged differences of the regressors as instruments for the equation in level along with the conventional use of lagged levels of regressors for the equation in first differences overcome the weak instrument problem and perform very well in terms of precision and bias (Blundell and Bond 1998).

The two-step system GMM estimator which provides more efficient estimators over the one-step system GMM was chosen to estimate the parameters of the model. Though the two-step GMM provides a covariance matrix which is robust to heteroskedasticity and autocorrelation, the standard errors show a downward bias and using robust standard errors gives consistent estimates in the presence of panel heteroskedasticity and autocorrelation. This issue has been taken care of in our study and all our final results of the model are corrected for heteroskedasticity. Moreover, unlike the one-step system GMM, the two-step GMM gives a robust Hansen *J*-test for over-identification. Thus, we chose the two-step system GMM procedure with robust standard errors to estimate our model.

2 The FDI and Economic Growth Controversy in Sub-Saharan Africa

Table 4 shows the results of the dynamic panel data estimated using various forms of difference GMM. Though an interpretation of the coefficients and their significance is delayed until we address the system GMM model, a cursory look at Table 4 shows that if the regression model does not account for the heteroskedasticity problem, several variables turn out to be significantly associated with the growth of per capita GDP. However, once we correct the dispersion in variance using the 'robust' option in Stata, a number of the variables that were significant become insignificant. The first and the second models used the second lags of the endogenous variables as instruments for the difference GMM model while the third and fourth models employed the third lags of the endogenous variables in the estimation of the difference GMM model. Besides, the standard errors given in the first and third models are not corrected for heteroskedasticity while those given in the second and fourth models take care of the heteroskedasticity problem that seems to be prevalent in the models.[4]

Though the various forms of the difference GMM model presented in Table 4 pass diagnostic tests, none of the variables is significant after we correct them for heteroskedasticity (see Models 2 and 4) except the institutional quality index which seems significant at the 10 percent significance level. Given the lack of good governance in SSA, this result is bizarre and should be taken with a pinch of salt.

Coviello and Islam's (2006) empirical results show that if the time series are persistent, for example, growth of GDP per capita, the difference GMM estimator can behave poorly because the lagged levels of the series only provide weak instruments. Further, they indicate that the difference GMM estimates of the coefficient on the lagged dependent variable tend to lie below the corresponding within-group (fixed effects) estimates which suggests that the difference GMM estimates are seriously biased (see the coefficients of the lagged dependent variable in Table 7). Hence, we deploy the system GMM estimators and rely on their results to interpret the coefficients and their significance.

---

[4]Compare the results in Table 4 under Models 1 and 2 as well as Models 3 and 4 to appreciate the impact that the uncorrected standard errors have on the significance of the coefficients.

Table 4 Estimating the GDP growth rate per capita using various forms of difference GMM

Explanatory variables	DiffGMM1 Model 1	DiffGMM2 Model 2	DiffGMM3 Model 3	DiffGMM4 Model 4
Lag of GDP per capita growth	−0.156***	−0.156	−0.057**	−0.057
	(0.01)	(0.10)	(0.02)	(0.12)
Gross capital formation	2.491***	2.491	3.515***	3.515
	(0.86)	(2.73)	(0.72)	(2.17)
Labor force	0.221	0.221	−11.617*	−11.617
	(5.54)	(17.25)	(5.94)	(19.18)
FDI	−0.118**	−0.118	−0.133***	−0.133
	(0.05)	(0.12)	(0.03)	(0.11)
Human capital	−25.257**	−25.257	−4.667	−4.667
	(10.53)	(23.51)	(10.91)	(33.29)
Inflation	−0.001	−0.001	−0.001**	−0.001
	(0.00)	(0.00)	(0.00)	(0.00)
FDI*human capital	−3.810***	−3.810	−6.091***	−6.091
	(1.02)	(3.07)	(1.05)	(4.12)
Exports	7.563***	7.563	6.278***	6.278
	(1.91)	(5.29)	(1.35)	(3.92)
Broad money	−5.003***	−5.003	−4.601***	−4.601
	(1.74)	(4.91)	(1.56)	(3.11)
Broad money*FDI	0.133	0.133	1.001***	1.001
	(0.27)	(0.52)	(0.27)	(0.86)
Government expenditure	−4.983***	−4.983	0.435	0.435
	(0.87)	(4.15)	(1.01)	(6.72)
ODA	2.655	2.655	−4.234**	−4.234
	(2.05)	(5.46)	(1.92)	(5.76)
Institutional quality index	4.871***	4.871*	3.430***	3.430
	(0.87)	(2.83)	(0.93)	(2.87)
Infrastructure	1.712***	1.712	1.314***	1.314
	(0.55)	(1.46)	(0.35)	(0.83)
Observations	505	505	505	505
Number of countries	43	43	43	43
F-test (p-value)	0.000	0.000	0.000	0.000
Hansen p-value	0.934	0.934	0.967	0.967
AR(1) p-value	0.010	0.042	0.003	0.016
AR(2) p-value	0.154	0.363	0.592	0.683

Notes All variables except human capital, inflation, infrastructure, the institutional quality index and dummy of resource abundance are given as a percentage of GDP. Moreover, all variables except FDI, inflation, ODA and the dummy for resource endowment are given in logarithmic values for ease of interpretation though logarithmic transformation also has other additional benefits. FDI and ODA are given as a percentage of GDP. The first and second models employ only the second of the endogenous variables as instruments whereas the third and fourth models use the third lag of the endogenous variables as instruments. The standard errors of the first and third models are not robust while those of the second and the fourth models are

The standard errors are given in parenthesis. (*$p < 0.10$, **$p < 0.05$, ***$p < 0.01$ signify the level of significance at 10, 5 and 1% levels respectively)

2 The FDI and Economic Growth Controversy in Sub-Saharan Africa

Table 5 presents the regression results obtained by using various forms of the system GMM. The interpretation of the model is mainly based on the coefficients of the variables in Model 2 which like Model 1 uses the second lag of endogenous variables as instruments but it is an improvement over Model 1 (Column 1) since the standard errors are robust and pass the different diagnostic tests. Models 1 and 2 use fewer instruments over Models 3 and 4. Thus, they offer more degrees of freedom which makes them preferable over the others that use deeper lags and consume more degrees of freedom.

As is the case in all dynamic panel data models, the lagged value of the growth of per capita GDP is incorporated into the model to capture persistence and feedback effects over time. Ceteris paribus, a 1 percent increase in the growth rate of per capita GDP in the previous year brings about an increase in the growth rate of per capita GDP by 0.101 percent at the 5 percent significance level. Moreover, the fact that the lagged dependent variable is significant in all the models implies that we are justified in using a dynamic model.

Gross capital formation is another variable that has a significant and positive effect on the growth of per capita GDP. In virtually all alternative models and scenarios formulated, this variable is consistent in having a positive and significant effect on the growth rate of per capita GDP at the 1 percent significance level. An increase of 1 percent in gross capital formation brings a large increase in the growth of per capita income which is 3.67 percent, ceteris paribus.

The growth of the labor force has a positive but statistically insignificant effect on the growth of GDP per capita. Given the poor productivity performance of the labor force in SSA countries, this insignificant outcome is not a big surprise. Of course, labor force is only marginally insignificant at the 10 percent significance level.

FDI as a percentage of GDP, the main variable of interest in our study, had a negative and significant effect on economic growth in SSA in the period under discussion. This result coincides with the findings of Ang (2009), Alfaro et al. (2004), Carkovic and Levine (2002) and Haddad and Harrison (1993) among many others.

The common trait in much of the empirical FDI-growth literature is that they take a cautious stand that FDI on its own does not

Table 5 Estimation of the GDP growth rate per capita using various forms of system GMM

Explanatory variables	SysGMM1 Model 1	SysGMM2 Model 2	SysGMM3 Model 3	SysGMM4 Model 4
Lag of GDP per capita growth	0.101***	0.101**	0.143***	0.143
	(0.01)	(0.04)	(0.01)	(0.09)
Gross capital formation	3.670***	3.670***	3.584***	3.584***
	(0.30)	(1.03)	(0.22)	(1.15)
Labor force	0.741***	0.741	0.721***	0.721*
	(0.20)	(0.54)	(0.20)	(0.42)
FDI	−0.138***	−0.138**	−0.099***	−0.099
	(0.02)	(0.07)	(0.02)	(0.08)
Human capital	2.874*	2.874	3.619*	3.619
	(1.63)	(4.05)	(2.08)	(3.94)
Inflation	−0.000***	−0.000	−0.000*	−0.000
	(0.00)	(0.00)	(0.00)	(0.00)
FDI*human capital	−1.365**	−1.365	−1.539***	−1.539
	(0.59)	(1.74)	(0.50)	(1.74)
Exports	2.796***	2.796**	2.534***	2.534
	(0.49)	(1.37)	(0.74)	(1.63)
Broad money	−3.182***	−3.182**	−1.767***	−1.767
	(0.24)	(1.38)	(0.33)	(1.51)
Broad money*FDI	0.287	0.287	0.229	0.229
	(0.18)	(0.38)	(0.17)	(0.40)
Government expenditure	−2.203***	−2.203	−1.842***	−1.842
	(0.40)	(2.51)	(0.44)	(3.28)
ODA	8.080**	8.080	5.192***	5.192
	(3.98)	(7.47)	(1.74)	(5.09)

(continued)

Table 5 (continued)

Explanatory variables	SysGMM1 Model 1	SysGMM2 Model 2	SysGMM3 Model 3	SysGMM4 Model 4
Institutional quality index	1.315***	1.315	0.698***	0.698
	(0.27)	(0.98)	(0.17)	(1.12)
Infrastructure	−0.131	−0.131	−0.433**	−0.433
	(0.16)	(0.52)	(0.17)	(0.38)
Dummy for resource endowment	−0.907	−0.907	−2.414***	−2.414
	(0.63)	(1.68)	(0.70)	(1.63)
Constant	−18.373***	−18.373	−19.196***	−19.196
	(4.26)	(11.92)	(5.44)	(11.62)
Observations	561	561	561	561
Number of countries	43	43	43	43
F-test (p-value)	0.000	0.000	0.000	0.000
Hansen p-value	0.978	0.984	0.987	0.988
AR(1) p-value	0.011	0.019	0.004	0.006
AR(2) p-value	0.228	0.241	0.653	0.534

Notes All variables except human capital, inflation, infrastructure, the institutional quality index and dummy of resource abundance are given as a percentage of GDP. Moreover, all variables except FDI, inflation, ODA and the dummy for resource endowment are given in logarithmic values for ease of interpretation though logarithmic transformation also has other additional benefits. FDI and ODA are given as a percentage of GDP

The first and second models employ only the second of the endogenous variables as instruments whereas the third and fourth models use the third lag of the endogenous variables as instruments. The standard errors of the first and third models are not robust while those of the second and the fourth models are. The standard errors are given in parenthesis. (*p < 0.10, **p < 0.05, ***p < 0.01 signify that the coefficients are significant at the 10, 5 and 1% level respectively)

immediately foster growth. For FDI to thrive and have a positive effect on economic growth there are conditions that need to be fulfilled such as the presence of a well-developed financial sector, a skilled and well-trained labor force and other institutional and infrastructural factors. In FDI-growth literature, these conditions are called the 'absorptive capacity' of the host country.

Proponents of FDI argue that it has a positive impact on aggregate demand of the host country in the short-run via productivity improvements and technology transfers while critics raise concerns over these supposed benefits. Their rationale is that the long-run balance of payments position of the host country is detrimentally affected after the initial financial outlay made by the investor. Once the initial investment starts turning profitable, it is inevitable that capital will return to the country it originated from which will negatively affect the growth prospects of the host country. Moreover, policies that offer preferential tax treatment and other incentives to induce inward FDI may introduce a distortion in the economy affecting domestic investments which eventually leads to a situation of FDI having a negative effect on economic growth. If the distortion between the return to foreign and domestic capital is of a huge magnitude, it will have a large negative effect on growth.

Based on the findings of our study, a unit increase in FDI as a percentage of GDP results in a decline in the growth of per capita income by as much as 13.8 percent. This result is troubling given the hype and attention given by SSA governments to attracting FDI. To put this result into perspective, an additional increase of FDI as a percentage of GDP by 10 units causes a further deterioration in the growth of per capita income (GDP) by 0.25 percent.

Human capital has an insignificant direct effect on the growth of per capita income even at the 10 percent significance level. Given the well-documented poor record of SSA countries in education attainment and other measures of human capital development, this finding is not surprising. However, this could partly be because of the poor proxy variable used here for human capital which is the average years of schooling. Many previous studies too have used this proxy and complain about its strength in representing human capital. Others have also used secondary-school enrolment as a proxy but the results are not any better. This result confirms that of Islam (1995) who found that human capital did not significantly affect output growth. He claims that it should affect growth through its impact on total factor productivity (TFP) growth. However, Miller and Upadhyay (2000) did find a positive and significant effect of human capital on income growth at the 10 percent significance level but failed to find any direct positive effect of human capital on TFP.

There exists a negative association between inflation and growth but the association is not statistically significant. High and erratically volatile inflation can reduce returns on capital and hence decrease investments on capital which reduce growth (Gillman et al. 2004).

Our study's estimation results show that the interactive term between FDI and human capital is negative but insignificant even at the 10 percent significance level. One plausible reason for this could be that the sector in which FDI is heavily concentrated might siphon off the skilled and educated labor force from domestic investment sectors which are more productive and make a more positive contribution to the growth of per capita income. This seems true as gross capital formation which is a proxy for domestic investments has a positive and significant effect on growth while FDI has an adverse effect.

Exports have positive and statistically significant effect on growth. Exports are deliberately selected to represent the openness of an economy. Most of the imports of SSA countries constitute petroleum products and other consumer items that do not have an appreciable contribution for further production. The a priori expected sign that exports have a positive contribution to economic growth is maintained and substantiated by our findings. Not only do exports have a positive impact as expected, they also have an enormous contribution. A 1 percent increase in exports brings about an increase in the much needed growth by nearly 2.78 percent.

The role of financial development in economic growth is captured by broad money. Using broad money as a proxy for financial development might make the whole essence of financial development narrow. But no matter how that characterization narrows the idea of financial development, it is difficult to discern and explain a situation where financial development affects growth negatively at a time when most SSA countries are adjudged to have liberalized their financial systems and markets. Keeping all else equal, an increase in broad money by 1 percent drags down growth by 3.18 percent as indicated in Table 5 (Model 2).

The interaction between FDI and broad money has a positive but an insignificant effect on the growth rate of per capita GDP but this could be due to the multiplicative outcome of their respective negative signs.

Our empirical findings suggest that SSA governments are destabilizing the markets and retarding growth possibly through distortionary policies which create a situation where government failure surpasses market failure. Governments could introduce inefficiencies, rent-seeking behavior, corruption and malpractices if they are not accountable to the electorate.

ODA is another variable which has a positive but insignificant effect on the growth of per capita income. This result is similar to Ogundipe et al.'s (2014) result who found that foreign aid did not significantly influence the growth of real GDP per capita in SSA.

The institutional quality index has the expected positive sign but it is not significant which coincides with the widespread perception about the poor quality of institutions in SSA, if any. Infrastructure which is proxied by the sum of the number of fixed line and mobile cell subscribers out of 100 people has a negative sign that is unexpected on a priori grounds. The reason could partly be due to the poor measurement of infrastructure only through access to telephones while infrastructure is a broad issue that should not be boiled down to a single variable like the case here.

The other variable that should be emphasized here is the endowment of natural resources and its impact on economic growth. The dummy variable is set to 1 for 'resource-rich' countries on the basis of the IMF (2013) classification. The categorization was made depending on the data about natural resources' contribution to the respective countries' economies between 2005 and 2010. The result is not significant though it is negative—an indication that the much maligned 'resource-curse' hypothesis might be at work. A separate growth regression for the resource-rich countries which are supposed to attract more FDI does not yield a statistically different result. When an independent regression is run for the resource-rich countries the FDI sign still remains negative.

The diagnostic tests in Table 5 suggest that the performance of the estimators is satisfactory. The *F*-test rejects the hypothesis that all the coefficients are zero, while the Hansen tests do not reject the hypothesis that the instruments are not correlated with the residual. This finding makes the instruments valid. We also detect first-order autocorrelation, AR(1) which is expected by the system GMM estimators. However, the detection of a second-order autocorrelation will cause problems as it makes the use of the second lag of the independent variables as instruments invalid. Finally, the AR(2) test results indicate no second-order autocorrelation in the residuals.

Linear dynamic panel data models include p lags of the dependent variable as covariates. In addition, they also have unobserved individual panel-level effects, assumed to be either fixed or random. By construction, the unobserved individual effects are correlated with the lagged dependent variables which makes the standard estimators inconsistent.

The dynamic fixed effects model has a disadvantage in that it may suffer from the so-called Nickell (1981) bias. The bias is a result of a correlation between the lagged dependent variable and fixed effects where the coefficient on the lagged dependent variable tends toward zero. If the explanatory variables are correlated with the lagged dependent variable then their estimated coefficients may inherit this Nickell bias. The size of the bias is a negative function of T and it becomes small when T exceeds 20 (see also Ashraf et al. 2016).

The main estimation method is a two-step system GMM with dynamics. A two-step difference GMM method and other static set-ups were also considered to check if the findings remained robust (Table 6). Static linear panel data models such as pooled-OLS, fixed effects and random effects are inconsistent in the presence of a lagged dependent variable which persists over time as is the case here. Though the results of the pooled-OLS and random effects estimators signal that the lagged value of the dependent variable is significant at the 1 percent significance level, we should be cautious in interpreting these results as the very existence of the lagged value of the dependent variable in the list of covariates renders those models irrelevant.

From the results in Table 6 under Model 5 we can see that the lagged value of the growth of per capita income significantly affects the current

Table 6 Estimating the GDP growth rate per capita for SSA using different methods (2001–2015)

Explanatory variables	Pooled OLS Model 1	RE Model 2	FE Model 3	DiffGMM Model 4	SysGMM Model 5
Lag of GDP per capita growth	0.180*** (0.04)	0.180*** (0.04)	0.045 (0.05)	−0.057 (0.12)	0.101** (0.04)
gross capital formation	2.383*** (0.69)	2.383*** (0.67)	4.079*** (0.98)	3.515 (2.17)	3.670*** (1.03)
Labor force	0.455*** (0.16)	0.455** (0.19)	−2.907 (6.74)	−11.617 (19.18)	0.741 (0.54)
FDI	−0.170* (0.09)	−0.170*** (0.05)	−0.182*** (0.05)	−0.133 (0.11)	−0.138** (0.07)
Human capital	0.254 (1.06)	0.254 (1.29)	−24.409** (9.85)	−4.667 (33.29)	2.874 (4.05)
inflation	−0.000 (0.00)	−0.000*** (0.00)	−0.000** (0.00)	−0.001 (0.00)	−0.000 (0.00)
FDI*Human capital	0.613 (0.59)	0.613 (0.58)	1.775* (0.89)	−6.091 (4.12)	−1.365 (1.74)
Exports	0.925* (0.55)	0.925* (0.51)	2.228** (1.10)	6.278 (3.92)	2.796** (1.37)
Broad money	−0.554 (0.41)	−0.554 (0.46)	−0.846 (0.68)	−4.601 (3.11)	−3.182** (1.38)
Broad money*FDI	0.163 (0.15)	0.163 (0.14)	0.066 (0.21)	1.001 (0.86)	0.287 (0.38)
Government expenditure	−0.382 (0.88)	−0.382 (1.13)	−1.473 (2.07)	0.435 (6.72)	−2.203 (2.51)
ODA	4.944** (2.50)	4.944*** (1.73)	7.240*** (2.53)	−4.234 (5.76)	8.080 (7.47)

(continued)

Table 6 (continued)

Explanatory variables	Pooled OLS Model 1	RE Model 2	FE Model 3	DiffGMM Model 4	SysGMM Model 5
Institutional quality index	0.346 (0.40)	0.346 (0.43)	2.538 (1.98)	3.430 (2.87)	1.315 (0.98)
Infrastructure	−0.439* (0.23)	−0.439* (0.26)	0.362 (0.68)	1.314 (0.83)	−0.131 (0.52)
Resource endowment	−0.389 (0.49)	−0.389 (0.51)	0.000 (.)		−0.907 (1.68)
Constant	−12.580*** (3.93)	−12.580*** (4.08)	35.372 (100.67)		−18.373 (11.92)
Observations	561	561	561	505	561
Number of countries	43	43	43	43	43
F-test (p-value)	0.000	0.000	0.000	0.000	0.000
Hansen p-value				0.934	0.984
AR(1) p-value				0.052	0.019
AR(2) p-value				0.113	0.241
R-squared	0.194		0.015		
Overall R-squared		0.194			

Note All standard errors are robust. (*p < 0.10, **p < 0.05, ***p < 0.01 significance of the coefficients at 10, 5 and 1% respectively)

growth rate of per capita income at the 5 percent significance level. To be specific, a 1 percent increase in the growth of per capita income in the previous year affects the growth of current income per capita by around 0.10 percent.

5.3 Robustness Check of the Base Specification

Since the dynamic panel data estimators are instrumental variables methods, it is particularly important to evaluate the Hansen test's results.

As far as heteroscedasticity is concerned, in a two-step estimation the standard covariance matrix is already robust but the reported two-step standard errors tend to be severely downward biased (Arellano and Bond 1991; Blundell and Bond 1998) which is the case in our study. Performing the Sargan test after the two-step estimator is an alternative, but Arellano and Bond (1991) found a tendency for this test to under-reject in the presence of heteroskedasticity.

It is worth mentioning that for a one-step estimation robust means that a robust estimator of the covariance matrix of the parameter estimates is calculated. The resulting estimates are consistent in the presence of heteroskedasticity and autocorrelation. In a two-step estimation, the standard covariance matrix is robust in theory, but the estimated standard errors are downward biased. A two-step robust estimation needs Windmeijer's finite-sample correction which is used for estimating the models adopted in this chapter (see Ashraf et al. 2016).

The *xtabond2*[5] tests over-identifying the restriction of whether the instruments as a group are exogenous. For a one-step, non-robust estimation the test gives the Sargan statistic which is the minimized value of the one-step GMM criterion function. The Sargan statistic has a weakness as it is not robust to heteroskedasticity or autocorrelation. In

---

[5]xtabond2 is a user-written Stata add-on command developed by Roodman (2009a, b) which helps to find difference GMM and system GMM of a linear dynamic panel data model. It is more flexible and has more functions not present in the xtabond, xtdpdsys and xtdpd commands available in the Stata package.

Table 7 'Three-Year Average' Estimation results of GDP growth rate per capita using various forms of static panel data models

Explanatory variables	POLS Model 1	RE Model 2	FE Model 3	BE Model 4	PA Model 5
Lagged GPD per capita growth	0.281***	0.281***	0.063	0.578***	0.359***
	(0.09)	(0.09)	(0.14)	(0.08)	(0.06)
Broad money	0.020	0.020	−3.415*	0.579	0.277
	(0.71)	(0.67)	(2.00)	(0.54)	(0.57)
Exports	1.514***	1.514***	4.010**	1.368**	1.432***
	(0.55)	(0.50)	(1.49)	(0.54)	(0.45)
FDI	0.065	0.065	0.103	−0.007	0.051
	(0.05)	(0.05)	(0.06)	(0.06)	(0.04)
Inflation	−0.000***	−0.000***	−0.000***	−0.000	−0.000***
	(0.00)	(0.00)	(0.00)	(0.00)	(0.00)
Government expenditure	−0.089	−0.089	−2.918	1.091	0.445
	(0.88)	(0.88)	(2.18)	(0.67)	(0.70)
Gross fixed capital formation	0.703	0.703	2.666	−0.346	0.297
	(0.73)	(0.84)	(1.99)	(0.60)	(0.65)
Labor force	0.365	0.365	11.019	0.287	0.272
	(0.63)	(0.42)	(19.28)	(0.50)	(0.36)
Population	0.205	0.205	−9.605	0.287	0.285
	(0.62)	(0.36)	(19.17)	(0.47)	(0.33)
ODA	−4.663	−4.663	−3.814	1.845	−3.626
	(3.81)	(4.14)	(8.08)	(3.89)	(3.34)
Institutional quality index	0.453	0.453	3.995*	−0.024	0.264
	(0.61)	(0.53)	(2.14)	(0.39)	(0.41)
Human capital	0.701	0.701	−20.567*	0.974	0.982
	(1.15)	(0.87)	(11.76)	(1.06)	(0.71)

(continued)

Table 7 (continued)

Explanatory variables	POLS Model 1	RE Model 2	FE Model 3	BE Model 4	PA Model 5
Infrastructure	−1.000***	−1.000***	−0.135	−0.458	−0.992***
	(0.27)	(0.26)	(0.83)	(0.53)	(0.26)
Resource endowment	−0.879	−0.879*	0.000	−0.776*	−0.841*
	(0.57)	(0.53)	(.)	(0.41)	(0.43)
Constant	−12.690***	−12.690***	−15.015	−16.562***	−13.362***
	(3.92)	(3.68)	(129.75)	(4.06)	(3.23)
Observations	172	172	172	172	172
F-statistic (p-value)	0.000		0.000	0.000	
R-squared	0.354				
Overall R-squared		0.354	0.191	0.254	
Wald-chi-squared		4622.29	22.65		2984.83
Wald-chi-square test (p-value)		0.000			0.000

Note *p < 0.10, **p < 0.05, ***p < 0.01 are the significance levels at 10, 5 and 1% respectively. The standard errors are given in parentheses. POLS, RE, FE, BE and PA stand for pooled OLS, random-effects estimator, fixed-effects estimator, the between-effects estimator and the population-averaged estimator respectively

addition to Sargan statistic the xtabond2 test also reports the Hansen J statistic, which is the minimized value of the two-step GMM criterion function and is robust (Roodman 2009a, b; Ashraf et al. 2016). This is another problem encountered here. Most of the coefficients that are significant when the robust option is not used become insignificant once the respective models are adjusted for heteroskedasticity.

We employed the Blundell and Bond (1998) difference GMM estimator to ensure the robustness of the results. Moreover, in order to overcome any possible Nickell bias and for a sensitivity analysis of the results in addition to GMM we also estimated static panel data regression models (see Ashraf et al. 2016).

The model was checked for robustness using the user-written add-on command 'checkrob' with different combinations of supposed 'core variables' (the variables to be retained in all the regressions) such as the lagged value of the growth of per capita GDP, FDI, gross capital formation, labor force, human capital and other 'testing variables' (the variables to be systematically included/excluded). The outcome of the robustness check indicates that the baseline model consistently performed better than the other alternatives.

To check for robustness, domestic investments were calculated by subtracting FDI from gross fixed capital formation (GFCF). This procedure was adopted because GFCF includes FDI as well as domestic investments. Many empirical studies, however, have used either gross capital formation (GCF) or GFCF in lieu of domestic investments (Mileva 2008; Mody and Murshid 2005; Wang 2010).

A closer inspection of the data for the FDI variable reveals that out of the 645 observations from 43 countries, in 146 (22.6 percent) cases the value of FDI as a percentage of GDP was less than 1. Roughly translated this means that nearly 10 of the 43 countries included in the study had FDI as a percentage of GDP of value less than 1 percent. The implication of this is that transforming this value into a logarithmic form will result in many negative values which will eventually change the nature of the relationship and the impact of FDI on economic growth. However, the robustness check undertaken here does not support this line of argument. Whether we take FDI as a percentage of GDP or transform it into a natural logarithmic value does not change the sign and significance of the variable.

Table 7 presents the result of the three-year average values for a number of variables. In the baseline regressions and extensions we used annual data to apply the GMM methods. However, to check robustness we averaged all variables over non-overlapping three-year periods and used the averaged data. The reason for averaging is justified as follows. The averaging of data dampens the influence of short-term shocks and business cycles and allows us to focus on the long-term relationship between FDI and the growth of per capita GDP. In empirical literature, 3-, 5-, and 10-year averages are widely used. We considered three-year averages for the following reasons. First, the three-year averages give us more observations on each variable and preserve the time series dimension of the data. Second, we include some variables for which only short series data are available (for example, Worldwide Governance Indicators and data on human capital).

One of the surprising results in Table 7 from the various regressions using the three-year average data is that the more resource endowed countries grew at a slower pace as opposed to their less resource endowed counterparts. In Table 7, when we use the three-year average FDI data which in effect is the stock of FDI, we see that the coefficient of FDI is positive in four out of the five models even though they are all statistically insignificant.

6 Conclusion and Policy Implications

6.1 Conclusion

The overarching objective of this paper was to delve into the FDI-growth controversy through empirical research and thereby contribute to the not so large literature in SSA on the topic. The study's main intention was analyzing the impact of FDI on SSA economies.

A debate is going on regarding the nexus between FDI and growth both at the theoretical and empirical levels. Both theoretical and empirical literature addresses these controversies. Theoretical literature is divided into two: those who advocate FDI's role in an economy (termed advocates or proponents of FDI) and those who are FDI skeptics (dissidents of FDI).

A simple *t*-test was used to compare the differences in FDI growth and inflows between resource-rich and resource-poor countries. The outcome of the comparison showed that there was no statistically significant difference between them.

The main finding of our paper was obtained using the system GMM which concludes that FDI had a negative and statistically significant impact on the growth of per capita GDP (income) for the 43 SSA countries included in the study between 2001 and 2015.

The other variables with a positive and significant contribution to GDP growth per capita included the lagged value of the growth rate per capita GDP itself, gross capital formation which is used as a proxy for domestic investments and exports.

Our empirical findings in this macro-panel data based literature do not support the exogenous positive effect of FDI on economic growth. The findings in this literature indicate that a country's capacity to exploit the full benefits of FDI spillover effects might be hampered by local conditions like the development of local financial markets or the level of educational attainments of its nationals. These are termed as absorptive capacities in literature on FDI.

6.2   Policy Implications

Our findings have the following policy implications:

FDI is a buzzword among development practitioners and MNCs and its positive impact on economic growth is highly acclaimed. Our study failed to find a positive effect of FDI on economic growth. Instead it found a negative effect. There are many reasons for this negative association which are outside the purview of our research. What our study would like to cautiously indicate is that FDI is not the panacea for all economic malaises in SSA.

Given the negative relationship between FDI and economic growth, it is time that the SSA leaders probed their policies and identified the areas that need more scrutiny. They should look into their domestic taxes and incentives and other investment policies and figure and sort out where the problem lies.

Governments, policymakers and development practitioners have a role to play by designing more appropriate FDI policies so that countries have necessary conditions to leverage the positive effects and mitigate the negative ones.

One may be tempted to argue that there is a plethora of empirical findings and researches regarding FDI and economic growth. However, our paper calls for more studies to find out what exactly are the reasons for the negative relationship between the two. Financial, human and infrastructural issues are captured here. They have negative but insignificant effects except for the financial development variable captured by broad money which has a negative and significant effect on economic growth. Future research should also look into the incentive and tax aspects of government policy.

Although the findings of our study suggest a negative effect of FDI on economic growth, these results should be interpreted with caution. This finding might purely be due to a different measure of the dependent variable, estimation method, sample and composition of countries selected as well as the FDI measure. For instance, the result is positive though insignificant when FDI stock of a longer duration is used rather than an FDI flow. This necessitates further analysis by incorporating more countries as data becomes available not only for FDI but also for other concomitant variables.

Foreign firms could positively affect domestic investments through knowledge spillovers by influencing factor costs downward and by promoting collateral benefits. But to reap these benefits governments should devise appropriate domestic policies and improve their administrative capabilities so that they can screen and select FDI projects that suit their economies. Governments should make sure that foreign firms do not displace local firms. Rather they should complement the activities of local firms and should have backward and forward linkages with them. If this happens, FDI could promote domestic investments.

Acknowledgements I would like to thank my main supervisor Professor Almas Heshmati, Jonkoping University, Sweden, for his contribution in improving the quality of this paper. I am also grateful for the help that I got from my co-supervisor Dr Adane Tuffa, Addis Ababa University, Ethiopia. Thanks are also due to my friends Fikru Debelie and Kahsay Berhane for their comments after reading certain sections of this paper. My special thanks also to the participants from the University of Rwanda (UR) International Scientific Conference Week that was held on 14–16 June 2017. However, all errors that are there are mine.

References

Acemoglu, D. and J.A. Robinson (2006). *Economic Origins of Dictatorship and Democracy*. New York: Cambridge University Press.

Addison, T. and A. Heshmati (2004). The New Global Determinants of FDI Flows to Developing Countries: The Importance of Ict and Democratization. *Monetary Integration, Markets and Regulation: Research in Banking and Finance* (4): 151–186.

Agrawal, G. (2011). Impact of FDI on GDP Growth: A Panel Data Study. *European Journal of Scientific Research*, 57(2): 257–264.

Agrawal, G. (2015). Foreign Direct Investment and Economic Growth in BRICS Economies: A Panel Data Analysis. *Journal of Economics, Business and Management*, 3(4): 421–428.

Alege, P. and A. Ogundipe (2013). Sustaining Economic Development of West African Countries: A System GMM Panel Approach. *Munich Personal RePEc Archive*. Available at: http://mpra.ub.uni-muenchen.de/51702/.

Alfaro, L., A. Chanda, S. Kalemi-Ozcan, and S. Sayek (2004). FDI and Economic Growth: The Role of Local Financial Markets. *Journal of International Economics*, 64(1): 89–112.

Anderson, J. (2006). 'What Happened to the MNCs?' *UBS Investment Research: Asia Focus*.

Ang, J.B. (2009). Financial Development and the FDI-growth Nexus: The Malaysian Experience. *Applied Economics*, 41(13): 1595–1601.

Arellano, M. and S. Bond (1991). Some Test of Specification for Panel Data: Monte Carlo Evidence and An Application to Employment Equations. *Review of Economic Studies*, 58(2): 277–297.

Arellano, M. and O. Bover (1995). Another Look at the Instrumental Variable Estimation of Error-components Models. *Journal of Econometrics*, 68(1): 29–51.

Ashraf, A., Herzer, D., and Nunnenkamp, P. (2016). The Effects of Greenfield FDI and Cross-border M&As on Total Factor Productivity. *The World Economy*, 39: 1728–1755. https://doi.org/10.1111/twec.12321.

Asiedu, E. and D. Lien (2011). Democracy, Foreign Direct Investment and Natural Resources. *Journal of International Economics*, 84(1): 99–111.

Barro, R. and J.W. Lee (1994). *Sources of Economic Growth*. Paper Presented at the Carnegie Rochester Conference Series on Public Policy.

Beugelsdijk, R.S. and R. Zwinkels (2008). The Impact of Horizontal and Vertical FDI on Host Country Economic Growth. *International Business Review*, 17: 452–472.

Blundell, R. and S. Bond (1998). Initial Conditions and Moment Restrictions in Dynamic Panel Data Models. *Journal of Econometrics Review*, 87(1): 115–143.

Borensztein, E., J. de Gregorio, and J.W. Lee (1998). How Does Foreign Direct Investment Affect Economic Growth? *Journal of International Economics*, 45: 115–135.

Bornschier, V. and C. Chase-Dunn (1985). *Transnational Corporations and Under-development*. New York: Prager Publishers.

Buckley, P.J. (2003). *FDI and Growth for Developing Countries: MNEs and the Challenges of the 'New' Economy*. Paper Presented at The Role of Industrial Development in the Achievement of the Millennium Development Goal. Proceedings of the Industrial Development Forum and Associated Round Tables, United Nations Industrial Development Organization, Vienna.

Carkovic, M. and R. Levine (2002). *Does Foreign Direct Investment Accelerate Economic Growth?* Minneapolis, MN: University of Minnesota.

Chika, O.G. (2014). Determinants of Foreign Direct Investment into Sub-Saharan Africa and Its Impact on Economic Growth. PhD thesis, Bournemouth University, UK.

Coviello, D. and R. Islam (2006). Does Aid Help Improve Economic Institutions? *World Bank Policy Research Working Paper No. 3990*.

De Mello, L.R. (1997). Foreign Direct Investment in Developing Countries and Growth: A Selective Survey. *Journal of Development Studies*, 34(1): 1–34.

Dollar, D. and A. Kraay. (2004). Trade, Growth, and Poverty. *Economic Journal*, 114(493): 22–49.

Fedderke, J.W. and A.T. Romm (2006). Growth Impact and Determinants of Foreign Direct Investment into South Africa (1953–2003). *Economic Modelling*, 23: 738–760.

Gholami, R., S.Y. Tom Lee, and A. Heshmati (2006). The Causal Relationship Between Information and Communication Technology and Foreign Direct Investment. *The World Economy*, 29(1): 43–62.

Gillman, M., M.N. Harris, and L. Mátyás (2004). Inflation and Growth: Explaining a Negative Effect. *Empirical Economics*, 29(1): 149–167.

Haddad, M. and A. Harrison. (1993). Are There Positive Spillovers from Direct Foreign Investment? Evidence form Panel Data for Morocco. *Journal of Development Economics*, 42: 51–74.

Heshmati, A. and R. Davis (2007). *The Determinants of Foreign Direct Investment: Flows to the Federal Region of Kurdistan*. Discussion Paper No. 3218. Institute for the Study of Labor (IZA).

IMF (2009). *World Economic Outlook 2009: Sustaining the Recovery*. Available at: https://www.imf.org/en/Publications/WEO/Issues/2016/12/31/World-Economic-Outlook-October-2009-Sustaining-the-Recovery-22576.

IMF (2013). *Boom, Bust, or Prosperity? Managing Sub-Saharan Africa's Natural Resource Wealth*. Washington D.C.

Islam, N. (1995). Growth Empirics: A Panel Data Approach. *Quarterly Journal of Economics*, 110(4). 1127–1270.

Kamara, Y.U. (2013). *Foreign Direct Investment and Growth in Sub-Saharan Africa: What are the Channels?* University of Kansas.

Lamine, K.M. (2010). Foreign Direct Investment Effect on Economic Growth: Evidence from Republic of Guinea in West Africa. *International Journal of Financial Research*, 1(1): 49–54.

Li, X. and X. Liu (2005). Foreign Direct Investment and Economic Growth: An Increasingly Endogenous Relationship. *World Development*, 33(3): 393–407.

Lucas, R. (1993). On the Determinants of Direct Foreign Investment: Evidence from East and Southeast Asia: 391–406. Available at: http://dx.doi.org/10.1016/0305-750X(93)90152-Y.

Mileva, E. (2008). *The Impact of Capital Flows on Domestic Investment in Transition Economies*. Working Paper Series. European Central Bank. Frankfurt, Germany.

Miller, S.M. and M.P. Upadhyay (2000). The Effects of Openness, Trade Orientation, and Human Capital on Total Factor Productivity. *Journal of Development Economics*, 63: 399–423.

Mody, A. and A.P. Murshid (2005). Growing Up with Capital Flows. *Journal of International Economics*, 65: 249–299.

Nickell, S. (1981). Biases in Dynamic Models with Fixed Effects. *Econometrica*, 49(6): 1417–1426.

Ogundipe, A.A., P. Ojeaga, and O.M. Ogundipe (2014). Is Aid Really Dead? Evidence from Sub-Saharan Africa. *International Journal of Humanities and Social Science*, 4(10): 300–314.

Osvaldo, S. (1969). National Development Policy and External Dependence in Latin America. *Journal of Development Studies* VI: 23–48.

Ramirez, M.D. (2000). Foreign Direct Investment in Mexico: A Cointegration Analysis. *Journal of Development Studies*, 37: 138–162.

Romer, P. (1986). Increasing Returns and Long Run Growth. *Journal of Political Economy*, 94(5): 1002–1037.

Roodman, D. (2009a). How to Do xtabond2: An Introduction to Difference and System GMM in Stata. *Stata Journal*, 9(1): 86–138.

Roodman, D. (2009b). A Note on the Theme of Too Many Instruments. *Oxford Bulletin of Economics and Statistics*, 71: 135–158.

Sala, H. and P. Trivin (2014). Openness, Investment and Growth in Sub-Saharan Africa. *Journal of African Economies*, 1–33. Available at: https://doi.org/10.1093/jae/ejt027.

Saqib, N., M. Masnoon, and N. Rafique (2013). Impact of Foreign Direct Investment on Economic Growth of Pakistan. *Advances in Management & Applied Economics*, 3(1): 35–45.

Solow, R.M. (1956). A Contribution to the Theory of Economic Growth. *Quarterly Journal of Economics*, 70(1): 65–94.

Stoneman, C. (1975). Foreign Capital and Economic Growth. *World Development*, 3(1): 11–23.

Suleiman, N.N., S.R. Kaliappan, and N.W. Ismail (2013). Foreign Direct Investments (FDI) and Economic Growth: Empirical Evidence from Southern Africa Customs Union (SACU) Countries. *International Journal of Economics and Management*, 7(1): 136–149.

UNCTAD (2006). *World Investment Report: FDI from Developing and Transition Economies: Implications for Development.*

UNCTAD (2014). *World Development Report: Investing in SDGs, An Action Plan.*

UNCTAD (2015). *World Investment Report: Reforming International Investment Governance.*

UNCTAD (2016). *FDI Data.*

Wang, M. (2010). Foreign Direct Investment and Domestic Investment in the Host Country: Evidence from Panel Study. *Applied Economics*, 42(29): 3711–3721.

World Development Report (2016). *Mind, Society, and Behavior.* World Bank. Washington, DC.

World Economic Outlook (2016). *World Economic Outlook (WEO) Database 2016.* IMF.

3

Determinants of Foreign Direct Investment Inflows to Africa

Alemayehu Geda and Addis Yimer

1 Introduction

While there exists a large body of literature on the determinants of FDI flows to the developing world in general, little has been done to investigate the determinants of FDI flows to Africa. The few available cross-country studies conducted on Africa generally identify the factors that explain FDI flows to the continent. However, they fail to provide an in-depth analysis and country specific factors that are crucial for attracting FDI. They also deal with the economic determinants of FDI inflows as if such inflows occur in a political and institutional vacuum. They are not theoretically and empirically systematic either. In addition, all these studies fail to account for possible cross-sectional dependence in their econometric analyses. Our study addresses this gap by developing a new

A. Geda (✉) · A. Yimer
Department of Economics, College of Business and Economics,
Addis Ababa University, Addis Ababa, Ethiopia

© The Author(s) 2018
A. Heshmati (ed.), *Determinants of Economic Growth in Africa*,
https://doi.org/10.1007/978-3-319-76493-1_3

analytical country classification which takes into account cross-country differences. We also offer an in-depth theoretical analysis by using a wide coverage of data tested for cross-sectional dependence to validate our results.

FDI flows to developing economies have reached a new high of US$778 billion, accounting for 54 percent of global inflows. Developing Asia continues to be the region with the highest FDI inflows (Table 1). Africa's share of world FDI inflows has been extremely low. By the second half of the 1990s, the average share of FDI in the GDP of African countries was not only very small but was also declining. Any positive trends were largely related to investments in countries with newly discovered resources. For instance, in 1996 FDI was a mere US$5.5 billion representing only 1.5 percent of global investment flows. Its distribution was also extremely skewed with Nigeria, Egypt, Morocco, Tunisia, South Africa, Algeria, Angola, Ghana and Côte d'Ivoire accounting for over 67 percent of FDI receipts

Table 1 FDI flows by region in 2011–2014 (US$ billion) (*Source* UNCTAD (2014))

Host region/economy	FDI inflows			FDI outflows		
	2011	2012	2013	2011	2012	2013
World	1700	1330	1452	1712	1347	1411
Developed Economies	880	517	566	1216	853	857
European Union	490	216	246	585	238	250
North America	263	204	250	439	422	381
Developing Economies	725	729	778	423	440	454
Africa	48	55	57	7	12	12
Asia	431	415	426	30-4	302	326
Latin America & Caribbean	2448	256	292	111	124	115
Percentage Share of World FDI						
Developed Economies	51.8	38.8	39.0	71.0	63.3	60.8
European Union	28.8	16.2	17.0	34.2	17.7	17.8
North America	15.5	15.3	17.2	25.6	31.4	27.0
Developing Economies	42.6	54.8	53.6	24.7	42.7	32.2
Africa	2.8	4.1	3.9	0.4	0.9	0.9
Asia	25.3	31.2	29.4	17.8	22.4	23.1
Latin America & Caribbean	14.3	19.2	20.1	6.5	9.2	8.1

to Africa. Between 1991 and 1996 ten countries (Nigeria, Morocco, Tunisia, Angola, South Africa, Ghana, Tanzania, Namibia, Uganda and Zambia) received almost 90 percent of the FDI inflows, with Nigeria alone absorbing a third of the amount.

Most of the flows emanated from France, UK, Germany and the US. Favored recipient sectors included oil, gas, metals and other extractive industries (UNCTAD 1998). The total value of FDI inflows to Africa in 2003 was about US$18 billion which increased to US$57 billion by 2013. This constituted about 4 and 7 percent of world and developing economies' FDI inflows respectively (Table 1). In 2013, North Africa managed to attract about US$15 billion while the rest of Africa attracted about US$42 billion, divided between US$14, 8, 6, and 13 billion for West, Central, Eastern and Southern Africa respectively.

Intra-Africa investments are also increasing and are dominated by South African, Kenyan and Nigerian firms. According to UNCTAD (2014), between 2009 and 2013, the share of announced cross-border Greenfield investment projects originating from within Africa increased to 18 percent, from less than 10 percent earlier. For many smaller, often landlocked or non-oil-exporting countries in Africa, intra-regional FDI is a significant source of foreign capital flows (UNCTAD 2014).

FDI flows to Africa are from traditional sources and the OECD countries are important in this. Despite the media's focus on China and other emerging economies investing on the continent, the combined share of China and India's FDI to Africa in the total FDI to the continent was just about 6 percent (Geda 2013). Generally, we note the following points about FDI to Africa in relation to China and India. First, it is highly unlikely that China and India as host countries will divert FDI that will come to Africa. Second, the level of FDI from China and India to Africa is not only very small but also located in a few countries. Third, these flows from China and India are largely motivated by the desire to secure sources of energy and raw materials and the desire to exploit preferential markets which are accessible to African countries (Geda 2013).

2   Determinants of FDI Flows: The Theory

This section briefly examines various theories on the determinants of FDI. The early neo-classical approach summarized by MacDougal (1960) hypothesized that capital flows across countries are governed by differential rates of return (within the neo-classical market setting). He also argued that such capital inflows were welfare enhancing for both parties engaged in capital movement. The MacDougal model assumes perfect competition, risk free capital movement, mobility in factors of production and no risk of default. The portfolio approach to FDI, presented in a reaction to the MacDougal model, emphasizes not only a returns differential, but also risk (Agarwal 1980).

Ohlin (1933) was one of the first to address the determinants of FDI. According to him FDI was motivated mainly by the possibility of high profitability in growing markets along with the possibility of financing these investments at relatively low rates of interest in the host country. Other determinants were the necessity of overcoming trade barriers and securing sources of raw materials. This is strengthened by a theory which emphasizes the positive relationship between FDI and output (sales in the host country) along the lines of Jorgenson's (1963) investment model (see Agarwal 1980; Geda 2002).

A major criticism of these theories is that they miss the relevance of market imperfections. Hymer (1960) and Kindleberger (1969) argue that if foreign firms were able to compete and succeed in the host country, then they must be in possession of a specific and transferable competitive advantage both over local firms and other potential entrants into the local markets. Building on Hymer's (1960) analysis Kindleberger (1969) posited that instead of multinational firms' behavior determining the market structure, it is the market structure (monopolistic competition) that determines the conduct of a firm by internalizing its production. Based on a microeconomic analysis of FDI Caves (1971), added to the link between industrial organization and FDI established by Hymer (1960). Caves argues that multinational companies invest overseas to protect the foreign market from tariffs or other trade related restrictions imposed by host countries. According to Caves (1971), overseas investments go where trade does not.

This FDI oligopolistic market theory claims that imperfect competition encourages multinational firms to differentiate products and engage in FDI (Kindleberger, 1969). For this strand of literature, foreign investments reflect the outcome of strategic rival reactionary behaviors between companies in the world market following the entry of competitors in certain markets (see Kindleberger, 1969).

Based on an analysis of oligopolistic market behaviour, Vernon (1966) provided the 'product-life-cycle' theoretical approach. According him, investment decisions faced by multilateral firms are a choice between exporting and investing in a foreign market as products move through a life cycle. In the early stages of a product's life-cycle, invention and production of a new product takes place in developed countries which have research and development capabilities and growing markets. When the product becomes standardized, there is technological transfer to firms in developing countries and production shifts to low-wage firms in these economies (Vernon, 1966). Thus, multinationals switch from exporting to foreign-based production to maximize their profits. Krugman (1979) formalized Vernon's (1966) theory in a dynamic setup. For Krugman (1979) technological innovations are the basis for FDI (Geda, 2002).

Recently, 'new trade theories' based on the original contributions of Hymer (1960), among others, have underscored the importance of specialization in production in explaining FDI (see Geda, 2002).

Based on the original contributions of Hymer (1960), Vernon (1966), Kindleberger (1969) and Caves (1971), Buckley and Casson (1976) extended FDI's industrial organization theory to include the concept of 'internationalization.' Based on Coase's (1937) original concept of internationalization in the theory of a firm Buckley and Casson (1976) extended its application to international firms (multinational companies). According to them firms choose to internationalize operations through FDI when market transaction costs are high as compared to the internationalization of operations (see Buckley and

Casson, 1976). More generally, in the context of FDI's internationalization theory any form of market imperfection is taken as a rationale for multinational companies to internationalize their production and engage in overseas investments (see Buckley and Casson, 1976; Agarwal, 1980; Dunning, 1993). The internationalization theory of FDI became one of the major building blocks on which Dunning's (1993) more integrated and comprehensive theory about the determinants of FDI was established (see Dunning, 1981, 1988 and 1993). This line of using transaction and related cost internalization as determinants of FDI is also emphasized by Buckley and Casson (1976) and Buckley (1985). Their arguments run mainly on the fact that transaction costs of intermediate products will be minimized when markets are integrated by multinational firms (MNFs). They argue that MNFs have proprietary assets regarding marketing, designs, patents, trademarks and innovative capacity among others (that is, ownership advantages) whose transfer may be costly for being intangible assets or due to a good sense of opportunity or even because they are diffused and thus difficult to sell or lease. According to Buckley and Casson (1976) and Buckley (1985), the main strength of the internalization theory is its capacity to address the dilemma between the licensing of production to a foreign agent and own production that can be done through FDI.

Dunning's (1981, 1988, 1993) comprehensive theoretical framework, termed as the eclectic approach, contributed to the determinants of FDI in literature by bringing together a number of complementary FDI theories that explain the location decisions of multinational firms when they opt for a particular place for their overseas investments (see Geda, 2002).

The OLI approach provides a micro-macroeconomic approach based on the advantages of ownership, location and internationalization (OLI) to analyze the determinants of FDI. According to this theory, FDI is advantageous when simultaneously there are also advantages of OLI. Ownership advantages are firm-specific competitive advantages which an investing firm possesses over local firms in serving particular markets.

These include the possession of certain valuable and organizationally embedded resources such as patents and marketing and managerial know-how. The location advantage arises when a company benefits from its presence in a given market as a result of specific advantages that the host country offers to foreign investors. These advantages can be a simple geographical location like proximity to a larger market (Porter, 1990) or the existence of cheap and abundant factors of production such as natural resources, energy, labor and other raw materials, or policy related incentives such as special preferential tax rights and tariffs and low cost access to land (Dunning, 1993). The advantages of internationalization relate to the concept of minimizing transaction costs that may arise due to market imperfections in alternative modes of entry into a particular market. FDI will occur when investing companies choose to exploit their ownership and location advantages through internationalization (Dunning, 1993). The OLI paradigm is popular in empirical applications because of its comprehensiveness and coherent integration of complementary FDI theoretical approaches for investigating the determinants of FDI (Helleiner, 1989).

Another strand of literature, which is often overlooked in mainstream analyses, is Marxist theories of FDI determination. Citing historical and other empirical evidence from Britain and the United States, Baran and Sweezy (1966) argue that FDI represents an outlet for investment-seeking surplus resulting from stagnation in the centers of capitalism. According to Marxist theories, FDI also represents a mechanism for extracting surplus from under-developed areas (Baran and Sweezy 1966). Magdoff (1992) argues that the 1970s and 1980s exhibited a slowdown in economic activity which itself is an inherent feature of capitalism according to Marxist theory and that this slowdown spurred capital to seek and create new profit opportunities. Thus, the speeded-up flow of direct investments from one country to another is seen as a reaction to stagnation in capitalist centers. According to Magdoff, the 1980s witnessed world FDI growing at an average annual rate of 29 percent and the pattern of such investments increasingly switching to finance and insurance, real estate, advertising and the media (as opposed to the traditional sectors of manufacturing and raw material extraction). Despite such changing patterns, Magdoff saw stagnation in the centers and the search for profit as representing the main reasons for FDI.

To sum up, a number of theoretical frameworks explain the location determinants of FDI. However, all of them are not equally applicable to Africa. For instance, the neoclassical theory of FDI is not relevant in Africa due to its assumption of a perfect market. Krugman's theory is not applicable either as it is workable in countries where there are better initial conditions for industrial expansion.

The Marxist version focuses primarily on the consequence of FDI which is not the prime focus of our empirical study. Besides, its stagnation thesis may not fully explain FDI destinations as much as its sources and might also be inferred from the industrial organization and international firm based theories.

On the other hand, Dunning's eclectic paradigm is a better option for explaining FDI in African states. The abundance of natural resources and low-cost factors of production, the path dependent nature of such flows based on colonial history (see Geda, 2002) and the wide range of policy related incentives that African countries provide for foreign investors make Dunning's OLI framework relevant for explaining FDI on the continent. Hence, in the next section we use the OLI theoretical approach for specifying the FDI model to be estimated. This theoretical insight is used in identifying the determinants of FDI for the construction of the model used for the empirical analysis in the next section.

3 Determinants of FDI Flows to Africa: Recent Evidence

Empirical literature on the determinants of FDI to LDCs is voluminous and is based both on country case studies (see, for example, Sunday and Lydie 2006; Seetanah and Rojid 2011) and cross-section analyses (see, for example, Asiedu 2002, 2006; Anyanwu 2012; Root and Ahmed 1979). An examination of the findings of these studies and how they are related to the theories reviewed earlier is informative for the approach in our study.

The findings from existing studies generally reveal that labor costs, country size, openness, the exchange rate regime, returns on investments, human capital and political factors are among the most important factors explaining FDI flows (see Table 2 for a summary). Notwithstanding these general findings we focus on the evidence found in African studies[1] which offer some insights into the empirical analysis conducted in our study.

Most studies on Africa report that FDI to the continent was largely motivated by natural resource endowments (Asiedu 2006; Asiedu and Gyimah-Brempong 2008, Basu and Krishna 2002; Morisset 2000, among others). Though natural resource abundance is a common factor explaining much of the FDI inflows, a few successful African countries have also managed to attract FDI by creating a favorable economic, social and political environment. For instance, Mauritius and Seychelles have managed to attract FDI by tailoring their FDI policies through liberalization, export orientation, tax and other investment incentives. Moreover, some countries like Lesotho and Swaziland have attracted FDI because they are near South Africa and investors wishing to serve the large market in South Africa have located their subsidiaries in these countries (Basu and Krishna 2002; UNCTAD 1998).

Asiedu (2002) analyzed 34 countries in sub-Saharan Africa over the period 1980–2000. Using a panel data analysis she found that openness to trade, higher income and better growth prospects and a better institutional framework and infrastructure were 'rewarded' with more investments. A later study by Asiedu (2006) shows the significant role of a country's market size and natural resource endowments in enhancing FDI. She found lower inflation, good infrastructure, an educated population, openness, less corruption, political stability and a reliable legal system to have a similar positive effect on FDI flows to the

---

[1] The empirical discussion presented here does not discuss the findings from country case studies in Africa. However, country case studies in Africa reported a similar result to the cross-sectional studies in Africa (see Geda and Yimer 2015).

Table 2 Result of recent empirical studies on major determinants of FDI flows to Africa (and other developing countries)

Determinant	FDI destinations	Method	Proxy	Effect	Author(s)
Market size	12 MENA, 24 DCs	Panel data	GDP	+	Mohamed and Sidiropoulos (2010)
	14 SADC	Panel data	GDP	+	Mhlanga et al. (2010)
	16 SSA countries,	Multivariate regression	GDP per capita	+	Cleeve (2008)
	22 SSA countries,	Panel data	GDP	+	Asiedu (2006)
	Africa (SSA and North Africa)	Panel data	urban population, as per cent of total population and GDP per capita	+	Anyanwu (2012)
	80 DCs	Multivariate regression	GNP per capita	+	Schneider and Frey (1985)
	SSA and 6 other non-SSA African countries, DCs	Panel data	total population	+	Abdoul (2012)
		Correlation analysis	Population	+	Nunnekamp (2002)
Openness of the economy	16 SSA countries,	Multivariate regression	(X+M)/GDP	+	Cleeve (2008)
	29 African Countries,	Panel data	(X+M)/GDP	+	Onyeiwu and Shrestha (2004)
	14 SADC	Multivariate regression	(X+M)/GDP	+	Mhlanga et al. (2010)
	12 MENA, 24 DCs	Panel data	(X+M)/GDP	0	Mohamed and Sidiropoulos (2010)
	SSA & North Africa,	Panel data	(X+M)/GDP	+	Anyanwu (2012)
	22 SSA countries,	Panel data	(X+M)/GDP	+	Asiedu (2006)
	SSA and 6 other non-SSA African countries,	Panel data	(X+M)/GDP	+	Abdoul (2012)
	DCs	Correlation analysis	(X+M)/GDP		Nunnekamp (2002)

(continued)

3 Determinants of Foreign Direct Investment Inflows to Africa

Table 2 (continued)

Determinant	FDI destinations	Method	Proxy	Effect	Author(s)
Factor endowments in natural resources	22 SSA countries,	Multivariate regression	X fuels+minerals/ total X	+	Asiedu (2006)
	12 MENA, 24 DCs	Multivariate regression	X fuels/total X	+	Mohamed and Sidiropoulos (2010)
	14 SADC	Multivariate regression	Investment in extractive industry (dummy)	0	Mhlanga et al. (2010)
	29 African countries,	Panel data	X fuels/total X	+	Onyeiwu and Shrestha (2004)
	Africa (SSA and North Africa)	Panel data	Oil exporters represent dummy for net oil exporters,	+	Anyanwu (2012)
Macroeconomic Stability	14 SADC	Multivariate regression	Inflation rate	0	Mhlanga et al. (2010)
	22 SSA countries	Panel data	Inflation rate	−	Asiedu (2006)
	12 MENA, 24 DCs	Panel data	Inflation rate	−	Mohamed and Sidiropoulos (2010)
	80 DCs	Multivariate regression	Inflation rate	−	Schneider and Frey (1985)
	29 African countries	Panel data	Inflation rate	−	Anyanwu (2012)
	16 SSA countries	Multivariate regression	Inflation rate	−	Cleeve (2008)
Governance Indicators	22 SSA countries	Panel data	Effectiveness of the Government Index (ICRG)	+	Asiedu (2006)
	16 SSA countries	Multivariate regression	Corruption Index	−	Cleeve (2008)
	African countries	Panel data	Rule of Law Index (IGRC)	+	Anyanwu (2012)

Notes DCs is Developing Countries; MENA is Middle East and North African Countries; SSA is Sub-Saharan Africa; SADC is Southern Africa Development Community; X is Exports and M is Imports

continent. Asiedu and Gyimah-Brempong (2008) validate these finding to a large extent and note that countries that are small or lack natural resources can attract FDI by improving their institutions and policy environments.

Based on a co-integration analysis for the period 1970–2000 using data from 19 sub-Saharan African countries, Bende-Nabende (2002) found market growth, export-oriented policies and liberalization were the most dominant long-run determinants of FDI in Africa. Using fixed and random effects models on a panel dataset for 29 African countries over the period 1975–1999, Onyeiwu and Shrestha (2004) identified economic growth, inflation, openness of the economy, international reserves and natural resource availability as important determinants of FDI to Africa. Contrary to conventional wisdom, political rights and infrastructure were found to be unimportant in their study. Krugell (2005) also empirically tested for the significance of a number of hypothesized determinants of FDI in sub-Saharan Africa. The pooled cross-country and time-series estimation covered the period 1980–1999 for 17 countries. Krugell's results are in line with the findings mentioned earlier, particularly with respect to economic growth and openness.

Dupasquier and Osakwe (2006) identified factors such as political and macroeconomic instability, low growth rate, weak infrastructure, poor governance, an inhospitable regulatory environment and ill-conceived investment promotion strategies as being responsible for the poor FDI record of the region. Naude and Krugell (2007) employed a cross-country econometric approach using a dynamic one-step generalized method of moment's estimator in their study. They identified government consumption, inflation rate, investment, governance and initial levels of literacy as being important. The authors concluded that geography did not seem to have a direct influence on FDI flows to Africa. Neither market-seeking nor re-exporting motives of FDI seemed to be the major determinants of FDI in their study. However, institutions in the form of political stability showed up as a significant determinant of FDI to the continent.

Among the most recent FDI studies on Africa, Abdoul (2012) estimates a model of FDI determination using a five-year panel data with the system-GMM technique over the period 1970–2009 for 53 African countries. He found that larger countries attracted more FDI. However, regardless of their size, more open and politically stable countries that offered higher returns on investments also attracted FDI. FDI inflows were also found to be persistent in the sense that countries that manage to attract FDI today are likely to attract more FDI in the future. Using cross-country data for 53 African countries for the period 1996–2008 Anyanwu (2012) found market size (whose proxy is urban population as percentage of total population and GDP per capita of the host country), openness to trade, rule of law, foreign aid, natural resources and past FDI inflows (increased agglomeration) to have a positive effect on FDI inflows. He also found that domestic financial developments had a negative effect on FDI inflows. Further, he found eastern and southern African sub-regions positively disposed towards obtaining higher levels of inward FDI.

In sum, market size, openness of an economy, natural resource endowments and political and macroeconomic stability are important determinants of FDI flows to Africa. We believe that these are important factors that any model on the determinants of FDI flows to Africa needs to consider. However, when examined in the light of theoretical literature on FDI, none of these African studies seem to formulate their empirical models by explicitly following one strand of the theoretical literature or the other. The variables used in their models, however, suggest the use of Dunning's eclectic paradigm without stating which variable is used as a proxy for which theoretical concept. This is partly the result of missing theoretical discussions and formulations in almost all these studies.

One important area emphasized in theory but not well addressed in the studies discussed earlier relates to the location of the 'eclectic paradigm' in the OLI framework. However, the effects of major determinants of FDI identified in African empirical literature vary across countries or groups of countries—thus location matters. We believe this is an important omission and some analytical classification of countries could be an important indicator of the location issues emphasized in the OLI theoretical framework. Thus, FDI models need to be fitted to different country groupings and these groupings need to be formed using rigorous analytical classifications.

With this perspective, in the model developed and estimated in our study, the modeling of the determinants of FDI inflows to Africa is framed in a new country classification framework. Moreover, in addition to incorporating broader governance indicators we also use longer data series and a panel error correction modeling (ECM) technique that accounts for cross-sectional dependence which is missing in existing African literature.

4 A New Analytical Country Classification

Country classification schemes are important both for analytical and operation activities of international and regional developmental organizations such as the World Bank and the African Development Bank (AfDB). A recent study by Brixiova and Ndkumana (2011) for AfDB proposes a new country classification for Africa. The authors' proposed classification scheme for Africa is based on four criteria: (a) level of income, (b) growth acceleration and resilience, (c) a robust macroeconomic framework and macroeconomic stability, and (d) an enabling business environment and private sector driven growth. However, the proxies used to measure these criteria are not clearly articulated in the study. Although the Brixiova-Ndikumana classification provides a fresh perspective on African country classifications, it is not a concrete proposal that can readily be used either for operational (except perhaps the fragile states category) or analytical work. This is because first, the stages of development used are not characterized in terms of their salient features except at the general impression level (like having a stock market and credit ratings). Second, it does not have systematic and quantifiable proxies that can be used for the purpose (except a limited use of per capita income). Third, it does not have a clear analytical basis for the classification. Finally, there is no dynamic and measurable story that indicates that one stage surely follows or precedes the other (say, along the Rostovian line of the 'dynamic theory of production'). Notwithstanding these weaknesses, it is an important starting point for the classification of African economies. It also offers an opportunity to build on this initiative and come up with a useful classification that is appropriate both for operational and analytical work on the continent. We make an attempt to do this and this also informs the FDI model estimated in our study.

Literature on the classification of countries by level of development (sometimes referred to as 'stage theories') is rife with debates and unsolved issues. Prominent contributions range from the two famous and dominant classifications scheme of stages of development[2] (Marxian and Rostovian; see Fig. 1) to that of Michael Porter's relatively recent effort. Departing from the dominant Marxian discourse on stages of development at the time, Rostow, in his …*Non-Communist Manifesto* offers a somewhat different classification of the 'stages' of economic development.

Some of the major weaknesses of the Rostovian approach which is relevant for our topic relates to Rostow's failure to elaborate more on the concept of 'stages' (defined as a concept indicating the discontinuous aspect of growth), the meaning of 'sequence of stages' (defined as indicating the continuous aspect of growth) and 'periodization.' He also fails to make an effective application of the 'dynamic theory of production' that he claims to use as an apparatus of stage analysis (see Itagaki 2007). In short, Rostow's analysis fails to impress his critics regarding the dynamic force that links one stage to the other or what Rostow called 'the inner logic of continuity: the analytic bone-structure.' According to Rostow, this sequence is rooted in a dynamic theory of production and leading sector analysis (see Rostow 1959, 1960). This notion was revisited by Michael Porter in the 1990s. Unlike Rostow, Porter's classification scheme has a lot to offer in classifying African countries at various stages of development.

Porter's (1990) classification of countries is based on his work *The Competitive Advantage of Nations* where he examines the pattern and characteristics of industrialization and exports in the global market place. For Porter each stage of development represents the development of different industries and industry segments as well as the required policy and company strategy (Porter 1990: 545). He structured his stages

---

[2]This section does not pretend to be exhaustive on stage theory.

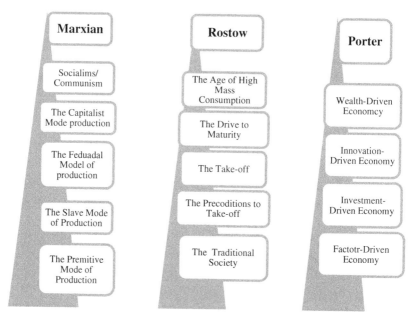

Fig. 1 Summary of literature on an analytical basis for classifications

in such a way that the ability to transit from one stage to the other is a function of a country's relative position in the global market where without the ability to export, the level of production and productivity will not rise (Porter 1990: 545). It is on the basis of this notion that his stages of development (see Fig. 1) are outlined.

In contrast, literature does not have an analytical classification of African countries. A recent comprehensive study of the political economy of growth in Africa by the African Economic Research Consortium (AERC), using 26 country case studies identified four political regimes that characterized the political and policy landscape of post-independence Africa—a potential basis for an analytical classification. The regimes are: the State Controls (SC) regime, the Adverse Redistribution (AR) regime, the Inter-temporally Unsustainable Spending (IUS) regime and the State Breakdown (SB) regime; also presented is the complementary Syndrome-Free (SF) category (Fosu 2008). The study notes that the quality of economic policies pursued by each of these regimes had a powerful effect on whether countries seized the growth opportunities implied by global technologies and markets and by their own initial conditions (Fosu 2008). According to Fosu (2008), this syndrome based classification aggregates a multi-dimensional policy into broad patterns that occur repeatedly in African countries. The evidence that syndromes reduce growth is strong in the AERC study. According to Fosu and O'Connell (2006) being syndrome-free can add as much as 2.5 percentage points per year to per capita growth. While this classification is used for a policy analysis, the same AERC study also comes up with an analytic-cum-geographic classification. This classification finds justification in the belief that the potential for growth in the continent is strongly associated with endowments and location (Collier and O'Connell 2008). As a result countries in Africa are also classified in the AERC study as 'land locked,' 'coastal,' and 'resource rich.'

These two classifications (policy opportunity/syndrome and geography) can also be mapped together (Fosu 2008). In this mapping we note, for instance, that state breakdown is common in landlocked economies while coastal economies are generally free from this. Further, all geographic locations are characterized by the syndrome of being regulatory and redistributive. However, this facet is more dominant in resource rich economies. Although AERC's analytic approach is excellent it is beleaguered by the same flaws as earlier studies (that is, it fails to show the trajectory of development stages for countries examined in the case studies) although the implicit assumption in the study is a 'syndrome free' status as the best direction. This makes the AERC classification fundamentally driven by policy analyses. This leaves economic dynamics and shifts in the growth frontier as a result of higher productivity largely untouched.

Finally, it is worth looking at the classifications of global financial market players, partly because the Brixiova-Ndikumana classification for Africa categorically borrows archetypal group names (such as 'emerging markets' and 'frontier markets') from that domain. For instance, Standard and Poor's (S&P) Global Broad Market Index (BMI) classifies countries as 'developed', 'emerging' and 'emerging plus' based on the relative size and performance of global stock markets. The motivation behind S&P's classification is gauging the global financial market.

S&P uses quantitative criteria as well as the opinions and experiences of global investors. The S&P methodology document notes that many of the issues in determining if a market is developed, emerging or frontier are not amenable to quantitative decisions. Regulations, rules and procedures for foreign exchange trading, trade settlements, availability of company financial data and other factors as well as operating costs imposed on investors by these factors vary from market to market and determine the classification of countries (see Standard and Poor 2011).

With regard to the relevance of adopting this global financial market based classification in Africa we note that if a country does not have publicly listed companies (with a market capitalization value of over US$100 million), classifications such as 'emerging' and 'frontier' are not usable and hence their usage (as in the case of Brixiova and Ndikumana's study) is problematic. In fact, S&P's (2011) classification shows only Egypt, Morocco and South Africa as 'emerging markets' in Africa; the rest of Africa is totally absent from all S&P's categories.

The broad lesson from the analysis so far is that a classification of countries by stages of development is an important matter for developmental institutions in Africa and also for analytical work on the continent. This is because countries at various stages of development face different challenges and exhibit diversified outcomes. This may entail different policy and assistance strategies that suit each of the stages (see Brixiova and Ndikumana 2011; Lin 2011; Porter 1990). If such a classification is important, what then is the lesson from literature for classifying African countries and what should be the criteria for them? For analytical work such as a FDI analysis in our study, the following criteria are important for classification of African countries into different categories:

(a) Needs to be guided by an attempt to capture the salient structural features of African economies in the global economy context including the position of its leading sectors.
(b) Needs to be informed by an indication of the existence of levels or stages of development governed by an inner logic of production and export dynamism in each country. It also needs to be forward looking.

3 Determinants of Foreign Direct Investment Inflows to Africa

(c) Should be helpful in identifying challenges and evaluating outcomes which are believed to be different at different stages of development and hence call for different intervention strategies.
(d) Finally, as much as possible the classification should be quantifiable to avoid arbitrariness.

Building on Porter's (1990) work which methodically adheres to criteria similar to those mentioned here and providing an excellent framework for depicting the stylized facts of countries we propose an alternative classification scheme for African countries. The main principle behind this classification is that each stage is a step in the productivity ladder which is qualitatively different in its structure. This could be inferred from the uniqueness of its product sophistication and productivity level in the global economy and market context. A global competitive position is also an indirect measure of domestic economic sophistications once an economy has moved out of, say, the factor-intensive stage of a competitive advantage position. Hence, one stage follows the other in a linear or non-linear way following a qualitative change in a country's economic structure and its accompanied socio-political (soft) and physical (hard) infrastructure.[3] This conceptualization relies heavily on the pattern of trade because this is invariably the best measure of sophistication of the domestic economy and hence a derived indicator of the relative position of a country vis-à-vis other economies in the world. Benchmarked with East Asia's fast growing economies (such as China, South Korea and Taiwan) such a scheme for Africa will help us see the diversity among African economies. Thus, primarily relying on Porter (1990) we outline and briefly define the following four categories for Africa. These are summarized, together with their possible proxies in the Appendix.

---

[3] The notion of hard infrastructure refers to the prevailing state of rationality, science, technology, the mode of organization and the degree of human development (human capital formation). Soft infrastructure refers to the corresponding distribution of income and levels of poverty, the social conditions under which production takes place, the mode of thought, ideology, culture and global perspective of citizens (see Geda 2002 and Lin 2011, among others).

(i) *Factor-Driven African Economies (Aspiring African Economies: Class A and B)*: African economies whose source of competitive advantage in the global economy comes from basic factors such as labor and other natural resources. Here technology is pretty much standard and at best imitated and competition by countries in this stage is sustained through prices. The peculiar feature of countries in this stage is the sensitivity of such economies to world economic cycles, exchange rates and interest rate movements and their effect on commodity speculators as well as the loss of factor advantages. This stage is relevant for a majority of African countries. It can also be further divided into agricultural (Class A) and non-agricultural (Class B) factor driven categories as the former is unique and dependent on climate change. In our study we use them as one category.

(ii) *Investment-Driven African Economies (Emerging African Economies)*: African economies with the ability and willingness to absorb and modify the best available technology through large investments and those who have made themselves competitive in the global economy. Like the factor-driven stage the competitiveness in this stage comes from standardized and price sensitive commodities.

(iii) *Innovation-Driven African Economies (Advanced [or Frontier] African Economies)*: African economies which have created unique value for their firms and cluster of firms that gives them an edge over competitors in the global market. They are also at the world technology frontier with regard to the goods they supply to both large domestic markets and the global economy.

(iv) *Fragile and Post-Conflict African Economies*: African economies characterized by a debilitating combination of weak governance, policies and institutions indicated by their ranking among the lowest (<3) on the World Bank's country's policies and institutional performance assessment (CPIA) index. These are states that have failed to provide comprehensive service entitlements to their citizens and lack authority and legitimacy owing to the failure of either capacity or political will or both. This category also entails differing policy needs and assistance compared to countries that are similar in every respect. One distinguishing characteristic is that there is a high(er) risk of reverting back into conflict. Economic performance has an important effect on the weight of this risk. Therefore, economic policy has the *additional* potential of helping reduce the risk of reverting into conflict.

The implications of our classification for an analytical macroeconomic analysis and cross-country econometrics work on Africa include: First, both from the operational and analytical perspective the 'fragile states' group is important. This group has unique features that require unique analyses, interventions and hence financing mechanisms. Thus, macroeconomic/international economic analyses such as the one conducted in our study need to consider this group as an important and unique category.

Second, non-fragile states in Africa make up other categories of countries with a different set of economic characteristics and challenges. At specific periods in time, each country may find itself at different stages on the ladder of growth and development. These economies also have unique developmental challenges and financing needs at the various stages of their development (from the factor-driven stage to the 'innovation-driven' stage). This underscores the need to take them as another unique analytical category. This helps us to come up with appropriate development policies including different financing schemes and financing instruments that are suitable to each group of countries.

Finally, all these categories need to be analyzed and understood in the context of a dynamic global economy where the trade and financing patterns of African countries are fast changing. For instance, the last decade shows a surge in Chinese and Indian economic engagement on the continent. They are in the course of significantly replacing the traditional dominant role of OECD countries as a source and destination of trade (market) and finance. Thus, analytical work such as ours and the accompanying modeling strategy needs to bring this issue onboard. This is what we attempt in our modeling of FDI flows to Africa as the nature of FDI for each category of countries may have different motivations and attractiveness criteria that are unique for each category.

5 The Empirical Methodology and Findings of the Study

5.1 The Econometric Approach and Definition of Variables

Following Johansen (1988, 1991) we consider a VAR model given by Eq. (1a), where Y represents a vector of variables with n lags:

$$Y_t = A_1 Y_{t-1} + A_2 Y_{t-2} + \ldots + A_4 Y_{t-n} + \mu_t \tag{1a}$$

Generally, economic time series exhibit a non-stationary process and hence VAR systems like Eq. (1a) can be expressed as Eq. (1b) through repeated parameterization to tackle this problem (Geda et al. 2012):

$$\Delta Y_t = -\sum_{i=1}^{n}(I - A_i)Y_{t-1} - \sum_{j=2}^{n} A_j \Delta Y_{t-1} - \sum_{j=3}^{n} A_j \Delta Y_{t-2} - \sum_{j=i}^{n} A_j \Delta Y_{t-n-1} + \phi D + \phi \mu_i \tag{1b}$$

where, D is a vector of exogenous variables.
Or

$$\Delta Y_t = \Pi Y_{t-1} \sum_{j-i+1}^{n-1} \Phi_i \Delta Y_{t-n+1} + \phi D + \phi \mu_i$$

with

$$\Pi = \left(I - \sum_{i=1}^{n} A_t\right) \quad \text{and} \quad \Phi_i = \left(I - \sum_{j=i+1}^{n} A_j\right) = -A * (L)$$

The model estimated in our study is based on the VECM formulation given as Eq. (1b) which is a traditional first difference VAR model, except for the term ΠX_{t-1}. The Johansen procedure is based on an examination of matrix Π, which contains information about long-run relationships. An analysis of a long-run relationship in the model is based on examining the rank of this matrix. The most interesting possibility is when $0 < \text{rank } \Pi = r < p$, which implies there are $p * r$ matrices α (the adjustment vector) and β (the long-run co-integration vector) such that $\Pi = \alpha\beta'$. The co-integration vector β has the property that $\beta'X_t$ is stationary even though X_t itself is non-stationary. The Johansen procedure helps determine and identify this/these co-integrating vector(s). The empirical analysis in our study uses the abovementioned approach to identify co-integrating vector(s).

Equation (1b) is estimated based on the autoregressive distribution lag model (ADL) formulation of VAR given as Eq. (1a) which is re-parameterized as Eq. (1b). In general, in an ADL formulation a long-run (equilibrium) relationship between two variables, Y and X, can be given as:

$$Y_t = KX_t^\gamma = \gamma_1 + \gamma_1 X_t \qquad (2)$$

where, K, γ_1 are and γ_2 constants and $\gamma_1 = \log K$.

As in this equilibrium a relationship cannot be observed, the observable disequilibrium formulation of this long run (equilibrium) relationship between Y and X in a simplified from can be given by Eq. (3) which is a simple $ADL\,(m, n, p)$ (where m is the number of lags, n and p the number of endogenous and exogenous variables respectively), $ADL(1, 1, 1)$ formulation of Eq. (2):

$$Y = \beta_0 + \beta_1 X_t + \beta_2 X_{t-1} + \alpha Y_{t-1} + u_t, 0 < \alpha < 1 \qquad (3)$$

With some re-parametrization[4] the ECM representation of Eq. (3) which is the estimable version of Eq. (1) can be given by Thomas (1993), Hendry (1995), Geda (2002), Morales and Raei (2013):

$$\Delta Y = \beta_1 \Delta X_t - (1-\alpha)\left[Y_{t-1} - \gamma_1 - \gamma_2 X_{t-1}\right] + u_t \qquad (4)$$

---

[4]Subtracting Y_{t-1} from either side of Eq. (3) and adding and subtracting X_{t-1} in the right hand side of the resulting equation gives Eq. (4).

where,

$\gamma_1 = \frac{\beta_0}{1-\alpha}$; $\gamma_2 = \frac{\beta_1+\beta_2}{1-\alpha}$; and $\{-(1-\alpha)\}$ is the ECM term and is expected to be negative.

This formulation can be generalized for a general ADL of the form:

$$Y_t = \beta_0 + \sum_{i=1}^{m+1} \beta_i X_{t-i+1} + \sum_{i=1}^{m+1} \alpha_i Y_{t-i} + u_t \quad (5)$$

The estimable ECM formulation of Eq. (5) can be derived in similar way as:

$$\Delta Y_t = \gamma_0 + \left(1 - \sum_{i=1}^{m} \alpha_i\right)\left[Y_{t=m} - \gamma_0 - \sum_{i=1}^{m} \gamma_i X_{t-m}\right] + \sum_{i=1}^{m} \beta_i \Delta X_{t-m+1} \quad (6)$$

where, $\gamma_0 = \frac{\beta_0}{1-\sum_{i=1}^{m}\alpha_i}$ is the constant and $\gamma_i = \frac{\sum_{i=1}^{m+1}\beta_i}{1-\sum_{i=1}^{m}\alpha_1}$

The final estimable version of Eqs. (1b) or (6) that we estimate as our FDI model is given as:

$$\Delta Y_t = -\Pi Y_{t-1} + \sum_{j-i+1}^{n-1} \Phi_i Y_{t-n+1} \phi D + u_t \quad (7)$$

with $\Pi = \left(I - \sum_{i=1}^{n} A_i\right)$ and $\Phi_i = -\left(\sum_{j=i+1}^{n} A_j\right) = -A * (L)$

Where: $Y = \begin{bmatrix} FDI_{it} \\ RGDPPC_{it} \\ INVGDP_{it} \\ RES_{it} \\ EXTDEBGDP_{it} \\ OPNESS_{it} \\ RER_{it} \\ INF_{it} \end{bmatrix}$ and $D = \begin{bmatrix} POLSTAB_{it} \\ GOVEFFE_{it} \end{bmatrix}$

in our FDI model.

The indices '*i*' and '*t*' refer to countries and time respectively. *Y* shows the vector of the endogenous variable that includes *FDI* which is measured as FDI inflows. Π is equal to $\alpha\beta'$ where β is the co-integrating vector and α is the vector of adjustment coefficients. The FDI data series is taken from UNCTAD (2014). The data series for the macro fundamentals and institutional indicators are taken from the World Bank's (2014a, b) African development indicators and world development indicators.

In specifying Eq. (7) we used the theoretical lines of Porter (1990) and Dunning's (1981, 1988, 1993) 'eclectic theory' of OLI advantages as determinants of FDI flows to Africa. Our analytical classification of African economies as fragile, factor-driven and investment-driven economies is presumed to capture the location advantage which is unique to each category of countries. Hence, the model is estimated for the three categories of countries discussed in the previous section. In addition to location advantage, Dunning's ownership and internalization advantages that may attract FDI to Africa can be proxied by market size, natural endowments and a stable macroeconomic and political environment as African empirical literature in the previous section shows. Thus, we used these variables as part of our empirical model given as Eq. (7).

Market size (RGDPPC): The size of the host market which also represents the host country's economic conditions and potential demand is an important element in FDI decision-making. Scaperlanda and Mauer (1969) argue that FDI responds positively to market size 'once it reaches a threshold level that is large enough to allow economies of scale and efficient utilization of resources.' This is akin to the concept of I in the OLI framework. The importance of market size has been confirmed in many previous empirical studies (see, for example, Schneider and Frey 1985; Wheeler and Mody 1992). Thus, following literature we used real GDP per capita as a proxy for market size. Its expected sign is positive.

Domestic investment as a percentage of GDP (INVGDP): Literature suggests that the availability of strong domestic investments should improve a country's position in the eyes of foreign investors. As noted by Ndikumana and Verick (2008), higher levels of private investments can help attract FDI inflows possibly due to a signaling effect as higher private investments are seen as an indication of high returns to capital. Higher levels of public investments, particularly in areas like infrastructure, are expected to reduce production and trade costs and hence provide a more profitable environment for foreign investors by raising FDI's marginal productivity. Thus, the expected sign for this variable is positive.

Natural resource abundance (RES): The availability of natural resources might be a major determinant of FDI for the host country. Foreign firms embark on vertical FDI in the host country to produce raw materials or/and inputs for their production processes at home. This means that certain FDI may be less related to profitability or market size of the host country. As posited by the eclectic theory, other things remaining the same, countries that are endowed with natural resources will receive more FDI in line with OLI advantages. As noted by Asiedu (2002), very few studies on FDI's determinants control for natural resource availability. The failure to do so may cause the estimates to be biased. We therefore included the share of minerals and oil in total merchandise exports of a country to capture the availability of natural resource endowments. This measure of natural resources has been employed in previous studies on FDI (see, for example, Asiedu 2002, 2006).

Openness (OPNESS): Openness to international trade as an indicator of the importance of trade for an economy is regarded as a very important factor that promotes FDI. This proxy is also important for foreign direct investors who are motivated by the export market potential of the host country. Empirical evidence (see Table 2) shows that higher levels of exports lead to higher FDI inflows. In Africa, for example, export-oriented economies such as Egypt, Mauritius, Morocco and Tunisia have tended to attract large amounts of FDI in their textiles and apparel industries (Ancharaz 2003). Following literature (see Table 2) we used the ratio of trade to GDP as a measure of a country's openness.

External debt as a percentage of GDP (EXTDEBTGDP): A higher level of indebtedness is considered a component of financial risk influencing FDI inflows negatively (Nonnenberg and Mendonca 2004). In addition, heavily indebted countries represent higher future taxes and higher transfer risks—risks of potential restrictions on the ability to transfer funds across national boundaries. Higher transfer risks may cause foreign capital to move out of a country and new FDI flows to be re-routed to safer locations. We used the debt to GDP ratio as a measure of indebtedness and its expected sign is negative.

Real exchange rate (RER): The effect of changes in exchange rates on FDI flows is ambiguous. For instance, Elbadawi and Mwega (1998) used the real exchange rate as an indicator of a country's international competitiveness, hypothesizing that a real depreciation would attract larger FDI flows. However, it may be argued that a real depreciation increases the costs of imported inputs and reduces the foreign-currency value of profit remittances, both of which have adverse effects on the profitability of FDI projects (Asiedu 2002). This effect will dominate if FDI is undertaken primarily to serve the domestic market. Thus, the expected sign for this variable depends on the type and motive of FDI coming to the region.

Inflation rate (INF): Is generally used as a macroeconomic instability indicator which could affect FDI negatively (see, for example, Asiedu 2002). More stable economies that reflect a lesser degree of uncertainty attract more FDI (Elbadawi and Mwega 1998). Thus, the expected sign for this variable is negative.

Political stability (POLSTAB): It is argued that political instability and the frequent occurrence of disorder 'create an unfavorable business climate which seriously erodes the risk-averse foreign investors' confidence in the local investment climate and thereby repels FDI away' (Schneider and Frey 1985). We used a political risk rating provided by the World Bank (2014b) as a proxy for political stability. The rating awards the highest value to the lowest risk country as a means of assessing the political and institutional condition of countries.

Government effectiveness (GOVEFFE): Finally, in order to take account of the impact of the institutional quality of a host country on FDI inflows we included an index of institutional quality using data on 'government effectiveness' compiled by the World Bank (2014a, b). This variable captures the government's ability and credibility to formulate and implement sound policies and regulations that promote private sector development. We argue that excessive and inefficient bureaucracy raises the costs of doing business and offers opportunities for corruption thereby deterring FDI inflows.

5.2 Findings of the Study

We used three separate models for factor-driven, investment-driven and fragile African economies. Our preference for three models was informed by our finding of statistically significant values for 'country classification' dummies that we incorporated in a single general FDI regression model estimated for all countries (not reported). This suggests that the various factors determining FDI had a different effect in each country depending on the analytical category in which the country was located.

The estimation of the models was preceded by all the necessary pre-estimation diagnostic tests including the unit root and co-integration tests. The results justified the use of the panel equilibrium error correction modeling technique. In addition, the Hausman test for random/fixed-effects models' specifications was carried out and this justified the use of the fixed-effects model in all the three models. In addition, potential long run relationships in such ARDL based models could also be tested by carrying out Pesaran's bound test (Pesaran and Shin 1999; Pesaran et al. 2001). As in conventional co-integration tests, the bound test is a test for the absence of a long-run equilibrium relationship between the variables if the null hypothesis (H_0) is accepted and vice versa. The results of this test further confirmed the existence of a long-run relationship among the variables in our model.

Having passed all pre-estimation tests, the model (given as Eq. 7) was estimated using the general to specific approach. The results from the estimation of this FDI model are given in Table 3. One of the major weaknesses of previous cross-sectional studies in estimating such models is their failure to test for cross-sectional dependence in their models in the presence of which the estimated results are problematic (see Pesaran 2006, 2007). We did a number of post-estimation cross-sectional dependence tests and observed no problem of cross-sectional dependence (see Table 3). In addition, a test for normality of the error terms showed that all the three models had no problem of non-normality.

Table 3 shows that for investment driven African economies real GDP per capita, natural resource abundance, the level of domestic investments and exchange rate had a positive impact in the short run

Table 3 Results of the FDI model

Dependent variable: Δ (Log of FDI)
Method: Fixed effect panel error correction model
Sample: 1996–2012

Variables	Estimated model Investment driven (N, T) = (10, 17)	Factor driven (N, T) = (20, 17)	Fragile (N, T) = (12, 17)
Short run effects			
Constant	−10.62	8.76	58.62
Δ (Log of Real GDP per capita)	0.97***	−2.02	0.32
Δ (Log of Natural Resource Abundance)	0.53**	0.12***	1.08*
Δ (Log of Domestic Investment to GDP Ratio)	1.39**	0.53	−0.37
Δ (Log Inflation)	−0.373**	0.06	0.02
Δ (Log of External Debt to GDP Ratio)	0.00	−0.15	−1.00
Δ (Log of Openness)	1.13	0.45	1.42
Δ (Log of Real Exchange Rate)	0.97**	−0.41	0.71
Error Correction Term	−0.98***	−0.70***	−0.88***
Long-run effects			
Log of Real GDP per capita (−1)	0.34**	0.54	0.32
Log of Log of Natural Resource Abundance (−1)	−0.01	0.17***	0.66**
Log of Domestic Investment to GDP Ratio (−1)	0.39	0.43	1.47***
Log of Inflation (−1)	−0.51	0.00	−0.15
Log of External Debt to GDP Ratio (−1)	−0.62***	−0.17	−2.08***
Log of Openness (−1)	5.13***	−0.06	1.72
Log of Real Exchange Rate (−1)	0.89	−0.03	0.12
Political Stability	1.28**	0.51***	1.26
Government Effectiveness	2.02*	0.53*	2.82**

(continued)

Table 3 (continued)

Dependent variable: Δ (Log of FDI)
Method: Fixed effect panel error correction model
Sample: 1996–2012

Variables	Estimated model		
	Investment driven $(N, T) = (10, 17)$	Factor driven $(N, T) = (20, 17)$	Fragile $(N, T) = (12, 17)$
Diagnostic tests			
Adjusted R-squared	0.83	0.55	0.58
F-statistic	13.22	5.73	3.97
Prob (F-statistic)	0.00	0.00	0.00
Jarque-Berra	0.14	0.98	2.86
Prob (Jarque-Berra)	0.93	0.61	0.24
Cross-section Dependence Tests: (Null hypothesis: Cross-sectional independence)			
Breusch-Pagan Chi-square P-value	0.32	1.00	1.00
Pearson LM normal P-value	0.69	0.17	0.84
Pearson CD normal P-value	0.45	0.59	0.50
Friedman Chi-square P-value	1.00	0.59	0.89

Note ***, ** and * indicate 1, 5, and 10 percent level of significance respectively and T are the number of cross-sections and years in the model

while inflation had a negative effect. The adjustment coefficient shows that a 98 percent deviation from the long run equilibrium path will be adjusted in one period. This shows very fast adjustments in investment-driven countries. However, this adjustment towards equilibrium becomes slower in fragile and factor-driven economies. In the long run, real GDP per capita and openness had a significant positive impact, while external debt had a negative effect on FDI flows to the continent. In addition, political stability and government effectiveness indices had a statistically significant positive relationship with increased FDI inflows to all economies.

Table 3 further shows that in both the factor-driven and fragile economies, abundance of natural resources had a statistically significant positive impact on FDI inflows both in the short and long run. Its effect is also found to be more important in fragile rather than in factor-driven economies. It is also interesting to see that government effectiveness was important in all the three categories while political stability was important in investment-driven and factor-driven economies only.

Macroeconomic stability (whose proxies are inflation and exchange rate indicators) in the short run and openness in the long run were important only in investment-driven economies. Similarly, market size was important only in investment-driven economies perhaps indicating that FDI to these economies is market-seeking while it is resource seeking in the factor-driven and fragile economies. Finally, financial risks as measured by the stock of external debt to GDP ratio affect FDI inflows negatively in investment-driven and fragile economies only with the effect being stronger in fragile economies. This suggests that if a country is rich in resources (that is, it is factor-driven), financial risks may not be an issue.

6 Conclusion

Based on a new analytical classification of African economies as fragile, factor and investment driven economies we identified the main determinants of FDI inflows to Africa. The empirical analysis was conducted using a panel co-integration approach for the period 1996–2012. Our empirical analysis supports the hypothesis that FDI flows to Africa are conditional on the nature of the country in question as outlined in our analytical country classification.

Among all FDI determinants only government effectiveness in the long run and natural resource abundance in the short run were important determinants of FDI to all countries in Africa. The second finding of the study is that adjustment towards equilibrium was the fastest in investment-driven (ID) country groups followed by fragile (FR) and factor-driven (FD) country groups. Third, our study also showed that natural resource endowments were not important in investment-driven countries while they were very important in fragile economies. Fourth, openness was not important for all countries as current literature suggests; it was found to be important only in investment-driven countries. Similarly, financial and fund transfer risks as can be seen read from the debt to GDP ratio were not important for factor-driven economies. Political instability was not important for fragile country groups while government effectiveness was. However, political instability was important for investment and factor driven country groups.

The findings of our study suggest the importance of emphasizing different policies in different countries/country groups as well as the need for designing different FDI related incentive systems in different country groupings. Moreover, our analysis also suggests that the new analytical classification that we have developed could be an important guide in the operational and analytical work of continental organizations such as AfDB, the Economic Commission for Africa and the African Union as it suggests using different intervention strategies or policies for different countries.

Appendix

Suggested Proxies for Empirical Application of the Country Classification:

3 Determinants of Foreign Direct Investment Inflows to Africa

Table 4 An alternative proposed country classification of African Economies

Country's stage of development	Suggested proxies for measuring the stage
(a) Innovation-Driven African Economies (Advanced [frontier] African Economies)	R&D spending as percent of total government spending and also as percent of GDP Number of patent applications (as proxy for innovation) Number of leading global companies Tertiary education enrolment share, gross secondary education enrolment share, gross internet users per 100; mobile users (per 100) Private sector development (entrepreneurship: stock market value) Competitive democracy (governance indicator) GDP per capita (in US$) (All proxy indicators above should be benchmarked/comparable to the level attained by East Asian countries or a sample of them such as China, India and Taiwan)
(b) Investment-Driven African Economies (Emerging African Economies)	Investment (GCF) as share of GDP Gross domestic saving (share of GDP) FDI as share of GDP Manufacturing sector as the share of GDP Manufacturing export as the share of total exports Existence of stock market and listed companies Stable macroeconomic regime (inflation, CAD and Fiscal deficit percent GDP) Private sector development (entrepreneurship: stock market value) Competitive democracy (governance indicator) Road, km; rail and mobiles per 100 people (All proxy indicator above should be at least half the level attained by East Asian countries or a sample of them such as China, India and Taiwan)
(c) Factor-Driven African Economies (Aspiring African Economies)	Share of primary commodities in total exports >75 percent Share of manufactured exports in total exports <25 percent Road, rail and mobile per capita (< half of East Asia)
(C1) Agricultural Commodity Driven Economies (Class A)	Agricultural commodity exports >75 percent of exports Agriculture in GDP (above 40 percent)
(C2) Non-Agricultural Commodity Driven Economies (Class B)	(Non-agricultural commodity exports >75 percent of exports) Agriculture in GDP (below 40 percent)
(d) Post-Conflict and Fragile African Economies	lowest (<3) country policies and institutional performance assessment (CPIA) index value Uncompetitive democracy Emerged from conflict (less than 10 years) Existence of active rebellion

Table 5 Final analytical country classification for the model

Fragile State African Economies (AfDB CPIA <3)	Investment-Driven African Economies (Emerging or Frontier African Economies)	Factor-Driven African Economies (Aspiring African Economies)	Comment
Burundi	North Africa	(Rest of Africa)	• No African economy has reached the innovation driven stage (advanced African), yet (except to some degree South Africa followed by Egypt and Algeria) • (Libya, Madagascar and Mozambique on the border line scoring 40 percent while the passing level for the scale of 10 indicators is 50 percent)
Central African Republic	Algeria	Angola	
Chad		Benin	
Comoros	Egypt	Burkina Faso	
Congo, Dem Rep	Tunisia	Cameroon	
Congo, Rep	Morocco	Equatorial Guinea	
Cote d'Ivoire,	Other Africa	Ethiopia,	
Central African Republic	Botswana	Gabon	
	Kenya,		
Djibouti		Gambia, Ghana	
Eritrea	Mauritius,	Lesotho, Libya	
Guinea	Malawi	Madagascar, Mali	
Guinea-Bissau	Namibia,	Mauritania	
Liberia	South Africa	Mozambique	
Sao Tome and Principe	Cape Verde	Niger Nigeria	
Sierra Leone		Rwanda, Senegal	
Somalia		Seychelles, Swaziland	
Sudan		Tanzania,	
Togo		Uganda,	
Zimbabwe		Zambia	

References

Abdoul, G. (2012). What Drives Foreign Direct Investments in Africa? An Empirical Investigation with Panel Data. African Center for Economic Transformation, Accra, Ghana.

Agarwal, J. (1980). Determinants of Foreign Direct Investment: A Survey. *Review of World Economics*, 116(4): 739–773.

Ancharaz, V. (2003). Determinants of Trade Policy Reform in Sub-Saharan Africa. *Journal of African Economies*, 12(3): 417–443.

Anyanwu, J. (2012), Why Does Foreign Direct Investment Go Where It Goes? New Evidence from African Countries. *Annals of Economics and Finance*, 13(2): 433–470.

Asiedu, E. (2002). On the Determinants of Foreign Direct Investment to Developing Countries: Is Africa Different? *World Development*, 30(1): 107–118.

Asiedu, E. (2006). Foreign Direct Investment in Africa: The Role of Natural Resources, Market Size, Government Policy, Institutions and Political Instability. *World Economy*, 29(1): 63–77.

Asiedu, E. and K. Gyimah-Brempong (2008). The Effect of the Liberalization of Investment: Policies on Employment and Investment of Multination Corporation Corporations in Africa. *African Development Review*, 20(1): 49–66.

Baran, P. and P. Sweezy (1966). *Monopoly Capital: An Essay on the American Economic and Social Order*. London: Penguin Books Limited.

Basu, A. and S. Krishna (2002). *Foreign Direct Investment in Africa—Some Case Studies*. IMF Working Paper, No. 61.

Bende-Nabende, A. (2002). Foreign Direct Investment Determinants in Sub-Sahara Africa: A Co-integration Analysis. *Economics Bulletin*, 6(4): 1–19.

Brixiova, Z. and L. Ndikumana (2011). Characterizing Africa's Economic Dynamism. *AfDB Africa Economic Brief*, 2(8).

Buckley, P. (1985). *Foreign Direct Investment and Multinational Enterprises*. London: Macmillan.

Buckley, P. and M. Casson (1976). *The Future of the Multinational Enterprises*. London: Macmillan.

Caves, R. (1971). Industrial Corporations: The Industrial Economics of Foreign Investment. *Economica*, 38: 1–27.

Cleeve, E. (2008). How Effective are Fiscal Incentives to Attract FDI to Sub-Saharan Africa? *The Journal of Developing Areas*, 42(1): 135–153.

Coase, R. (1937). The Nature of the Firm. *Economica*, New Series, 4(16): 386–405.
Collier, P. and S. O'Connel (2008), 'Opportunities and Choices', in B. Ndulu, S. O'Connell, R. Bates, P. Collier, and C. Soludo (eds.), *The Political Economy of Economic Growth in Africa, 1960–2000*, Volume 1. Cambridge: Cambridge University Press, pp. 76–136.
Dunning, J. (1981). Explaining the International Direct Investment Position of Countries Towards a Dynamic or Development Approach. *Weltwirtschaftliches Archiv*, 117: 30–64.
Dunning, J. (1988). The Eclectic Paradigm of International Production: A Restatement and Some Possible Extensions. *Journal of International Business Studies*, 19(1): 1–31.
Dunning, J. (1993). *Multinational Enterprises and the Global Economy.* Reading, MA: Addison-Wesley.
Dupasquier, C. and P. Osakwe (2006), Foreign Direct Investment in Africa: Performance, Challenges, and Responsibilities. *Journal of Asian Economics*, 17(2): 241–260.
Elbadawi, I. and F. Mwega (1998). 'Regional Integration, Trade, and Foreign Direct Investment in Sub-Saharan Africa', in Z. Iqbal and M. Khan (eds.), *Trade Reform and Regional Integration in Africa*. Washington, DC: IMF, pp. 369–394.
Fosu, A. (2008). 'Anti-Growth Syndrome in Africa: A Synthesis of the case Studies,' in B. Nudulu, S. O'Connell, R. Bates, P. Collier, and C. Soludo (eds.), *The Political Economy of Economic Growth in Africa 1960–2000*. Cambridge: Cambridge University Press, pp. 68–82.
Fosu, A. and S. O'Connell (2006). 'Explaining African Economic Growth: The Role of Anti-Syndromes', in F. Bourguignon and B. Pleskovic (eds.), *Annual Bank Conference on Development Economics (ABCD)*. Washington, DC: The World Bank, pp. 31–66.
Geda, A. (2002). *Finance and Trade in Africa: Macroeconomic Response in the World Economy Context*. Basingstoke and New York: Palgrave Macmillan.
Geda, A. (2013). 'African Economic Engagement with China and Other Emerging South', Background Study for African Export-Import Bank, Afrixim Bank, Cairo.
Geda, A. and A. Yimer (2015). *Determinants of Foreign Direct Investment Inflows to Africa: A Panel Co-integration Evidence Using New Analytical Country Classification*, Addis Ababa University, Department of Economics Working Paper, No. 4.

Geda, A., N. Njuguna, and D. Zerfu (2012). *Applied Time Series Econometrics: A Practical Guide for Macroeconomic Researchers in Africa.* Nairobi: University of Nairobi Press.

Helleiner, G. (1989). 'Transnational Corporations and Direct Foreign Investment', in H. Chenery and T. Srinivasan (eds), *Handbook of Development Economics,* Volume III. Amsterdam: Elsevier, pp. 1452–1485.

Hendry, D. (1995). *Dynamic Econometrics.* Oxford: Oxford University Press.

Hymer, S. (1960). The International Operations of National Firms: A Study of Direct Foreign Investment. PhD Dissertation. Cambridge, MA: The MIT Press, Published Posthumously.

Itagaki, Y. (2007). Criticisms of Rostow's Stage Approach: The Concept of Stage, System and Type. *The Developing Economies,* 1(1): 1–17.

Johansen, S. (1988). Statistical Analysis of Cointegrating Vectors. *Journal of Economic Dynamics and Control,* 12: 231–254.

Johansen, S. (1991). Estimation and Hypothesis Testing of Cointegrating Vectors in Gaussian Vector Autoregressive Models. *Econometrica,* 59(6): 1551–1580.

Jorgenson, D. (1963). Capital Theory and Investment Behavior. *American Economic Review,* Supplement 53(2): 247–259.

Kindleberger, C. (1969). *American Business Abroad.* New Haven, CT: Yale University Press.

Krugell, H. (2005). 'The Determinants of Foreign Direct Investment in Africa', in T. Gries and W. Naude (eds.), *Foreign Direct Investment and Growth in Africa: South African Perspectives.* Berlin: Springer, pp. 49–71.

Krugman, P. (1979). A Model of Innovation, Technology Transfer, and the World Distribution of Income. *Journal of Political Economy,* 87(2): 253–266.

Lin, Y. (2011). New Structural Economics: A Framework for Rethinking Development. *The World Bank Research Observer,* 26(2): 193–221.

MacDougall, D. (1960). The Benefits and Costs of Private Investment from Abroad: A Theoretical Approach. *Economic Record,* 36: 13–35.

Magdoff, H. (1992). 'Globalization—To What End?' in M. Ralph and P. Leo (eds.), *Socialist Register.* London: The Merline Press, pp. 235–257.

Mhlanga, N., G. Blalock, and R. Christy (2010). Understanding Foreign Direct Investment in the Southern African Development Community: An Analysis Based on Project Level Data. *Agricultural Economics,* 41: 337–347.

Mohamed, S. and M. Sidiropoulos (2010). Another Look at the Determinants of Foreign Direct Investment in MENA Countries: An Empirical Investigation. *Journal of Economic Development,* 35(2): 75–95.

Morales, R. and F. Raei (2013). *The Evolving Role of Interest Rate and Exchange Rate Channels in Monetary Policy Transmission in EAC Countries*, IMF Working Paper, No. WP/13/X. Washington, DC: IMF.

Morisset, J. (2000). Foreign Direct Investment in Africa: Policies Also Matter. *Transnational Corporation*, 9(2): 107–125.

Naude, W. and H. Krugell (2007). Investigating Geography and Institutions as Determinants of Foreign Direct Investment in Africa Using Panel Data. *Applied Economics*, 39: 1223–1233.

Ndikumana, L. and S. Verick (2008). The Linkage Between FDI and Domestic Factor Markets: Unraveling the Developmental Impact of Foreign Investment. *Development Policy Review*, 26(6): 713–726.

Nonnenberg, M. and M. Mendonca (2004). *The Determinants of Direct Foreign Investment in Developing Countries*, Institute of Applied Economic Research Working Paper, January.

Nunnekamp, P. (2002). *Determinants of FDI in Developing Countries: Has Globalization Changed the Rules of The Game?* Kiel Working Paper. No. 1122.

Ohlin, B. (1933). *Interregional and International Trade*. Cambridge, MA: Harvard University Press.

Onyeiwu, S. and H. Shrestha (2004). Determinants of Foreign Direct Investment in Africa. *Journal of Developing Societies*, 20(1/2): 89–106.

Pesaran, H. (2006). Estimation and Inference in Large Heterogeneous Panels with a Multifactor Error Structure. *Econometrica*, 74: 967–1012.

Pesaran, H. (2007). A Simple Panel Unit Root Test in the Presence of Cross Section Dependence. *Journal of Applied Econometrics*, 22: 265–312.

Pesaran, H and Y. Shin (1999). An Autoregressive Distributed-Lag Modeling Approach to Cointegration Analysis. *Econometric Society Monographs*, 31: 371–313.

Pesaran, H., Y. Shin, and R. Smith (2001). Bounds Testing Approaches to the Analysis of Level Relationships. *Journal of Applied Econometrics*, 16: 289–326.

Porter, M. (1990). *The Competitive Advantage of Nations*. New York: The Free Press.

Root, E. and A. Ahmed (1979). Empirical Determinants of Manufacturing Direct Foreign Investment in Developing Countries. *Economic Development and Cultural Change*, 27: 751–767.

Rostow, W. (1959). The Stage of Economic Growth. *The Economic History Review*, 12(1): 1–16.

Rostow, W. (1960). *The Stages of Economic Growth: A Non-Communist Manifesto*. Cambridge: Cambridge University Press.

Scaperlanda, A. and L. Mauer (1969). Determinants of U.S. Investments in the EEC: Revisited. *American Economic Review*, 1: 381–390.

Schneider, F. and B. Frey (1985). Economic and Political Determinants of Foreign Direct Investment. *World Development*, 13(2): 161–175.

Seetanah, B. and S. Rojid (2011). The Determinants of FDI in Mauritius: A Dynamic Time Series Investigation. *African Journal of Economic and Management Studies*, 2(1): 24–44.

Standard and Poor (2011). *S&P Global BMI, S&P/IFCI Index Methodologies*. September.

Sunday A. and T. Lydie (2006). 'An Analysis of Foreign Direct Investment Flows to Cameroon,' in I. Ajayi (ed.), *Foreign Direct Investment in Sub-Saharan Africa: Origins, Targets, Impact and Potential*. Nairobi: AERC, pp. 235–252.

The World Bank (2014a). *African Development Indicators*. Washington, DC: WB.

The World Bank (2014b). *World Development Indicators*. Washington, DC: WB.

Thomas, R. (1993). *Introductory Econometrics: Theory and Application*. London: Longman.

UNCTAD (1998). *World Investment Report: Trends and Determinants*. New York and Geneva: United Nations.

UNCTAD (2014). *World Investment Report: Investing in the SDGs: An Action plan*. New York and Geneva: United Nations.

Vernon, R. (1966). International Investment and International Trade in the Product Cycle. *Quarterly Journal of Economics*, 80(2): 190-207.

Wheeler, D. and A. Mody (1992). International Investment Location Decisions: The Case of US Firms. *Journal of International Economics*, 33: 57–76.

4

Impact of Foreign Direct Investment on Economic Growth in Eastern Africa

Biratu Bekere and Mekonnen Bersisa

1 Introduction

In recent years, developing countries have acknowledged the significant role that FDI plays in their development agendas. In Africa in particular it is considered as an important ingredient in filling the gaps between domestically available savings supplies and investment demands; technology transfers; enhancing job creation; adding value to human skills; and increasing aggregate productivity of the host country (Todaro and Smith 2012).

B. Bekere (✉)
Department of Development Economics, Bole Campus,
Rift Valley University, Addis Ababa, Ethiopia

M. Bersisa
Department of Economics, Addis Ababa University,
Addis Ababa, Ethiopia

© The Author(s) 2018
A. Heshmati (ed.), *Determinants of Economic Growth in Africa*,
https://doi.org/10.1007/978-3-319-76493-1_4

Globally, the flow of FDI increased from US$13.3 billion in 1970 to US$1.76 trillion in 2015. At the same time developing countries' share of FDI increased from US$3.8 billion to US$0.8 trillion. Similarly, the inflow of FDI to Africa increased from US$1.8 billion in 1970 to US$57.2 billion and Eastern Africa's share went from US$0.1 to US$15.7 billion. The growth rate of FDI inflows to Africa and Eastern Africa increased in absolute terms between 1970 and 2015. Eastern Africa has also been attracting a large number of foreign investors (UNCTAD 2016).

However, a major concern for developing countries including those in East Africa is how to achieve sustainable growth in output over a long period of time and improve the standard of living of the people. This fundamental question of achieving sustained economic development in Africa and Eastern Africa remains a serious challenge for the regional economies. The region is not meeting its investment demands due to capital constraints, low saving rates, poor regional infrastructure development, structural and institutional rigidities, political instability, high crime rates, continuous civil conflicts, droughts and famines and unclear and arbitrary decisions about land ownership (Anyanwu 2012).

On the other hand, FDI's economic role in developing countries has not been supported unequivocally by all writers; it has both proponents and opponents. The proponents argue that FDI is an alternative source of capital which stimulates economic growth in the host economy, transfers technology and skill gains, increases production and trade networks, enhances socioeconomic development, promotes employment opportunities, helps in integration with global production networks and access to high quality goods and reduces disparities between revenues and costs (OECD 2008). However, the fruits of this can be harnessed under the condition that the host country has the right policy environment and minimum levels of educational, technological and infrastructure development (Borensztein et al. 1998).

Opponents of FDI argue that it has a negative or insignificant effect on the host economy and at worst it can also retard economic growth through its crowding-out effects on domestic infant industries, deteriorating balance of payments, exploiting local resources, repatriating profits to home countries, risks of political changes and opening the door to corruption by some public officials (Abadi 2011; Agrawal 2011; Alege and Ogundipe 2013). Several empirical studies have confirmed the negative effects of FDI on the economies of host countries. At an extreme FDI leads to modern day economic colonialism.

For sub-Saharan African countries considerable research findings show that FDI has had a positive impact on the economic growth of the region. For instance, Demelew (2014) examined the impact of FDI on the economic growth of 47 sub-Saharan African (SSA) countries. The study showed that FDI had a positive and significant effect on economic growth in the region. Similarly, a study by Zekarias (2016) confirmed a positive effect of FDI on economic growth in 14 East Africa countries. The study showed that FDI had spillover effects on economic growth in the region.

Besides the inconclusive empirical results about the impact of FDI on economic growth, clear causality between the two has not been established as yet in the Eastern African region. As a result, our study examines the causes and effects of these variables for the region. To provide up to date evidence in East African countries, we provide additional insights into the impact of FDI on economic growth in Eastern African countries. Moreover, we also examine political instability, problems of institutional quality, financial constraints, low saving rates, infrastructure development and other variables as the determinants of FDI inflows into the region.

The primary objective of our study is investigating the impact of FDI on economic growth in Eastern African countries and see the determinants of FDI in the region. Specifically, we address the following objectives:

- Identifying FDI's short run and long run contribution to economic growth in East Africa.
- Examining the causal relationship between FDI and economic growth.
- Investigating the effects of institutional quality and political stability in attracting FDI to the region.

2   Literature Review

Both theoretical and empirical literature on FDI abounds. Contending theories are available for the concepts, definitions, benefits and costs of FDI to the overall performance of an economy. Conceptually, FDI is one of the three components of international capital flows: portfolio investments, foreign direct investments and other flows like bank loans from developed economies to developing economies (Todaro and Smith 2012).

FDI is defined differently by various organizations. For instance, OECD (2008) defines FDI as establishing a lasting interest by a resident enterprise in one economy (direct investor) in an enterprise (direct investment enterprise) that is resident in an economy other than that of the direct investment. Lasting interest implies the existence of a long-term relationship between the direct investor and the direct investment enterprise with a significant degree of influence on the management of the enterprise. A significant degree of influence and a long-term relationship are key terms that distinguish FDI from portfolio investments which are short-term activities undertaken by institutional investors through the equity market. A 'lasting interest' in a foreign entity emphasizes the difference between FDI and other forms of capital flows and occurs in the form of know-how or the transfer of management skills. It also refers to a direct or indirect ownership of 10 percent or more of the voting powers of an enterprise residing in one economy (OECD 2008).

Different types of FDI have been identified on the basis of various criteria. Based on the strategic motive of an investment, FDI is classified as: market-seeking FDI, resource-seeking FDI, efficiency-seeking FDI and strategic asset seeking FDI. Resource-seeking investments seek to acquire factors of production that are more efficient than those obtainable in the home economy of the firm. Market-seeking investments aim at either penetrating new markets or maintaining existing ones. Efficiency-seeking investments target enhancing firms' efficiencies by exploiting the benefits of economies of scale, scope and common ownership (Kinyondo 2012; UNCTAD 1998).

Foreign direct investment is also classified into horizontal and vertical FDI. Horizontal FDI refers to foreign manufacturing products and services similar to those produced in the home market. Vertical FDI refer to those multinationals that fragment production process geographically. It is called vertical because a multinational enterprise (MNE) produces a product that has multiple stages with different production activities (Beugelsdijk and Zwinkels 2008).

Further, FDI can be classified into Greenfield investments, brownfield investments and cross-border mergers and acquisitions. Greenfield investments refer to direct investments in new facilities or an expansion of existing facilities. Greenfield investments are a primary target of a host nation's promotional efforts because they create new production capacities and jobs, transfer technology and knowledge and can lead to linkages to the global marketplace. In brownfield investments a company or government entity purchases or leases existing production facilities to launch a new production activity. It is one strategy for getting FDI. Mergers and acquisitions transfer existing assets from local firms to foreign firms and are common practices of this category of FDI (Kiyondo 2012; Solomon 2008; UNCTAD 2013).

Several theories of FDI have been postulated to explain its roles and effects including the product life cycle theory, exchange rates on imperfect capital markets theory, internalization theory and the eclectic paradigm of Dunning theory. The production cycle theory was developed by Vernon (1966) to explain four stages of production: innovation, growth, maturity and decline (Denisia 2010; Vernon 1966). The exchange rates on imperfect capital markets theory analyzes foreign exchange risk from the view of international trade along with the influence of uncertainty as a factor of FDI. The internalization theory was developed by Buckley and Casson (1976) and then elaborated by Casson (1983) and it explains the growth of transnational companies and their motivations for achieving FDI. The eclectic paradigm of Dunning theory was developed by Dunning (1973). This paradigm includes three different types of FDI: Ownership advantages, location-specific and internalization.

2.1 Evolution of FDI and Role of Institutional Quality in Attracting It

Developing countries as well as countries in transition have been attracting FDI and exploring ways of increasing its inflows. Buckley (1991) distinguished four phases in the history of growth of international private investments. The first phase (1870–1914) focused on the role of multinational enterprises (MNEs) as entrepreneurs and transfer of intangible assets in these 40 years. FDI during this period was transfer of resources between different countries and was used as a means of controlling the use of resources and complementary local inputs. The second phase (1918–1938) was followed by World War I where several challenges in levels, form and structure of international production were encountered. The war itself caused several European countries to aggressively sell some of their pre-war investments. There were also some challenges in its geographical distribution. The size of West European investments in central Europe and USA continued to attract more than two-third of the US direct investment stakes. There were a number of new MNEs which participated in the developing world in the inter-war years including new oil investments in the Mexican gulf, the Dutch East Indies and in the Middle East, copper and iron ore in Africa, bauxite in Dutch and British Guyana, nitrate in Chile, precious metals in South Africa and non-iron metals in South America.

The third phase (1939–1960), witnessed the increasingly important role of European, Japanese and some third world countries as international direct investors. Between 1960 and 1970 the world capital stock increased to US$18 billion of which USA accounted for 48 percent and West Germany and Japan for 18 percent.

Finally, the fourth phase (1960–1978) was a period when the rate of growth of international capital stock reached its peak in the late 1960s, reduced in the early and mid-1970s, UK and USA's shares kept falling and there was an increase in the shares of West Germany, Japan and Switzerland. In the late 1970s regions such as Eastern Europe and China opened up. The growth in MNEs' activities in different service sectors like banking, insurance, advertising and tourism and the increasing use of cross-border arrangements through multilateral agreements were some of the development indices during this time.

Several factors are responsible for increasing international flows of investments. Institution as a determinant of FDI was established in the distant past. The quality of institutions may matter in attracting FDI. Wei (2000) investigated the lack of institutional quality reflected in corruption by civil servants which generated mistrust and was unhealthy for the business community and for both domestic and foreign investors.

However, FDI has shown an increasing trend over time. In particular, the growth rate of FDI inflows to Africa and Eastern Africa increased in absolute terms between 1970 and 2015. Africa's FDI share in developing countries fell from 33 percent in 1970 to 7.3 percent in 2013, but the share of East Africa in Africa as a whole rose from 6.3 percent in 1970 to 25.5 percent in 2013 and the total FDI inflows into Africa were approximately 12.6 percent in 2014 (AEO 2016).

To examine the role of FDI in economic growth, it is important to study its theoretical foundation. Its roles have been analyzed in a theoretical framework of the classical international trade theory of comparative advantage and differences in factor endowments between countries (Sala and Trivin 2014). Further, the importance of capital in an economy has been well stated in Keynesian, neoclassical and endogenous growth theories.

Most recently, the new growth theory acknowledged the importance of FDI in starting economic growth through financing new investments and technology transfers (Sala and Trivin 2014). Unlike previous theories, the new growth models emphasize the role of research and development, human capital accumulation and externalities in economic growth (Romer 1994).

Moreover, one can find vast empirical evidence on the nexus between FDI and economic growth. While there is consensus on the theoretical outcomes of FDI on economic growth, there is a disagreement in the empirical findings. There are mixed results from this perspective. Balasubramanyam (1996) analyzed the relationship between FDI and economic growth in developing countries using cross-sectional data and ordinary least squares. His findings showed that FDI had a positive impact in developing countries that had adopted export-oriented strategies but not in countries that had implemented import-oriented strategies.

Borensztein et al. (1998) examined the impact of FDI on economic growth by focusing on the role of technological diffusion in 69 developing countries. Their findings indicate that FDI was an important driving factor for transfer of technology, which eventually contributed more to economic growth than domestic investments. The study concluded that FDI had a positive impact on economic growth, but the amount of growth depended on the availability of human capital. DeMello (1999) extended Borensztein et al. (1998) study accounting for both developing and developed countries. The findings of this study showed the existence of a positive impact of FDI on economic growth for both developed and developing countries. The study found that FDI inflows had a positive impact on economic growth in countries with higher income levels and substantial privatization.

In contrast, some studies have found a negative relationship between FDI and economic growth. For instance, Herzer et al. (2008) indicate that the relationship between FDI and economic growth in selected sample countries was indeterminate. Apergis (2008) found that FDI had a negative effect on economic growth in countries that had lower income levels and ineffective liberalization policies.

Sukar and Hassan (2011) investigated FDI's effects on economic growth in sub-Saharan African countries by using 25 years' panel data over the period 1975–1999. They found that FDI had a positive effect on the economic growth of these countries. On the other hand, Alege and Ogundipe (2013) found a negative effect of FDI on economic growth in the ECOWAS region. Their study indicated that the negative effect got stronger with the level of under-development; the growth-stimulating effect of FDI depended on human capital, the quality of institutions, infrastructure and other country specific factors.

Sala and Trivin (2014) examined the relationship between trade openness, investments and economic growth in sub-Saharan African countries using the GMM estimation method to the dynamic growth model. They examined the existence of both conditional and unconditional convergence models. Their findings show that globalization (trade openness) and FDI had a significant effect on economic growth in the past three decades.

Agrawal (2015) analyzed FDI's impact on economic growth in BRICS economies using panel data. The study focused on integration and a causality analysis at the panel level, which indicated the presence of a long run relationship between FDI and economic growth in BRICS.

Existing empirical literature provides mixed results on the determinants of FDI inflows. Valeriani and Peluso (2011) examined the impact of institutional quality on economic growth in 69 developed and developing countries using the fixed effect model. Their results revealed that a country with better institutional quality had better economic growth and attracted more FDI inflows. Basemera et al. (2012) analyzed the role of institutions in determining FDI inflows to East Africa between 1987 and 2008 based on the Dunning eclectic paradigm using the fixed effects and random effects models. Their study found that economic risk rating, financial risk rating and corruption significantly influenced FDI inflows to East Africa. However, governance and law and order were insignificant in influencing FDI inflows.

Baklouti and Boujelbene (2014) explain the impact of institutional quality in attracting FDI in the Middle East and North America (MENA) region over the period 1996–2008 using fixed effects models of panel data in eight selected countries. Their result indicate that corruption and regulatory quality had a negative influence on FDI. Nondo et al. (2016) found an insignificant relationship between institutional quality and FDI inflows to 45 sub-Saharan African countries in 1996–2007 using the fixed effects estimation technique. Many sub-Saharan African countries scored very low on all dimensions of institutional quality. However, these findings should be interpreted very cautiously as they do not discount the importance of institutional quality in the sustainable development process in SSA. Accordingly, it is possible that institutional quality may affect FDI indirectly by stimulating other variables including human capital, infrastructure and the health of workers which in turn directly affect FDI. This study revealed that institutional quality was hindering foreign investors in most African countries.

A recent study by Zekarias (2016) investigated FDI's impact on economic growth in 14 Eastern African countries using the GMM estimation method. The findings of the study indicate that FDI had a positive and marginally significant impact on economic growth in the region. However, the findings did not find any impact of political instability and institutional quality on economic growth in East African countries.

Hence, it can be seen that there is scant empirical evidence on FDI's impact on economic growth in East Africa and even this evidence has mixed results which may justify further studies. Our study explores the determinants of FDI by filling the missing variables in Zekarias' (2016) study. Our study thus contributes to existing knowledge by taking into account the impacts of political stability and institutional quality on economic growth and FDI flows in the region.

3 Data and Methodology

3.1 Types and Source of Data

We used secondary data to analyze FDI's impact and its determinants in Eastern African countries. Panel data was collected from the World Development Indicator database of the World Bank, the World Governance Indicator (WGI) database of the World Bank and Political Risk Services International's Country Risk Guide (PRS) database. The study used 20 years panel data (1996–2015) for 14 Eastern African countries.

3.2 Population and Sample

Based on the UNCTAD classification, Eastern Africa comprises of 18 countries: Burundi, Comoros, Ethiopia, Kenya, Madagascar, Malawi, Mauritius, Mozambique, Seychelles, Rwanda, Uganda, Tanzania, Zambia, and Zimbabwe, Djibouti, Eritrea, Somalia and South Sudan. However, we excluded the last four countries from our study due to data limitations. Data for these countries was missing in the indicated sources. Therefore, the first 14 countries were included in the econometric analysis.

3.3 Model Specification

FDI is required for reducing the capital and income gap between developing and developed countries under endogenous growth. FDI impacts growth by improving the productivity of domestic and foreign capital. We estimated two models in our study. The first model was developed to examine FDI's effects on economic growth and the second one was used for exploring the relationship between FDI and explanatory variables such as institutional quality and political instability. To find the impact of FDI on economic growth, we used a Solow-swan aggregate production (Solow 1956) from the augmented Cobb-Douglas production function as a theoretical foundation. The model is specified as:

Model one:

$$Y = f(K_d, K_f, L, E) = AL^\alpha K^\beta E^{1-\alpha-\beta} \tag{1}$$

Where, Y is growth of output, K_d is domestic capital, K_f is foreign capital, L is labor force and E is the multiplier effect from FDI, α and β are the elasticity of labor and capital to output (Y) respectively and A refers to efficiency of production. The human capital augmented Lucas model (Lucas 1988; Romer 1994) divides labor into human capital (HC) and labor force (LF). Based on its productivity the rate of economic growth is affected by capital (K), the level of infrastructure (INFRA), inflation (INF), foreign trade (OPEN), political stability (POLSTA) and institutional factors. We used regulatory quality as a proxy for institutional quality. Using these variables, our modified model is:

$$Y = f \begin{pmatrix} \text{FDI, GFCF, HC, LF, INFRADEV,} \\ \text{OPEN, INFL, POLSTA, INS, } \varepsilon \end{pmatrix} \tag{2}$$

where, Y is the GDP growth rate, FDI is foreign direct investment, GFCF is gross fixed capital formation (earlier known as domestic private investment), HC is human capital, LF is the labor force, INFRADEV is infrastructure development, OPEN is the value of foreign trade which is the sum of exports and imports, INF is the rate of inflation, POLSTA is political instability, INST is the institutional quality proxied by regulatory quality and ε is the general error term. Since the relationship between growth in output (dependent variable) and the independent variables is non-linear, the explicit form of the model given in Eq. (2) is:

$$Y = \text{AFDI}^{\beta_1}\text{GFCF}^{\beta_2}\text{HC}^{\beta_3}\text{LF}^{\beta_4}\text{INFRDEVE}^{\beta_5} \\ \text{OPEN}^{\beta_6}\text{INFL}^{\beta_7}\text{POLSTA}^{\beta_8}\text{INST}^{\beta_9}\,\varepsilon \qquad (3)$$

where, $\beta_1\ldots\beta_9$ are respective factor contributions to growth and ε is the error term.

As panel models comprise both longitudinal and cross-sectional data they have dynamic dimensions across space, time and variables (Wooldridge 2005). In our study, there are 14 cross-countries, 20 years' data and 13 variables. Therefore, Eq. (3) was further modified to include cross-sectional units and time. Thus, the dynamic cross-country growth model is given by:

$$Y_{it} = \text{AFDI}_{it}^{\beta_1}\text{GFCF}_{it}^{\beta_2}\text{HC}_{it}^{\beta_3}\text{LF}_{it}^{\beta_4}\textit{INRDEV}_{it}^{\beta_5} \\ \text{OPEN}_{it}^{\beta_6}\text{INF}_{it}^{\beta_7}\text{POLSTA}_{it}^{\beta_8}\text{INST}_{it}^{\beta_9}\,\varepsilon_{it} \qquad (4)$$

where, i refer to cross-sectional units, that is, countries, t refers to time units in years (1996–2015) and ε_{it} is the composite disturbance term. For computational convenience and easier understanding, the non-linear equation is converted into a linear equation through a logarithmic transformation as:

$$\text{Ln}Y_{it} = \beta_0 + \beta_1\text{FDI}_{it} + \beta_2\text{GFCF}_{it} + \beta_3\text{HC}_{it} \\ + \beta_4\text{LF}_{it} + \beta_5\text{INFRDEV}_{it} + \beta_6\text{OPEN}_{it} \\ + \beta_7\text{INF}_{it} + \beta_8\text{POLSTA}_{it} + \beta_9\text{INST}_{it} + U_{it} \qquad (5)$$

where, β_0 is the intercept, $\beta_1, \beta_2 \ldots \beta_9$ are coefficients of the respective explanatory variables, Y_{it} is growth rate of GDP which is the dependent variable, all the variables as explained earlier are transformed into a natural logarithm and U_{it} is the error term which is natural logarithm of ε_{it}.

Model two:

An alternative model was formulated to examine the determinants of FDI (Eq. 6). Institutional quality, political instability and human capital were used as explanatory variables.

$$\ln FDI_{it} = \beta_0 + \beta_1 \ln FDI_{it-1} + \beta_2 INST_{it} + \beta_3 POLSTA_{it} + \varepsilon_{it} \quad (6)$$

where, FDI is foreign direct investment, INST is regulatory quality proxy for initutional quality, POLSTA is political stability to indicate the level of political instability and ε_{it} is the error term.

3.4 Estimation Technique

To investigate FDI's impact on economic growth in East Africa we used the generalized method of moments (GMM) of dynamic panel data. GMM is a statistical method that combines observed economic data with information in population conditions to produce estimates of unknown parameters of the economic model (Zsohar 2012). The advantage of dynamic panel estimation methods like GMM is that they address the endogenity problem, work to eliminate the serial correlation and easily eliminate the hetroscedasticity problem. GMM is a general framework for deriving estimators that are consistent under weak distributional assumptions (Wooldridge 2001).

We used the Arellano-Bond dynamic panel estimator in our study. This method starts by transforming all regressors, usually by differencing and uses the generalized method of moments and is called difference GMM. The difference GMM estimator is designed for a panel analysis and embodies the assumptions about data generating of the dynamic model, with current realizations of the dependent variable which are influenced by past realizations but in this case there may be arbitrarily distributed fixed individual effects (Arellano and Bond 1991; Hansen 1982).

3.5 Diagnostic Tests

We conducted several diagnostic tests to confirm the appropriateness of the method and the adequacy of the variables among which are cross-sectional dependence, over-identification, autocorrelation and the panel unit root test. First, we tested the existence of cross-sectional dependence. DeHayos and Sarafidis (2006) have shown that if there is cross-sectional dependence in the disturbances all estimation procedures that employ the generalized method of moments such as Anderson and Hsiao (1981), Arellano and Bond (1991), and Blundell and Bond (1998) are inconsistent as N (the cross-sectional dimension) grows large for fixed T (the panel's time dimension). As a result, our study also conducted a cross-sectional dependence test.

We also conducted the Sargan and Hansen tests of over-identifying restrictions. Here the crucial assumption for the validity of GMM is that the instruments are exogenous. If the model is identified exactly, the detection of invalid instruments is impossible. Even when $E(Ź\epsilon) \neq 0$, the estimator will choose so that $E(Ź\epsilon) = 0$. However, if the model is over-identified, a test statistic for the joint validity of the moment conditions falls naturally out of the GMM framework.

Arellano and Bond (1991, 1995) have developed a test for a phenomenon that would render some lags invalid as instruments due to the existence of autocorrelation in the idiosyncratic disturbance term, v_{it}. If v_{it} are themselves serially correlated of order one then y_{it-2} will be endogenous to v_{it-1} in the error term in differences, $\Delta\varepsilon_{it} = v_{it} - v_{it-1}$ making them potentially invalid instruments. To test for autocorrelation aside from the fixed effects, we applied the Arellano-Bond test to the residuals in differences. To check for first-order serial correlation in levels or for second-order correlation in differences a test for correlation between the v_{it-1} in Δv_{it} and the v_{it-2} in Δv_{it-1} is needed. The Arellano-Bond test for autocorrelation has a null hypothesis of no autocorrelation and is applied to the differenced residuals. The test for the AR (1) process in first differences usually rejects the null hypothesis (though not in our case), but this is expected since:

$$\Delta e_{it} = e_{it} - e_{it-1} \text{ and } \Delta e_{it-1}$$
$$= e_{it-1} - e_{it-2} \text{ both have } e_{it-1} \text{ in common} \tag{7}$$

We also conducted the panel unit root test and the panel Granger causality test. Stationarity of individual variables has to be tested before estimating any model. A time series is said to be stationary if its mean, variance and auto covariance remain the same. If time series is non-stationary, the persistence of shocks will be infinite. As we used panel data the Hadri LM test was also done. This LM test has a null of stationary and is distributed as standard normal under the null (Hadri 2000). For each cross-sectional panel in $i = 1\ldots N$, at time $t = 1\ldots T$, suppose that:

$$Y_{it} = \alpha_i Y_{it-1} + \delta_i Z_{it} + \varepsilon_{it}, t = 1\ldots T, i = 1,\ldots N \qquad (8)$$

where, Z_{it} represents the exogenous variables in the model including any fixed effects or individual trends, T is time span of the panel, N represents the number of cross-sections, α_i is the autoregressive coefficient and error term ε_{it} is assumed to be mutually independent of idiosyncratic disturbances. Here if $|\alpha_i| < 1$, then Y_{it} is said to be stationary. On the other hand, if $|\alpha_i| = 1$ and then Y_{it} contains a unit root.

Further, we also tested the Granger causality. A variable Y is said to Granger cause another variable X if at time t, X_{t+1} can be better predicted by using past values of Y. Because panel data gives us more variability, degree of freedom and efficiency and also considering the time series individual regionally disaggregated we introduce panel techniques to improve the validity of our Granger causality test.

Finally, we specified and tested panel cointegration and vector error correction. The use of cointegration techniques to test for the presence of long run relationships among integrated variables has enjoyed growing popularity in empirical literature. Since the panel unit root tests presented earlier indicate that the variables are integrated of order one I (1) we conducted a test for cointegration using the panel cointegration test developed by Pedroni (1999). If two or more series are individually integrated (in the time series sense) but some linear combination of them has a lower order of integration then the series are said to be cointegrated. Besides, once we determined that the two variables were cointegrated we performed a panel-based vector error correction model (VECM) to conduct the Granger causality test to account for both short run and long run causality. We did this using Engle and Granger's

(1987) two-step procedure. In the first step, we estimated the long run model specified in Eq. (9) to obtain the estimated residuals ε_{it}:

$$Y_{it} = \alpha_i + \delta_t + \gamma x_{it} + \varepsilon_{it} \quad (9)$$

where, $\alpha_i + \delta_t$ are fixed cross-section and trend effects respectively. We included them only when redundant fixed effects showed that this was necessary. Then we estimated the second stage using:

$$\Delta Y_{it} = \Phi_j + \sum_1 \Phi_1 k \Delta Y_{it-k} + \sum_2 \Phi_2 k \Delta Y_{it-k} + \lambda \text{ECT}_{it-1} + U_{it} \quad (10)$$

where, Δ is the first difference of the variable, k is the lag length, ECT is the error correction term which is estimated by residuals from the first stage and U_{it} are the residuals of the model. Here the significance of causality results is determined by the Wald F-test.

3.6 Definition of the Variables

The dependent variable for the first model is growth of national income denoted by Y. We used annual percentage growth rate of GDP at constant 2010 prices in terms of USD. In fact, a higher economic growth rate coupled with stable and credible macroeconomic policies attracts foreign investors (Onyeiwu and Shrestha 2004).

We also identified several variables as independent variables for the first model. Their definitions and expected signs are:

Foreign direct investment (FDI): the net inflows of FDI as a percent of GDP in the host country. It is the sum of equity capital, reinvestments of earnings, other long-term capital and short-term capital as shown in the balance of payments. This series shows net inflows (new investment inflows less disinvestment) in the reporting economy from foreign investors. We expect that FDI positively effects economic growth in East African countries.

Gross fixed capital formation (GFCF): earlier known as gross domestic private investment. Private investment covers gross outlays by the private sector on additions to its fixed domestic assets including land improvements (fences, ditches, drains); plant, machinery and equipment purchases; and the construction of roads and railways including schools, offices, hospitals, private residential dwellings and commercial and industrial buildings. It is measured as private sector investment as a percentage of GDP. It is also expected that this variable will have a positive effect on economic growth in the region.

Human capital (HC): is the aggregation of health, education, on-job training and social welfare. Human capital is one of the determinants of economic growth. Countries with good education and healthcare facilities also have developed economies. There is a positive correlation among economic growth, FDI and level of human capital. We used expenditure on education and health as a percentage of GDP as proxy to human capital. Human capital is expected to have a positive effect on economic growth and attract more FDI.

Institutional quality (INST): regulatory quality was used as proxy for institutional quality which reflects perceptions of people about the ability of the government to formulate and implement sound policies and regulations that permit and promote private sector development. Countries with good institutional quality have better economic development and attract more international investors to boost their economies.

Political stability (POLSTA): measures perceptions about the likelihood of political instability and/or politically motivated violence, including terrorism. A stable political situation leads to higher economic growth and attracting more FDI.

Infrastructure development (INFR): one of the well-recognized factors for economic growth and for attracting FDI. The main argument is that well-established infrastructure such as roads, airports, electricity, water supply, telephones and internet access reduce the cost of doing business and help maximize the rate of returns. It is suggested that the availability of good quality infrastructure subsidizes the cost of total investments and leads to increasing efficiency in production and marketing. To measure the overall infrastructural development of the region we used the number of mobile subscription per 100 population.

Trade openness (OPEN): is the sum of exports and imports as a percent of gross domestic product. A country's openness can be expressed in different ways—trade restrictions, tariffs and foreign exchange control laws. As the openness of an economy is believed to foster economic growth and level of FDI, the more open an economy, the more likely it is to grow and attract FDI.

Labor force (LF): labor force participation rate is the proportion of the population aged 15–64 years, that is, economically active people who supply labor for the production of goods and services during a specified period.

Inflation rate (INF): inflation as measured by the consumer price index reflects the annual percentage change in costs for an average consumer acquiring a basket of goods and services that may be fixed or may change at specified intervals, such as yearly. A nation's macroeconomic stability affects both economic growth and FDI flows.

4 Results and Discussion

4.1 Descriptive Statistics of Variables

Our study's primary focus was examining FDI's effect on economic growth in East African countries and the role of institutional quality and political stability in attracting FDI to the region. Country level descriptive data on GDP growth rate, FDI, GFCF, human capital, institutional quality, political stability, labor force, inflation rate, trade openness and infrastructure development for 14 East Africa countries for the period of 1996–2015 is presented in Table 1.

As can be seen from Table 1 during the past two decades, Seychelles attracted the highest share of FDI as percentage of its GDP in the region. For the stated period on average it attracted about 12.39 percent share of GDP with a variation of about 10.91. The share of FDI to GDP ranged from 3.95 to 54.06 percent for Seychelles. Mozambique was the second highest FDI recipient country in the region. On average, the country attracted about 11.87 percent FDI as a share of its GDP. Zambia was the third recipient of international investors (on average

Table 1 Summary statistics of share of FDI in GDP by country (*Source* Authors' computation using Stata 13)

Country	Obs.	Mean	St. dev	Min	Max
Burundi	20	0.614479	1.132043	0.0013049	4.300125
Comoros	20	0.843107	1.023333	0.0094295	3.938068
Ethiopia	20	2.429813	1.621524	0.2565531	5.392123
Kenya	20	0.633925	0.656430	0.0408334	2.281243
Madagascar	20	4.622954	4.489862	0.2351848	15.126020
Malawi	20	3.140974	3.296864	0.1485800	10.180350
Mauritius	20	2.215993	1.800518	0.6100591	5.796793
Mozambique	20	11.877900	12.81055	1.5234410	41.809640
Rwanda	20	1.298351	1.297509	0.0949419	3.992169
Seychelles	20	12.396430	10.91984	3.9563830	54.062100
Tanzania	20	3.862751	1.254259	1.8437990	5.773068
Uganda	20	3.826471	1.280041	2.0017920	6.479821
Zambia	20	5.713476	1.721872	3.2552910	9.418112
Zimbabwe	20	1.688352	1.622256	0.0560688	6.940053

5.71 percent). Burundi got the least among the East African countries during the study period (on average 0.61 percent).

FDI inflows to the regions have been increasing over time. In particular, they have has shown an increasing trend internationally after the financial crisis (2008–2009). FDI flows were volatile depending on various shocks in the international economy. From Fig. 1 it can be seen that FDI inflows to the region were volatile. Seychelles followed by Mozambique attracted more foreign private investments than other countries in the region.

4.2 Results of Diagnostic Tests

We conducted various diagnostic tests on each variable before running the actual model. First, we tested the stationarity of each variable. We used the Hadri Lagrange Multiplier (LM) test to conduct the panel unit root test. The results are given in Table 2.

The test statistics confirm that all the variables were not stationary at level. All the variables (GDP, gross capital formation, FDI, human capital, inflation rate, openness, political stability and institutional quality) become stationary at first difference.

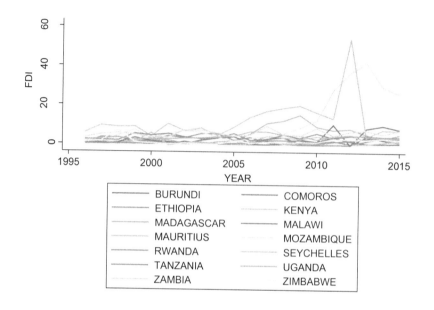

Fig. 1 Net inflows of foreign direct investment (1996–2015)

Table 2 Panel unit root test for all variables (*Source* Authors' computation using Stata 13)

Variables	Statistics	p-value
Difference of GDPGR	−2.2229	0.986
Difference of FDI	−3.0529	0.998
Difference of GFCF	−1.7055	0.956
Difference of HC	−0.4701	0.680
Difference of INF	−3.5279	0.999
Difference of OPEN	−1.3639	0.913
Difference of PLOSTA	0.5612	0.287
Difference INS	0.7330	0.231

Besides, we also conducted an autocorrelation test of the dynamic panel data using the Sargan test and Hansen statistic. The results are given in Table 3.

The test results provide sufficient evidence to reject the null hypothesis of autocorrelation. This indicates that there is no autocorrelation problem in our models as the probability of the Sargan and Hansen tests is greater than the 5 percent level of significance. We used the

4 Impact of Foreign Direct Investment on Economic Growth ...

Table 3 Autocorrelation test of variables

Variables	Coefficient	Robust St.	T stat	p > |t|
DGDPGR	0.3929087	0.0437690	8.98	0.000
FDI	0.0477607	0.0326863	1.46	0.168
GFCF	0.0328513	0.0361883	0.91	0.381
INF	0.0001851	0.0000143	12.95	0.000
HC	0.0730388	0.0122672	5.95	0.000
INST	0.1432963	0.0372915	3.84	0.002
INFRADEV	0.0961568	0.0519566	1.85	0.087
LF	−1.4116790	0.3433706	−4.11	0.001
OPEN	0.0038710	0.0078375	0.49	0.630
POLSTA	0.0346090	0.0171885	0.20	0.844
Cons	1.7940700	1.0251030	1.75	0.104

Arellano-Bond test for AR (1) in first differences: $z = -1.28$ Pr $> z = 0.202$
Arellano-Bond test for AR (2) in first differences: $z = -2.80$ Pr $> z = 0.233$
Sargan test of overid. Restrictions: $\chi^2(248) = 789.32$ Prob $> \chi^2 = 0.12$
Hansen test of overid. Restrictions: $\chi^2(248) = 7.67$ Prob $> \chi^2 = 0.45$

robust standard error to remove the problem of hetroscedasticity in the panel data. Moreover, Arreano-Bond AR (1) probability was greater than the 5 percent significance level. Therefore, there was no autocorrelation in our dataset.

We also tested a null hypothesis of the absence of cross-sectional dependence for which we used Pesaran's test of cross-sectional independence. The test results are given in Table 4 and these do not provide us sufficient evidence to reject the null hypothesis.

Therefore, our model has no problem of panel cross-sectional dependence.

Similarly, we did the cointegrated test using both Johansen and Fisher cointegration tests. The results of the Fisher cointegration test, which is system based are given in Table 5.

We can reject the null hypothesis of no cointegration between the variables of interest. Therefore, there is cointegration between the GDP growth rate and FDI inflows.

Finally, we estimated the panel vector error correction model to see the long run dynamics of the model.

As we can see from Table 6 the coefficient of C_1 (error correction term) is negative and significant. This indicates that there is long run

Table 4 Cross-sectional dependence test (*Source* Authors' computation using Stata 13)

Variables	Fixed effect model Coefficient	Robust Std. error	p > |z|	Random effect model Coefficient	Robust Std. error	p > |z|
DGDPGR	−0.4092829	0.0812359	0.001	−0.3608371	0.0632569	0.000
DFDI	0.1814331	0.1325841	0.201	0.0446622	0.0585386	0.445
DGFCF	0.0145540	0.0741949	0.848	0.0665304	0.0516201	0.197
DHC	0.1319314	0.0293109	0.001	0.1189323	0.0697123	0.088
D INF	0.0001841	0.0000234	0.001	0.0001669	0.0001304	0.201
DINST	−0.0739660	0.0732641	0.337	−0.0089595	0.0712787	0.900
DINFRADEV	0.1603613	0.1262307	0.233	0.0833399	0.0561279	0.138
DLF	−1.1160740	0.4784722	0.042	−0.7767940	0.3387792	0.022
DPOLSTA	0.0003242	0.0286603	0.991	−0.0009563	0.0321035	0.766
DOPEN	0.0237874	0.0320562	0.475	0.0263030	0.0161076	0.102
Cons	−0.5571521	0.4241773		−1.0401880	0.7060838	0.141
Sigma u	0.4320248					
Sigma e	4.3716911			4.3993984		
Rho	0.0096715					

Notes Pesaran's test of cross-sectional independence = 0.420, Pr = 0.6747
Average absolute value of the off-diagonal elements = 0.201

Table 5 Cointegration test of FDI and GDPGR (*Source* Authors' computation using Stata 13)

Hypothesized No. of CE(s)	Fisher stat.* (from trace test)	Prob.	Fisher stat.* (from max-Eigen test)	Prob.
None	57.60	0.0008	64.33	0.0001
At most 1	17.43	0.9396	17.43	0.9396

Table 6 Long run causal relationship between FDI and GDPGR (*Source* Authors' computation using Stata 13. Eview 9)

	Coefficient	Standard error	t-statistic	Prob.
C(1)	−0.005219	0.007060	−0.739153	0.0462
C(2)	−0.523831	0.064266	−8.150923	0.0000
C(3)	−0.202577	0.065183	−3.107847	0.0020
C(4)	0.081804	0.081063	1.009142	0.3134
C(5)	0.089638	0.067329	1.331347	0.1837
C(6)	0.369947	0.284353	1.301013	0.1939
C(7)	0.034451	0.006171	5.582308	0.0000
C(8)	−0.048651	0.056175	−0.866057	0.3869
C(9)	−0.080104	0.056976	−1.405923	0.1604
C(10)	−0.218639	0.070856	−3.085661	0.0022
C(11)	−0.121305	0.058852	−2.061207	0.0398
C(12)	0.001664	0.248551	0.006695	0.9947
Determinant residual covariance		261.1073		

causality from the independent to the dependent variable. There is long run causality from international private investments to GDP in the region.

4.3 Estimation Results of the Difference GMM

We used the difference GMM estimation method to examine the determinants of economic growth in East African countries. The results provide long run as well as short run effects of the covariates on the GDP growth rate. In particular, FDI had a positive and marginally significant effect on economic growth in the region. However, in the short run foreign private investments had a positive but insignificant effect on the GDP growth rate. Our results are consistent with some other studies (Demelew 2014; Zekariyas 2016).

As can be seen from Table 7, human capital and infrastructure development were negatively related to GDP growth. Since human capital and infrastructure are still poor in East Africa, our results justify the reality of the region. Despite the theoretical importance of human capital in growth and development, its practical contribution to Eastern African countries is not clear in the short run. There are many reasons for this including: (i) usually human capital development is gained through education, and it takes a long time to realize its returns, (ii) the

Table 7 Effects of independent variables on GDP growth rate (*Source* Authors' computation using Stata 13)

Variables	Difference GMM results		
	Coefficient	Standard error	$p > t$ value
DIGDPGR	3.38967	0.1424	0.000
DIFDI	0.19766	0.1121	0.080
DGFCF	0.03290	0.0263	0.213
DHC	−0.00246	0.0236	0.917
DINST	−0.21728	2.3899	0.928
DINFRADE	−0.00734	0.0069	0.291
DOPEN	0.00408	0.0069	0.558
DLF	0.03480	0.1049	0.741
DINF	−0.00860	0.0213	0.684
POLSTA	−0.01364	0.0101	0.179

cost of education and hence human capital is huge so that poor households may not be able to afford its cost in the short run and the government hardly provides the required education for all citizens at a time, (iii) brain drain is one of the serious challenges in the sub-region; competent productive forces are migrating to advanced economies, and (iv) the existing manpower may be placed in wrong positions which reduces the motivation and productivity of labor. Given these pitfalls of human resource utilization, our findings confirm the actual situation in East Africa.

Trade openness benefits small economies rather than large economies because small economies cannot affect world supply and hence world prices. This means their influence in world supply is insignificant and does not affect world demand and price levels. Small countries (Eastern Africa) are price takers in the global market. According to Krugman and Obstfeld (2006), a country gains from international trade at least in the form of a comparative advantage. Although most of these countries are too small to impact the world market, foreign trade has a positive effect on their economic growth.

Most of the time the sub-region faces trade deficit but the contribution of trade to growth is positive and insignificant. The reason for this could be that they import more capital goods (which induce investments and growth) than consumer goods. This signals how foreign trade integration is important for continuous economic growth in the sub-region. Empirically, Sala and Trivin's (2014) work confirms our findings.

After examining FDI's role in the economic growth of the region, we examined the determinants of FDI. FDI inflows to host countries are influenced by an array of factors which can be categorized as characteristics of the market (doing business), investment incentives and environmental policies. Characteristics of doing business encompass factors like economic and political stability, geographical position, factors of production (costs and quality), the institutional environment, technology levels, purchasing power of domestic demand and the business environment. Investment incentives include variables like tax policy and incentives and the trade policies of host countries. Contemporary development is facing stricter challenges from the environmental effects of development. As a result, several countries have formulated and implemented environmental policies. This to a larger extent is becoming a bottleneck for FDI. Therefore, the extent and strictness of environmental policies in host countries are important determinants of FDI. Our study was constrained by the availability of data for the selected countries and so it examined the effect of some of the determinants of FDI in East African countries. The results are given in Table 8.

As we can see from the results in Table 8, a one period lag of FDI had a positive and significant effect on FDI. This implies that the previous year's inflow of FDI determined its inflows in the current year. This could be due to the fact that successful experiences of previous investors impacted others to come and invest in the area. A one period lag of institutional quality had a positive but insignificant effect in attracting FDI. A country with better institutional quality attracted more inflows from international investors and vice versa and there was a negative relationship between the two variables.

Political instability negatively affected foreign investment flows. The negative coefficient of a one period lag in political instability though insignificant signals this fact. Lack of good governance, civil conflict, unclearly defined land property rights and corruption reduced FDI flows and its effects on economic growth in the region. In the end, there was a positive correlation between gross fixed capital formation and FDI

Table 8 Relationships between FDI and its determinants (*Source* Authors' computation using Stata 13)

Variables	Difference GMM estimation results		
	Coefficient	Standard error	$p > t$ value
D(lnFDI(−1))	1.082652	0.244450	0.000
D(lnFDI (−2))	0.295528	0.159718	0.060
lnINST(−1)	−0.217285	2.389904	0.928
lnINST(−2)	−1.734791	1.744488	0.321
lnPOLSTA(−1)	−1.704065	1.184330	0.152
lnPOLSTA(−2)	0.197979	0.837256	0.813
D(ln LF(−1))	−66.537450	32.79312	0.040
D(lnLF(−2))	−33.287660	33.68673	0.324
D(lnINRADEV(−1))	−1.891683	0.864115	0.030
D(lnINFRADEV (−2))	0.591224	0.877820	0.502
D(lnGFCF(−1))	0.238707	0.689403	0.730
D(lnGFCF(−2))	−0.437656	0.461172	0.344

inflows. In the long run, gross fixed capital formation had a positive effect on FDI inflows to the region, though this was insignificant.

The coefficients of infrastructure development of a one period lag were negative. Infrastructure development affected international investments directly or indirectly. Empirical evidence shows that there was poor infrastructure development in the region. There were more international investors in a country that had suitable infrastructure development like roads, electricity, railways, airways, and so on. A one period lag of labor force had a negative and significant effect. Improved infrastructure provided attractive investment conditions, and may lead to more production, income and ultimately economic growth. Infrastructure was negatively related to the growth rate in the short run, but was positive and significant in the long run.

5 Summary and Conclusion

Our study analyzed the impact of FDI on economic growth in 14 East African countries using dynamic GMM estimators after conducting appropriate diagnostic tests. All the hypothesized variables were tested to be valid. First, FDI had a positive and marginally significant impact on economic growth in East African countries in the long run. However, institutional quality and political stability had an insignificant effect in attracting FDI to the region. This could raise questions about the nature of FDI flows to the region.

A pairwise Granger causality test indicated the existence of a unidirectional causality running from GDPGR to FDI inflows in the region. Hence, foreign investors came to a country which had a good economic performance. FDI is becoming significant for economic growth in the region. Eastern African countries need to attract more FDI by improving their investment environments, building key infrastructure, investing more in human capital, increasing regional integration, strengthening internal coordination and external relations, following up on export-oriented investments and doing careful impact evaluations. However, care should be taken about the composition of FDI and its maturity stage profit repatriation and low tax collection due to tax holidays to attract more FDI. A detailed study is needed to see the environmental effects of FDI in the region since this may undo its positive effects in economic growth in the region.

References

Abadi, B.M. (2011). The Impact of Foreign Direct Investment on Economic Growth in Jordan. *International Journal of Recent Research and Applied Sciences*, 8(2): 253–258.

AEO (2016). *African Economic Outlook 2016: Sustainable Cities Structural Transformation*. African Development Bank.

Agrawal, G. (2011). Impact of FDI on GDP Growth: A Panel Data Study. *European Journal of Scientific Research*, 57(2): 257–264.

Agrawal, G. (2015). Foreign Direct Investment and Economic Growth in BRICS Economies: A Panel Data Analysis. *Journal of Economics, Business and Management*, 3(4): 421–424.

Alege, P. and A. Ogundipe (2013). *Sustaining Economic Development of West African Countries: A System GMM Panel Approach*. MPRA Paper, 51702. Ota, Ogun: Covenant University.

Anderson, T.W and C. Hsiao (1981). Estimation of Dynamic Models with Error Components. *Journal of the American Statistical Association*, 76: 598–606.

Anyanwu, J.C. (2012). Why Does Foreign Direct Investment Go Where It Goes? New Evidence from African Countries. *Annals of Economics and Finance*, 13(2): 425–462.

Apergis, N. (2008). The Relationship Between Foreign Direct Investment and Economic Growth: Evidence from Transition Countries. *Transition Studies Review*, 15: 37–51.

Arellano, M. and S. Bond (1991). Some Tests of Specification for Panel Data: Monte Carlo Evidence and Application to Employment Equation. *Review of Economic Studies*, 58(2): 277–297.

Arellano, M. and O. Bover (1995). Another Look at the Instrumental-Variable Estimation of Error Components Models. *Journal of Econometrics*, 68(1): 29–52.

Baklouti, N. and Y. Boujelbene (2014). Impact of Institutional Quality on the Attractiveness of Foreign Direct Investment. *Journal of Behavioral Economics, Finance, Entrepreneurship, Accounting and Transport*, 2(4): 89–93.

Balasubramanyam, M.S. (1996). Foreign Direct Investment and Growth in EP and is Countries. *The Economic Journal*, 106(434): 92–105.

Basemera, S., J. Mutenyo, E. Hisali, and E. Bbaale (2012). Foreign Direct Investment Inflows to East Africa: Do Institutions Matter? *Journal of Business Management and Applied Economics*, 5. Available at: http://jbmae.scientificpapers.org.

Beugelsdijk, R.S. and R. Zwinkels (2008). The Impact of Horizontal and Vertical FDI on Host Country's Economic Growth. *International Business Review*, 17: 452–472.

Blundell, R. and S. Bond (1998). Initial Conditions and Moment Restrictions in Dynamic Panel Data Models. *Journal of Econometrics*, 87: 15–143.

Borensztein, E., J. De Gregorio, and J.W. Lee (1998). How Does Foreign Direct Investment Affect Economic Growth? *Journal of International Economics*, 45: 115–135.

Buckley, P.J. (1991). Development in International Business Theory in the 1990s. *Journal of Marketing Management*, 7: 15–24.

Buckley, P. and M. Casson (1976). *The Future of the Multinational Enterprises*. London: Macmillan.

Casson, M. (1983). *Internalization as General Theory of Foreign Direct Investment*. Cambridge: MIT Press.

DeHoyos, R.E. and V. Sarafidis (2006). Testing for Cross-Sectional Dependence in Panel-Data Models. *The Stata Journal*, 6(4): 482–496.

Demelew, T.Z. (2014). *Foreign Direct Investment Led Growth and Its Determinants in Sub-Saharan African Countries*. Masters thesis, Paper 1284. Available at: http://thekeep.eiu.edu/theses/1284.

DeMello, L.R. (1999). Foreign Direct Investment-Led Growth: Evidence from Time Series and Panel Data. *Oxford Economic Papers*, 51(1): 133–151.

Denisia, V. (2010). Foreign Direct Investment Theories: An Overview of the Main FDI Theories. *European Journal of Interdisciplinary Studies*, 3: 53–59.

Dunning, J.H. (1973). The Determinants of International Production. *Oxford Economic Papers*, 25: 289–336.

Engle, R.E. and C.W.J. Granger (1987). Cointegration and Error-Correction: Representation, Estimation, and Testing. *Econometrica*, 55(2): 251–276.

Hadri, K. (2000). Testing for Stationarity in Heterogeneous Panel Data. *Econometrics Journal*, 3: 148–161.

Hansen, L.P. (1982). Large Sample Properties of Generalized Method of Moments Estimators. *Econometrica*, 50: 1029–1054.

Herzer, D., S. Klasen, and D.F. Nowak-Lehmann (2008). In Search of FDI-Led Growth in Developing Countries: The Way Forward. *Economic Modelling*, 25: 793–810.

Kinyondo, M. (2012). Determinants of Foreign Direct Investment. *Global Journal of Management and Business Research*, 12(18): 20.

Krugman, P. and M. Obstfeld (2006). *International Economics: Theory and Policy* (9th ed.). English: Pearson Addison Wesley.

Lucas, R.E. (1988). On the Mechanics of Economic Development. *Journal of Monetary Economics*, 22(1): 3–42.

Nondo, C., M.S. Kahsai, and Y.G. Hailu (2016). Does Institutional Quality Matter in Foreign Direct Investment? Evidence from Sub-Saharan African Countries. *African Journal Economic and Sustainable Development*, 5(1): 12–30.

OECD (2008). *OECD Benchmark Definition of Foreign Direct Investment*. Paris: OECD.

Onyeiwu, S. and H. Shrestha (2004). Determinants of Foreign Direct Investment in Africa. *Journal of Developing Societies*, 20(1–2): 89–106.

Pedroni, P. (1999). Critical Values for Co-integration Test in Heterogeneous Panels with Multiple Regressors. *Oxford Bulletin of Economics and Statistics*, Special Issue: 653–670.

Romer, P.M. (1994). The Origins of Endogenous Growth. *The Journal of Economic Perspectives*, 8(1): 3–22.

Sala, H. and P. Trivin (2014). Openness, Investment and Growth in Sub-Saharan Africa. *Journal of African Economies*: 1–33.

Solomon, W.D. (2008). *Determinants of Foreign Direct Investment in Ethiopia*. Maastricht, The Netherlands: Maastricht University.

Solow, R.M. (1956). A Contribution to the Theory of Economic Growth. *The quarterly Journal of Economics*, 70(1): 65–94.

Sukar, A. and S. Hassan (2011). The Effects of Foreign Direct Investment on Economic Growth: The Case of Sub-Sahara Africa. *South Western Economic Review*, 34(1), 61–73.

Todaro, M.P. and S.C. Smith (2012). *Economic Development* (11th ed.). New York, San Francisco, and Upper Saddle River: Addison-Wesley.

UNCTAD (1998). *World Investment Report 1998: Trends and Determinants*. New York and Geneva: UNCTAD.

UNCTAD (2013). *Global Value Chains: Investment and Trade for Development. World Investment Report*. New York: United Nations.

UNCTAD (2016). *World Investment Report 2016: Investor Nationality: Policy Challenges.* New York: United Nations, UNCTAD.

Valeriani, E. and S. Peluso (2011). *The Impact of Institutional Quality on Economic Growth and Development.* Italy: University of Modena and Reggio Emilia.

Vernon, R. (1966). International Investment and International Trade in the Product Cycle. *The Quarterly Journal of Economics*, 80(2): 190–207.

Wei, S. (2000). How Taxing is Corruption on International Investors? *Review of Economics and Statistics*, 82(1): 1–11.

Wooldridge, J.M. (2001). Applications of Generalized Method of Moments Estimation. *Journal of Economic Perspectives*, 15(4): 87–100.

Wooldridge, J.M. (2005). *Introductory Econometrics: A Modern Approach* (2nd ed.). Thomson South-Western.

Zekarias S.M. (2016). The Impact of Foreign Direct Investment (FDI) on Economic Growth in Eastern Africa: Evidence from Panel Data Analysis. *Applied Economics and Finance*, 3(1): 145–160.

Zsohar, P. (2012). Short Introduction to the Generalized Method of Moments. *Hungarian Statistical Review*, Special Number 16.

5

The Role of Remittances, FDI and Foreign Aid in Economic Growth in Low and Middle Income African Countries

Gutu Gutema

1 Introduction

Developing countries are striving to achieve and sustain long run economic growth and in this process, they are confronted with various questions and policy options. The most prominent question that every country faces is: What actually determines economic growth? This is a complicated question as the complex nature of economic structures means that there are various factors that can influence the economic growth of a country.

External factors such as FDI, migrant remittances (remittances hereafter), official development assistance (ODA) (foreign aid hereafter) play an important role in boosting economic growth and development in developing countries (Almfraji and Almsafir 2014; Imai et al. 2014; Tahir et al. 2015). However, researchers and policymakers have not been able to agree about the effects of these external factors

---

G. Gutema (✉)
Department of Economics, Addis Ababa University, Addis Ababa, Ethiopia

© The Author(s) 2018
A. Heshmati (ed.), *Determinants of Economic Growth in Africa*,
https://Doi.org/10.1007/978-3-319-76493-1_5

on economic growth in developing countries. The reality is that FDI, remittances and foreign aid have grown significantly over the last couple of decades. However, despite their increased importance the combined impact of these variables on economic growth in developing nations is not considered sufficiently studied.

The neoclassical growth theory has been widely employed at the macroeconomic level to understand the impact of FDI on economic growth. Lucas (1988) and Barro (1991) argue that FDI not only supplements domestic investments but it also provides technology transfers that generate positive spillover effects in local firms in host countries which ultimately spur growth. However, FDI's effect on economic growth has been an issue of long debate in development literature. Existing theories and empirical evidence on the effect of FDI on economic growth in developing countries can be categorized into the following broad views: first, those that claim a negative or neutral effect (Agosin and Machado 2005; Gui-Diby 2014; Herzer et al. 2008). Herzer et al. (2008) for example claim that 'in the vast majority of countries, there exists neither a long-term nor a short-term effect of FDI on growth; in fact, there is not a single country where a positive unidirectional long-term effect from FDI to GDP is found.' Their results also indicate that there is no clear association between the growth impact of FDI and the level of per capita income, the level of education, the degree of openness and the level of financial market development in developing countries. Second, those who claim positive effects mainly rooted in endogenous growth theories (De Mello 1997; Driffield and Jones 2013). Their findings are based on the argument that FDI's effect depends on the degree of complementarities and substitution between FDI and domestic investments, macroeconomic stability, the institutional and legal framework, knowledge and human capital, trade openness and other socioeconomic and demographic characteristics.

In addition to FDI, the role of foreign aid in promoting economic growth is also a debatable issue and remains unsettled at both theoretical and empirical levels. Riddell (2007) summarizes the issues of foreign aid and economic growth from the proponents' point of view. The issues include arguments based on an optimistic view of the impact of foreign aid on economic growth. This argument is primarily based on solidarity or humanitarian imperatives that stem as a response to extreme poverty and inequalities faced by individuals in the developing world. The opponents of aid take the view that it is a form of wealth distribution whereby poor people in rich countries send money directly to rich people in poor countries (Bauer 1972). Chenery and Strout (1966) suggest that foreign aid increases income levels and the rate of investments in the receiving economy by supplementing available resources. Studies such as those by Ehrenfeld (2004) explain that donor countries are to be blamed for the unproductive outcome of aid in most receiving countries as aid-tying practices and conditionalities redirect aid to benefit political elites. Burnside and Dollar (2000) argue that aid has a positive impact on growth in developing countries with good fiscal, monetary and trade policies but has little effect in the presence of poor policies. Easterly et al. (2004) re-estimated Burnside and Dollar's (2000) results using new data and found far less evidence that aid had a positive impact on growth even when accounting for institutions. The effectiveness of foreign aid may be heterogeneous across countries and its impact varies over time depending on the type of aid. This is one reason that prompted us to categorize Africa into low and middle-income countries based on their income levels. Since growth is a complex process in which many other variables should be taken into account it is not surprising that literature has yielded such mixed result.

There is also controversy regarding the relationship between remittances and economic growth. Imai et al. (2014) argue that remittance flows have been beneficial to economic growth in developing countries through their direct effects on poverty reduction. However, the volatility of remittances harms economic growth. Giuliano and Ruiz-Arranz (2009) found that remittances had a positive impact on economic growth in countries that had lower levels of financial sector development. Catrinescu et al. (2009) argue that in countries with good financial intermediates, sound economic policies and institutions remittances have positive effects on growth. This is because they help reduce poverty, smooth consumption and relieve the capital constraints of the poor. According to their findings remittances exert a weak positive impact on long-term macroeconomic growth. This implies that there is a threshold that countries have to pass which renders the effects of remittances minimal. In contrast, Ahortor and Adenutsi (2009) found that remittances had a negative effect on economic growth since they drained highly skilled and active workers through migration and created over dependency on the external economy. Another argument concerning the harmful nature of remittances is that they are not used for direct productive investment purposes. Rather, these funds are spent on consumption, housing and land, which are seen as a loss of resources that would have otherwise been used for promoting long-term growth and development (Ekanayake and Halkides 2008). Since the effects of remittances might be different across different countries with different income levels existing literature has to be tested under the categorization that we make based on income levels. The weakness of existing literature on remittances and economic growth is that they do not fully take into consideration the simultaneity effects with other external factors like FDI and foreign aid.

One common strand in empirical growth literature is that it examines the impact of the three external factors in isolation ignoring the impact of other known external growth factors. However, including all the three factors in the same growth regression model can explain the ambiguous results discussed earlier. So, allowing a simultaneity relationship between the variables gives more insights into the points of argument than dealing with the effect of a single variable in isolated terms. Specifically, FDI, foreign aid and remittances are all vital for economic growth and failure to control for them in a growth regression might result in an omitted variable bias. In the meantime, the problem of endogeneity in relation to estimation also needs to be addressed. Therefore, these kinds of problems heavily rely on the choice and use of the appropriate methodology.

Like Nwaogu and Ryan (2015) and Driffield and Jones (2013) our study also examines the effects of FDI, foreign aid and remittances on economic growth in developing countries. Nwaogu and Ryan (2015) examined the effects of these three external factors on regional economic growth in developing countries in Africa, Latin America and the Caribbean by employing a dynamic spatial model that allowed them to capture how growth in one country affected growth in neighboring countries. Their argument is that the income growth rate in one country may be affected by the growth rates in its surrounding countries. Driffield and Jones (2013) investigated the relative contributions of FDI, foreign aid and migrant remittances to economic growth in developing countries using the three-stage least squares method to account for the inherent endogeneities in these relationships.

We explore the relative contribution of these three factors in economic growth in low and middle income African countries using the system GMM based on its advantages over other methods. We also examined the effects of these variables by considering countries' income levels based on the World Development Indicators' 2016 dataset.

A number of studies have examined the impact of variables on economic growth in isolation, some of the researchers have studied pairs of variables without considering the effects of differences in countries' income levels. Hence, their results depend on and are affected by a mix of host country and growth factors that they examine (Bhandari et al. 2007; Kosack and Tobin 2006; Ndambendia and Njoupouognigni 2010). The lack of a systematic study of these three variables and their joint impact on economic growth by taking countries' income levels into consideration represents a serious gap in literature. Therefore, our study controls for all three external growth variables by categorizing African countries into low and middle income ones. Controlling for all three external factors eliminates possible omitted variable bias problems.

To the best of our knowledge, all the studies conducted on the effects of external factors on economic growth do not analyze the effects of FDI, foreign aid and remittances on economic growth by considering the differences in income levels in the developing countries (that is, low and middle income countries). The effects of these three external factors on economic growth might differ depending on the countries' current income levels. Their effects might not be the same for low and middle-income countries.

2   The Theoretical Framework

The base growth model that we follow is derived from a model in the style of Solow (1956) where θ is equal to 1. FDI, foreign aid and remittances are all introduced as components of investments by Burnside and Dollar (2000) and Catrinescu et al. (2009). Driffield and Jones (2013) also use this approach. We follow the approach model introduced by Herzer and Morrissey (2009) and Driffield and Jones (2013). The assumption is that foreign financial inflows finance investments that determine economic growth. The impact of each variable can be represented in an aggregate production function of the form:

$$Y_t = \beta_t K_t^\theta, \quad (0 \leq \theta \leq 1) \tag{1}$$

where, Y_t is output, β_t is total factor productivity, K_t is capital stock and the parameter θ measures the marginal product of the capital. For simplicity, we assume that the capital stock depreciates fully in each period so that the end-of-period capital stock K_t is equal to domestic investments ID_t. Assuming further that investments are the aggregate of public and private investments and that public investments are partly financed by aid, whereas private investments are composed of gross capital formation, FDI and remittances, we can write the production function as:

$$Y_t = \beta_t (G_t + A_t + DI_t + FDI_t + R_t)^\theta, \tag{2}$$

where, G_t is government investment spending, A_t is foreign aid, DI_t is domestic investments, FDI_t is FDI and R_t is remittances. Foreign aid can influence growth directly or through public investments, whereas FDI and remittances generate growth through external private sources. Even though remittances are commonly considered only for financing domestic consumption a few studies point out the importance of remittances in economic growth through financing domestic investments (see Giuliano and Ruiz-Arranz 2009).

3   Data and Estimation Methodology

The issue of endogeneity is something that literature is trying to address. This problem is common in most cross-country growth research. In our case FDI, foreign aid and remittances are typically endogenous since they are common features of growth regression models. Burnside and Dollar (2000) argue for endogeneity of aid in growth regressions; Kosack and Tobin (2006) assert the endogeneity of aid and FDI on economic growth; and Giuliano and Ruiz-Arranz (2009) stress the endogeneity of remittances for growth. Therefore, we need to adopt an econometric approach that is consistent and efficient in the presence of endogenous variables to ensure that the estimation of our model is unbiased. Different approaches can be followed to address the endogeneity problem by introducing an instrumental variable into the model. Consider the following equation:

$$Y_{it} = \gamma Y_{it-1} + BX_{it} + \alpha_i + U_{it} \qquad (3)$$

Equation (3) contains country fixed effects which are correlated with the regressors and because of this the exogeneity assumption is violated. Therefore, we cannot apply the fixed and random effects models. Applying OLS/GLS, within group fixed effects and first difference fixed effects generates biased and inconsistent results because of $\text{corr}(Y_{it-1}, \alpha_i \neq 0)$, $\text{cov}[(Y_{it-1} - \bar{Y}_i), (U_{it} - \bar{U}_i \neq 0)]$ and $\text{cov}(\Delta Y_{it-1}, \Delta U_{it} \neq 0)$ respectively. This implies that this method of estimation does not solve the endogeneity problem. What is required is an instrumental variable estimator that can correct for correlated fixed effects and account for the endogeneity of regressors. Anderson and Hsiao (1981) proposed the IV two-stage least square (2SLS) method to solve this problem which will not generate an efficient estimator in case the model is over identified. Due to this limitation, Arellano and Bond (1991) proposed the difference-GMM estimator. The difference-GMM estimator is a IV estimator that uses the lagged value of all endogenous regressors and all the exogenous regressors as an instrument. If we use the two-step difference-GMM under the hetroscedasticity problem the standard error is downward biased. The correction for this two-step difference-GMM is proposed by Windmeijer (2005). The difference-GMM removes country-specific characteristics when using the time invariant regression included in the model. The bias and imprecision in the difference-GMM estimator occurs due to the double lagged level instruments for the difference. As Blundell and Bond (1998) state the instruments used in the standard first-difference-GMM estimator become less informative in two important cases: first, as the value of the coefficients of the autoregressive parameter increase towards unity; and second, as the variance of the country-specific effects increases relative to the variance of the transitory shock. Given these two cases the IV estimator performs poorly. Blundell and Bond (1998) attribute the bias and poor precision of the first difference-GMM-estimator to the problem of weak instruments. So, Arellano and Bover (1995) and Blundell and Bond (1998) proposed the system-GMM method.

Generally, even if the two-stage least squares and three-stage least squares are used in a simultaneous equation, our decision to use the system GMM is reasonable because according to the discussion earlier and those in Gui-Diby (2014), the two-stage least squares and three-stage least squares methods are special cases of generalized methods of moments.

Therefore, technically system GMM-estimators embody the assumption of endogeneity and employ moment conditions to generate a set of valid instruments for the endogenous regressors that can significantly improve efficiency (Blundell and Bond 1998; Kosack and Tobin 2006; Roodman 2006). The application of system GMM is thus justified in empirical growth research as an effective approach to deal with endogeneity bias and omission bias associated with growth regressions. We estimated the following equations to examine the effects of FDI, net ODA received and personal remittances received on economic growth as well as what affected their levels using the system GMM:

$$lnGDP_{it} = \beta_0 + \beta_1 lnFDI_{it} + \beta_2 lnODA_{it} + \beta_3 lnREM_{it} + \beta_4 lnGDP_i + \beta \mathbf{X_{it}} + u_{it} \quad (4)$$

$$lnFDI_{it} = \alpha_0 + \alpha_1 lnGDP_{it} + \alpha_2 lnODA_{it} + \alpha_3 lnREM_{it} + \alpha_4 lnGDP_i + \alpha \mathbf{Z_{it}} + \gamma_{it} \quad (5)$$

$$lnODA_{it} = \varphi_0 + \varphi_1 lnGDP_{it} + \varphi_2 lnFDI_{it} \\ + \varphi_3 lnREM_{it} + \varphi_4 lnGDP_i + \varphi \mathbf{N_{it}} + \xi_{it} \quad (6)$$

$$lnREM_{it} = \aleph_0 + \aleph_1 lnGDP_{it} + \aleph_2 lnFDI_{it} \\ + \aleph_3 lnODA_{it} + \aleph_4 lnGDP_i + \aleph \mathbf{M_{it}} + \Psi_{it} \quad (7)$$

As given in Eq. (4) our dependent variable is gross domestic product (GDP) per capita growth (GDP_{it}). The other endogenous variables are FDI as a percentage of (FDI_{it}), official development assistance as a percentage of GDP (ODA_{it}) and migrant remittances as a percentage of GDP (REM_{it}).

The vector $\mathbf{X_{it}}$ contains a number of additional control variables: gross capital formation, trade as a percentage of GDP, total labor force, population growth, rate of inflation, broad money as a percentage of GDP (financial depth) and government expenditure on education and primary school enrolments.

We use cross-country unbalanced panel data for African countries (low and middle-income groups) in the period 1980–2016. The data is obtained from the World Development Indicators' 2016 database. The sample consists of 25 low income countries and 25 middle income countries.[1]

However, the use of system GMM depends on the validity of additional instrument variables. To assess the validity of these additional instruments, Arellano and Bond (1991) and Arellano and Bover (1995) proposed the Sargan test of over-identification. Table 1 gives the Sargan test of over-identification which tests the validity of the instruments. The high P-values of these tests in our estimations ensure the validity of our model.

---

[1]Grouping of the African countries into low and middle-income countries is based on the World Development Indicators.

4 Empirical Findings

4.1 Description of the Data

Table 1 gives the summary statistics of the data for our dependent and independent variables. The average GDP growth rate in Africa was 3.8 with a standard deviation of 7.99. The maximum GDP growth rate was 149 recorded in 1997 by Equatorial Guinea. This might be because in 1996 Equatorial Guinea recorded the maximum FDI net inflows as a percentage of GDP in the history of Africa. And the least GDP growth rate was recorded in Libya in 2011 (62.07 percent). On average FDI net inflows as a percentage of GDP were 3.33 which, on average, deviated by 8.87 from the center. The average net ODA received as a percentage of GDP was 54.98. It varied from −11.96 to 666.79 with a standard deviation of 56.56. Average personal remittances received as a percentage of GDP were 4.18 which varied from zero to 99.82 with

Table 1 Descriptive statistics for African countries

Variables	Mean	Standard deviation	Minimum	Maximum
Gross domestic product growth rate	3.813120	7.9986	−62.07592	149.9730
Foreign direct investment net inflows as % of GDP	3.332586	8.8775	−82.8921	161.8238
Net ODA received as a % of GDP	54.985630	56.5685	−11.9666	666.7904
Personal remittance received as a % of GDP	4.180523	9.4635	0	99.8218
Broad money as a % of GDP (financial depth)	96.505260	2652.7720	−99.8700	108,613.3000
Openness (trade as a percentage of GDP)	72.583170	44.9830	6.3203	531.7374
Gross capital formation as a % of GDP	21.280660	15.6393	−2.4243	219.0694
Government total expenditure on education as a % of GDP	4.396016	2.7125	0	44.3339
Inflation rate	42.263010	673.5358	−31.5659	26,762.0200
Population growth rate annually	2.560653	1.0976	−6.3428	8.3549

a dispersion of 9.46 around the mean value. The average inflation rate recorded for African countries was 42.26 which is high. It varied in the interval of −31 and 26,762. The minimum inflation rate was recorded in Equatorial Guinea in 1998 and the maximum was recorded in the Democratic Republic of Congo in 1994. The value of broad money as a percentage of GDP (financial depth) significantly varied in the dataset. Its mean was 96.50 with a large standard deviation of 2652.77 and it varied in the interval of −99.87 and 108,613.3.

4.2 FDI, ODA, Migrant Remittances and Economic Growth

Table 2, columns 1–3 give the results from estimating Eq. (4) using the sample of low and middle income African countries and all African countries pooled together. According to column 1 the coefficients of FDI net inflows, net ODA received and personal remittances received had positive and statistically significant effects on economic growth in low income African countries. This implies that these three sources of development financing were very helpful in economic growth in low income countries in Africa. Our result is consistent with Driffield and Jones (2013), Burnside and Dollar (2000), and Imai et al. (2014). According to their findings FDI (Driffield and Jones 2013), foreign aid (Burnside and Dollar 2000; Driffield and Jones 2013) and remittances (Imai et al. 2014) had positive effects on economic growth in developing countries. In contrast, Chami et al. (2003) found that remittances had a negative effect on economic growth in both developing and developed countries. They argue that income from remittances may be plagued by a moral hazard problem, permitting migrants' families to reduce their work efforts. At the same time control variables like openness (trade as a percentage of GDP) and gross capital formation were positive and significantly associated with economic growth in low income African countries.

Gross capital formation had a positive and significant effect in both low and middle income African countries, but when we compare the strength of the magnitude, middle income countries had a stronger

Table 2 Growth regression using the system GMM

Dependent variable: LN of gross domestic product	Low income countries	Middle income countries	Pooled Regression
Independent variable			
Lag of LN of gross domestic product	0.663***	0.671***	0.805***
	(0.0557)	(0.0640)	(0.0315)
LN of foreign direct investment net inflows	0.00313*	0.00717	0.00161
	(0.00184)	(0.00572)	(0.00173)
LN of net ODA received	0.0147**	0.000502	0.00229
	(0.00595)	(0.00589)	(0.00374)
LN of personal remittances received	0.0559***	−0.00270	0.00416
	(0.0156)	(0.00406)	(0.00409)
Broad money as a % of GDP (financial depth)	6.35e-05	0.0500**	0.0175
	(0.00306)	(0.0207)	(0.0200)
Openness (trade as a percentage of GDP)	0.00120***	0.000226	−0.000381*
	(0.000426)	(0.000292)	(0.000216)
LN of gross capital formation	0.0219***	0.0395***	0.0399***
	(0.00773)	(0.00970)	(0.00755)
LN of Gov. total exp. on education	0.0157	0.00254**	0.0449***
	(0.0102)	(0.00127)	(0.0164)
Inflation rate	−0.00150*	−0.000213	−1.73e−05
	(0.000816)	(0.000207)	(0.000225)
LN of total population	0.0290	0.224***	0.0836**
	(0.0671)	(0.0767)	(0.0425)
Constant	4.744***	1.822**	0.984*
	(0.898)	(0.794)	(0.509)
Sargan test (p-value)	0.6147	0.0653	0.151

Note Robust standard errors in parentheses. ***$p < 0.01$, **$p < 0.05$, *$p < 0.1$

magnitude than low income countries—a 10 percent increase in gross capital formation increased economic growth by 3.95 and 2.19 percent in low and middle income African countries respectively. This implies that the effect of gross capital formation was more effective in middle-income countries than in low income countries. Economic theories have also shown that capital formation plays a crucial role in models of economic growth and our results suggest that income growth can occur when developing countries are able to maintain capital formation. This result confirms the results obtained by Nwaogu and Ryan (2015). Inflation rate had a negative and statistically significant effect on economic growth in low income countries but it had a positive and no significant effect in middle-income countries. The lagged value of GDP was positively and significantly associated with economic growth in both low and middle income African countries.

However, according to column 2 in Table 2 which is estimated using a sample of middle income African countries the coefficients of FDI, foreign aid and remittances had no significant impact on economic growth in middle income African countries. This might be because of some institutional factors such as government effectiveness, political stability, rule of law and control of corruption which we do not include in our regression due to lack of data. It is not surprising that FDI, foreign aid, remittances and the other variables had different effects across countries. Easterly et al. (2004) also claim that the effectiveness of variables like foreign aid was heterogeneous across countries. In contrast, the lagged value of GDP, government expenditure on education, population growth and gross capital formation had a positive and statistically significant effect at the 1 percent level of significance while financial depth (broad money as a percentage of GDP) was significant at the 5 percent level of significance for economic growth in middle income African countries. The pooled regression in Table 2, column 3 shows that the coefficients of FDI, foreign aid and remittances had no significant impact on economic growth. This confirms that the impact of these three factors on economic growth was different across low and middle-income groups.

4.3 FDI and Economic Growth

Columns 1 and 2 in Table 3 give the results from estimating Eq. (5) using a sample of African low and middle-income countries. According to this table the lagged value of FDI net inflows, GDP, personal remittances received and gross capital formation were positively and significantly associated with the level of FDI in both low and middle income African countries. But the magnitude and level of significance of the

Table 3 Foreign direct investment regression using the system GMM

Dependent variable: LN of foreign direct investment net inflows	Low income countries	Middle income countries
Independent variable		
Lag of LN of foreign direct investment net inflows	0.208**	0.141**
	(0.0866)	(0.0563)
LN of gross domestic product	1.513*	1.880**
	(0.854)	(0.851)
LN of net ODA received	−0.300	−0.0624
	(0.241)	(0.0791)
LN of personal remittances received	0.193**	0.370***
	(0.0837)	(0.0517)
Openness (trade as a percentage of GDP)	0.00248	0.00726**
	(0.00321)	(0.00339)
LN of gross capital formation	0.594***	0.522***
	(0.194)	(0.170)
Inflation rate	−0.00403	−0.00202
	(0.00455)	(0.00297)
Broad money as a percentage of GDP (financial depth)	−0.0812	0.250
	(0.263)	(0.290)
LN of total population	−0.531	−4.224*
	(2.909)	(2.377)
LN of total labor force	0.777	2.296
	(2.613)	(1.795)
Primary school enrolments as a percentage of gross		0.00270
		(0.00700)
Constant	−30.48***	−17.02
	(11.02)	(16.68)

Note Robust standard errors in parentheses. ***$p < 0.01$, **$p < 0.05$, *$p < 0.1$

variables was different. For example, personal remittances received was significant at the 5 percent level of significance for low income counties whereas it was statistically significant at the 1 percent level of significance for middle-income countries. This implies that the personal remittances received were more effective in pushing up FDI levels in middle income African countries.

The results in Table 3 also show that population growth had a negative and significant effect on FDI net inflows in middle-income countries whereas they had no effect in low income countries. Openness was positively and significantly associated with FDI net inflows in middle income African countries but it was not significant for low income African countries. Since openness gives rise to opportunities for importing the goods needed for production, foreign investors are encouraged to get investments. The effect of GDP was higher in middle income countries than in low income countries in Africa in terms of both magnitude and level of significance. Interestingly, the effect of gross capital formation on FDI was almost the same for both low and middle income African countries in terms of magnitude as well as level of significance. A 10 percent increase in gross capital formation increased FDI inflows by 5.9 and 5.2 percent for low and middle income African countries respectively. It was also significant at the less than 1 percent level of significance for both low and middle income African countries.

4.4 Official Development Assistance and Economic Growth

The results from estimating Eq. (6) using the sample of low and middle income African countries are presented in Table 4. The results in column 1 indicate that the lagged value of net ODA received, trade openness, gross capital formation and labor force had a positive and statistically significant relation with the level of net ODA received in low income African countries.

Column 2 also indicates that a lag of net ODA received, inflation rate, financial depth and primary school enrolments had a positive and

Table 4 Official development assistance regression using the system GMM

Dependent variable: LN net ODA received	Low income countries	Middle income countries
Independent variable		
Lag of LN of net ODA received	0.558***	0.418***
	(0.0562)	(0.0630)
LN of gross domestic product	−0.0671	−0.395
	(0.150)	(0.544)
LN of foreign direct investment net inflows	−0.0135	−0.0250*
	(0.0152)	(0.0147)
LN of personal remittances received	0.000758	0.0202
	(0.0180)	(0.0396)
Openness (trade as a percentage of GDP)	0.00104**	
	(0.000468)	
LN of gross capital formation	0.0949***	0.0699
	(0.0236)	(0.100)
Inflation rate	0.00143	0.00983*
	(0.00107)	(0.00563)
Broad money as a percentage of GDP (financial depth)	0.102	1.009***
	(0.0962)	(0.377)
LN of total population	−0.00611	−0.728
	(0.0151)	(0.982)
LN of total labor force	0.356***	−0.516
	(0.115)	(0.893)
Primary school enrolments as a percentage of gross		0.00738*
		(0.00432)
Constant	1.060	15.91
	(1.341)	(10.18)

Note Robust standard errors in parentheses. ***$p < 0.01$, **$p < 0.05$, *$p < 0.1$

statistically significant relationship with foreign aid received in middle income African countries. FDI net inflows had a negative and statistically significant relationship with foreign aid received in middle income African countries. The results in Table 4 indicate that the factors that significantly affected the level of foreign aid received were different for the two groups of countries. This implies that low and middle income African countries need to adopt different policies and approaches for attracting foreign aid.

4.5 Migrant Remittances and Economic Growth

The results from estimating Eq. (7) are given in Table 5. According to this table the lagged value of personal remittances received, FDI net inflows, openness (trade as a percentage of GDP) and primary school enrolments had a positive and statistically significant effect on the level of personal remittances received in both low and middle income African countries. Gross capital formation had a negative and statistically

Table 5 Official development assistance regression using the system GMM

Dependent variable: LN of personal remittances received	Low income countries	Middle income countries
Independent variable		
Lag of LN of personal remittances received	0.608***	0.564***
	(0.0797)	(0.0731)
LN of gross domestic product	−0.0883	−0.111
	(0.375)	(0.401)
LN of foreign direct investment net inflows	0.0965***	0.109***
	(0.0373)	(0.0225)
LN of net ODA received	0.0364	0.0345
	(0.0878)	(0.0397)
Openness (trade as a percentage of GDP)	0.00531*	0.00712***
	(0.00274)	(0.00186)
LN of gross capital formation		−0.287***
		(0.0793)
Inflation rate	−0.000559	0.00127
	(0.00231)	(0.00166)
Broad money as a percentage of GDP (financial depth)	−0.202	−0.0316
	(0.169)	(0.113)
LN of total population	0.552	1.744
	(1.468)	(1.093)
LN of total labor force	0.215	−0.398
	(0.824)	(0.708)
Primary school enrolments as a percentage of gross	0.0119***	0.0112***
	(0.00448)	(0.00385)
Constant	−2.731	
	(8.924)	

Note Robust standard errors in parentheses. ***$p < 0.01$, **$p < 0.05$, *$p < 0.1$

significant effect on the level of personal remittances received in middle income African countries only. Even though the factors that affected the level of personal remittances received by both low and middle-income countries were the same, the effect of personal remittances on economic growth was not the same for both groups of countries.

5 Summary, Conclusion and Policy Implications

This study analyzed the relative effect of FDI, net ODA and personal remittances on economic growth in African countries using the system GMM approach. It used data from the World Development Indicators' 2016 dataset for the period 1985–2015 for 50 African countries. It analyzed the effects of these three external factors by categorizing African countries into low and middle-income countries.

The results show that FDI, net ODA received and personal remittances had a positive impact on economic growth in low income African countries. When we compare the effects of FDI, net ODA received and personal remittances received for low income African countries based on their coefficients and level of significance, personal remittances received were stronger than FDI and net ODA received in magnitude as well as in the level of significance. This implies that remittances are more important for economic growth in low income African countries. This result might also imply that migrant transfers in the form of remittances can ease families' immediate budget constraints by strengthening crucial spending needs on food, healthcare and schooling expenses for children in low-income countries. This is expected to pave the way for the development of a formal financial sector which is essential for economic growth and development in these countries (Giuliano and Ruiz-Arranz 2009). Remittances by and large serve as an alternative to debt that helps alleviate individuals' credit constraints in countries where micro-financing is not widely available (Giuliano and Ruiz-Arranz 2009). Therefore, policies that encourage migrants to remit via formal money transfer networks by reducing the cost of remittances, encouraging investments in the items that promote long term growth and encouraging formal migration will have a significant impact on improving economic growth in low income African countries via remittances.

Another finding of our study is that in addition to encouraging remittances, countries interested in increasing economic growth need to adopt suitable policies that attract FDI and also use the foreign aid received efficiently and effectively.

In middle income African countries FDI, net ODA received and personal remittances received were not significant determinants of economic growth. This implies that there should be certain conditions under which these factors have a significant impact on economic growth in the countries. As supported by other studies, poor governance indicated by high corruption forced the host countries to make less efficient use of funds (Curvo-Cazurra 2006). This implies that institutions are the key determinants of growth as perceived corruption in the host country and less property rights discourage FDI (Acemoglu and Johnson 2005). Therefore, it is important to test the effect that institutions have and their interaction terms with the targeted variables.

Our study also shows that gross capital formation, inflation rate and trade openness were significant determinants of economic growth in low income African countries and financial depth, gross capital formation, government expenditure on education, population and total population were significant determinants of economic growth in middle income African countries. Hence, policies that are suitable for good financial depth, increasing human capital through education, higher capital formation via investments, controlling inflation and greater trade openness stimulate economic growth in developing counties.

This shows that GDP, personal remittances received and gross capital formation were significant determinants FDI inflows in low income African countries and GDP, personal remittances received, gross capital formation, openness, financial depth and primary school enrolments were significant determinants in middle income African counties. This implies that countries interested in attracting more FDI flows on a sustained basis must adopt suitable policies. Policymakers in these countries should provide incentives and make efforts at greater trade openness, higher capital formation, reasonable financial depth and investing in human capital like education.

Trade openness, gross capital formation and total labor force were significant determinants of net ODA received in low income African countries and financial depth, inflation and primary school enrolments were significant determinants in middle income African countries. Our results also show that FDI net inflows, trade openness and primary school enrolments were significant determinants of personal remittances received in low income African countries and gross capital formation, FDI net inflows, trade openness and primary school enrolments were significant determinants in middle income African countries.

The policy implications of our findings are that countries should encourage remittances, foreign aid and FDI for economic growth in low income countries.

However, our study has limitations. One major limitation is that our model does not include the effect of institutions and their interaction terms with FDI, net ODA received and remittances received due to data constraints. It will be interesting and beneficial if the effects of institutions and their interaction terms with the targeted variables are also tested.

Appendix

See Table 6.

Table 6 Low and middle income African countries

Middle income countries	Low income countries
1. Algeria	1. Benin
2. Angola	2. Burkina Faso
3. Botswana	3. Burundi
4. Cabo Verde	4. Central African Republic
5. Cameroon	5. Chad
6. Congo, Rep.	6. Comoros
7. Cote d'ivoire	7. Congo, Dem. Rep.
8. Djibouti	8. Ethiopia
9. Egypt, Arab Rep.	9. Gambia, The
10. Equatorial Guinea	10. Guinea
11. Gabon	11. Guinea-Bissau
12. Ghana	12. Liberia
13. Kenya	13. Madagascar
14. Lesotho	14. Malawi
15. Libya	15. Mali
16. Mauritania	16. Mozambique
17. Mauritius	17. Niger
18. Morocco	18. Rwanda
19. Namibia	19. Senegal
20. Nigeria	20. Sierra Leone
21. South Africa	21. Somalia
22. Sudan	22. Tanzania
23. Swaziland	23. Togo
24. Tunisia	24. Uganda
25. Zambia	25. Zimbabwe

References

Acemoglu, D. and S.H. Johnson (2005). Unbundling Institutions. *Journal of Political Economy*, 113(5): 949–995.

Agosin, M. and R. Machado (2005). Foreign Investment in Developing Countries: Does it Crowd in Domestic Investment? *Oxford Development Studies*, 33(2): 149–162.

Ahortor, C.R.K. and D.E. Adenutsi (2009). The Impact of Remittances on Economic Growth in Small-Open Developing Economies. *Journal of Applied Sciences*, 9: 3275–3286.

Almfraji, M. and K.M. Almsafir (2014). Foreign Direct Investment and Economic Growth Literature Review from 1994 to 2012. *Procedia-Social and Behavioral Sciences*, 129: 206–213.

Anderson, T.W. and C. Hsiao (1981). Estimation of Dynamic Models with Error Components. *Journal of the American Statistical Association*, 976: 589–606.

Arellano, M. and O. Bover (1995). Another Look at Instrumental Variable Estimation of Error-Component Models. *Journal of Econometrics*, 68(1): 29–51.

Arellano, M. and S. Bond (1991). Some Tests for Specification of Panel Data: Monte Carlo Evidence and an Application to Employment Equations. *Review of Economic Studies*, 58: 277–297.

Barro, R.J. (1991). Economic Growth in a Cross Section of Countries. *The Quarterly Journal of Economics*, 106(2): 407–443.

Bauer, P.T. (1972). *Dissent on Development*. Cambridge, MA: Harvard University Press.

Bhandari, R., D. Dharmendra, P. Gyan, and K. Upadhyaya (2007). Foreign Aid, FDI and Economic Growth in East European Countries. *Economic Bulletin*, 6: 1–9.

Blundell, R. and S. Bond (1998). Initial Conditions and Moment Restrictions in Dynamic Panel Data Models. *Journal of Econometrics*, 87(1): 115–143.

Burnside, C. and D. Dollar (2000). Aid, Policies, and Growth. *American Economic Review*, 90(4): 847–868.

Catrinescu, N., M. Leon-Ledesma, P. Matloob, and B. Quillin (2009). Remittances, Institutions and Economic Growth. *World Development*, 37: 81–92.

Chami, R., C. Fullenkamp, and S. Jahjab (2003). Are Immigrant Remittance Flows a Source of Capital for Development? IMF WP/03/189.

Chenery, H. and A. Strout (1966). Foreign Assistance and Economic Development. *American Economic Review*, 56: 679–733.

Curvo-Cazurra, A. (2006). Who Cares About Corruption? *Journal of International Business Studies*, 37: 807–822.

De Mello, L.R. (1997). Foreign Direct Investment in Developing Countries and Growth: A Selective Survey. *Journal of Development Studies*, 34: 1–34.

Driffield, N. and C. Jones (2013). Impact of FDI, ODA and Migrant Remittances on Economic Growth in Developing Countries: A Systems Approach. *The European Journal of Development Research*, 25(2): 173–196.

Easterly, W., R. Levine, and D. Roodman (2004). Aid, Policies, and Growth: Comment. *American Economic Review*, 94(3): 774–780.

Ehrenfeld, D. (2004). Foreign Aid Effectiveness, Political Rights and Bilateral Distribution. *Journal of Humanitarian Assistance*. Available at: http://sites.tufts.edu/jha/archives/75.

Ekanayake, E.M. and M. Halkides (2008). Do Remittances and Foreign Direct Investment Promote Growth? Evidence from Developing Countries. *Journal of International Business and Economics*, 8: 58–68.

Giuliano, P. and M. Ruiz-Arranz (2009). Remittances, Financial Development and Growth. *Journal of Development Economics*, 90(1): 144–152.

Gui-Diby, S.L. (2014). Impact of Foreign Direct Investments on Economic Growth in Africa: Evidence from Three Decades of Panel Data Analyses. *Research in Economics*, 68: 248–256.

Herzer D. and O. Morrissey (2009). *The Long-Run Effect of Aid on Domestic Output*. Discussion Papers 09/01, University of Nottingham.

Herzer, D., S. Klasen, and F. Nowak-Lehmann (2008). In Search of FDI-Led Growth in Developing Countries: The Way Forward. *Economic Modelling*, 25: 793–810.

Imai, K., R. Gaiha, A. Ali, and N. Kaicker (2014). Remittances, Growth and Poverty: New Evidence from Asian Countries. *Journal of Policy Modeling*, 36: 524–538.

Kosack, S. and J. Tobin (2006). Funding Self-Sustaining Development: The Role of Aid, FDI and Government in Economic Success. *International Organization*, 60: 205–243.

Lucas, R.E. (1988). On the Mechanics of Economic Development. *Journal of Monetary Economics*, 22: 3–42.

Ndambendia, H. and M. Njoupouognigni (2010). Foreign Aid, Foreign Direct Investment and Economic Growth in Sub-Saharan Africa: Evidence from Pooled Mean Group Estimator. *International Journal of Economic and Finance*, 2: 39–45.

Nwaogu, U. and M. Ryan (2015). FDI, Foreign Aid, Remittance and Economic Growth in Developing Countries. *Review of Development Economics*, 19(1): 100–115.

Riddel, R.C. (2007). *Does Foreign Aid Work?* Oxford: Oxford University Press.

Roodman, D. (2006). *How to Do Xtabond2: An Introduction to 'Difference' and 'System' GMM in Stata*. Center for Global Development Working Paper 103. Available at: http://www.cgdev.org/files/11619_file_HowtoDoxtabond6_12_1_06.pdf/.

Solow, R.M. (1956). A Contribution to the Theory of Economic Growth. *Quarterly Journal of Economics*, 70(1): 65–94.

Tahir, M., I. Khan, and A.M. Shah (2015). Foreign Remittances, Foreign Direct Investment, Foreign Imports and Economic Growth in Pakistan: A Time Series Analysis. *Arab Economics and Business Journal*, 10: 82–89.

Windmeijer, F. (2005). A Finite Sample Correction for the Variance of Linear Efficient Twostep GMM Estimators. *Journal of Econometrics*, 126(1): 25–51.

6

The Role of Financial Development and Institutional Quality in Economic Growth in Africa in the Era of Globalization

Kahsay Berhane

1 Introduction

Every country in Africa strives to achieve a higher level of economic growth. Many macroeconomic factors contribute towards the economic growth of a country that have received much attention in literature such as financial development, institutional quality, macroeconomic stability, foreign direct investment (FDI), natural resource endowments and globalization. In the 1980s and 1990s, most African countries undertook significant efforts to expand the depth, efficiency and stability of their financial systems to promote diversification and economic growth so as to manage shocks and enhance macroeconomic stability. However, the efforts that have been made have typically not brought economic growth and macroeconomic stability due to several remaining significant structural challenges, particularly the lack of quality institutions or good governance and financial constraints on the continent.

K. Berhane (✉)
Department of Economic, Addis Ababa University, Addis Ababa, Ethiopia

Several empirical studies have used cross-sectional and panel data analyses to investigate the impact of financial development on economic growth (see, for example, Beck et al. 2000; Cojocaru et al. 2016; Hassan et al. 2011; Khan and Senhadji 2003; King and Levine 1993; Law and Singh 2014; Levine et al. 2000; Levine and Zervos 1998; Lu et al. 2017; Menyah et al. 2014; Samargandi et al. 2015; Valickova et al. 2015; Zhang et al. 2012). Other studies have analyzed the relationship between financial development and economic growth employing time-series analyses (Christopoulos and Tsionas 2004; Demetriades and Hussein 1996; Luintel et al. 2008; Odedokun 1996). Besides financial development, several empirical studies have also investigated the role of institutional quality on economic growth using individual country time-series data and using cross-sectional country data (Acemoglu and Johnson 2005; Acemoglu and Robinson 2013; Bozoki and Richter 2016; Krasniqi and Desai 2016; Rodríguez-Pose 2013; Sarmidi et al. 2014).

Recently, growth literature has combined both financial development and institutional quality to investigate the effect of financial development on economic growth conditional on a country's institutional quality in the globalized world. The objective of our study is to examine the effect of financial development, institutional quality and globalization on economic growth in the entire sample of 40 African countries and in sub-groups of those countries classified as low-income, lower-middle-income and upper-middle-income countries following the World Bank classification (2015). Based on per capita income,[1] these 40 countries consist of 19 low-income, 14 lower-middle-income and seven upper-middle-income countries. So far, evidence of such a relationship is mixed and inconclusive. Further, our study also examines whether globalization is a key factor in stimulating institutional quality that generates a conducive environment for technological change and innovation and financial development to enhance economic growth in Africa.

---

[1] Low-income economies are defined as those with a GNI per capita, calculated using the World Bank Atlas method, of $1025 or less in 2015; lower middle-income economies are those with a GNI per capita between $1026 and $4035; upper middle-income economies are those with a GNI per capita between $4036 and $12,475.

This study also helps fill the following research gaps. First, it uses a new broad-based financial development index. Constructed by the International Monetary Fund (IMF) this index captures both developments in financial institutions, including banks, insurance companies, mutual funds, pension funds and other types of non-bank financial institutions and financial markets, including stock and bond markets (Svirydzenka 2016). Moreover, it uses comprehensive measures of globalization and institutional quality as regressors: the KOF index of globalization index which includes economic globalization, social globalization and political globalization, and the World Bank's Worldwide Governance Indicators (WGIs) which consist of six different indicators. Second, our study considers country-specific growth responses to financial development, variations in institution quality and their interaction, allowing for parameter heterogeneity and correcting for cross-sectional dependence. Third, the panel dataset covers the period 1980–2014, with a larger number of countries in Africa included over a significantly longer time span than in previous studies. Finally, our analysis complements its main findings for the entire sample of 40 African countries by considering analogous estimates in three sub-groups—low, lower-middle and upper-middle-income countries. To the best of our knowledge, this is the first study to undertake an assessment of how growth is affected in the long-run by financial development, institutional quality and globalization using a non-stationary dynamic panel allowing for parameter heterogeneity and correcting for cross-sectional dependence.

2   Literature Review

2.1   Theoretical Review

Over the past four decades, endogenous growth models have generally been the theoretical basis of studies on the financial development and economic growth nexus. Theoretically, the channels through which financial development affects saving and investment decisions and hence growth have been discussed extensively in literature. In literature the nexus between financial development and economic growth is characterized by optimistic and skeptical approaches.

According to the optimistic approach, efficient financial systems help countries acquire and process information on firms, managers and economic conditions thereby leading to more efficient resource allocations and enhancement of total factor productivity that can stimulate economic growth (Boyd and Prescott 1986; Greenwood and Jovanovic 1990). Second, under better financial systems, the shareholders and creditors monitor firms more effectively and enhance corporate governance which makes savers more willing to finance production and innovations in profitable investments which in turn boost productivity, capital accumulation and economic growth (Bencivenga et al. 1995; Harrison et al. 1999; Stiglitz and Weiss 1983; Sussman 1993). Third, a well-developed financial system mobilizes savings and facilitates efficient allocation of resources (Greenwood et al. 2013; King and Levine 1993). Fourth, financial arrangements play pivotal roles in reducing agency transaction and information costs and enhancing innovation activities and growth (Aghion et al. 2005). Finally, sound financial systems can also contribute to high-return investments through risk-sharing like investments in human capital and research development that accelerate economic growth (Aghion et al. 2009; Bencivenga and Smith 1991; De Gregorio 1996; Devereux and Smith 1994; Galor and Zeira 1993; Greenwood and Jovanovic 1990; Obstfeld 1994; Saint-Paul 1992)

According to the skeptical approach, high systemic risks[2] can lead to increased economic growth and financial volatility with potential negative impacts on economic growth in the short to long term. Financial sectors may take neglected risky loans, insure risky assets and may be affected by external shocks due to asymmetric information that increase banking instability and are capable of generating systemic financial crises (see, for example, Allen and Carletti 2006; Gai et al. 2008; Gennaioli et al. 2012) and misallocation of natural resources and labor into the fast growing financial sector when ideally those inputs should be used

---

[2]Higher systemic risks imply more frequent and/or more severe crises which in turn negatively affect economic growth rates in the short and medium term.

in other sectors. The financial sector attracts more skilled workers while the other real sectors are left behind due to absence of sufficient human resources that can have negative repercussions for growth (Bolton et al. 2016; Philippon 2010; Santomero and Seater 2000). Moreover, deviation from the unique optimal size of the financial sector creates inefficiencies and high costs for the economy (Santomero and Seater 2000), sub-optimal low savings, growth due to financial deregulation (Jappelli and Pagano 1994) and informational overshooting that expands the economy to a new capacity due to financial liberalization which is unknown until it is reached (Zeira 1999). These are some of the main factors that lead financial development to higher systemic risks and then lower economic growth. Therefore, theoretically it is not clear whether financial sector development contributes to economic growth or not particularly in developing countries like those in Africa.

2.2 Empirical Literature

Building on theoretical evidence, there is extensive empirical literature on the role of financial development in economic growth in developing countries. Like in theoretical studies the evidence shows mixed and inconclusive results and differs among countries as per individual characteristics of financial development, institutional quality, globalization, the development stage of the country and country-specific macroeconomic factors.

In finance growth literature, most research has found a positive relationship between financial development and economic growth (Adu et al. 2013; Akinlo and Egbetunde 2010; Christopoulos and Tssionas 2004; Goldsmith 1969; Hassan et al. 2011; Kargbo and Adamu 2009; King and Levine 1993; Levine et al. 2000; Levine and Zervos 1996; Luintel et al. 2008; Odedokun 1996; Rafindadi and Ozturk 2016; Shahbaz and Rahman 2012; Zhang et al. 2012).

Notwithstanding the early empirical evidence, some studies have found a negative relationship between financial development and economic growth (Friedman and Schwartz 2008; Kaminsky and Reinhart 1999; Loayza and Ranciere 2006; Lucas 1988; Rousseau and Wachtel 2011).

Kaminsky and Reinhart (1999) suggest a possible negative channel of the effect of financial development on economic growth through triggering financial instability. Loayza and Ranciere (2006) found evidence of the co-existence of a positive relationship between financial intermediation and output in the long run and a negative short-run relationship due to financial instability.

Other related studies have shown that the positive effect of financial deepening weakens over time regardless of the country's level of development (Beck et al. 2014; Rousseau and Wachtel 2011). Levine et al. (2000) suggest that a larger financial sector increases growth and reduces volatility over the long run while enhancing growth at the cost of higher volatility over short-term horizons.

Further, recent studies document the existence of a certain threshold of financial development beyond which additional deepening generates decreasing returns to economic growth and stability. Using a sample of 87 developed and developing countries, Law and Singh (2014) provide a threshold analysis of the finance-growth link. Their findings reveal that finance is beneficial for growth up to a certain level; beyond the threshold level further development of finance tends to affect growth adversely. Similarly, Arcand et al. (2012), Cecchetti and Kharroubi (2012), Deidda and Fattouh (2002), Huang and Lin (2009), Samargandi et al. (2015), and Shen and Lee (2006) have also found that the nexus between financial development and economic growth has an inverted U-shape effect where a higher level of financial development tends to slow down economic growth.

Existing empirical evidence on the relationship between financial development and growth shows dependence on the income levels of the countries. De Gregorio and Guidotti (1995) and Huang and Lin (2009) found that the positive effect of financial development on economic growth is much more significant in low-income and middle-income countries than in high-income countries. Calderón and Liu (2003) suggest that financial deepening contributes more to growth in developing countries than in industrial countries. A similar result is found by Masten et al. (2008) who analyzed a sample of European countries. They show a strong and positive effect on economic growth only for countries with intermediate levels of development.

Seven and Coskun (2016) examined whether financial development reduced income inequalities and poverty in 45 emerging countries for the period 1987–2011. They found that although financial development promoted economic growth this did not necessarily benefit low-income emerging countries.

To show the existence of an optimal level of financial development, Ductor and Grechyna (2015) employed the first difference generalized Method of Moment estimator (FD-GMM) in 101 developed and developing countries over the period 1970–2010. They empirically examined the relationship between financial development and real sector output and its effect on economic growth. Their results show that the effect of financial development on economic growth depended on the growth of private credit relative to growth in real output.

Further, financial development also affects growth indirectly through positive spillovers from foreign direct investment (FDI) to stimulate economic growth in a well-functioning financial system. Empirically, Alfaro et al. (2004), Hermes and Lensink (2003), Shahbaz et al. (2013) among many others have shown that financial development encourages FDI inflows and transfer of technology and managerial skills that have positive spillover effects on economic growth. Donaubauer et al. (2016), using gravity-type models show that bilateral FDI increases with better developed financial markets in both the host and source countries which have positive economic growth impacts.

Several works in recent years show that strong legal and institutional frameworks are critical for creating an environment in which the financial sector facilitates economic growth. Al-Yousif (2002) argues that the relationship between financial development and economic growth cannot be generalized across countries because economic policies are country-specific and their success depends on the efficiency of the institutions implementing them. Similarly, Demetriades and Law (2006) extend Arestis and Demetriades (1997) and Demetriades and Andrianova's (2004) studies on the role of institutions in the financial-growth nexus and using a sample of 72 countries for the period 1978–2000 and employing cross-sectional and panel data estimation find that financial development had a greater effect on growth when the banking system was operating within a sound institutional framework.

Law et al. (2013) using a sample of 85 countries over the period 1980–2008 and employing the threshold estimation technique found that the impact of finance on growth was positive and significant only after a certain threshold level of institutional development had been attained. Specifically, the qualities of formal institutions like control of corruption, rule of law, bureaucratic quality or government effectiveness and the overall institution had a vital role in the finance-growth nexus. As per their results, the effect of finance on growth was non-existent until the optimal level of institution was reached. Similarly, Ng et al. (2016) employed threshold estimation techniques to a cross-section of 85 jurisdictions during the post-crisis period. They found that the impact of stock market liquidity on growth was positive and significant only in jurisdictions where there was a high level of property rights protection but there was mixed evidence in the low to medium degrees of protection. Moreover, using broader governance indicators as threshold variables and instrumental variables the threshold regressions confirmed the main finding of identifying a threshold level above which institutional quality can positively shape the impact of the stock market on economic growth.

In other work, Le et al. (2016) used a panel dataset of 26 countries over the period 1995–2011 to investigate the impact of institutional quality, trade and financial development on economic growth using the dynamic generalized Method of Moments model. They found that better governance and improved institutional quality impacted on financial development in developing economies while economic growth and trade openness were vital determinants of financial depth in developed economies. Therefore, the effect of financial development on economic growth may vary as per the level of the financial indicator itself, institutional quality, income level and other country-specific conditions.

3   Data Description and Methodology

3.1   Data Source and Descriptive Statistics

Our dataset comprises of annual time series data of selected macroeconomics indicators for 40 African countries (see the list of countries in Appendix A, Table 1) on an annual frequency over the period

Table 1 Description of symbols, definitions of variables and data source

Variable defined	Data source
Real GDP per capita at chained PPPs (in million 2011 US$) in log	PWT 9.0
Human capital index	PWT 9.0
Capital formation in log	PWT 9.0
Financial development index	IMF
Overall globalization index	ETH Zurich 2016
Institutional quality: Estimate	WGI of World Bank
Inflation, consumer prices (annual %)	WDI
Foreign direct investment, net inflows (% of GDP)	WDI

Notes PWT 9.0: Penn World Tables version 9; IMF: International Monetary Fund; WGI: World Governance Indictor of the World Bank; WDI: World Development Indicator of the World Bank; and ETH Zurich 2016: The KOF index of globalization http://globalization.kof.ethz.ch/

1980–2014. The number of countries included and the time period of the study were dictated by data availability. All the variables used in the descriptive and econometrics analysis along with their symbols and sources are given in Table 1.

3.1.1 Dependent Variable

The dependent variable is the logarithm of real GDP per capita at chained PPPs (in million 2011 US$) obtained from the Penn World Table (PWT 9.0)

3.1.2 Independent Variables

The Financial Development Index: To capture the overall size and depth of financial development, most previous empirical studies on financial development have used monetary aggregates (such as M2 and M3 as a ratio of GDP), the ratio of private credit as a ratio of GDP and to a lesser extent the ratio of stock market capitalization to GDP. However, financial development is multidimensional including enhancements in financial institutions and financial markets. Therefore, to investigate the finance-growth relationship more accurately our study uses the financial development index, a new broad-base measure constructed by Sahay et al. (2015) and obtained from IMF. They constructed this index for 183 countries on annual frequency from 1980 to 2014 capturing both financial institutions and financial markets. This index is an improvement over the conventional measures of financial development. Conceptually, it incorporates information on a broader range of financial institutions including banks, insurance companies, pension and mutual funds and financial markets such as the stock and bond markets. For this index, financial development is defined as a combination of depth (size and liquidity of markets), access (ability of individuals and companies to access financial services) and efficiency (institutions' ability to provide financial services at low costs and with sustainable revenue and the level of activity of capital markets) in both financial institutions and financial markets.

The financial development index ranges from 0 (lowest level of development) to 1 (highest level of development) as do its sub-indices on financial institutions' development and financial markets' development.

The Institutional Quality Index: For a measure of institutional quality our study employs the World Bank's Worldwide Governance Indicators (WGIs) for all countries over the period 1996–2014. Governance includes both traditions and institutions through which authority is exercised in a country. The WGI indicators have six dimensions of governance—voice and accountability, political stability and absence of violence, government effectiveness, regulatory quality, rule of law and control of corruption.[3] The data for each variable was normalized to the standard normal distribution with values ranging between −2.5 (lowest quality governance) and 2.5 (highest quality governance).

---

[3] *Voice and Accountability* (*VA*)—capturing perceptions of the extent to which a country's citizens can participate in selecting their government, as well as freedom of expression, freedom of association and a free media. *Political Stability and Absence of Violence/Terrorism* (*PV*) capture perceptions of the likelihood that the government will be destabilized or overthrown by unconstitutional or violent means, including politically-motivated violence and terrorism. *Government effectiveness* (*GE*): Measures the quality of public and civil services, along with their independence from political pressures. Further, it assesses the quality of policy implementation and the

The Globalization Index: We used the KOF[4] index of globalization which was introduced in 2002 (Dreher 2006), its construction details can be found in other studies (Dreher et al. 2008). It was retrieved from the ETH database. The overall index combines economic, social and political dimensions into a measure of total globalization, ranging from 0 to 100, with higher numbers indicating more globalization.

A correlation matrix among the dependent and independent variables and their level of significance is reported in Table 2. The results in column 1 indicate that financial development, globalization and institutional quality variables have positively significant correlations with real gross domestic per capita at the 5 percent level of significance. Similarly, the results in columns 2–5 show that there is a positive and significant correlation between financial development, globalization, institutional quality, human capital and capital formation.

Table 2 Pair-wise correlation of important variables for the all 40 African countries

No.	Variables	1	2	3	4	5	6
1	Real GDP per capita	1					
2	Financial development index	0.62*	1				
3	Institutional quality index	0.37*	0.43*	1			
4	Globalization index	0.61*	0.58*	0.50*	1		
5	Human capital index	0.66*	0.50*	0.40*	0.68*	1	
6	Capital stock per capita	0.76*	0.41*	0.25*	0.52*	0.58*	1

Note * The 5 percent level of significance

---

reliability of government enforcement about such policies. *Regulatory quality* (RQ): Assesses the government's ability to apply sound policies to stimulate private sector development. *Rule of law* (RL): Captures perceptions concerning the degree of confidence possessed by agents in a society based on the protection of property rights, contract enforcement, police, courts and the possibility of violence. *Control of corruption* (CC): Evaluates the ability of public power to prevent corruption and the degree of influence on the state wielded by private interest groups.

[4]Note: The KOF index is available at: http://globalization.kof.ethz.ch/.

Figure 1 gives information about the overall financial development, financial institutions' development and financial markets' development by income groups. As can be seen in the figure, financial institutions' development is relatively higher than financial markets' development in all income groups. The overall financial development index and its components on average improve with higher income.

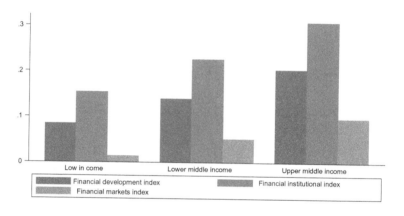

Fig. 1 Financial development indicators by income group for 40 African countries (*Source* Author's calculation based on the International Monetary Fund (IMF))

Figure 2 shows a plot of mean values over the sample period regarding indicators of institutional quality for different income levels. In this figure we can see that each of the six institutional quality indicators is the highest in upper-middle-income countries, followed in order by lower-middle-income and low-income countries with one exception: the voice and accountability indicator is on average higher in low-income countries than in lower-middle-income countries.

3.2 Theory and Model Specifications

Recently, both endogenous and exogenous growth theories have been used to investigate the determinants of economic growth across countries. Following Mankiw et al. (1992) and Demetriades and Law (2006)

6 The Role of Financial Development and Institutional Quality ...

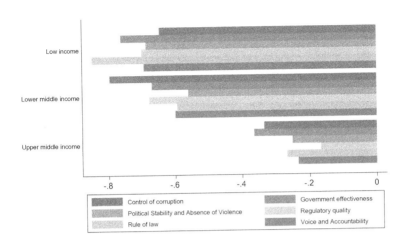

Fig. 2 World governance indicators by income group for 40 African countries (1996–2014) (*Source* Author's calculations based on the WGI dataset obtained from the World Bank—control of corruption, political stability and absence of violence/terrorism, rule of law, government effectiveness, regulatory quality and voice and accountability)

we used a Cobb–Douglas production function for the aggregate economy as a theoretical base but this function was augmented with financial development, institutional quality and other control variables. Based on literature and the framework posited by León-Ledesma et al. (2015), Omri et al. (2015), Rahman et al. (2015), and Zerihun (2014), we determined labor-augmenting technology A not only by technological improvements but also by financial development, institutional quality and globalization within the augmented Cobb–Douglas production function.

Theoretically, there are many channels through which financial development, institutional quality, globalization and their interactions can affect economic growth and the level of technology and efficiency. Higher degrees of financial development and institutional quality can encourage accumulation of physical capital, human capital, FDI inflows and transfer of technological knowledge. These factors in turn help improve the level of technology and efficiency thereby promoting economic growth in a country. Globalization also contributes to economic growth by inducing more efficient allocation of internal and external resources and by helping shift technological advancements from developed countries to developing economies with the less-developed countries exploiting innovations of developed countries through learning-by-doing effects. Besides, using both OLS and SYS-GMM on 21 sub-African countries for the period 1980–2010, Effiong (2015) found evidence of threshold effects by the introduction of a linear interaction term between financial development and institutional quality in growth regressions. In his model, financial development contributed positively to growth but only in good policy environments. Various studies (for example, Acemoglu 2006; Acemoglu and Robinson 2008, 2010; Rodrik and Subramanian 2003) have provided new impetus to empirical research by showing that institutions affect the economic growth of individual firms and countries.

To examine the linkage between financial development, institutional quality, globalization and growth we used the production function with constant returns to scale and productivity growth that is purely labor augmenting or 'Harrod-neutral' for each country i at time t. This is presented as:

$$Y_{it} = K_{it}^{\alpha}(A_{it}L_{it})^{1-\alpha} \tag{1}$$

where, Y_{it} is real gross domestic product (GDP) in country i ($i = 1, 2, 3, \ldots, 40$) at time t ($t = 1, 2, 3, \ldots, 35$), K_{it} is capital, including both human and physical capital, L_{it} is the stock of raw labor and A_{it} is a labor-augmenting factor measuring the level of technology and efficiency in country i at time t in an economy. This equation assumes that $0 < \alpha < 1$, implying decreasing returns to all capital.

In existing literature, the elasticities in the production function are typically estimated under the assumption of country homogeneity and cross-sectional independence which are strong assumptions. We used a flexible framework to estimate the elasticities from a panel of countries allowing for slope heterogeneity and taking into account cross-sectional dependence. There are theoretical and empirical reasons to expect that there will be important heterogeneity and cross-sectional dependence across countries.

6 The Role of Financial Development and Institutional Quality ...

Hence, under the assumption of slope heterogeneity across countries the capital stock, raw labor and labor-augmenting technology were assumed to evolve exogenously at rate n_i and g_i, and are presented as:

$$L_{it} = L_{i0} e^{n_i t} \tag{2}$$

$$A_{it} = A_{i0} e^{g_i t + x_{it} \theta_i} e^{\mu_{it}} \tag{3}$$

where, n_i is the exogenous labor force growth rate in each country, A_{i0} is time-invariant country specific technology and g_i is the exogenous rate of technological progress in each country in the panel. Moreover, x_{it} is a vector of financial development, institutional quality and globalization indices that can affect the level of technology and its efficiency in country i at time t, and θ_i is a vector of coefficients related to these variables. The term μ_{it} represents the error term. The production function in Eq. (1) can be written in a per-worker form such that:

$$y_{it} = \frac{Y_{it}}{L_{it}} = A_{it}^{1-\alpha} k_{it}^{\alpha} \quad \text{where} \quad k_{it} = \frac{K_{it}}{L_{it}} \tag{4}$$

Taking the log transformation of both sides of Eq. (4) yields:

$$\ln y_{it} = (1-\alpha) \ln A_{it} + \alpha \ln k_{it} \tag{5}$$

Taking the log of Eq. (3) and then substituting the result into Eq. (5) leads to:

$$\ln y_{it} = \ln A_{i0} + (1-\alpha) g_i t + (1-\alpha) \theta_i x_{it} + \alpha \ln k_{it} + \mu_{it} \tag{6}$$

The variable x_{it} in Eq. (6) shows variations across countries which implies that different countries may converge to different steady states based on their steady state levels of financial development, institutions and globalization.

Plugging-in Z_{it}, representing cross-interaction terms between financial development, institution quality and globalization into Eq. (6) gives the final theoretical specification as:

$$\ln y_{it} = \ln A_{i0} + (1-\alpha)g_i t + (1-\alpha)\theta_i x_{it} \\ + \phi_i Z_{it} + \alpha \ln k_{it} + \mu_{it} \quad (7)$$

Rewriting Eq. (7) as a standard panel model specification we get:

$$\ln y_{it} = \beta + \beta_{1i} \ln k_{it} + \beta_{2i} X_{it} + \beta_{3i} Z_{it} + \gamma_t + \eta_i + \mu_{it} \quad (8)$$

where, $\ln y_{it}$ is the log-transform of real GDP per capita PPP chained 2011 US$, $\ln k_{it}$ represents log of capital formation per capital, X_{it} consists of variables representing the degree of financial development, institutional quality and globalization while Z_{it} represents the cross-interaction term between the variables represented by X_{it}. Moreover, γ_t and η_i correspond to the time effect and the unobserved country-specific effect respectively and μ_{it} refers to the regression random error term. Finally, the lagged value of the dependent variable is included as a regressor in Eq. (8) to make a dynamic panel model.

In our study in addition to the slope heterogeneity we also take into account the impact of cross-section dependence, both the unobservable and the observable parts of the empirical model. The conventional panel specification assumes that there is slope homogeneity and cross-section independence. That is, all the elasticity and semi-elasticity parameters in Eq. (8) will then be equal across countries (β_{1i}, β_{2i} and β_{3i} do not vary by i) and the regression error term will show no systematic patterns of correlation across countries. The slope homogeneity restriction implies that each country with a different level of economic development such as low-income (for example, Ethiopia, Uganda and Tanzania), upper-middle-income (Botswana, Namibia and South Africa) and higher-income (for example, Equatorial Guinea and Seychelles)[5] countries should have the same parameters in a growth regression. However, this is a strong assumption which is likely to be violated in reality. Moreover, due to strong inter-economy relationships, global technological and financial shocks, co-movements of macroeconomic aggregates and worldwide environmental changes the assumption of cross-section

---

[5]Income categories of African countries based on the World Bank's Development Indicators.

independence is unrealistic and that the covariance of the residual is zero can be easily violated. Westerlund and Edgerton (2008) support this point, 'When studying long macroeconomic and micro cross country regression cross-sectional dependencies are likely to be the rule rather than the exception, due to the existence of common shocks and unobserved factors.'

3.3 Econometric Methodology

The methodology in our paper follows four steps. First, cross-sectional independence of each variable is tested using the Pesaran (2004) test for $N = 40$ and $T = 35$, where N is the cross-section dimension and T is the time dimension. Second, the integration levels of the variables using appropriate panel unit root tests are investigated. That is, in case cross-sectional dependence is rejected, the first-generation panel unit root test by Maddala and Wu (1999) is used. Instead, if there is evidence of cross-sectional dependence we employ the CADF test suggested by Pesaran (2007), a second-generation panel unit root test that controls for cross-sectional dependence. Third, depending on the integration levels of the variables, slope heterogeneity and cross-sectional dependence, both first and second generation panel co-integration tests are used: the Pedroni (1999, 2001, 2004) residual-based test and the Westerlund (2007) error-correction-based test. Finally, given the importance of slope heterogeneity and cross-country dependence in the African context a recently developed model that allows for slope heterogeneity and cross-sectional dependence was also used.

We tried three dynamic panel data estimation techniques that address the issue of non-stationarity—the pooled mean group (PMG) estimators by Pesaran et al. (1999), the mean-group (MG) estimator by Pesaran and Smith (1995) and a PMG estimator with a common correlated effects correction (PMG-CCE)—as suggested in a non-dynamic setting by Pesaran (2006).

The PMG estimator imposes homogeneity on the long-run parameters across individual units (countries in our case) while maintaining heterogeneous short-run dynamics. This estimator yields efficient and consistent estimates when the long-run coefficients are equal across all individual units and when there is no cross-sectional dependence in the panel. Often, however, the hypothesis of long-run slope homogeneity and cross-sectional independence are rejected empirically. The MG estimator relaxes the assumption of long-run slope homogeneity compared to the PMG estimator. The PMG-CCE estimator attempts to correct for cross-sectional dependence by augmenting the regression with cross-section means of the explanatory variables.

3.3.1 Cross-Sectional Dependency Test

In a macroeconomic panel cross-sectional dependence can be introduced because of a finite number of unobservable and/or observed common factors that may have different effects on total factor productivity (TFP) across countries. Such factors include spatial spillovers, aggregate technological shocks, similar national policies intended at raising the level of technology, oil price shocks that influence TFP through their effects on production costs, world financial crises and interaction effects through trade or other networks. Therefore, in a cross-country macroeconomic panel study performing a cross-sectional dependence test is a vital step. That is why of late there has been increasing research interest in characterizing and modeling cross-sectional dependence and its impacts on estimation.

To determine the presence of CD we used the simple test suggested by Pesaran (2004) for all the variables in which the test statistic is based on an average of all pair-wise correlations (for cross-section pairs) of the ordinary least squares (OLS) residuals from the regression of the panel data model:

$$y_{it} = \hat{\alpha}_i + \hat{\beta}_i x_{it} + \hat{\mu}_{it} \quad (9)$$

where, y_{it} is the dependent variable, ($i = 1, \ldots, N$), N is the number of panel members, ($t = 1, \ldots, T$) is time period and x_{it} is the vector of observed explanatory variables. $\hat{\alpha}_i$ and $\hat{\beta}_i$ refer to the estimated intercepts and the slope coefficients which can vary across panel members.

The Pesaran (2004) CD-test statistic can generally be expressed as:

$$CD = \sqrt{\frac{2T}{N(N-1)}} \left(\sum_{i=1}^{N-1} \sum_{j=i+1}^{N} \hat{\rho}_{ij} \right) \to N(0,1) \qquad (10)$$

where, $\hat{\rho}_{ij}$ refers to the sample estimate of the pair-wise correlation of the OLS residuals, $\hat{\mu}_{it}$ and $\hat{\mu}_{jt}$ associated with Eq. (9).

$$\hat{\rho}_{ij} = \frac{\sum_{t=1}^{T} \hat{\mu}_{it} \hat{\mu}_{jt}}{\sqrt{\sum_{t=1}^{T} \hat{\mu}_{it}^2} \sqrt{\sum_{t=1}^{T} \hat{\mu}_{jt}^2}} = \hat{\rho}_{ji} \qquad (11)$$

The null hypothesis for this test is cross-sectional independence and under this the statistics are distributed as standard normal for $T > 3$ and a large value (Pesaran 2004). The CD-test statistics from various simulations show robustness to non-stationarity, structural breaks, parameter heterogeneity and above all, they perform well in small samples. This test is applicable both on the variables and on the estimated residuals.

3.3.2 Panel Unit Root Test

Since our dataset covers a long time period (35 years) it is very likely to observe that the macroeconomic variables will follow a unit root process (Nelson and Plosser 1982) Hence, we employed Pesaran's (2007) second-generation panel unit root test, referred to as cross-sectionally augmented Dickey-Fuller (CADF) test. This test is based on the assumption that the data generating process is:

$$\Delta X_{it} = \alpha_i + \beta_i X_{it-1} + v_{it} \qquad (12)$$

where, $v_{it} = \rho_i \theta_t + \mu_{it}$, θ_t is the common factor and μ_{it} is white noise. The regression model to be estimated for the CADF test is:

$$\Delta X_{it} = \alpha_i + \beta_i X_{it-1} + \phi_i \bar{X}_{it-1} + \gamma_i \Delta \bar{X}_{it-1} + \varepsilon_{it} \qquad (13)$$

where, for each cross-section, a *t*-statistic is obtained for each of the estimated β_i. The test statistics for the CIPS test are the mean of these *t*-statistics. Pesaran (2007) provides the critical values for the CIPS test statistics. In comparison to the first-generation panel unit root tests the CIPS test provides more precise and reliable results in the presence of cross-sectional dependence.

3.3.3 Panel Co-integration Test

The idea of co-integration was first introduced in literature by Engle and Granger (1987). Co-integration means the existence of a long-run relationship among two or more non-stationary variables. The principle of testing for co-integration is to show if the variables in question move together over time so that a short-term sudden shock will be corrected in the long run with the variables in the long run returning to a steady-state linear relationship. Otherwise, if two or more variables are not co-integrated they may wander randomly far away from each other.

Therefore, to determine the existence of a long-run equilibrium relationship among the variables in the panel data two groups of panel co-integration tests have been developed in literature. The first group consists of first generation panel co-integration tests developed by Pedroni (1999, 2001, 2004) which solve the problem of small samples and allow for heterogeneity in the intercepts and slopes across the different members of the panel but these tests ignore cross-sectional dependence in cross-country panel analyses. Pedroni (1999, 2001, 2004) developed seven panel co-integration statistics based on the residuals of the Engle and Granger (1987) co-integrating regression in a panel data model that allows for considerable heterogeneity. Four of these statistics are within-dimension ('panel') and the other three statistics are between-dimension ('group') test statistics and in all cases the null hypothesis being tested is no co-integration.[6]

---

[6]Since the seven Pedroni panel co-integration statistics have been extensively discusses in the literature all the procedure will not be discussed in this paper.

The second group of tests is second-generation co-integration tests developed by Westerlund (2007) that take cross-sectional dependence into account. The Westerlund tests consist of four statistics based on the speed that the adjustment parameter in an error-correction model equals zero. Two of these statistics are group mean statistics (Gt and Ga) which investigate co-integration in at least one panel and the other two statistics are panel statistics (Pt and Pa) which investigate co-integration for panel members as a whole. Gt and Pt are computed with the conventional standard error of the parameters of the error correction model whereas Ga and Pa are adjusted for heteroscedasticity and auto-correlations based on two standard errors developed by Newey and West (1994). The null hypothesis tested by all the four tests is the hypothesis of no co-integration.

The second-generation panel co-integration tests have the following advantages. First, they allow for a large degree of heterogeneity both in the long-run co-integration relation and in short-run dynamics and can deal with different integration levels in the variables as long as the dependent variable is not I(0) (Persyn and Westerlund 2008). Second, they take into account cross-sectionally dependent data among the members of the panel. Third, there is an optional bootstrap procedure developed for the test which is quite robust against cross-sectional dependencies thereby allowing for various forms of heterogeneity. Fourth, the Westerlund panel co-integration tests show both better size accuracy and higher power than the residual-based tests developed by Pedroni. The difference in power arises mainly because the residual-based tests ignore potentially valuable information by imposing a possibly invalid common factor restriction whereas Westerlund avoids the common factor restriction problem.

Hence, we used Westerlund's (2007) error-correction-based co-integration tests in addition to Pedroni's (2004) tests to examine the long-run relationship between economic growth, financial development, institutional quality and globalization in African countries.

The Westerlund tests for the absence of co-integration are based on the error-correction model for individual or for panel members as a whole. Consider the error-correction model given as:

$$\Delta y_{it} = \alpha_i' d_t + \phi_i(y_{it-1} - \beta_i' x_{it}) + \sum_{j=1}^{p_i} \lambda_{ij} \Delta y_{it-j}$$
$$+ \sum_{j=-q_i}^{p_i} \theta_{ij} \Delta x_{it-j} + \varepsilon_{it} \quad (14)$$

where, $t = 1, 2, \ldots, T$ and $i = 1, 2, \ldots, N$ show the time period and cross-sectional index respectively, d_t is a variable that includes any deterministic components and x_{it} is a variable that includes a set of exogenous variables. We can rewrite Eq. (14) as:

$$\Delta y_{it} = \alpha_i' d_t + \phi_i y_{it-1} - \phi_i \beta_i' x_{it} + \sum_{j=1}^{p_i} \lambda_{ij} \Delta y_{it-j}$$
$$+ \sum_{j=-q_i}^{p_i} \theta_{ij} \Delta x_{it-j} + \varepsilon_{it} \quad (15)$$

From Eqs. (14) and (15), the deterministic component d_t has three distinct possibilities. The first case is when $d_t = 0$, in which case Eqs. (14) and (15) have no deterministic term. Second, when $d_t = 1$, the implication is that Eqs. (14) and (15) have a constant intercept term but no trend. Third, having $d_t = (1, t)$ indicates that Eqs. (14) and (15) have both a constant intercept and a trend. Moreover, ϕ_i is the parameter for the error-correction term and determines the speed at which the system corrects back to the long-run equilibrium relationship $y_{it-1} - \beta_i' x_{it} = 0$ after a sudden shock. Therefore, given that β_i is not a zero vector, if the value of $\phi_i < 0$, then the model is error correcting which implies that y_{it} and x_{it} are co-integrated whereas if the value $\phi_i = 0$ then the model is not error correcting and thus there is no co-integration among the variables. The two group co-integration tests state the null hypothesis of no co-integration as $H_0: \phi_i = 0$ for all i and the alternative hypothesis $H_1: \phi_i < 0$ for at least one i. In contrast the panel co-integration tests state the null hypothesis no co-integration as $H_0: \phi_i = 0$ for all i versus the alternative hypothesis of a co-integration presence among the whole panel $H_1: \phi_i = \phi < 0$ for all i. In other words, the group mean statistics G_a and G_t are used to test the null hypothesis of no co-integration against the alternative hypothesis of at least one element of panel co-integration and the panel statistics P_a and P_t are used to test the null hypothesis of co-integration against the simultaneous alternative of panel co-integration. Hence, based on the group mean and panel test, rejection of H_0 should be taken as evidence of co-integration in at least one of the cross-sectional units or for the whole panel respectively.

3.3.4 Empirical Estimation Technique

The estimation strategy in our study largely follows an extended version of the Pesaran (2006) common correlated effects (CCE) estimator which allows for a heterogeneous coefficient. The CCE estimator has been used in empirical application in Bond and Eberhardt (2013), Eberhardt (2012), LeMay-Boucher and Rommerskirchen (2015), McNabb and LeMay-Boucher (2014) in panel models with strictly exogenous regressors. Pesaran's (2006) baseline specification given independent explanatory variables and a single common factor is:

$$\begin{aligned} y_{it} &= \alpha_i + \beta_i x_{it} + \mu_{it} \\ \mu_{it} &= \gamma_i' f_t + \varepsilon_{it} \end{aligned} \quad (16)$$

where, y_{it}, as used in our paper is the logarithm of real gross domestic per capita for country i at time t and x_{it} is a vector of regressors. f_t and its coefficient γ_i are an unobserved common factor and a heterogeneous loading factor respectively. To account for cross-sectional dependence induced by the unobserved common factor this model is augmented with cross-sectional averages of the dependent variable as well as the regressors, and to account for slope heterogeneity, mean-group regression is used instead of pooled regression.

Nevertheless, Chudik and Pesaran (2015) and Everaert and De Groote (2016) have shown that the CCE estimator is consistent in a non-dynamic panel model only. A dynamic panel model where the lagged dependent variable is added as a regressor to Eq. (16) is given as:

$$y_{it} = \alpha_i + \lambda_i y_{i,t-1} + \beta_i x_{it} + \mu_{it} \tag{17}$$

where, the idiosyncratic errors μ_{it} are cross-sectionally weakly dependent and the mean of the coefficients of the one-time lag of the dependent is homogenous. The lagged dependent variable in Eq. (17) is no longer strictly exogenous, and hence the coefficient estimates become inconsistent. Chudik et al. (2015) however, show that these estimates become consistent by adding $\sqrt[3]{T}$ lags of the cross-sectional means. The equation is given as:

$$y_{it} = \alpha_i + \lambda_i y_{i,t-1} + \beta_i x_{it} + \sum_{l=0}^{q} \delta'_{i,l} \bar{z}_{t-l} + \varepsilon_{it} \tag{18}$$

where, $\bar{z}_t$ represents a vector of the cross-sectional means of the dependent and independent variables with q time lags of the $\bar{z}$ vector. Moreover, Chudik and Pesaran (2015) used a 'half-panel' jack-knife and recursive mean adjustment to help correct for the small sample bias. Our approach is based on the distributed lag and an error-correction model (ECM) representation of Eq. (18), which can be easily written as:

$$\Delta y_{it} = \alpha_i + \theta_i (y_{i,t-1} - \beta_i x_{it}) + \sum_{l=1}^{q} \phi_{i,l} \Delta y_{i,t-l} + \sum_{l=0}^{q} \psi'_{i,l} \Delta x_{t-l}$$
$$+ \sum_{l=0}^{q} \delta'_{i,l} \bar{z}_{t-l} + \varepsilon_{it} \tag{19}$$

Equation (19) can be rewritten as:

$$\Delta y_{it} = \alpha_i + \theta_i y_{i,t-1} + \gamma_i x_{it} + \sum_{l=1}^{q} \phi_{i,l} \Delta y_{i,t-l} + \sum_{l=0}^{q} \psi'_{i,l} \Delta x_{t-l}$$
$$+ \sum_{l=0}^{q} \delta'_{i,l} \bar{z}_{t-l} + \varepsilon_{it} \tag{20}$$

where, $\gamma_i = \theta_i \beta_i$.

4 Empirical Analysis

We report the cross-sectional dependence tests based on Pesaran (2004) in this section. Secondly, we also report on the panel unit root for the entire sample as well as sub-groups of countries based on income levels. We used the Pedroni and Westerlund panel co-integration tests to investigate the existence of a long-run relationship among the variables. Finally, this section also gives the estimates from error-correction models.

4.1 Cross-Sectional Dependence Test

The tested cross-sectional dependence results among the variables with the CD test are presented in Table 3 for the entire sample as well as for the different income levels of the countries. The table gives the CD statistics and their *p*-values, the cross-sectional correlation for each variable, where ρ measures the magnitude of correlation and avg |ρ| indicates the average of such correlation in absolute value in the noted income category. From these statistics, the null hypothesis that there is no cross-sectional dependence can be rejected at the 5 percent significance level for all the variables in all income categories except for institutional quality in the upper-middle-income category and in the full sample of countries.

The results indicate that even after including the regressors that are expected to affect economic growth in each country, the regression disturbance terms among the countries also affect one another. Therefore, the results show that all the countries and countries in each income group examined in this study have highly integrated economies and when a shock occurs in one of them it will also affect the other countries.

4.2 Panel Unit Root Test Allowing for Cross-Sectional Dependence

Since the previous section gives cross-sectional dependency among the variables, Pesaran's (2007) second-generation panel unit root test was used to investigate the integration levels of the variables. CIPS tests were carried out including an intercept only as well as with an intercept and

Table 3 Results of Pesaran's (2004) cross-sectional dependence test by income category

Variables	Full sample countries			Low-income countries		
	CD-test	P	abs (ρ)	CD-test	P	abs (ρ)
Log of real GDP per capita	49.41***	0.3	0.47	13.17***	0.17	0.38
GDP per capital growth	10.10***	0.06	0.17	3.02***	0.04	0.15
Log of human capital	148.73***	0.9	0.91	74.60***	0.96	0.96
Log of capital stock per capita	83.55***	0.51	0.7	30.82***	0.4	0.65
Log of foreign direct investment, net inflows (% of GDP)	37.73***	0.23	0.32	25.03***	0.34	0.39
Inflation, consumer prices (annual %)	35.63***	0.24	0.31	13.89***	0.2	0.33
Financial development index	20.74***	0.13	0.44	7.34***	0.09	0.41
Institutional quality index	−0.38	0	0.42	2.10***	0.05	0.4
Globalization index	139.98***	0.85	0.85	68.83***	0.89	0.89

Notes (1) ρ is the cross-sectional correlation of the variable and abs (ρ) is absolute value of the correlation. (2) Under the null hypothesis of cross-sectional independence, CD ~ $N(0, 1)$, *p*-values close to zero indicate data are correlated across panel groups. (3) *** and ** represent 1 and 5 percent level of significance respectively

linear trend in levels and in first differences for all income categories.[7] As indicated in Table 4, when using the full sample of countries almost all the variables appear non-stationary in levels but after taking the first difference they become stationary under the specifications without trend (constant only) and with trend (constant and trend) at the 1 percent level of significance except for human capital and capital stock per capital.

4.3 Panel Co-integration Test Allowing for Cross-Sectional Dependence

The previous sections show that there is typically cross-section dependence based on the Pesaran (2004) test and the variables appear non-stationary in levels based on Pesaran's (2007) CIPS test. Following the CD test and panel unit root test, the next step is to check the existence of co-integration among the variables. For this purpose, the results from both the Pedroni (1999, 2001, 2004) and Westerlund (2007) tests, that is, the first and second generation panel co-integration tests respectively are presented in Table 5.

In the case of the entire sample of 40 countries, the results suggest that six out of the seven Pedroni tests (panel and group) reject the null hypothesis of no co-integration, indicating that financial development, institutional quality and globalization have a long-run relationship with economic growth. Similarly, six out of seven Pedroni tests reject the null hypothesis of no co-integration in low-income countries, five out of seven do so regarding lower-middle-income countries and four out of seven do so regarding upper-middle-income countries.

On the other hand, considering the presence of potential cross-sectional dependence across the entire sample of 40 countries and all sub-groups of countries, it is more robust to apply Westerlund's (2007) panel co-integration tests. Under the presence of cross-sectional dependence, recent papers have shown that the asymptotic p-values without bootstrapping are inefficient and inconsistent as compared to the robust p-values with bootstrapping. The Westerlund tests based on

---
[7]The CIPS test results for each income category are given in Appendix A.

Table 4 Pesaran's (2007) Panel Unit Root test results for the full sample of countries

Variable	In levels				In first differences			
	Specification without trend		Specification with trend		Specification without trend		Specification with trend	
	Zt-bar	p-value	Zt-bar	p-value	Zt-bar	p-value	Zt-bar	p-value
Log of real GDP per capita	−0.70	0.258	2.40	0.992	−10.90	0.000	−8.80	0.000
Log of human capital	2.70	0.996	6.00	1.000	2.40	0.992	2.40	0.992
Log of capital stock per capita	2.10	0.980	−0.50	0.312	−2.00	0.023	0.70	0.766
Log of foreign direct investment, net inflows (% of GDP)	−9.30	0.000	−6.80	0.000	−19.20	0.000	−16.10	0.000
Inflation, consumer prices (annual %)	−11.00	0.000	−8.50	0.000	−20.80	0.000	−17.20	0.000
Financial development index	−5.40	0.000	−2.10	0.020	−16.00	0.000	−12.90	0.000
Institutional quality index	0.10	0.535	0.60	0.737	−14.40	0.000	−11.50	0.000
Globalization index	−3.80	0.000	−3.40	0.000	−15.40	0.000	−11.70	0.000

Notes Null for CIPS test: series is I (1) and the CIPS test assumes that the cross-section dependence is in form of a single unobserved common factors

the ECM approach and the robust *p*-values based on 800 bootstrap replications are reported in Table 5. All four of the Westerlund tests clearly reject the null of no co-integration at the 1 percent level of significance in the entire sample and in all sub-groups of countries. Consequently, the results indicate the presence of a strong co-integration relationship among economic growth, financial development, institutional quality and globalization in the entire sample of countries as well as in each of the three income categories.

4.4 Long and Short Run Estimation Using the Panel Error Correction Model

The results of estimated error correction models with long-run relationships of financial development, institutional quality and globalization indicators on economic growth for the full sample of countries are reported in Table 6. Columns 1 and 2 in Table 6 report the results for the pooled-mean group (Pesaran et al. 1999) and mean-group (Pesaran and Smith 1995) estimated models. Based on the test, presented in Appendix A, Table 2, the calculated Hausman statistic is 1.67 with its *p*-value 0.644 and is distributed $\chi^2(2)$. Hence, the PMG estimator is preferred to the MG group estimator.[8]

Column 3 gives a PMG model similar to that in column 1 with the difference that the estimates are performed using ordinary least squares (OLS) as advocated by Ditzen (2016), whereas column 1 follows the maximum-likelihood strategy of Pesaran et al. (1999). We refer to the estimates in column 3 as PMG-OLS estimates. The null hypothesis of the absence of weak cross-sectional dependence is rejected in column 3, in which there is no attempt to correct for cross-sectional dependence.

For non-dynamic models with independent explanatory variables in which there is cross-sectional dependency, Pesaran (2006) suggested the correction of MG estimators by augmenting the regression model with cross-sectional means of the explanatory variables which is referred to

---

[8]For the PMG estimator, the long coefficients are homogenous but not the short run coefficients.

Table 5 Co-integration tests by income category

Statistics	Entire sample of countries	Low-income countries	Lower-middle-income countries	Upper-middle-income countries
Pedroni's statistics of panel tests				
v statistic	0.5	0.39	0.47	0.5
ρ statistic	−4.089***	−3.204***	−1.99**	−2.193**
t statistic	−15.63***	−12.68***	−7.883***	−6.881***
ADF statistic	−5.931***	−4.034***	−5.868***	1.42
Pedroni's statistics of group tests				
ρ statistic	−1.885**	−1.703**	−0.71	−1.336*
t statistic	19.72***	−15.72***	−10.02***	−8.68***
ADF statistic	−4.395***	−2.287**	−5.376***	2.74
Westerlund's test				
Gt	−4.09***	−3.80**	−4.42***	−4.36***
Ga	−10.66***	−11.37***	−12.68***	−10.34**
Pt	−23.62***	−16.65**	−13.68***	−10.71**
Pa	−10.71**	−11.70**	−9.03**	−11.02**

Notes (1) In Pedroni statistics 'All test statistics are distributed $N(0,1)$ under a null of no co-integration, and diverge to negative infinity [under the alternative] (save for panel v).' (2) The Bartlett kernel window width set according to $\sqrt[3]{T}$, that is approximately equal to 2 in Westerlund. (3) Akaike Information Criterion (AIC) with a maximum lag length 2 and lead length of 1 is used for optimal lag/lead length selection in the Westerlund test. (4) Bootstrapped p-values robust against cross-sectional dependencies are obtained from bootstrapping 800 times in the Westerlund test. (5) ***, **, and * represent 1, 5 and 10 percent level of significance respectively. (6) The tests are employed using STATA 14 with the 'xtpedroni' (Neal 2013) and 'xtwest' command (Persyn and Westerlund 2008)

Table 6 Long run and short run estimation following the error correction model

Long run coefficients	PMG[a] (1)	MG[b] (2)	PMG-OLS[c] (3)	PMG-CCE[d] (4)
Overall globalization index	0.036***	0.025*	0.034***	0.011*
Average of six institutional quality indices	−0.555***	−0.116	−0.008	0.171*
Financial development index	6.552***	4.637***	3.297**	1.528*
Short run coefficients				
Speed of adjustment	−0.115***	−0.351***	−0.139***	−0.721***
Δ Financial development index[e]	−0.382	−0.270	−0.007	0.514
Δ Overall globalization index[e]	0.003	−0.000	0.002	0.001
Δ Average of six institutional quality indices[e]	0.045	0.002	0.023	−0.052
Number of observations	720	720	720	720
CD test statistics[f]			4.500	0.660
CD P-value[f]			0.000	0.507
Constant	0.593***	2.323***	0.835***	0.494

Notes ***, **, and * is 1, 5 and 10 percent level of significance respectively
Columns 1 and 2 are based on the results from the STATA package xtpmg (by Edward F. Blackburne III and Mark W. Frank), whereas columns 3 and 4 are based on results from the STATA package xtdcce2 (by Jan Ditzen)
[a]PMG: Estimates using pooled mean group estimator which does not account for cross-sectional dependence
[b]MG: Estimates mean group estimators that take into account slope heterogeneity
[c]PMG-OLS: Pooled-mean-group estimates using OLS estimates rather than maximum likelihood
[d]PMG-CCE: Pooled-mean-group estimates using OLS estimates, with standard CCE correction
[e]Δ is the first difference operator: $\Delta x = x_t − x_{t−1}$
[f]CD test statistic = Pesaran (2015) weakly cross-sectional dependence statistics and CDP-value = the related *p*-value of cross-sectional dependency test

as the CCE (common correlated effects) approach. Column 4 modifies the model in column 3 (Table 6) by augmenting it with cross-sectional means of the explanatory variables to correct for common correlated effects with the resulting estimates referred to as PMG-CCE estimates as given in column 4. The CD test is applied with this model also with the result that the hypothesis that there is no weak cross-sectional dependence is rejected, lending credence that this is the most legitimate model among the ones presented in Table 6.

Table 7 presents the PMG-CCE regression results for financial development and its components—financial institutions' development and financial markets' development in addition to institutional quality and globalization indices for the entire sample. The results reported in column 1 in Table 7 show that financial development is positively related to economic growth in the long-run and it is statistically significant at the 10 percent level. All else being equal, a 0.1 unit increase in financial development leads to greater economic growth by 15.3 percent, which shows that financial development plays a vital role in increasing economic growth in the long run, a finding that is in line with Beck et al. (2014) and Loayza and Ranciere (2006). Similarly, the estimated results show that in the long-run higher institutional quality and greater globalization have significantly positive impacts on economic growth at the 10 percent significance level. Having 1.1 and 1.7 percent economic growth in the long-run is linked with 1 unit and 0.1 unit increase in the globalization and institutional quality indices respectively.

To examine the role of financial development in economic growth it would be better to consider the simultaneous and separate impact of financial institutions' development and financial markets' development across countries and income categories. The results in columns 2 and 3 in Table 7 indicate that greater financial institutions' development has a positive and significant impact on growth. However, the same cannot be said for greater financial markets' development. The estimated results indicate that African countries are predominantly financial institution-based economies and financial markets are still very little developed to affect economic growth. This is consistent with the descriptive statistics in Fig. 1. Moreover, in column 4 in Table 7 the interaction between financial development and institutional quality is included in addition

Table 7 Estimates of pooled mean group model with common correlated effects correction, for entire sample of 40 African countries

Long Run Coefficients	1 Coef	2 Coef	3 Coef	4 Coef
Overall globalization index	0.011*	0.008	−0.002	0.004
Average of six institutional quality indices	0.171*	0.168*	0.135**	0.380**
Financial development index	1.528*			−0.076
Financial institutions index		1.575***		
Financial markets index			−0.547	
Financial development and institutional quality interaction				−2.946***
Short run coefficients				
Speed of adjustment	−0.721***	−0.623***	−0.835***	−0.880***
Δ Overall globalization index	0.001	−0.001	−0.000	−0.223
Δ Average of six institutional quality indices	−0.052	−0.013	−0.054	−0.681*
Δ Financial development index	0.514			−3.654
Δ Financial institutions index		−0.360		
Δ Financial markets index			0.795	
Δ Finance and institution interaction				2.124
Number of observations	1320	1265	720	720
CD test statistics	−1.35	−1.14	0.66	0.6
CD p-value	0.1763	0.2532	0.507	0.5459
Constant	0.494	1.210	1.095	−3.712

Notes (1) ***, **, and * is 1, 5 and 10 percent level of significance respectively. (2) N = number of observations, CD test statistic = Pesaran (2015) weakly cross-sectional dependence statistics and CDP-value = the related P-value of cross-sectional dependency test. (3) Δ is the first difference operator: $\Delta x = x_t - x_{t-1}$

Table 8 Estimates of dynamic common correlated effects by income level

Long run coefficients	Low-income countries 1 Coef	2 Coef	3 Coef	4 Coef	Lower-middle-income countries 1 Coef	2 Coef	3 Coef	4 Coef	Upper-middle-income countries 1 Coef	2 Coef	3 Coef	4 Coef
Financial development index	2.793**			−6.40**	2.450**			0.309	1.163			11.49**
Overall Globalization index	0.013*	0.01	0.011	0.013	−0.008	−0.006	−0.001		−0.007	−0.01	−0.01	−0.01
Average of six institutional quality indices	0.388***	0.325***	0.353***	1.27***	0.019	0.113	−0.015	0.039	−0.077	0.05	−0.04	1.00*
Financial institutions index		1.312				1.644*				0.81		
Financial markets index			−0.13				1.515				0.53	
Finance and institution interaction				−11.58***				0.694				−3.20*
Short run coefficients												
Speed of adjustment	−0.960***	−0.982***	−0.899***	−0.85***	−0.623***	−0.624***	−0.711***	−0.624***	−0.811***	−0.92***	−0.62***	−0.69***
ΔFinancial development index	0.194			0.67	−0.103			0.169	−0.122			−18.22
Δ Overall globalization index	−0.010**	−0.006	−0.010**	0.12	−0.001	0.002	−0.001		0.007	0.00	0.01*	0.00
Δ Average of six institutional quality indices	−0.081	−0.1	−0.057	0.53	0.086	0.095	0.181	0.235	−0.014	−0.15	−0.14***	−0.62

(continued)

Table 8 (continued)

	Low-income countries				Lower-middle-income countries				Upper-middle-income countries			
Long run coefficients	1	2	3	4	1	2	3	4	1	2	3	4
	Coef	Coef	Coef	Coef	Coef	Coef	Coef	Coef	Coef	Coef	Coef	Coef
Δ Financial institutions index		−0.065				−0.271				−0.44		
Δ Financial markets index			−6.276*				8.395*				−0.04	
Δ Finance and institution interaction				0.64				−0.648				9.78
Number of observations	583	342	342	342	252	252	252	252	126	126	126	126
CD test statistic	−1.82	−1.16	−2.00	0.72	−0.9	−1.7	−1.89	−0.5	−2.10	−2.25	−2.74	0.49
CD P-value	0.068	0.245	0.045	0.47	0.37	0.088	0.058	0.615	0.036	0.25	0.006	0.63
Constant	0.38	0.829	1.396	0.89	−0.135	−0.153	−0.254	−0.353	−0.112	−0.50	0.24	−0.94

Notes (1) ***, **, and * is 1, 5 and 10 percent level of significance respectively. (2) N = Number of observations, CD test statistic = Pesaran (2015) weakly cross-sectional dependence statistics and CDP-value = the related P-value of cross-sectional dependency test. (3) Δ is the first difference example ($\Delta x = x_t − x_{t−1}$)

to the financial development index and the results show an insignificantly negative impact of financial development on growth being exacerbated by better institutional quality.

The findings reported in Table 8 are similar to the ones in Table 7 with the difference that Table 8 presents the estimates for each of the three sub-groups of countries (low, lower-middle and upper-middle-income). The results suggest that the three primary explanatory variables (financial development, institutional quality and globalization) have statistically significant positive effects on economic growth in the low-income countries, while such effects are insignificant in the upper-middle-income countries. The findings for the lower-middle-income countries also show that only financial development had a positive and significant effect on economic growth. Moreover, another interesting finding comes from considering the impact of financial institutions and financial markets separately on economic growth in each of the income groups. The results reveal that financial institutions' development had significantly positive long-run and short-run effects on economic growth in lower-middle-income countries only and financial markets' development had no significant effect on growth in any of the income categories.

The results in Table 8 also indicate that when the interaction term between financial development and institutional quality is also included in the regression along with the financial development index, the results indicate that financial development has a negative effect on economic growth and that higher institutional quality aggravates the negative effect of financial development on economic growth in low-income countries. In contrast, in upper-middle-income countries financial development has a positive and significant impact on economic growth while institutional quality adversely affects that positive impact. The empirical findings in Table 8 which show that financial development has positive and significant effects on low and lower-middle-income countries is consistent with Calderón and Liu (2003) and Huang and Lin (2009).

5 Conclusion and Policy Recommendations

This study examined the short and long-run relationships among financial development, institutional quality, globalization and economic growth for 40 African countries and three sub-group panels (low, lower-middle and upper-middle-income panels) over the period 1980–2014. It used a new broad based financial development model generated with the help of a principal component with two sub-components (financial institutions and financial markets), a broad measure of institutional quality having six dimensions of governance and broad coverage of the globalization index comprising economic, social and political globalization variables.

Moreover, it used the recently developed macro-econometrics panel data estimation techniques to address the problems of cross-sectional dependence, variable non-stationarity, dynamics and slope heterogeneity. First, we conducted a cross-sectional dependence test to decide appropriate panel unit root tests and panel co-integration tests. Depending on the CD results appropriate panel unit root tests were conducted in the second step. In the third step, the long run relationship among the variables was tested using the Pedroni and Westerlund co-integration tests. Finally, the dynamic commonly correlated effect estimator which is an extension of the Mean Group Common Correlated Effects estimator developed by Chudik and Pesaran (2015) that allows for the inclusion of lagged dependent variables and weakly exogenous regressors in the panel data modeling was employed.

Our empirical results indicate the existence of cross-sectional dependence among the variables and all variables are integrated at I(1) which is confirmed by the second-generation panel unit root tests. The findings of both Pedroni and Westerlund co-integration tests established that economic growth, financial development, institutional quality and globalization have a long-run relationship. Further, based on the dynamic CCE estimates our empirical results suggest that financial development, institutional quality and the globalization indices have a positive and significant effect on long-run economic growth in the entire sample of countries and also in low-income countries. However, three of these regressors were insignificant in upper-middle-income countries while only financial development had a positive effect on economic growth. Hence, the impact of financial development and institutional quality on economic growth in the globalization world varies across income levels and across countries due to the heterogeneous nature of economic structures, the way countries are integrated into the global economy, institutional set-ups and financial development.

Our study has some specific policy implications. Countries should reform and strengthen their financial sectors to accelerate economic growth. A strong financial sector mainly relaxes credit constraints and provides instruments to withstand adverse shocks. However, financial institutions should be monitored carefully because financial development might also increase the propagation and amplification of shocks. African governments must have strong legal and institutional frameworks to create an environment in which the financial sector stimulates and accelerates economic growth. Moreover, policymakers need to design and implement active development strategies to benefit from FDI flows, technological innovations, efficiency and economies of scale which are components of globalization but also to counteract the negative effects of the immutable forces of globalization on social and political systems.

This study focused more on macro-panel econometrics, hence future researchers can look at country-level studies using a time series analysis or at the firm level for a micro-panel data analysis.

Appendix A

See Tables 9 and 10.

Table 9 List of countries

No.	Country	Code	Code_Id	Country group	No.	Country	Code	Code_Id	Country group
1	Algeria	DZA	612	EM	21	Malawi	MWI	676	LIDC
2	Angola	AGO	614	EM	22	Mali	MLI	678	LIDC
3	Benin	BEN	638	LIDC	23	Mauritania	MRT	682	LIDC
4	Botswana	BWA	616	EM	24	Mauritius	MUS	684	EM
5	Burkina Faso	BFA	748	LIDC	25	Morocco	MAR	686	EM
6	Burundi	BDI	618	LIDC	26	Mozambique	MOZ	688	LIDC
7	Cameroon	CMR	622	LIDC	27	Namibia	NAM	728	EM
8	Central African Rep.	CAF	626	LIDC	28	Niger	NER	692	LIDC
9	Congo, Dem. Rep.	ZAR	636	LIDC	29	Nigeria	NGA	694	LIDC
10	Congo, Republic of	COG	634	LIDC	30	Rwanda	RWA	714	LIDC
11	Cote D'Ivoire	CIV	662	LIDC	31	Senegal	SEN	722	LIDC
12	Egypt	EGY	469	EM	32	Sierra Leone	SLE	724	LIDC
13	Ethiopia	ETH	644	LIDC	33	South Africa	ZAF	199	EM
14	Gabon	GAB	646	EM	34	Sudan	SDN	732	LIDC
15	Gambia, The	GMB	648	LIDC	35	Swaziland	SWZ	734	EM
16	Ghana	GHA	652	LIDC	36	Tanzania	TZA	738	LIDC
17	Kenya	KEN	664	LIDC	37	Togo	TGO	742	LIDC
18	Lesotho	LSO	666	LIDC	38	Tunisia	TUN	744	EM
19	Liberia	LBR	668	LIDC	39	Uganda	UGA	746	LIDC
20	Madagascar	MDG	674	LIDC	40	Zambia	ZMB	754	LIDC

Table 10 Hausman test on the MG and PMG models

Coefficients				
	(b)	(B)	(b−B)	sqrt (diag (V_b−V_B))
	MG	PMG	Difference	S.E.
FDI	4.636916	6.551868	−1.914952	2.774944
OVGL	0.0246016	0.0361285	−0.0115269	0.0233311
INQ	−0.1161565	−0.5550853	0.4389289	0.471968

b = Consistent under Ho and Ha; obtained from xtpmg
B = Inconsistent under Ha, efficient under Ho; obtained from xtpmg
Test: Ho: difference in coefficients not systematic
$\chi^2(3) = (b - B)'[(V_b - V_B)^{(-1)}](b - B) = 1.67$
Prob > χ^2 = 0.6440

References

Acemoglu, D. (2006). *Modeling Inefficient Institutions*. Cambridge, MA: National Bureau of Economic Research.

Acemoglu, D. and S. Johnson (2005). Unbundling Institutions. *Journal of Political Economy*, 113(5): 949–995.

Acemoglu, D. and J.A. Robinson (2008). Persistence of Power, Elites, and Institutions. *The American Economic Review*, 98(1): 267–293.

Acemoglu, D. and J.A. Robinson (2010). *The Role of Institutions in Growth and Development*. World Bank Publications.

Acemoglu, D. and J.A. Robinson (2013). *Why Nations Fail: The Origins of Power, Prosperity, and Poverty*. Crown Business.

Adu, G., G. Marbuah, and J.T. Mensah (2013). Financial Development and Economic Growth in Ghana: Does the Measure of Financial Development Matter? *Review of Development Finance*, 3(4): 192–203.

Aghion, P., P. Bacchetta, R. Ranciere, and K. Rogoff (2009). Exchange Rate Volatility and Productivity Growth: The Role of Financial Development. *Journal of Monetary Economics*, 56(4): 494–513.

Aghion, P., P. Howitt, and D. Mayer-Foulkes (2005). The Effect of Financial Development on Convergence: Theory and Evidence. *The Quarterly Journal of Economics*, 120(1): 173–222.

Akinlo, A.E. and T. Egbetunde (2010). Financial Development and Economic Growth: The Experience of 10 Sub-Saharan African Countries Revisited. *The Review of Finance and Banking*, 2(1): 17–28.

Al-Yousif, Y.K. (2002). Financial Development and Economic Growth: Another Look at the Evidence from Developing Countries. *Review of Financial Economics,* 11(2): 131–150.

Alfaro, L., A. Chanda, S. Kalemli-Ozcan, and S. Sayek (2004). FDI and Economic Growth: The Role of Local Financial Markets. *Journal of International Economics,* 64(1): 89–112.

Allen, F. and E. Carletti (2006). Credit Risk Transfer and Contagion. *Journal of Monetary Economics,* 53(1): 89–111.

Arcand, J.L., E. Berkes, and U. Panizza (2012). *Too Much Finance?* IMF Working Paper WP/12/161.

Arestis, P. and P. Demetriades (1997). Financial Development and Economic Growth: Assessing the Evidence. *The Economic Journal,* 107(442): 783–799.

Beck, T., H. Degryse, and C. Kneer (2014). Is More Finance Better? Disentangling Intermediation and Size Effects of Financial Systems. *Journal of Financial Stability,* 10: 50–64.

Beck, T., R. Levine, and N. Loayza (2000). Finance and the Sources of Growth. *Journal of Financial Economics,* 58(1): 261–300.

Bencivenga, V.R. and B.D. Smith (1991). Financial Intermediation and Endogenous Growth. *The Review of Economic Studies,* 58(2): 195–209.

Bencivenga, V.R., B.D. Smith, and R.M. Starr (1995). Transactions Costs, Technological Choice, and Endogenous Growth. *Journal of Economic Theory,* 67(1): 153–177.

Bolton, P., T. Santos, and J.A. Scheinkman (2016). Cream Skimming in Financial Markets. *The Journal of Finance,* 71(2): 709–736.

Bond, S. and M. Eberhardt (2013). Accounting for Unobserved Heterogeneity in Panel Time Series Models. *Universidad de Oxford, Inédito.*

Boyd, J.H. and E.C. Prescott (1986). Financial Intermediary-Coalitions. *Journal of Economic Theory,* 38(2): 211–232.

Bozoki, E. and M. Richter (2016). Entrepreneurship, Institutions and Economic Growth: A Quantitative Study About the Moderating Effects of Institutional Dimensions on the Relationship of Necessity-and Opportunity Motivated Entrepreneurship and Economic Growth. Sweden: Jönköping International Business School, Jönköping University.

Calderón, C. and L. Liu (2003). The Direction of Causality Between Financial Development and Economic Growth. *Journal of Development Economics,* 72(1): 321–334.

Cecchetti, S.G. and E. Kharroubi (2012). *Reassessing the Impact of Finance on Growth. Bank for International Settlement.* BIS Working Papers No 381.

Christopoulos, D.K. and E.G. Tsionas (2004). Financial Development and Economic Growth: Evidence from Panel Unit Root and Cointegration Tests. *Journal of Development Economics,* 73(1): 55–74.

Chudik, A. and M.H. Pesaran (2015). Common Correlated Effects Estimation of Heterogeneous Dynamic Panel Data Models with Weakly Exogenous Regressors. *Journal of Econometrics,* 188(2): 393–420.

Chudik, A., K. Mohaddes, M.H. Pesaran, and M. Raissi (2015). Long-Run Effects in Large Heterogenous Panel Data Models with Cross-Sectionally Correlated Errors. Cambridge University, UK.

Cojocaru, L., E.M. Falaris, S.D. Hoffman, and J.B. Miller (2016). Financial System Development and Economic Growth in Transition Economies: New Empirical Evidence from the CEE and CIS Countries. *Emerging Markets Finance and Trade,* 52(1): 223–236.

De Gregorio, J. (1996). Borrowing Constraints, Human Capital Accumulation, and Growth. *Journal of Monetary Economics,* 37(1): 49–71.

De Gregorio, J. and P.E. Guidotti (1995). Financial Development and Economic Growth. *World Development,* 23(3): 433–448.

Deidda, L. and B. Fattouh (2002). Non-linearity Between Finance and Growth. *Economics Letters,* 74(3): 339–345.

Demetriades, P. and S. Andrianova (2004). Finance and Growth: What We Know and What We Need to Know. *Financial Development and Economic Growth*: 38–65. Springer.

Demetriades, P. and S. Law (2006). Finance, Institutions and Economic Development. *International Journal of Finance and Economics,* 11(3): 245.

Demetriades, P.O. and K.A. Hussein (1996). Does Financial Development Cause Economic Growth? Time-Series Evidence From 16 Countries. *Journal of Development Economics,* 51(2): 387–411.

Devereux, M.B. and G.W. Smith (1994). International Risk Sharing and Economic Growth. *International Economic Review,* 35(3): 535–550.

Ditzen, J. (2016). 'xtdcce: Estimating Dynamic Common Correlated Effects in Stata', in *United Kingdom Stata Users' Group Meetings 2016* (No. 08). Stata Users.

Donaubauer, J., E. Neumayer, and P. Nunnenkamp (2016). *Financial Market Development in Host and Source Countries and Its Effects on Bilateral FDI.* Kiel Working Paper 2029.

Dreher, A. (2006). Does Globalization Affect Growth? Evidence from a New Index of Globalization. *Applied Economics,* 38(10): 1091–1110.

Dreher, A., Gaston, N. et al. (2008). *Measuring Globalization: Gauging its Consequences.* New York: Springer.

Ductor, L. and D. Grechyna (2015). Financial Development, Real Sector, and Economic Growth. *International Review of Economics & Finance*, 37: 393–405.

Eberhardt, M. (2012). Estimating Panel Time-Series Models with Heterogeneous Slopes. *Stata Journal*, 12(1): 61.

Effiong, E. (2015). Financial Development, Institutions and Economic Growth: Evidence from Sub-Saharan Africa. Department of Economics, University of Uyo.

Engle, R.F. and C.W. Granger (1987). Co-integration and Error Correction: Representation, Estimation, and Testing. *Econometrica: Journal of the Econometric Society*: 251–276.

Everaert, G. and T. De Groote (2016). Common Correlated Effects Estimation of Dynamic Panels with Cross-Sectional Dependence. *Econometric Reviews*, 35(3): 428–463.

Friedman, M. and A.J. Schwartz (2008). *A Monetary History of the United States, 1867–1960*. New Jersey: Princeton University Press.

Gai, P., S. Kapadia, S. Millard, and A. Perez (2008). Financial Innovation, Macroeconomic Stability and Systemic Crises. *The Economic Journal*, 118(527): 401–426.

Galor, O. and J. Zeira (1993). Income Distribution and Macroeconomics. *The Review of Economic Studies*, 60(1): 35–52.

Gennaioli, N., A. Shleifer, and R. Vishny (2012). Neglected Risks, Financial Innovation, and Financial Fragility. *Journal of Financial Economics*, 104(3): 452–468.

Goldsmith, R.W. (1969). *Financial Structure and Development*. New Haven, CT: Yale University Press.

Greenwood, J. and B. Jovanovic (1990). Financial Development, Growth, and the Distribution of Income. *Journal of political Economy*, 98: 1076–1107.

Greenwood, J., J.M. Sanchez, and C. Wang (2013). Quantifying the Impact of Financial Development on Economic Development. *Review of Economic Dynamics*, 16(1): 194–215.

Harrison, P., O. Sussman, and J. Zeira (1999). Finance and Growth: Theory and New Evidence. *Handbook of Economic Growth*, Chapter 12, Volume 1A, 865–934.

Hassan, M.K., B. Sanchez, and J.S. Yu (2011). Financial Development and Economic Growth: New Evidence from Panel Data. *The Quarterly Review of Economics and Finance*, 51(1): 88–104.

Hermes, N. and R. Lensink (2003). Foreign Direct Investment, Financial Development and Economic Growth. *The Journal of Development Studies,* 40(1): 142–163.

Huang, H.C. and S.C. Lin (2009). Non-linear Finance–Growth Nexus. *Economics of Transition,* 17(3): 439–466.

Jappelli, T. and M. Pagano (1994). Saving, Growth, and Liquidity Constraints. *The Quarterly Journal of Economic,* 109(1): 83–109. Available at: http://www.jstor.org.proxy.library.ju.se/stable/pdf/2118429.pdf.

Kaminsky, G.L. and C.M. Reinhart (1999). The Twin Crises: The Causes of Banking and Balance-of-Payments Problems. *American Economic Review*: 473–500.

Kargbo, S.M. and P.A. Adamu (2009). Financial Development and Economic Growth in Sierra Leone. *Journal of Monetary Economics Integration,* 9(2): 30–61.

Khan, M.S. and A.S. Senhadji (2003). Financial Development and Economic Growth: A Review and New Evidence. *Journal of African Economies,* 12(suppl 2): ii89–ii110.

King, R.G. and R. Levine (1993). Finance, Entrepreneurship and Growth. *Journal of Monetary Economics,* 32(3): 513–542.

Krasniqi, B.A. and S. Desai (2016). Institutional Drivers of High-Growth Firms: Country-Level Evidence from 26 Transition Economies. *Small Business Economics,* 47(4): 1075–1094.

Law, S.H., W. Azman-Saini, and M.H. Ibrahim (2013). Institutional Quality Thresholds and the Finance–Growth Nexus. *Journal of Banking & Finance,* 37(12): 5373–5381.

Law, S.H. and N. Singh (2014). Does Too Much Finance Harm Economic Growth? *Journal of Banking & Finance,* 41: 36–44.

Le, T.H., J. Kim, and M. Lee (2016). Institutional Quality, Trade Openness, and Financial Sector Development in Asia: An Empirical Investigation. *Emerging Markets Finance and Trade,* 52(5): 1047–1059.

LeMay-Boucher, P. and C. Rommerskirchen (2015). An Empirical Investigation Into the Europeanization of Fiscal Policy. *Comparative European Politics,* 13(4): 450–470.

León-Ledesma, M.A., P. McAdam, and A. Willman (2015). Production Technology Estimates and Balanced Growth. *Oxford Bulletin of Economics and Statistics,* 77(1): 40–65.

Levine, R., N. Loayza, and T. Beck (2000). Financial Intermediation and Growth: Causality and Causes. *Journal of Monetary Economics,* 46(1): 31–77.

Levine, R. and S. Zervos (1996). Stock Market Development and Long-Run Growth. *World Bank Economic Review*, 10(2): 323–339.

Levine, R. and S. Zervos. (1998). Stock Markets, Banks, and Economic Growth. *American Economic Review*: 537–558.

Loayza, N.V. and R. Ranciere (2006). Financial Development, Financial Fragility, and Growth. *Journal of Money, Credit and Banking*: 1051–1076.

Lu, X., K. Guo, Z. Dong, and X. Wang (2017). Financial Development and Relationship Evolvement Among Money Supply, Economic Growth and Inflation: A Comparative Study from the US and China. *Applied Economics*, 49(10): 1032–1045.

Lucas Jr, R.E. (1988). On the Mechanics of Economic Development. *Journal of Monetary Economics*, 22(1): 3–42.

Luintel, K.B., M. Khan, P. Arestis, and K. Theodoridis (2008). Financial Structure and Economic Growth. *Journal of Development Economics*, 86(1): 181–200.

Maddala, G.S. and S. Wu (1999). A Comparative Study of Unit Root Tests with Panel Data and a New Simple Test. *Oxford Bulletin of Economics and Statistics*, 61(S1): 631–652.

Mankiw, N.G., D. Romer, and D.N. Weil (1992). A Contribution to the Empirics of Economic Growth. *The Quarterly Journal of Economics*, 107(2): 407–437.

Masten, A.B., F. Coricelli, and I. Masten (2008). Non-linear Growth Effects of Financial Development: Does Financial Integration Matter? *Journal of International Money and Finance*, 27(2): 295–313.

McNabb, K. and P. LeMay-Boucher (2014). *Tax Structures, Economic Growth and Development*. ICTD Working Paper 22.

Menyah, K., S. Nazlioglu, and Y. Wolde-Rufael (2014). Financial Development, Trade Openness and Economic Growth in African Countries: New Insights from a Panel Causality Approach. *Economic Modelling*, 37: 386–394.

Neal, T. (2013). Using Panel Co-Integration Methods To Understand Rising Top Income Shares. *The Economic Record*, 89(284): 83–98.

Nelson, C.R. and C.R. Plosser (1982). Trends and Random Walks in Macroeconmic Time Series: Some Evidence and Implications. *Journal of Monetary Economics*, 10(2): 139–162.

Newey, W.K. and K.D. West (1994). Automatic Lag Selection in Covariance Matrix Estimation. *The Review of Economic Studies*, 61(4): 631–653.

Ng, A., M.H. Ibrahim, and A. Mirakhor (2016). Does Trust Contribute to Stock Market Development? *Economic Modelling*, 52: 239–250.

Obstfeld, M. (1994). Risk-Taking, Global Diversification, and Growth. *American Economic Review,* 84(5): 1310–1329.

Odedokun, M.O. (1996). Alternative Econometric Approaches for Analysing the Role of the Financial Sector in Economic Growth: Time-Series Evidence from LDCs. *Journal of Development Economics,* 50(1): 119–146.

Omri, A., S. Daly, C. Rault, and A. Chaibi (2015). Financial Development, Environmental Quality, Trade and Economic Growth: What Causes What in MENA Countries. *Energy Economics,* 48: 242–252.

Pedroni, P. (1999). Critical Values for Cointegration Tests in Heterogeneous Panels with Multiple Regressors. *Oxford Bulletin of Economics and Statistics,* 61(s1): 653–670.

Pedroni, P. (2001). 'Fully Modified OLS for Heterogeneous Cointegrated Panels', in *Nonstationary Panels, Panel Cointegration, and Dynamic Panels,* Volume 15. Emerald Group Publishing Limited, Elsevier Science Inc, pp. 93–130.

Pedroni, P. (2004). Panel Cointegration: Asymptotic and Finite Sample Properties of Pooled Time Series Tests with an Application to the PPP Hypothesis. *Econometric Theory,* 20(03): 597–625.

Persyn, D. and J. Westerlund (2008). Error-Correction-Based Cointegration Tests for Panel Data. *Stata Journal,* 8(2): 232–241.

Pesaran, M.H. (2004). General Diagnostic Tests for Cross Section Dependence in Panels. Faculty of Economics, Cambridge University.

Pesaran, M.H. (2006). Estimation and Inference in Large Heterogeneous Panels with a Multifactor Error Structure. *Econometrica,* 74(4): 967–1012.

Pesaran, M.H. (2007). A Simple Panel Unit Root Test in the Presence of Cross-Section Dependence. *Journal of Applied Econometrics,* 22(2): 265–312.

Pesaran, M.H. (2015). Testing Weak Cross-Sectional Dependence in Large Panels. *Econometric Reviews,* 34(6–10): 1089–1117.

Pesaran, M.H. and R. Smith (1995). Estimating Long-Run Relationships from Dynamic Heterogeneous Panels. *Journal of Econometrics,* 68(1): 79–113.

Pesaran, M.H., Y. Shin, and R.P. Smith (1999). Pooled Mean Group Estimation of Dynamic Heterogeneous Panels. *Journal of the American Statistical Association,* 94(446): 621–634.

Philippon, T. (2010). Financiers Versus Engineers: Should the Financial Sector be Taxed or Subsidized? *American Economic Journal: Macroeconomics,* 2(3): 158–182.

Rafindadi, A.A. and I. Ozturk (2016). Effects of Financial Development, Economic Growth and Trade on Electricity Consumption: Evidence from

Post-Fukushima Japan. *Renewable and Sustainable Energy Reviews, 54*: 1073–1084.

Rahman, M.M., M. Shahbaz, and A. Farooq (2015). Financial Development, International Trade, and Economic Growth in Australia: New Evidence from Multivariate Framework Analysis. *Journal of Asia-Pacific Business,* 16(1): 21–43.

Rodríguez-Pose, A. (2013). Do Institutions Matter for Regional Development? *Regional Studies,* 47(7): 1034–1047.

Rodrik, D. and A. Subramanian (2003). The Primacy of Institutions. *Finance and Development,* 40(2): 31–34.

Rousseau, P.L. and P. Wachtel (2011). What is Happening to the Impact of Financial Deepening on Economic Growth? *Economic Inquiry,* 49(1): 276–288.

Sahay, R., C. Martin, N. Papa, B. Adolfo, B. Ran, A. Diana, G. Yuan, K. Annette, N. Lam, S. Christian, S. Katsiaryna, and R. Seyed (2015). Rethinking Financial Deepening: Stability and Growth in Emerging Markets. *IMF Staff Discussion Note* 15/08. Washington, DC: International Monetary Fund.

Saint-Paul, G. (1992). Technological Choice, Financial Markets and Economic Development. *European Economic Review,* 36(4): 763–781.

Samargandi, N., J. Fidrmuc, and S. Ghosh (2015). Is the Relationship Between Financial Development and Economic Growth Monotonic? Evidence from a Sample of Middle-Income Countries. *World Development,* 68: 66–81.

Santomero, A.M. and J.J. Seater (2000). Is there an Optimal Size for the Financial Sector? *Journal of Banking & Finance,* 24(6): 945–965.

Sarmidi, T., S. Hook Law, and Y. Jafari (2014). Resource Curse: New Evidence on the Role of Institutions. *International Economic Journal,* 28(1): 191–206.

Seven, U. and Y. Coskun (2016). Does Financial Development Reduce Income Inequality and Poverty? Evidence from Emerging Countries. *Emerging Markets Review,* 26: 34–63.

Shahbaz, M., S. Khan, and M.I. Tahir (2013). The Dynamic Links Between Energy Consumption, Economic Growth, Financial Development and Trade in China: Fresh Evidence from Multivariate Framework Analysis. *Energy Economics,* 40: 8–21.

Shahbaz, M. and M.M. Rahman (2012). The Dynamic of Financial Development, Imports, Foreign Direct Investment and Economic Growth: Cointegration and Causality Analysis in Pakistan. *Global Business Review,* 13(2): 201–219.

Shen, C.H. and C.C. Lee (2006). Same Financial Development Yet Different Economic Growth: Why? *Journal of Money, Credit and Banking*: 1907–1944.

Stiglitz, J.E. and A. Weiss (1983). Incentive Effects of Terminations: Applications to the Credit and Labor Markets. *The American Economic Review*, 73(5): 912–927.

Sussman, O. (1993). A Theory of Financial Development. *Finance and Development: Issues and Experience, 29*. Faculty of Economics, University of Oxford.

Svirydzenka, K. (2016). *Introducing a New Broad-Based Index of Financial Development*. IMF Working Paper WP/16/5.

The World Bank (2015). *World Bank Country and Lending Group*. Avaliable at: https://datahelpdesk.worldbank.org/knowledgebase/articles/906519.

Valickova, P., T. Havranek, and R. Horvath (2015). Financial Development and Economic Growth: A Meta-Analysis. *Journal of Economic Surveys*, 29(3): 506–526.

Westerlund, J. (2007). Testing for Error Correction in Panel Data. *Oxford Bulletin of Economics and Statistics*, 69(6): 709–748.

Westerlund, J. and D.L. Edgerton (2008). A Simple Test for Cointegration in Dependent Panels with Structural Breaks. *Oxford Bulletin of Economics and Statistics,* 70(5): 665–704.

Zeira, J. (1999). Informational Overshooting, Booms, and Crashes. *Journal of Monetary Economics*, 43(1): 237–257.

Zerihun, T. (2014). *Human Capital and Economic Growth: Causality and Co-integration Analysis*. Jimma University, Ethiopia.

Zhang, J., L. Wang, and S. Wang (2012). Financial Development and Economic Growth: Recent Evidence from China. *Journal of Comparative Economics,* 40(3): 393–412.

Part II
Sources of Productivity Growth

7

The Determinants of the Level and Growth of Total Factor Productivity in Sub-Saharan Africa

Yemane Michael

1 Introduction

Our study probes the determinants of economic growth in SSA with special focus on total factor productivity (TFP) along with capital accumulation, human capital, institutions, governance and FDI. We parametrically estimate TFP based on a production function. The main model is estimated using a system GMM linear dynamic panel model. Moreover, we also look at growth literature to find the factors that explain sub-Saharan Africa's growth slumber,[1] especially in per capita incomes for more than three decades starting from the 1960s up until

---

[1] Slumber here is defined as negligible or negative growth extending over many years.

Y. Michael (✉)
Department of Economics, College of Business and Economics,
Addis Ababa University, Addis Ababa, Ethiopia

Y. Michael
University of Gondar, Gondar, Ethiopia

© The Author(s) 2018
A. Heshmati (ed.), *Determinants of Economic Growth in Africa*,
https://doi.org/10.1007/978-3-319-76493-1_7

the second half of the 1990s. Theoretical literature claims that FDI is an important factor for technology transfers and improving TFP. Notwithstanding the persuasive theoretical arguments, the question as to whether FDI spurs productivity growth is ultimately an empirical one.

The recent upsurge in economic growth in SSA is another area of investigation that warrants a closer scrutiny. For this we analyze some of the factors that contributed to growth in SSA in recent times.

2 Sub-Saharan Africa's Growth Slumber

Over the last five decades or so, issues pertaining to economic growth have attracted the attention of both theoretical and empirical research. Despite this, what explains economic growth is poorly understood (Easterly 2001). This is partly attributed to the lack of a unifying and coherent economic theory and the reductionist way in which mainstream economics approaches the topic (Artelaris et al. 2006).

Literature differentiates between medium and long-term determinants of growth. Long-term determinants can be viewed as so-called deep determinants in growth literature or in other words, integration (mainly trade), institutions and geography. Following growth literature the rest of the determinants which serve the medium-term view can be referred to as proximate.

No matter how hard one tries, one cannot come up with the whole list of factors to which SSA's under-development can be attributed. There are a number of studies in empirical literature on SSA's under-development, each of which focuses on a given set of variables including colonial legacy, slave trade, low savings, weak and inefficient institutions, inadequate supply of a skilled and educated labor force (human capital), secular stagnation in terms of trade, physical capital, financial capital, infrastructure, governance problems and corruption, ethnic tensions and conflicts, geography and poor property rights which fall under economic institutions.[2]

---

[2] See Acemoglu et al. (2001), Collier (2000), Collier and Gunning (1999), Easterly and Levine (1997, 1998), Fosu (2012), Ndulu et al. (2007) and Sachs and Warner (1997, 1999, 2001).

Africa's colonial history, its ethnic and tribal divisions and its climate and geography are some of the issues that recur in literature while explaining the continent's slow growth during the three decades spanning the 1960s to the 1990s.[3] Sachs and Warner (1997) state that Africa's slow growth can be explained according to the same variables (for example, measuring economic policy, initial conditions, demography and physical geography) that account for the growth performance of other parts of the developing world. They argue that there is no need for a special 'Africa theory' at least regarding proximate causes of economic growth.

Ndulu et al. (2007) argue that it is slower productivity growth rather than lower levels of investment that more sharply explain and distinguish Africa's slower growth performance from that of the rest of the world.

Easterly (2001) speculates that worldwide factors like the increase in world interest rates, the increased debt burden of developing countries, the growth slowdown in the industrial world and skill-biased technical changes may have contributed to the developing countries' stagnation, especially in SSA.

In terms of economic development, SSA experienced two decades of stagnation in the 1980s and the 1990s. Economic growth was only 1.7 percent per annum in the 1980s and only 2.1 percent on average over the two decades. Growth rates reached higher levels, 5.8 and 6.3 percent for the whole region, only since 2004. This means that between 2006 and 2008 SSA achieved remarkable growth and grew faster than Latin America. The stagnation was mainly due to the poor performance of the agricultural sector. In the 1980s growth recovery in much of SSA was slow and both in academic and popular perceptions the growth outlook for the region's economies turned increasingly pessimistic.

Africa remains a continent plunged in the quagmire of abject poverty despite recent successes in terms of an increase in economic growth, reduced conflicts, expanded political liberalization and substantial improvements in governance.

---

[3]The terms 'Africa' and 'sub-Saharan Africa, SSA' are used interchangeably.

Fosu and O'Connell (2005) substantiate the argument that 'policy syndromes'[4] have substantially contributed to the generally poor growth of SSA economies in the post-independence period. Had SSA not had these syndromes, its per capita GDP growth could have averaged approximately 2 percentage points higher during the post-independence period.

Real income growth in SSA failed to keep pace with population growth between 1970 and 2000. The average annual growth rate in real per capital income registered a modest 0.7 percent during the 1970s but this was followed by negative rates of −1.0 and −0.5 percent during the 1980s and 1990s respectively. SSA countries have posted improved growth rates since 2000, largely due to commodity-driven recoveries. However, real per capita income is still barely higher than the level that prevailed in 1970. To make a bad situation worse, this weak and erratic growth performance has been accompanied by regressive trends in income distribution with a significantly marked drop in the average per capita income for the poorest quantile in the region (Alemayehu 2006). This adverse scenario is not only likely to undermine the efforts to develop human resources and the efforts to strengthen political cohesion in SSA but it is also likely to restrict future growth prospects.

Sachs and Warner (1997) argue that geography effects growth independently from institutions through its impact on public health and transport costs, although Rodrik (2004) challenges this view and maintains that it is more likely that geography effects growth through institutions.

Over 1960–1990, SSA countries under-performed in growth as compared to the other developing countries. Growth literature is fraught with many factors as potential causes of SSA's poor economic performance ranging from external shocks to domestic policies. During the 1980s, the overvalued exchange rate, deteriorating terms of trade and tight trade policies were seen as the culprits for the growth slumber. In the 1990s, the exchange rate and trade policies were reversed.

---

[4]'Policy syndromes' comprise of the following regimes: 'state controls,' 'adverse redistribution,' 'sub-optimal inter-temporal resource allocation' and 'state breakdown.' Note that the 'classification is based on policies, not growth outcomes' (Fosu 2009).

Domestic policies also played a role in retarding growth in SSA. Some of the domestic factors which are important in explaining the growth performance include poor quality education, political instability, lack of economic infrastructure, bad institutions and under-developed financial intermediaries.

However, in recent times there has been a reversal in fortunes as the World Economic Forum (2015) in its publication *The African Competitiveness Report* states that for 15 years growth rates on the continent averaged over 5 percent and rapid population growth was taken as a good omen as it held the promise for a large emerging consumer market as well as unprecedented labor force that, if properly harnessed, could provide growth opportunities.

3 Growth Accounting and Total Factor Productivity

One of the stylized facts in empirical macroeconomics is that a typical worker in a rich country such as Switzerland or the United States is 20 or 30 times more productive and hence more affluent than a typical worker in a poor country such as Niger or Chad. These between-country differences in worker productivity are several times bigger than the differences in worker productivities within a country. The common trait in growth literature is: Why are there such large differences in productivities and therefore incomes across countries?

A difference in natural resource endowments is one factor that explains differences in international incomes. Some countries are rich because they have a large per capita endowment of oil but such countries are small in number and do not have large populations. A much more important determinant of differences in international incomes are differences in the capital per worker. Capital per worker is exceedingly higher in rich countries and is an important reason why workers in rich countries are more productive than their counterparts in poor countries. However, capital per worker is not the whole story. There is more to this enormous difference in per capita incomes than capital per worker, total factor productivity (Prescott 1998).

The large differences in output per worker that cannot be accounted for by differences in capital per worker constitute differences in TFP. Because total factor productivities are high in rich countries, capital per worker is also high in rich countries. Differences in savings rates also effect capital stocks but these effects are relatively small. TFP determines labor productivity not only directly but also indirectly by determining the capital per worker.

In recent times economic growth literature has emphasized the importance of productivity growth[5] as an engine of sustained per capita growth (Hall and Jones 1999). A great deal of literature has examined the factors that account for cross-country differences in productivity growth. This literature stresses on the key role of macroeconomic and institutional factors, trade openness and human capital in aggrandizing productivity growth (Acemoglu et al. 2001; Edwards 1992). Notwithstanding the literature on the topic, there is still a heated debate on the factors that enhance productivity growth.

Growth of total factor productivity (TFP) creates ample opportunities for improving the welfare of society. Hence, it is worth asking: What determinants should policy give due attention to boost TFP's performance?

Our study contributes something positive to this debate. It uses a principal component analysis (PCA) to overcome the multiplicity of potential determinants of growth and reduces the dimensions of the variables that plausibly effect productivity growth. The PCA statistical technique helps identify the key combination of policy, human capital, institutional and governance aspects associated with productivity growth. Moreover, we also use a dynamic panel data model to investigate the nexus between productivity growth and several other variables that are used in extant empirical literature including education, health, infrastructure, imports, institutions, openness, competition, financial development, geographical predicaments and absorptive capacity (including capital intensity). These are termed determinants of productivity growth. The determinants of TFP growth can be studied at micro, sectoral and macro levels.

---

[5]Unless otherwise stated, productivity and total factor productivity are used interchangeably.

TFP can also be measured using the TFP index measures and a data envelopment analysis (DEA) which are non-parametric in nature. The parametric approaches include Cobb-Douglas and transcendental logarithmic (translog), constant elasticity of substitution (CES) production function employing GMM and other semi-parametric estimation approaches like those by Olley and Pake (1996) and Levinsohn and Petrin (2003). Another strand of literature also distinguishes TFP measures by the type of data used as cross-sectional data based, time series data based and panel data based.

Our study focuses on macro cross-country measures since the scope of our research is SSA countries.

Nowadays there is widespread consensus among academicians, growth theorists and development practitioners that factor accumulation (including human capital) and technological changes alone cannot adequately explain the differences in growth performance across countries. Demetriades and Law (2004) contend that institutions and finance are separately emerging as the key fundamental determinants of economic growth in recent literature.

TFP can be influenced by both external shocks and domestic policies through different ways. For example, when the government controls access to foreign exchange, preferential treatment is given to the imports of investment goods which could foster TFP growth. Besides, greater openness facilitates the adoption of more efficient techniques of production which contribute to the enhancement of TFP (Isaksson 2007). Miller and Upadhyay (2000) assert that the main bottleneck which hinders the adoption of new technologies in SSA is lack of human capital. Further, poor infrastructure which makes the supply of inputs unreliable can also impede growth by depressing the marginal product of private investments. Excessive regulation of financial markets and institutions too might have a negative impact on TFP growth.

Not many studies analyze sources of growth from a growth accounting perspective in SSA. A bulk of the existing studies point to factor accumulation as the main source of growth in SSA, while the contribution of TFP is deemed negligible. However, Fosu's (2012) study based on Bosworth and Collins' (2003) decomposition claims that the growth in GDP in the 1960s through the mid-1970s was caused equally by investments and TFP growth.

Abramovitz (1986), Devarajan et al. (2003), Durlauf et al. (2005), Easterly and Levine (2001b), Klenow and Rodríguez-Clare (2005), Nelson and Pack (1999), Romer (1990) and Temple (1999) who are proponents of total factor productivity as a major cause of the enormous gap in per capita incomes between economies believe that it is low productivity rather than the level of investments that has been the binding constraint in SSA's growth conundrum. They hold the view that the causes of low productivity should be addressed before we start talking about increasing investments to boost growth.

(A) Production Function

We need to express a production function with respect to inputs as explanatory variables to estimate production frontiers. The production function is expressed as $y = f(x_1, x_2, \ldots, x_n)$, where, y is output and x_i's are inputs with $i = 1, \ldots, n$.[6] A variety of mathematical forms of the production function are proposed in literature including Cobb-Douglas, translog, normalized quadratic, constant elasticity of substitution and generalized Leontief. Of all these production functions, the most common functional form in applied economics literature is the linear Cobb–Douglas function. This form is also supported by the standard neo-classical production function $Y = f(L, K)$ where, L denotes labor and K denotes capital stock. If we want a linear regression framework the parameters of the production function must be in linear form. Implementing the Cobb-Douglas function requires taking the logarithms of both sides of the function.

Both the neo-classical and endogenous growth models make use of the aggregate production function. A specific example of a Cobb-Douglas production function is given as:

$$Y_t = A_0 e^{\varphi t} K_t^{\alpha} L_t^{1-\alpha} \tag{1}$$

---

[6]The input can be classified into five main categories: capital (K), labor (L), energy (E), material inputs (M) and purchased services (S).

where, t is a time index, total aggregate output is measured as Y. L is an index of aggregate labor inputs. K is an index of aggregate capital, α is the contribution of capital to output, $1-\alpha$ is the contribution of labor and the expression $A_0 e^{\varphi t}$ is TFP. TFP—technological progress and other elements that effect the efficiency of the production process—measures the shift in the production function at given levels of capital and labor. The fixed component of TFP is assumed to grow at rate φ. Dividing both sides of Eq. (1) by L and taking the natural logarithms of the left and right sides yields:

$$y_t = \alpha_0 + \varphi t + \alpha k_t \qquad (2)$$

where, the lowercase variables y and k denote the natural logarithms of output and physical capital in per capita terms respectively. α_0 which is the natural logarithm of A_0 is unobservable and is captured through the residuals of Eq. (2). This type of Cobb–Douglas production function is frequently used to approximate the production possibilities of the economy because it has several properties that ease calculation and avoid complications such as the assumption of perfect competition, constant returns to scale (CRS) and constant factor income shares.

If we are given a more general type of Cobb–Douglas production function of the form $Y = AL^\beta K^\alpha$, the geometric index version of TFP is calculated by dividing both sides of the production function by $L^\beta K^\alpha$, to produce a measure of TFP:

$$TFP = A = \frac{Y}{L^\beta K^\alpha}$$

The growth rate measure of TFP is then calculated as an arithmetic index generated by taking time derivatives of the logarithms of both sides of the TFP expression:

Typically, Y, L and K are independently measured while A, α and β are statistical estimations. A is an index of the aggregate state of technology called total factor productivity. Since A is not a pure number, it carries no interesting information. But changes in the number indicate shifts in the relation between measured aggregate inputs and outputs and in this aggregate model these changes are assumed to be caused by changes in technology (or changes in efficiency and/or in the scale of operations of firms):

$$\frac{\dot{A}}{A} = \frac{\dot{Y}}{Y} - \beta \frac{\dot{L}}{L} - \alpha \frac{\dot{K}}{K} \tag{3}$$

The dot superscript denotes the time derivative (growth rates). α and β are the shares of output/income accruing to capital and labor respectively. That is:

$$\beta = \frac{wL}{Y}, \quad \text{and} \quad \alpha = \frac{\pi}{Y} = \frac{rK}{Y}$$

where, w is wages paid to labor, π is total profits and r is the real rental rate of capital.

These shares imply:

$$\frac{wL}{Y} + \frac{\pi}{Y} = 1 \quad or \quad \frac{wL}{Y} + \frac{rK}{Y} = 1$$

Provided we have measures of the physical inputs of labor and capital, Eq. (3) defines a Divisia index of inputs which is the percentage change in each input weighted by its relative share in input costs.

Once we estimate the parameter α in Eq. (2), we can decompose output growth into the contribution of the increases in labor and capital and the contribution of TFP. Assuming that the production function exhibits constant returns to scale (CRS) and that goods and factor markets are competitive, we can write the growth rate of output $\left(\frac{\Delta Y}{Y}\right)$ as:

$$\left(\frac{\Delta Y}{Y}\right) = \alpha \left(\frac{\Delta K}{K}\right) + \beta \left(\frac{\Delta L}{L}\right) + \frac{\Delta A}{A} \tag{4}$$

where, $\beta = 1 - \alpha$

TFP $\left(\frac{\Delta A}{A}\right)$ is the only term that cannot be measured directly in Eq. (4). It is measured indirectly by reorganizing Eq. (4) which yields:

$$\left(\frac{\Delta A}{A}\right) = \left(\frac{\Delta Y}{Y}\right) - \alpha \left(\frac{\Delta K}{K}\right) - \beta \left(\frac{\Delta L}{L}\right) \tag{5}$$

Hence, TFP growth is a residual—a 'measure of our ignorance' (Abramovitz 1956). It is also popularly known as 'Solow residual' in macroeconomics literature.

TFP is the remnant that is left after subtracting the weighted rate of growth of factor inputs from income growth where the weights are the corresponding input shares. The decomposition of growth into input and TFP contribution is a crude measure and masks important information as it does not give a clue about policy implications. This is true because this kind of decomposition fails to provide information regarding the factors behind the estimated TFP growth rates. Cognizant of this downside of the growth accounting framework most studies nowadays complement growth accounting exercises with growth regressions for a country or group of countries (Nachega and Fontaine 2006).

One of the tenets of the neo-classical model is that steady-state growth and improvements in the standard of living over time are made possible due to TFP growth. Supposing that the key parameter (α) of the Solow-Swan model is stable over time which can be tested and confirmed through a recursive estimation of Eq. (2) for sustained increases in real wage (W/P) and hence standards of living, labor productivity (Y/L) should increase. Since the growth rate of capital per unit of labor is zero in the steady state (Solow 1956),[7] the growth accounting formula in Eq. (5) can be written simply in terms of the labor productivity growth rate:

$$\frac{(\Delta Y/\Delta L)}{(Y/L)} = \frac{\Delta A}{A} \qquad (6)$$

The point here is that in equilibrium, TFP growth equals the productivity of labor. Probing the determinants of TFP growth is very crucial for identifying ways of boosting growth and improving living standards over time. Equation 6 holds in the steady state.

---

[7] In the Solow growth model, steady-state income is a function of total factor productivity.

Existing empirical and theoretical literature identifies several potential determinants of productivity growth including inflation, trade openness, the level of education and FDI.

(B) TFP's empirical model

Following a modified version of Shiu and Heshmati (2006) and Loko and Diouf (2009) TFP growth is modeled as a function of several determinants including economic policy factors, human capital, institutional quality, foreign aid, inflation, imports, FDI, investments, financial development and government expenditure. The regression equation is formulated as:

$$\ln TFP_{it} = \eta_0 + \eta \ln TFP_{it-1} + \delta FDI_{it} + \beta \ln GCF_{it} \\ + \alpha INF_i + \phi FAID_{it} + \varphi \ln GOVEXP_{it} \\ + \theta \ln BM_{it} + \gamma \ln IMP_{it} + \kappa \ln HC_{it} \\ + \lambda \ln IQI_{it} + \mu_i + v_t + \varepsilon_{it} \quad (7)$$

Or Eq. (7) can be more compactly written as:

$$\ln TFP_{it} = \eta_0 + \eta_1 \ln TFP_{it-1} + \delta FDI_{it} \\ + \beta X_{it} + \mu_i + \lambda_t + \varepsilon_{it} \quad (7a)$$

where, TPF represents the growth rate of total factor productivity; GCF is gross capital formation which is a proxy for the investment rate; INF is average inflation; FDI is the ratio of foreign direct investments to GDP; FAID is foreign aid; GOVEXP is government consumption expenditure which is a proxy for government size; BM is broad money which is a proxy for financial development; IMP is imports; HC is the level of education which is a proxy for human capital; IQI is the institutional quality index; μ_i is a country-specific effect; v_i is a time-specific effect; and e_{it} is the common error term. For each indicator, i represents the country and t the period. The dynamic process related to productivity growth is captured by a dynamic panel data model. The dynamic panel data also helps in addressing omitted variables and serial correlation problems. X_{it} is the vector of control variables.

Our study hypothesizes that these variables are primarily determinants of TFP growth rather than physical capital accumulation which is captured by gross capital formation. If they influence growth primarily through their impact on physical capital accumulation one should not expect them to appear significant in Eq. (7) which already incorporates the rate of physical capital accumulation as an explanatory variable (Benhabib and Spiegel 2002). Moreover, we should expect the coefficient β to be numerically very close to α in Eq. (2). All the variables except FDI, inflation and foreign aid (FAID) are transformed into logarithmic values. Inflation is given as the annual growth rate of the consumer price index. Transforming the values of the foreign aid variable will yield negative values since the ratio of foreign aid as a percentage of GDP is a fractional value, a number below 1, for most SSA countries.

(C) Description of Variables

Lagged value of TFP: The inclusion of the lagged TFP variable helps in capturing the dynamic productivity growth process. Moreover, it also enables us to control for the omission of relevant variables and mitigates the problem of serial correlation.

Financial development: We use the ratio of broad money to GDP as a proxy in our research.

Inflation: Inflation as proxied by the change in the consumer price index is used as a macroeconomic stability indicator.

Investment: The growth rate of gross (fixed) capital formation is used as a proxy for investment. Besides, FDI is subtracted from gross fixed capital formation to find domestic investments to check for the robustness of the results.

Institutions: The institutional quality index is developed by calculating the average of the World Bank's six worldwide governance indicators (WGIs database) which include control of corruption, government effectiveness, political stability and absence of violence/terrorism, regulatory quality, rule of law and voice and accountability.

Human capital: The average number of years of schooling of the labor force (retrieved from Barro and Lee's 2011 dataset) as well as from the Penn World Tables 9.0 is used as a proxy for human capital accumulation.

Foreign aid: The ratio of official development assistance-to-GDP (ODA-to-GDP) is used as a proxy variable for foreign aid.

Government expenditure: We use government consumption expenditure as a percentage of GDP to represent government expenditure.

FDI: We use net FDI inflows as a percentage of GDP.

Imports: We use imports as a share of GDP as the variable of interest. Moreover, the sum of exports and imports to the GDP ratio is used as an indicator of openness to check for robustness.

4 A Brief Methodology of the Study

We use the system-GMM method developed and improved by Arellano and Bover (1995) and Blundell and Bond (1998) to estimate Equation 7. The main advantage of the system-GMM method is that it addresses the endogeneity problem by generating instruments using the lagged values of the covariates. The other advantages of the system-GMM method over other estimation methods include:

- When there is heteroskedasticity in error variance, system-GMM yields more efficient estimates over other models including least squares. This primarily happens when it is unknown what form the heteroskedasticity takes (Baum et al., 2003). Thus, Equation 7 can be consistently estimated using two-stage least squares (2SLS) but the presence of heteroskedasticity makes it an inefficient estimator.
- The lagged values of TFP, gross capital formation, imports, FDI, government expenditure and broad money in Eq. (7) are presumed to be endogenous meaning that there is a correlation between these series and the error term which varies over time and across countries. By using the lagged values of the endogenous variables as explanatory variables the system-GMM helps us avoid the problem of a dynamic panel bias. When the endogenous variables are instrumented on their own lagged

values, they become exogenous which helps satisfy the identifying moment conditions $E(X_{it}\varepsilon_{it+j}) = 0$ and $E(Z_{it}\varepsilon_{it+j}) = 0$ for $j > 0$. Hansen test for over-identification can be used to check the validity of instruments.
- Roodman (2009) argues that the system-GMM performs better than difference GMM in estimating empirical growth models when the time dimension of the panel dataset is short and the outcome variable shows persistence.

All these factors lead to a situation where the difference GMM estimators become inapplicable for drawing statistical inferences. The equation in levels uses lagged differences of the regressors as instruments while in the first differences it uses the lagged levels of the regressors as instruments. This helps us to mitigate the problem of weak instruments. Further, this approach performs better in terms of precision and bias (Blundell and Bond 1998).

Within the system-GMM, there are two options: The one-step system-GMM and the two-step system-GMM. The two-step system-GMM yields more efficient estimators than the one-step system-GMM even though both are asymptotically equivalent when the disturbances are spherical (Blundell and Bond 1998). The two-step system-GMM gives the covariance matrix which is robust to heteroskedasticity and autocorrelation but the standard errors show a downward bias. Hence, the presence of panel heteroskedasticity and autocorrelation necessitate the use of robust standard errors that generate consistent estimates. Finally, contrary to the one-step system-GMM, the two-step system-GMM provides robust Hansen J-test for over-identification. Taking all these issues into consideration, we chose the two-step GMM method with its robust standard errors to estimate Eq. (7).

5 Data Sources

Output is measured by real GDP (in 2010 US$) from the World Development Indicators (WDI) 2016 online database; gross capital formation (in 2010 US$) which is used as a proxy for domestic investments is obtained from the WDI (2016) online database and the labor input is represented by the labor force (the number of people of working age, defined as being from 15 to 64 years old) from the WDI (2016) online database. A better measurement tool for labor input could be employment time average hours worked but data for this is difficult to come by. Hence, we follow the usual practice of using labor force as a measure of labor input. Broad money, gross capital (fixed) formation, FDI, imports, government expenditure and foreign aid all as a percentage of GDP are retrieved from the WDI (2016) online database.

Inflation rate and the sum of fixed line and mobile cell subscribers out of 100 people (a proxy for infrastructure) were also retrieved from the same online database. The institutional quality index was constructed using a simple and unweighted index from the six main indicators of governance from the Worldwide Governance Indicators (WGIs database) online database. Human capital was proxied by the average years of schooling and the source of data for it is the Penn World Tables (version 9.0). The data for this variable is available only up to 2014 and hence linear extrapolation was used to get the data for 2015. We used 43 countries for which data was available on a whole host of supposed determinants of TFP since a priori theoretical and past empirical findings in our study.[8]

6 Estimation of the Econometric Model and a Discussion of the Main Findings

The sole combination of inputs such as labor, capital and other intermediate inputs does not entirely explain output creation. The remaining share of output variation which cannot be explained by such

---

[8] The SSA countries included in the study are Angola, Benin, Botswana, Burkina Faso, Burundi, Cameroon, Cape Verde, Central African Republic, Chad, Comoros, Congo (Brazzaville), Congo (Democratic Republic), Côte d'Ivoire, Equatorial Guinea, Ethiopia, Gabon, The Gambia, Ghana, Guinea, Guinea-Bissau, Kenya, Liberia, Madagascar, Malawi, Mali, Mauritania, Mauritius, Mozambique, Namibia, Niger, Nigeria, Rwanda, Senegal, Seychelles, Sierra Leone, South Africa, Sudan, Swaziland, Tanzania, Togo, Uganda, Zambia and Zimbabwe.

endowments of inputs is a measurement of technical efficiency and provides insights into aggregate economic growth.

The focus of our study is on the macro aspects of TFP mainly for two reasons. First, overall or macro TFP is the main driver of economic growth in the long-run (Easterly and Levine 2001a) and it is assumed that FDI effects TFP and hence long-run growth via the introduction of new and cutting-edge technologies, acquisition of skills and spillover effects for local firms. Therefore, by focusing on TFP we gain valuable insights into how FDI may or may not effect economic growth. Second, FDI-productivity literature mainly consists of firm-level studies. Even though studies fail to capture the macroeconomic productivity effect holistically they do provide important insights regarding the productivity of multinational firms and likely externality effects of productivity for domestic firms. Studies on the impact of FDI on overall TFP are scarce and inconclusive in SSA.

Since there is no database providing information on the level of TFP,[9] we can construct it in two ways. One method of constructing TFP is given by $TFP = Y/K^{\alpha}L^{\beta}$ where, $\beta = 1-\alpha$. Y denotes output, K stands for capital stock and L denotes labor input. α is the output share of capital and $\beta = 1-\alpha$ is labor's share of the output.

Though Karabarbounis and Neiman (2014), Piketty (2014) and Piketty and Zucman (2014) document a pervasive decline in the labor's share of income since 1975 and highlight its co-movement of decreasing relative prices of investment goods, it is a common practice in literature to assume and use a constant labor share of two-third of the income. However, we increased the share of labor from the total income to 0.7 to better reflect the realities of developing regions like SSA.

The other method is to find TFP as a residual after regressing output on capital and labor (see Eq. 5). The flaw in this approach is that it attributes the remnant or the unexplained part of the regression to TFP

---

[9]The Penn World Tables (version 9.0) report TFP growth rates and relative TFP levels (relative to the US). The database contains no data on the absolute level of TFP. Besides, it is limited to a handful of SSA countries.

while in effect some portion of it could be due to idiosyncratic shocks. In fact, both methods yield similar results.

Next, we examined the effects of FDI and other covariates on total factor productivity using different forms of system-GMM with the second and third lags of the endogenous variables as instruments. The second and third lags are not correlated with the current error term while the first lag is highly correlated with the current error term.

The results of the model (given in Column 2 in Table 1) confirm that only the lagged values of TFP, gross (fixed) capital formation and macroeconomic stability as proxied by inflation positively and significantly affected the level of TFP in SSA.

The negative association between FDI and the level of TFP can be attributed to the lack of absorptive capacity of the host countries. The fact that a number of SSA countries have low absorptive capacity which is manifested in poor educational attainments (despite the sometimes positive but insignificant effect here) and under-developed financial systems may inhibit spillover effects of knowledge from MNCs. If domestic firms cannot make adequate investments which enable them to absorb foreign technologies, knowledge spillovers will be highly restricted. It is also possible that spillover effects may not take place. There is another possibility that MNCs may not apply modern technology in a host country with low quality human capital. There is a real danger in this as foreign firms take stringent measures to protect leakages of technology to local firms. By offering excessively high wages relative to the payments made by local firms, MNCs may prevent labor turnover to domestic firms thereby restricting the diffusion of technology. An unfair competition effect may also push local firms out of the market. Due to these reasons, knowledge spillover effects may have very limited scope in technology diffusion to local firms.

The human capital, broad money and imports variables used in the model effect the growth of TFP negatively but their effects are not significant whereas foreign aid, government expenditure and the institutional quality index have a positive but insignificant effect on TFP. Given the abysmal record of SSA regarding TFP, these results are not surprising. The TFP conundrum in SSA is expounded, among others, by Devarajan et al. (2003) and Durlauf et al. (2005).

Table 1 Estimation results of the level of TFP using various forms of system GMM

Explanatory variables	sysGMM1 1	sysGMM2 2	sysGMM3 3	sysGMM4 4
Lagged value of TFP	0.993***	0.993***	0.985***	0.985***
	(0.00)	(0.01)	(0.00)	(0.01)
Gross capital formation	0.078***	0.078**	0.064***	0.064**
	(0.01)	(0.03)	(0.01)	(0.03)
Inflation	0.000***	0.000***	0.000***	0.000***
	(0.00)	(0.00)	(0.00)	(0.00)
FDI	−0.000	−0.000	−0.001***	−0.001
	(0.00)	(0.00)	(0.00)	(0.00)
Foreign aid	0.056***	0.056	0.058***	0.058
	(0.02)	(0.06)	(0.02)	(0.06)
Government expenditure	0.002	0.002	−0.003	−0.003
	(0.00)	(0.02)	(0.00)	(0.02)
Broad money	−0.012***	−0.012	−0.016***	−0.016
	(0.00)	(0.01)	(0.00)	(0.01)
Imports	0.008	0.008	0.003	0.003
	(0.01)	(0.02)	(0.00)	(0.02)
Human capital	−0.018	−0.018	0.013	0.013
	(0.02)	(0.07)	(0.02)	(0.05)
The institutional quality index	0.007**	0.007	0.007**	0.007
	(0.00)	(0.01)	(0.00)	(0.01)
Constant	−0.060	−0.060	0.073	0.073
	(0.06)	(0.18)	(0.07)	(0.17)
Observations	592	560	560	560
Number of countries	43	43	43	43
F-test (p-value)	0.000	0.000	0.000	0.000
Hansen p-value	0.976	0.976	0.976	0.976
AR(1) p-value	0.001	0.001	0.001	0.001
AR(2) p-value		0.119	0.126	0.126

Notes Gross capital formation, FDI, foreign aid, government expenditure, broad money and imports are given as a percentage of GDP. All variables except FDI, inflation and foreign aid are transformed into 'log' form to ease interpretation. The first and second columns employ only the second lag of the endogenous variables as instruments whereas the third and fourth columns use the third lag of the endogenous variables as instruments. The standard errors of the first and third columns are not robust while those of the second and the fourth columns are *p < 0.05, **p < 0.01, ***p < 0.001 signify the level of significance

Some of the results are at odds with the Ssozi (2015) who found positive and significant effects of FDI, foreign aid, openness and remittances on TFP even though his model did not pass the instrument over-identifying tests and the first-order autocorrelation test as indicated by a very high p-value (0.374).

The lagged value of TFP which captures its persistence and dynamism over time has a significant and positive association with its current value. In the four different scenarios of the system GMM model, gross (fixed) capital formation has a positive and significant impact on TFP. All else being equal, a 1 percent increase in gross capital formation increases TFP by 0.078 percent.

Krugman (1994) argues that growth in East Asian economies was unsustainable because it was largely driven by capital accumulation and increasing the quantity of labor rather than gains in productivity. A similar situation seems to have unfolded in SSA countries in the period under discussion. Gross (fixed) capital formation is the only variable that is reliable in terms of having a positive and significant effect under the various circumstances of the static and dynamic panel data estimation approaches except the own lagged value of TFP. All other factors remaining constant, a 1 percent increase in gross capital formation increases TFP by around 0.078 percent as stated earlier (see Table 1, Column 2).

The fact that inflation has a positive impact can be taken as an indicator of the prevalence of macroeconomic stability in the region during the period under study. A high, erratic and volatile inflation plausibly stifles business and innovation but its absence is likely to boost confidence and hence innovation and entrepreneurship. Besides, on the basis of the Tobin–Mundell model Ghura and Goodwin (2000) argue that a rise in the inflation rate reduces the real interest rate which encourages investments by lowering money balances. An increase in investments can boost productivity. Bitros and Panas (2001) argue that inflation can make prices a less efficient coordination mechanism thus reducing the information content of prices and can hinder the gains in productivity without articulating the threshold level of inflation above which its impact on TFP becomes deleterious.

In most cases of the various alternative models provided in Tables 1 and 5, FDI has a negative but statistically insignificant effect on TFP. This finding does not cement the widely held view that FDI strengthens competition and enhances the productivity of local firms and industries

Table 2 Estimation of TFP growth using a GMM model with various lags of the dependent and explanatory variables as internal instruments (dependent variable: TFP growth)

Explanatory variables	Model22 1	Model23 2	Model24 3	Model25 4	Model33 5
Lag of TFP growth	−0.024	−0.079	−0.083	−0.083	−0.127
	(0.11)	(0.11)	(0.10)	(0.09)	(0.37)
Gross capital formation	−0.007	0.002	−0.001	−0.003	0.000
	(0.01)	(0.01)	(0.01)	(0.01)	(0.01)
Inflation	−0.000**	0.000	0.000	0.000	0.000*
	(0.00)	(0.00)	(0.00)	(0.00)	(0.00)
FDI	−0.008	−0.005	−0.002	−0.003	−0.001
	(0.01)	(0.00)	(0.00)	(0.00)	(0.01)
Foreign aid	−0.033	−0.029	−0.036	−0.034	−0.006
	(0.02)	(0.03)	(0.03)	(0.02)	(0.02)
Government expenditure	−0.035*	−0.003	−0.001	−0.000	−0.009
	(0.02)	(0.02)	(0.01)	(0.01)	(0.03)
Broad money	−0.035***	−0.037***	−0.034***	−0.036***	−0.042**
	(0.01)	(0.01)	(0.01)	(0.01)	(0.02)
Imports	0.039***	0.022***	0.019**	0.023**	0.017
	(0.01)	(0.01)	(0.01)	(0.01)	(0.01)
Human capital	−0.048**	−0.039	−0.044*	−0.038	−0.016
	(0.02)	(0.03)	(0.02)	(0.02)	(0.03)
Institutional quality index	0.030***	0.018**	0.016**	0.017**	0.023**
	(0.01)	(0.01)	(0.01)	(0.01)	(0.01)
Constant	0.076**	0.062**	0.072**	0.064**	0.089
	(0.04)	(0.03)	(0.03)	(0.03)	(0.06)
Observations	521	521	521	521	521
Number of countries	43	43	43	43	43
Number of instruments	21	29	37	45	21
F-test (p-value)	0.000	0.000	0.000	0.000	0.000
Hansen p-value	0.643	0.236	0.357	0.710	0.360
AR(1) p-value	0.051	0.008	0.024	0.021	0.382
AR(2) p-value	0.409	0.455	0.464	0.490	0.515

Notes Model22 shows that the equation is estimated using the second lag of both the dependent and explanatory variables as internal instruments whereas Model23 shows that the equation is estimated by using lags 2–3 of both the dependent and explanatory variables as internal instruments. All the other models here and in Tables 3 and 4 can be interpreted analogously

*$p < 0.10$, **$p < 0.05$, ***$p < 0.01$ show the significance of the coefficients of the variables at 10, 5 and 1 percent respectively

Table 3 Robustness check of the TFP level using deeper lags of the dependent and explanatory variables as internal instruments (dependent variable: TFP level)

Explanatory variables	Model34 1	Model35 2	Model44 3	Model45 4	Model55 5
Lag of TFP	1.079***	1.060***	1.042***	1.019***	0.968***
	(0.04)	(0.03)	(0.10)	(0.05)	(0.07)
Gross capital formation	−0.054	−0.007	0.008	0.064	0.073
	(0.11)	(0.08)	(0.19)	(0.08)	(0.09)
Inflation	0.000***	0.000***	0.000	0.000	0.000
	(0.00)	(0.00)	(0.00)	(0.00)	(0.00)
FDI	−0.012	−0.014	−0.011	−0.019	0.011
	(0.02)	(0.01)	(0.02)	(0.01)	(0.02)
Foreign aid	0.246*	0.221**	0.115	0.114	−0.006
	(0.13)	(0.10)	(0.17)	(0.13)	(0.13)
Government expenditure	0.037	0.034	0.010	-0.019	−0.191
	(0.09)	(0.07)	(0.17)	(0.08)	(0.15)
Broad money	−0.069*	−0.070	−0.123**	−0.116**	−0.021
	(0.04)	(0.04)	(0.05)	(0.05)	(0.06)
Imports	0.060	0.044	0.057	0.047	0.003
	(0.05)	(0.04)	(0.05)	(0.04)	(0.06)
Human capital	−0.239	−0.156	−0.174	−0.051	0.048
	(0.19)	(0.13)	(0.37)	(0.21)	(0.20)
The institutional quality index	0.050	0.040	0.072	0.057	0.067
	(0.04)	(0.03)	(0.07)	(0.04)	(0.05)
Constant	−0.982**	−0.809**	−0.515	−0.305	0.529
	(0.44)	(0.38)	(1.33)	(0.66)	(0.83)
Observations	541	541	541	541	541
Number of countries	43	43	43	43	43
Number of instruments	29	37	21	29	21
F-test (p-value)	0.000	0.000	0.000	0.000	0.000
Hansen p-value	0.328	0.388	0.411	0.434	0.506
AR(1) p-value	0.002	0.003	0.005	0.005	0.014
AR(2) p-value	0.251	0.248	0.357	0.208	0.712

Note $^*p < 0.10$, $^{**}p < 0.05$, $^{***}p < 0.01$ show the significance of the coefficients of the variables at 10, 5 and 1 percent respectively

through knowledge and technology transfers because of the negative sign it bears in its relation to TFP though that is statistically insignificant. These results imply that there is no guarantee that FDI will boost productivity all the time.

Table 4 Robustness check of TFP growth using deeper lags of the dependent and explanatory variables as internal instruments (dependent variable: TFP growth)

Explanatory variables	Model34 1	Model35 2	Model44 3	Model45 4	Model55 5
Lag of TFP growth	0.142	−0.001	0.177	0.135	0.141
	(0.20)	(0.20)	(0.23)	(0.23)	(0.39)
Gross capital formation	−0.002	−0.003	−0.019	−0.015	−0.011
	(0.01)	(0.01)	(0.02)	(0.02)	(0.02)
Inflation	0.000***	0.000*	0.000	0.000	0.000
	(0.00)	(0.00)	(0.00)	(0.00)	(0.00)
FDI	−0.003	−0.003	−0.004	−0.005	−0.004
	(0.00)	(0.00)	(0.01)	(0.00)	(0.01)
Foreign aid	−0.022	−0.014	−0.027*	−0.018	0.000
	(0.02)	(0.02)	(0.01)	(0.02)	(0.02)
Government expenditure	0.007	−0.000	−0.020	−0.012	−0.034
	(0.02)	(0.02)	(0.06)	(0.03)	(0.03)
Broad money	−0.036***	−0.035***	−0.029*	−0.034***	−0.021
	(0.01)	(0.01)	(0.01)	(0.01)	(0.01)
Imports	0.018**	0.016*	0.029	0.027**	0.020
	(0.01)	(0.01)	(0.02)	(0.01)	(0.02)
Human capital	−0.020	−0.015	−0.027	−0.014	−0.008
	(0.02)	(0.03)	(0.03)	(0.02)	(0.03)
Institutional quality index	0.015**	0.016**	0.024*	0.023***	0.022**
	(0.01)	(0.01)	(0.01)	(0.01)	(0.01)
Constant	0.048	0.069*	0.077	0.072*	0.095
	(0.03)	(0.04)	(0.06)	(0.04)	(0.08)
Observations	521	521	521	521	521
Number of countries	43	43	43	43	43
Number of instruments	29	37	21	29	21
F-test (p-value)	0.000	0.000	0.001	0.004	0.016
Hansen p-value	0.219	0.327	0.122	0.223	0.066
AR(1) p-value	0.035	0.065	0.026	0.003	0.137
AR(2) p-value	0.801	0.593	0.635	0.266	0.924

Note $^*p < 0.10$, $^{**}p < 0.05$, $^{***}p < 0.01$ show the significance of the coefficients of the variables at 10, 5 and 1 percent respectively

Some authors argue that FDI's role in technology transfer and hence TFP growth is unambiguous but we take a different stand and contend that this claim is not settled as the findings of our paper and also of some others indicate that the results are not conclusive. Of course,

Table 5 Estimation results of the level of TFP using various methods (2001–2015)

Explainable	Pooled OLS 1	Random effects 2	Fixed effects 3	Difference GMM 4	System GMM 5
Lagged value of TFP	0.992*** (0.01)	0.984*** (0.01)	0.587*** (0.04)	0.238** (0.11)	0.993*** (0.01)
Gross capital formation	0.071*** (0.01)	0.090*** (0.02)	0.227*** (0.02)	0.241*** (0.04)	0.078** (0.03)
Inflation	0.000 (0.00)	0.000*** (0.00)	0.000 (0.00)	−0.000 (0.00)	0.000*** (0.00)
FDI	−0.001 (0.00)	−0.001 (0.00)	−0.001 (0.00)	−0.004** (0.00)	−0.000 (0.00)
Foreign aid	0.046 (0.04)	0.047 (0.04)	−0.088 (0.08)	0.010 (0.04)	0.056 (0.06)
Gov. Exp	0.002 (0.01)	−0.001 (0.02)	−0.007 (0.02)	−0.030 (0.03)	0.002 (0.02)
Broad money	−0.009 (0.01)	−0.010 (0.01)	0.004 (0.01)	−0.006 (0.02)	−0.012 (0.01)
Imports	−0.007 (0.01)	−0.006 (0.01)	−0.042** (0.02)	−0.006 (0.03)	0.008 (0.02)
Human capital	−0.012 (0.02)	−0.004 (0.03)	0.701*** (0.11)	2.215*** (0.51)	−0.018 (0.07)
Instit. quality index	0.003 (0.01)	0.004 (0.01)	0.079*** (0.03)	0.054 (0.03)	0.007 (0.01)
Constant	−0.033 (0.09)	0.021 (0.13)	4.375*** (0.49)		−0.060 (0.18)

(continued)

Table 5 (continued)

Explainable	Pooled OLS	Random effects	Fixed effects	Difference GMM	System GMM
	1	2	3	4	5
Observations	592	592	592	549	592
No. of countries	43	43	43	43	43
F-test (p-value)	0.000	0.000	0.000	0.000	0.000
Hansen p-value				0.912	0.976
AR(1) p-value				0.314	0.119
AR(2) p-value				0.349	0.001
R-squared	0.993				
Overall R-squared		0.993	0.937		

Notes Gross capital formation, FDI, foreign aid, government expenditure, broad money and imports are given as a percentage of GDP. Moreover, all variables except FDI, inflation and foreign aid are transformed into 'log' form to ease interpretation. Columns 4 and 5 use the second lag of the endogenous variables as instruments

The standard errors of the first and third columns are not robust while those of the second and the fourth columns are. The standard errors are given in parenthesis. * $p < 0.05$, ** $p < 0.01$, *** $p < 0.001$ show the significance level at 10, 5 and 1 respectively

theoretically FDI is expected to increase productivity in the host country through the transfer of up-to-date technology and managerial knowledge as proposed by Caves (1974) and De Mello (1997). FDI is also assumed to create stiff and cut-throat competition, that is, foreign firms put pressure on domestic firms. However, Aghion et al. (2008) dispute this assertion using a Schumpeterian growth model explaining why more FDI could have positive growth effects only where local production is relatively close to the technological frontier whereas growth will remain unchanged or will even reduce where local producers lack absorptive capacity since they lag far behind the technological frontier.

More than four decades ago, Findlay (1978) argues that if developing host countries are to take advantage of FDI-related technology transfers, the gap in technology should not be extremely wide. Aitken and Harrison (1999) assert that if the entry of foreign firms supplants domestic competitors, FDI could reduce productivity.

Government size as captured by government expenditure does not have a statistically significant effect on the level of TFP. The coefficient of government size is a mixture of positive and negative signs but is statistically insignificant suggesting that government spending could be productive and enhance productivity growth especially when it does not distort the market and complements the private sector.

A heated debate is on about the effectiveness of foreign aid on economic growth and productivity both at theoretical and empirical levels. On the one hand, some claim that aid is 'dead' and 'ineffective.' Skeptics of the positive association between aid and economic growth argue that aid could hurt growth because it displaces domestic savings and finance consumption, leads to overvaluation of the real exchange rate (Dutch-Disease) and weakens the recipient country's institutions (see Devarajan et al. 2003; Rajan and Subramanian 2007).

On the other hand, some economists and development practitioners fervently advocate aid and say that it can be effective in promoting growth and dragging millions of people out of the quagmire of abject poverty provided the right institutions exist. The findings of our study are more inclined towards supporting this line of argument. Foreign aid has a positive but an insignificant effect on the level of TFP which casts doubts on the line of argument propounded by the dissidents of aid. Foreign aid has a positive but insignificant impact on TFP.

It might cautiously be said that aid, especially development aid, can be utilized for improving productivity if properly harnessed and provided the right institutional set up exists. One possible explanation about the perverse effect of foreign aid on TFP, as its exponents argue, is attributed to the weakening and distortion of institutions induced by aid. For example, if aid is associated with weak governance and increased rent-seeking activities, it might reduce efficiency and profitability of investments that will ultimately limit growth (Rajan and Subramanian 2007).

Broad money which is meant to capture the impact of financial development on TFP has a negative but an insignificant effect. Financially repressed economies could affect the health of an economy by damaging economic efficiency, slowing job creation and distorting the country's economic structure. Empirical findings suggest that development of the financial sector that facilitates the channeling of money to unproductive and wasteful investment ventures may have a deleterious impact on TFP.

Contrarily, financial development theories suggest that financial developments can promote technological progress and long-term economic growth. When firms increase their holdings of monetary deposits these monetary holdings have an opportunity cost, that is, allocating firms' financial capital into monetary deposits means that investments in real assets are reduced which could eventually affect TFP adversely. However, in the framework of the new Schumpeter model, King and Levine (1993) suggest that financial development lowers agency costs (due to the economies of scale) and then promotes technological innovations and economic growth. They also indicate that a financial system diversifies the risks of innovation activities which will also improve technological innovations. Our study surmises that the variable used as a proxy for financial development, which in this case is M2 or broad money, is a narrow measure and incorporating additional measures such as private sector credit to GDP, financial institutions' assets to GDP and deposits to GDP might yield better results.

There is a plethora of empirical findings that state that well-functioning financial institutions strongly augment technological innovations and capital accumulation and foster entrepreneurial activities that finally lead to economic development. McKinnon (1974) argues that the development of capital markets is a necessary and sufficient condition to foster the 'adoption of best-practice technologies and learning-by-doing.' In other words, limited access to credit markets restricts entrepreneurial development.

Financial sector development is found to have a negative impact on the level of TFP. If the development of the financial sector facilitates channeling credit to unproductive investments and wasteful activities it may have an adverse impact on TFP. Empirical findings suggest that there is a threshold effect on the finance-growth relationship. Financial development is beneficial for growth only up to a certain point; beyond this threshold level further development of the financial sector effects growth negatively. However, this does not seem to be the case in SSA given its weak and undeveloped financial systems. It is more plausible to argue that the negative effect is due to the inefficiency on the part of the financial system in allocating resources rather than exceeding a certain threshold level.

Imports of goods and services have a positive coefficient which is also statistically significant. Though the bulk of SSA imports are petroleum and other consumer items this result suggests that the countries in the region import technologically cutting-edge products which could be used for further production.

Human capital which is proxied by the average years of schooling has an unexpected negative coefficient but it is statistically insignificant. SSA countries are languishing at the bottom of the human development rankings. The human capital achievements of almost all the SSA countries barring Mauritius and Seychelles are well below average. UNDP's (2015) Human Development Report shows that except for these two nations which stood 63rd and 64th respectively all other SSA countries ranked below 100 out of the 188 countries included in the study. With this background one can only deduce that the human capital on the continent has a long way to go before it can start contributing significantly to productivity and growth. On a priori theoretical grounds, human capital is supposed to be an important determinant of both economic and TFP growth. However, empirical findings on the topic are mixed. For example, Klenow and Rodríguez-Clare (2005) and Prichett (2001) did not find any relation between schooling and economic growth. Further, one cannot rule out measurement errors and the 'poor' proxy used for human capital.

The other variable of interest in our study is the institutional quality index which is supposed to capture the quality of economic and social institutions and their role in boosting productivity. The index is developed based on a simple and unweighted average of the six governance indicators retrieved from the WGI online database. A priori this variable too has a positive coefficient as expected. And again its effect is not statistically significant. Empirical findings substantiate that productivity is low in countries with poor institutions (see Daniele and Marani 2011).

The models pass all the diagnostic tests as illustrated in the bottom-halves of Tables 1 and 5. The small f-test values signify that all the variables included in the model are jointly significant. The Hansen over-identifying test of instrument restrictions indicates that the restrictions being made on the instruments are valid. By construction, the system GMM dynamic model of this type suffers from first-order autocorrelation of the error terms which is validated by the small p-value of AR(1) while the p-value of AR(2) attests the null-hypothesis that there is no second-order autocorrelation between the error terms.

We assume that all the variables except foreign aid and the institutional quality index are endogenous in this system-GMM model of TFP growth. We used various lags of the endogenous variables as internal instruments to check the robustness of the model for different lags applied as internal instruments. Roodman (2009) warns that instrument proliferation might lead to biased standard errors, biased estimated parameters and a weak over-identification test. To overcome this hurdle, we used the 'collapse' option in 'xtabond2' which is a Stata routine to limit the number of instruments; it also restricts the number of lagged instruments of the endogenous variables.

In addition to the TFP level, it is helpful to see TFP growth because it measures technological change. Table 2 illustrates the impact of the explanatory variables on TFP growth.

The sign of human capital is negative but it is insignificant. This suggests that human capital as measured by the average years of schooling of the population over 25 years of age did not affect TFP growth. There is ample empirical evidence that high levels of human capital facilitate technology adoption but SSA's low educational attainments and poor quality of education which are well-documented do not fit this narration. Besides, in Table 4 we can observe that in three out of the five models, financial development which is proxied by broad money negatively affected TFP growth at the 1percent significance level. FDI, foreign aid and government expenditure which are a proxy for the size of the government have negative signs but they are not significant.

However, trade openness (measured by the ratio of the sum of exports and imports to GDP) has a positive and significant effect on TFP growth. Moreover, the institutional quality index positively and significantly affected TFP growth. This is also true with inflation rate when deeper lags of the dependent and explanatory variables are used as internal instruments.

6.1 Robustness Checks and Diagnostic Tests

The models in Table 5 are meant to check the robustness of the system-GMM model of the TFP level when viewed in light of other models.

A common practice in empirical economic studies is undertaking a robustness check or sensitivity analysis where how the regression coefficients of certain 'core variables' behave when the regression specification is modified by adding or removing some regressors are examined. The model is then interpreted as structurally valid if the coefficients are plausible and robust. However, the critics of this approach argue that it has pitfalls and is flawed when not applied properly. Further, skeptics claim that robustness checks do not give necessary or sufficient evidence of structural validity.

One of the approaches for a robustness check that we performed was by keeping the significant variables of the lagged value of TFP, gross capital formation and inflation as the 'core variables' with the others remaining as 'testing variables.' Our results show that the model is robust.

The model's diagnostic tests show that the system-GMM model given in column 2 in Table 1 and column 5 in Table 5 is well specified and satisfies all the tests. However, the difference GMM model given in column 4 in Table 5 fails to pass the AR(1) test, the test of first-order error autocorrelation implying that the model is not adequate enough for its coefficients to have an interpretable value.

We can further check the robustness of the TFP model in level and its growth rate using deeper lags of the dependent variable and the covariates. However, care should be taken as taking deeper lags may result in weak instruments in addition to consuming degrees of freedom.

7 Conclusion and Policy Implications

7.1 Conclusion

There is no empirical evidence about what causes sluggish TFP growth in SSA especially at a macro level. This chapter sought to find out the macro determinants of TFP.

TFP at a macro level can be estimated by either of two methods. The first method assigns the labor share of income between two-third and 0.7 with the remaining share going to capital under the assumption of a Cobb-Douglas type of production function of the form $Y = AK^{\alpha}L^{\beta}$. The production function further assumes constant returns to scale and a perfectly competitive market where factors of production are remunerated with an amount of income that is commensurate with their marginal contribution/productivity. Given this, the Cobb-Douglas production function can be rewritten to express 'A,' the parameter that captures TFP in terms of the others as: $A = \frac{Y}{K^{\alpha}L^{\beta}}$ where, $\beta = 1-\alpha$. Using a simple log-linearization, the growth of 'A' which is also popularly known as 'Solow Residual' can be rewritten as $g_A = g_Y - \alpha * g_K - (1-\alpha) * g_L$ where, g_Y denotes the growth rate of aggregate output, g_K the growth of aggregate capital, g_L the growth of aggregate labor and α the capital share of output while $\beta = 1-\alpha$ is the labor share of output.

This in effect is the other approach that involves regressing output (GDP) growth on the growth in the labor force and capital and predicting TFP as a residual. This is done by subtracting the growth of the labor force and capital growth from GDP growth (see Eq. 5).

This chapter estimated the impact of FDI on both the growth rate and level of TFP which in effect is a way of assessing the technological spillover effects of FDI in the host country. We focused on 43 SSA countries based on a balanced panel data for the period 2001–2015. We applied the system-GMM panel data method to estimate the models. The estimated coefficients show that FDI did not have any significant impact on the growth rate and the level of TFP.

Using the system-GMM estimation technique for the linear dynamic panel data model of TFP developed here; our study found that the lagged value of TFP, gross capital formation and inflation had a positive and significant effect on TFP growth.

On the other hand, foreign aid, government expenditure and the institutional quality index had a positive but insignificant effect on TFP growth.

There is also another group of variables that comprises foreign aid and human capital that had an insignificant negative effect on TFP growth.

There is a view within policy circles that FDI enhances productivity of the host countries and enhances economic development. This notion emanates from the perception that FDI will not only provide direct capital financing but also positive spillover effects via the adoption of improved foreign technology and know-how. However, empirical evidence on the existence of such positive productivity spillover effects is far from conclusive.

7.2 Policy Implications

Our study shows that the disappointing performance of TFP in SSA can be attributed to the poor performance of a range of macroeconomic variables including FDI, imports and human capital. Therefore, it is incumbent upon policymakers and governments in SSA to figure out the areas that need amelioration to boost TFP and attain a growth path that is sustainable in the future. Besides, economists working in the region have the added burden of identifying and understanding what actually drives TFP growth.

Poor TFP in SSA indicates that the region can climb up the value chain by focusing on higher productivity activities through technological changes and innovations. Relying on technology in particular can maximize efficiency gains. This can be done through either maximizing the benefits of information technology or exploiting technological catch-up by combining different existing technologies and adapting them in a way that boosts growth and productivity in the region.

Acknowledgements I would like to express my gratitude to my main supervisor, Professor Almas Heshmati of Jonkoping International Business School, Jonkoping University, Sweden for giving me tremendous support while writing this paper. I am also grateful to my co-supervisor Dr Adane Tuffa, Department of Economics, Addis Ababa University, Ethiopia for his constructive comments.

References

Abramovitz, M. (1956). Resource and Output Trends in the United States since 1870. *American Economic Review*, 46: 5–23.

Abramovitz, M. (1986). Catching Up, Forging Ahead, and Falling Behind. *Journal of Economic History*, 46: 385–406.

Acemoglu, D., S. Johnson, and J.A. Robinson (2001). Colonial Origins of Comparative Development: An Empirical Investigation. *American Economic Review*, 91: 1369–1401.

Aghion, P., U. Akcigit, and A.P. Howitt (2008). *What Do We Learn From Schumpeterian Growth Theory?* Harvard University Press, Harvard University.

Aitken, B.J. and A.E. Harrison (1999). Do Domestic Firms Benefit from Direct Foreign Investment? Evidence from Venezuela. *The American Economic Review*, 89: 605–618.

Alemayehu, G. (2006). *Openness, Inequality and Poverty in Africa*. DESA Working Paper No. 25. Department of Economic and Social Affairs, UN.

Arellano, M. and O. Bover (1995). Another Look at the Instrumental Variable Estimation of Error-components Models. *Journal of Econometrics*, 68(1): 29–51.

Artelaris, P., P. Arvanitidis, and G. Petrakos (2006). *Theoretical and Methodological Study on Dynamic Growth Regions and Factors Explaining Their Growth Performance.* Dynamic Regions in a Knowledge-Driven Global Economy, Lessons and Policy Implications for the EU, Working Paper.

Barro, R.J. and J.W. Lee (2011). *A New Data Set of Educational Attainment in the World, 1950–2010.* Available at: http:/www.barrolee.com/.

Baum, C., M.E. Schaffer, and S. Stillman (2003), Instrumental Variables and GMM: Estimation and Testing. *Stata Journal*, 3(1): 1–31.

Benhabib, J. and M.M. Spiegel (2002). *Human Capital and Technology Diffusion.* FRBSF Working Paper #2003-02. New York University and Federal Reserve Bank of San Francisco.

Bitros, G.C. and E.E. Panas (2001). Is There an Inflation-Productivity Trade-off? Some Evidence from the Manufacturing Sector in Greece. *Applied Economics*, 33(15): 19–61.

Blundell, R. and S. Bond (1998). Initial Conditions and Moment Restrictions in Dynamic Panel Data Models. *Journal of Econometrics*, 87: 115–143.

Bosworth, B.P. and S.M. Collins (2003). *The Empirics of Growth: An Update.* mimeo, Washington, DC: Brookings Institution.

Caves, E.R. (1974). Multinational Firms, Competition, and Productivity in Host-Country Markets. *Economica*, 41(1–2): 176–193.

Collier, P. (2000). *Economic Causes of Civil Conflict and Their Implications For Policy.* Development Research Group, The World Bank.

Collier, P. and J.W. Gunning (1999). Why Has Africa Grown Slowly. *Journal of Economic Perspectives*, 13(3): 3–22.

Daniele, V. and U. Marani (2011). Organized Crime, the Quality of Local Institutions and FDI in Italy: A Panel Data Analysis. *European Journal of Political Economy*, 27(1): 132–142.

De Mello, L.R. (1997). Foreign Direct Investment in Developing Countries and Growth: A Selective Survey. *Journal of Development Studies*, 34(1): 1–34.

Demetriades, P. and S.H. Law (2004). *Finance, Institutions and Economic Growth.* Working Paper. Department of Economics, University of Leicester, UK.

Devarajan, S., W. Easterly, and H. Pack (2003). Low Investment is Not the Constraint on African Development. *Economic Development and Cultural Change*, 51(3): 547–571.

Durlauf, S., P. Johnson, and J. Temple (2005). 'Growth Econometrics', in P. Aghion (ed.), *Handbook of Economic Growth*. North Holland: Elsevier.

Easterly, W. (2001). *The Elusive Quest for Growth: Economists' Adventures and Misadventures in the Topics.* Cambridge, MA: MIT Press.

Easterly, W. and R. Levine (1997), Afric's Growth Tragedy: Policies and Ethnic Divisions. *The Quarterly Journal of Economics,* 112(4): 1203–1250.

Easterly, W. and R. Levine (1998). Troubles with the Neighbors: Africa's Problem, Africa's Opportunity. *Journal of African Economies,* 7(1): 120–142.

Easterly, W. and R. Levine (2001a). It's Not Factor Accumulation: Stylized Facts and Growth Models. *World Bank Economic Review,* 15(2): 177–219.

Easterly, W. and R. Levine (2001b). What Have We Learned from a Decade of Empirical Research on Growth? It's Not Factor Accumulation: Stylized Facts and Growth Models. *The World Bank Economic Review,* 15(2): 177–219.

Edwards, S. (1992). Trade Orientation, Distortions and Growth in Developing Countries. *Journal of Development Economics,* 39: 31–57.

Findlay, R. (1978). Relative Backwardness, Direct Foreign Investment, and the Transfer of Technology: A Simple Dynamic Model. *The Quarterly Journal of Economics,* 92(1): 1–16.

Fosu, A.K. (2009). *Charting the Future of Africa: Avoiding Policy Syndromes and Improving Governance.* Paper presented at the UNU/UNESCO International Conference on 'Africa and Globalization: Learning from the Past, Enabling a Better Future', Tokyo, Japan, 28–29 September.

Fosu, A.K. (2012). Growth of African Economies: Productivity, Policy Syndromes and the Importance of Institutions. *Journal of African Economies,* 22(4): 523–551.

Fosu, A.K. and S.A.O'Connell (2005). *Explaining African Economic Growth: The Role of Anti-Growth Syndromes.* Paper presented at the Annual Bank Conference on Development Economics (ABCDE), Dakar, Senegal.

Ghura, D. and B. Goodwin (2000). Determinants of Private Investment: A Cross-Regional Empirical Investigation. *Applied Economics,* 32(14): 1819–1829.

Hall, R.E. and C.I. Jones (1999). Why do Some Countries Produce So Much More Output Per Worker Than Others? *Quarterly Journal of Economics,* 114(1): 83–116.

Isaksson, A. (2007). *Determinants of Total Factor Productivity: A Literature Review.* Research and Statistics Branch, United Nations Industrial Development Organization (UNIDO).

Karabarbounis, L. and B. Neiman (2014). *Capital Depreciation and Labor Shares Around the World: Measurement and Implications.* University of Chicago and NBER.

King, R. and R. Levine (1993). Finance and Growth: Schumpeter Might Be Right. *Quarterly Journal of Economics*, 108(3): 717–738.

Klenow, P.J. and A. Rodríguez-Clare (2005). 'Externalities and Growth Volume 1', in A.P. Aghion and S.N. Durlauf (eds.), *Handbook of Economic Growth*. Elsevier. Edited by Philippe Aghion and Steven N. Durlauf.

Krugman, P. (1994). The Myth of Asia's Miracle. *Foreign Affairs*, 73: 62–78.

Levinsohn, J. and A. Petrin (2003). Estimating Production Functions using Inputs to Control for Unobservables. *Review of Economic Studies*, 70: 317–341.

Loko, B. and M.A. Diouf (2009). *Revisiting the Determinants of Productivity Growth: What's New?* IMF Working Paper.

McKinnon, R.I. (1974). Money and Capital in Economic Development. *The American Political Science Review*, 68(4): 1822–1826.

Miller, S.M. and M.P. Upadhyay (2000). The Effects of Openness, Trade Orientation, and Human Capital on Total Factor Productivity. *Journal of Development Economics*, 63: 399–423.

Nachega, J.C. and T. Fontaine (2006). *Economic Growth and Total Factor Productivity in Niger*. IMF Working Paper.

Ndulu, B., L. Chakraborti, L. Lijane, V. Ramachandran, and J. Wolgin (2007). *Challenges of African Growth: Opportunities, Constraints and Strategic Directions*. Washington, DC: The International Bank for Reconstruction and Development/The World Bank.

Nelson, R.R. and H. Pack (1999). The Asian Miracle and Modern Growth Theory. *The Economic Journal*, 109(457): 416–436.

Olley, S.G. and A. Pake (1996). The Dynamics of Productivity in the Telecommunications Equipment Industry. *Econometrica*, 64(6): 1263–1297.

Piketty, T. (2014). *Capital in the Twenty-First Century*. Harvard University Press, Harvard University.

Piketty, T. and G. Zucman (2014). Capital is Back: Wealth-Income Ratios in Rich Countries 1700–2010. *Quarterly Journal of Economics*, 129(3): 1255–1310.

Prescott, E.C. (1998). Needed: A Theory of Total Factor Productivity. *International Economic Review*, 39: 552–551.

Prichett, L. (2001). Where has All the Education Gone? *World Bank Economic Review*, 15: 367–391.

Rajan, R.G. and A. Subramanian (2007). Does Aid Affect Governance? *American Economic Review*, 97(2): 322–327.

Rodrik, D. (2004). *Rethinking Growth Policies in the Developing World*. Harvard University.

Romer, P. (1990). Endogenous Technological Change. *Journal of Political Economy*, 98: 71–102.

Roodman, D. (2009). A Note on the Theme of too Many Instruments. *Oxford Bulletin of Economics and Statistics*, 71: 135–158.

Sachs, J.D. and A.M. Warner (1997). Sources of Slow Growth in African Economies. *Journal of African Economies*, 6(3): 335–376.

Sachs, J.D. and A.M. Warner (1999). The Big Push, Natural Resource Booms and Growth. *Journal of Development Economics*, 59: 43–76.

Sachs, J.D. and A.M. Warner (2001). The Curse of Natural Resources. *European Economic Review*, 45: 827–838.

Shiu, A. and A. Heshmati (2006). *Technical Change and Total Factor Productivity Growth for Chinese Provinces: A Panel Data Analysis*. Discussion Paper No. 2133. Bonn, Germany: Institute for the Study of Labor (IZA).

Solow, R.M. (1956). A Contribution to the Theory of Economic Growth. *Quarterly Journal of Economics*, 70(1): 65–94.

Ssozi, J. (2015). *The Comparative Economics of Catch-Up in Output Per Worker, Total Factor Productivity and Technological Gain in Sub-Saharan Africa*. Yaoundé, Cameroon: African Governance and Development Institute (AGDI).

Temple, J. (1999). The New Growth Evidence. *Journal of Economic Literature*, XXXVII: 112–156.

World Economic Forum. (2015). *The African Competitiveness Report*. Retrieved from Cologny/Geneva, Switzerland. Accessed 16 August 2017 at: https://www.weforum.org/reports/africa-competitiveness-report-2015.

8

Human Capital and Economic Growth in Developing Countries: Evidences from Low and Middle Income African Countries

Jonse Bane

1 Introduction

The theory of human capital was formally introduced in early 1960s by prominent thinkers like Schultz (1961) and Becker (1962). It entered mainstream economic growth theories in the late 1980s and early 1990s following the seminal work of two famous endogenous growth theorists—Romer (1986, 1990) and Lucas (1988). Lucas (1988) emphasized the role of human capital as central in explaining economic growth and added that it had spillover effects that increased the level of technology by the external effects whereas Romer (1990) asserted that economic growth depended on research and development (R&D) and spillovers from the R&D process. Both Romer and Lucas asserted that human capital (mainly ideas and knowledge) was not subject to diminishing returns as it generated productivity spillovers for the rest

J. Bane (✉)
Department of Economics, Addis Ababa University,
Addis Ababa, Ethiopia

© The Author(s) 2018
A. Heshmati (ed.), *Determinants of Economic Growth in Africa*,
https://doi.org/10.1007/978-3-319-76493-1_8

of the economy. Thus, according to literature on economic growth and health economics, human capital is a key input in enhancing economic growth. The integral components of human capital are education and health which are crucial in directly and indirectly affecting labor productivity and thereby economic growth and hence the wellbeing of society. In general, economic growth literature emphasizes human capital's important role in affecting the pace and dynamics of economic growth and its characteristics. Several studies show the importance of human capital in explaining differences in income growth across countries (Benhabib and Speigel 1994; Barro and Lee 1996; Mankiw et al. 1992; Romer 1990; Sachs and Warner 1997).

Historically, human capital is defined as 'labor skills, managerial skills, and entrepreneurial and innovative abilities-plus such physical attributes as health and strength.' In the early 1990s, human capital was proxied by education attainments like adult literacy rates and school enrolment ratios (Romer 1990). These proxies, however, did not measure the aggregate stock of human capital available in an economy adequately. Therefore, they were soon replaced with proxies that better conformed to the development of human capital, most notably 'average years of schooling' in the adult population (see, for instance, Islam 1995). Some authors proxied human capital by health indicators like adult survival rate (Bhargava et al. 2001); life expectancy at birth (Acemoglu and Johnson 2007; McDonald and Roberts 2002); and healthcare expenditure (Heshmati 2001). Broadly speaking, in literature on health and development economics, human capital is measured using indicators like education, health and the productivity of individuals (Gyimah-Brempong and Wilson 2004). However, most empirical studies deal with the role of human capital on income growth by focusing on education and health as proxies for human capital (see, for instance, Acemoglu and Johnson 2007; Barro 1991; Bhargava et al. 2001; Gyimah-Brempong and Wilson 2004; Levine and Renelt 1992; Mankiw et al. 1992; McDonald and Roberts 2002).

Several debates are taking place in literature on development economics regarding the role of human capital in economic growth. Some of the debates are on the lack of standardized indicators to measure human capital stock and investments as different authors have used different measures of human capital indicators (health and education expenditure, school enrolments, adult literacy rates, average years of schooling, mortality, life expectancy and adult survival rates). The other issue is related to the econometric problem of simultaneity as there may be a bidirectional relationship between human capital and economic growth. Several studies (for instance, Colantonio et al. 2010; Pelinescu 2015; Qadri and Waheed 2014; Sulaiman et al. 2015) suffered from possible endogeneity problems. Others (for instance, Borojo and Yushi 2015; Gebrehiwot 2014; Sulaiman et al. 2015) applied time series models by focusing on specific countries and hence ignored the importance of panel regression in controlling unobserved country-specific effects and dealing with potential endogeneity problems in the regressors. Several studies (see, for instance, Islam 1995) point out the limitations of cross-sectional and cross-country estimation techniques. As far as we know there is no study that divides African countries into low and middle-income countries. Hence, our study contributes to the ongoing debates and econometric issues in human capital and growth literature by examining the impact of human capital investments (proxied by education and health expenditure) and human capital stock (proxied by average years of schooling and life expectancy at birth) on economic growth in African countries using the GMM dynamic panel data approach which was initially proposed by Arellano and Bond (1991) to address the endogeneity problem.

2 Literature Review

The effects of human capital on economic growth in developed countries are mixed. Using education (enrolment rate, adult literacy, average years of schooling, etc.) as proxy for human capital, several studies found the positive and significant impacts of human capital on economic growth (Barro 1991; Mankiw et al. 1992; McDonald and Roberts 2002; Pelinescu 2015; Romer 1990). Some authors used life expectancy (Knowles and Owen 1995) and healthcare expenditure (Heshmati 2001) as proxy for health human capital and found statistically significant positive effects of health human capital on GDP growth. Some authors, however, found that better life expectancy had an insignificant impact on economic growth and even reduced per capita incomes due to higher population growth (Acemoglu and Johnson 2007; McDonald and Roberts 2002). Hartwig (2010) found no evidence that healthcare expenditure and increase in life expectancy positively Granger-caused-per capita GDP growth in OECD countries. However, Bhargava et al. (2001) claim a negative correlation between adult survival rates and economic growth in developed countries. However, as the authors argue, higher adult survival rates may not be harmful for growth rates; rather some developed countries (like US and France), which have achieved high adult survival rates experienced slower growth rates owing to 'historical and institutional reasons.'

Several cross-country and country-specific empirical studies in developing countries in general and in African countries in particular have reported mixed results regarding the impact of human capital on economic growth. Using a panel of five Asian countries, Narayan et al. (2010) found positive effects of health human capital on GDP growth. Similarly, Mayer-Foulkes (2001) found in Latin America, health human capital had a positive effect on economic growth. Several authors also found positive impacts of education human capital on GDP growth in African countries (Colantonio et al. 2010; Gyimah-Brempong and Wilson 2004; Oketch 2006). Country-specific empirical evidence also confirms the positive effects of human capital on income growth. For instance, Fleisher et al. (2010); Li and Huang (2009); and Zhang and Zhuang (2011) found positive effects of education human capital on economic growth in China. Qadri and Waheed (2014) assert that in Pakistan spending on education had a positive impact on economic growth via enhancing labor productivity. Similarly, in Nigeria both health and education expenditures as proxy for human capital positively affected GDP growth (Sulaiman et al. 2015; Victoria 2015). Similar findings were reported in Ethiopia where school enrolment as a proxy for human capital stock and health and education expenditure as indicators of investments in human capital had positive and significant impacts on income growth (Borojo and Yushi 2015). Some authors, however, found statistically insignificant effects of human capital on GDP growth in oil rich African countries (Daghighiasli et al. 2014).

Similarly, in Asia, education human capital had insignificant effects on economic growth (Narayan et al. 2010). In Ethiopia, tertiary education had no significant effect on growth (Borojo and Yushi 2015). However, Eggoh et al. (2015) found negative effects of human capital investments (public expenditure on health and education) on economic growth in African countries mainly due to high inefficiency in public expenditure.

Thus, both in developed and developing nations in general and in African countries in particular the impact of human capital on economic growth is at best mixed indicating a continuous debate on the role of human capital in economic growth in development economics literature.

3 Theoretical Framework and Econometric Models

3.1 Theoretical Framework

The starting point for our theoretical framework is Mankiw et al.'s (1992) extended neoclassical Solow growth model. Several studies have applied MRW's (1992) model in analyzing the impact of human capital on income growth (see, for instance, Heshmati 2001; Knowles and Owen 1995; and McDonald and Roberts 2002). Following Gyimah-Brempong and Wilson (2004), the generalized human capital augmented Solow growth model takes the form:

$$y_{it} = f(k_{it}, e_{it}, h_{it}, Z) \qquad (1)$$

where, y_{it} is GDP of country i at time t; k_{it} is fixed physical capital formation of country i at time t; e_{it} is education human capital of country i at time t; h_{it} is health human capital of country i at time t and Z is a vector of control variables. Equation (1) postulates that a country's GDP (y_{it}) depends, among other things, on stock of and investments in human capital (education and health) and physical capital.

Assuming absence of capital depreciation, the evolution of human capital is given by:
Health human capital:

$$h_{it} = h_{it-1} + \Delta h_{it} \quad \text{and} \quad \Delta h_{it} = \mu s_t^h y_{it} \qquad (2)$$

Education human capital:

$$e_{it} = e_{it-1} + \Delta e_{it} \quad \text{and} \quad \Delta e_{it} = \eta s_t^e y_{it} \qquad (3)$$

where, s_t^h and s_t^e represent the proportion of income allocated for healthcare and education respectively. Parameters μ and η are productivity parameters of healthcare and education expenditures respectively.

The two forms of capital—health human capital and education human capital—are endogenous variables because income growth depends on changes in the stock of and investments in human capital which in turn changes the stocks of and investments in this capital in economic growth. Second, since the resources available for investments in human capital development are limited, investments in physical as well as human capital may be contemporaneously substitutes or complements. This implies that there are bidirectional relationships between physical and human capital. Thus, the theoretical framework for estimating the impact of human capital on economic growth is expressed using the following three systems of simultaneous equations (by ignoring physical capital as we are interested in human capital):

$$\begin{cases} y_{it} = y(\Delta e_{it}, e_{it}, \Delta h_{it}, h_{it}, k_{it}, Z) \\ \Delta e_{it} = e(y, e_{it-1}, \Delta h_{it}, k_{it}, X) \\ \Delta h_{it} = h(y, h_{it-1}, \Delta e_{it}, k_{it}, Y) \end{cases} \qquad (4)$$

where, Z, X and Y are vectors of control variables that affect GDP growth and investments in education and health human capital respectively. The specific functional form, which can take a double log, can be derived using the standard neoclassical production function augmented by several variables like human capital, external sectors and other variables. That is, the specific functional forms for the system of the simultaneous equation are:

$$\ln y_{it} = \beta_0 + \beta_1 \ln K_{it} + \beta_1 \ln FDI_{it} + \beta_1 \ln L_{it} \\ + \beta_1 \ln H_{it} + \beta_1 \ln E_{it} \qquad (5)$$

$$\ln E_{it} = \beta_0 + \beta_1 \ln K_{it} + \beta_1 \ln FDI_{it} + \beta_1 \ln L_{it} \\ + \beta_1 \ln H_{it} + \beta_1 \ln y_{it} \quad (6)$$

$$\ln H_{it} = \beta_0 + \beta_1 \ln K_{it} + \beta_1 \ln FDI_{it} + \beta_1 \ln L_{it} \\ + \beta_1 \ln y_{it} + \beta_1 \ln E_{it} \quad (7)$$

Equations (5–7) are the estimable models as a single equation using the GMM estimation technique.

3.2 Estimation Technique: Dynamic Panel Estimator

Using the generalized method of moment (GMM) estimation technique, we estimated the income growth equation, education investment equation and health investment equation with panel data from 52 African countries over the period 1985–2015 by dividing the continent into low (27 countries) and middle (25 countries) income countries. Since the system of equations contains country specific fixed effects, which are correlated with explanatory variables, the orthogonality between error terms and regressors does not hold and hence the generalized least square (GLS) and fixed effects' (FE) estimators are both biased and inconsistent. The orthogonality issue can be addressed via appropriate differencing of the data. However, since the equations contain endogenous regressors and effects of lagged endogenous variables, the error terms in the differenced equations are correlated with the lagged dependent variable (Gyimah-Brempong and Wilson 2004). Consequently, both GLS and FE estimation techniques end up producing inconsistent estimates if applied to differenced equations. Thus, the solution is opting for an IV estimation technique which corrects the correlated fixed effects and hence cures the endogeneity problem.

Since getting appropriate IVs is a challenging task in applied research, Arellano and Bond (1991) came up with a dynamic panel estimator based on the GMM technique that optimally exploits linear moment restrictions. According to Arellano and Bond (1991), the dynamic GMM estimators are IV estimators where lagged values of all endogenous regressors and purely exogenous independent variables are used as instruments. After some computations, the GMM estimator is given as:

$$\hat{\theta} = (\bar{X}'ZA_N\bar{X})^{-1}\bar{X}'ZA_NZ'\bar{y} \qquad (8)$$

where, $\hat{\theta}$ is the vector of coefficient estimates on both the endogenous and exogenous regressors, $\bar{X}$ and $\bar{y}$ are the vectors of first differences of all the explanatory variables, Z is the vector of instruments and $\mathbf{A_N}$ is a vector used to weight the instruments. This IV estimator is equivalent to an efficient three stage least squares (3SLS) estimator.

4 Data

Our study uses data from the World Bank's World Development Indicators over 35 years—1980 to 2015—for all countries in Africa by splitting countries into low and middle-income ones based on the World Bank's classification. Data on GDP was generated in millions of constant 2010 USD, which is the dependent variable (in log form) in the growth equation. The major variables of interest in the growth model are both stock and flow of human capital indicators: education (total spending on education as a flow measure of the education human capital) and primary school enrolment as a measure of stock of education human capital. Health human capital was also measured using flow (total expenditure on health) and stock (life expectancy at birth). Other control variables include inflation rate as proxied by the growth rate of the GDP deflator; broad money as percentage of GDP to measure financial depth; domestic credit to the private sector; physical capital (fixed capital formation or investments); openness as measured by trade (imports + exports) as percentage of GDP; and net inflow of foreign direct investments (FDI). Land and labor are omitted from the growth regression model as land is a fixed factor and hence could not be expanded and physical labor alone has not attracted the attention of policymakers; instead quality-augmented labor (health, education, training, skills) is important. Since we consider the health and education aspects of labor (in terms of flow and stock), not using labor has no effect on the estimated coefficients of the growth equation. Due to lack of data on institutions, we also do not use the relevant variables related to institutions in our growth and human capital investment equations. This could be an interesting further research area which combines traditional inputs, human capital and institutions.

Table 1 presents the descriptive statistics of variables for both middle and low-income countries in Africa to see the central tendencies and variations in the variables used in the regression analyses. For low income countries, the GDP at 2010 USD constant prices was averaged at about US$6.4 billion over the period 1985–2015 ranging from US$240 million to US$24.6 with a standard deviation of about US$7 billion indicating significant variations in GDP among low income African countries. During the same period, the average value of GDP at the 2010 USD constant prices was US$45.1 billion for middle income African countries, which was about seven-fold that of the low-income countries on the continent. The standard deviation is about US$76.2 billion among middle income countries in Africa indicating that income variations are more severe for middle income countries compared to low income countries. The average inflation rate as measured by the GDP deflator growth rate amounted to 63.6 and 26.5 percent per annum for low and middle-income countries respectively over the period 1985–2015 indicating a high inflation rate in low income countries compared to middle income countries. The average total credit to the private sector was US$806 million and US$23,000 million for low and middle-income countries respectively over 1985–2015 indicating that private sector credit in middle income countries was about 29 times that of low income countries. The flow measure of education human capital is given using expenditure on education, which averaged at about US$287 million and US$2070 million respectively for low and middle-income countries over the period 1985–2015. This implies that there were significant differences between education expenditures in low and middle-income countries as education expenditure in middle income countries was over seven times that of low income countries. We measured the stock of education human capital by the

Table 1 Definitions and descriptive statistics of variables used in regression analyses (1985–2015) (*Source* Author's computation based on the WDI database)

Variables	Low income African countries Mean	SD	Middle income African countries Mean	SD
GDP at 2010 constant USD (in million USD)	6430.00	6970.00	45,100.00	76,200.00
Inflation (growth rate of GDP deflator)	63.6	984.7	26.5	214.7
Broad money as percentage of GDP	24.7	19.4	150.8	3725.20
Gross capital formation in current USD (in million)	1080.00	2150.00	7760.00	14,400.00
FDI net inflows in current USD (in million USD)	172	502	618	1480.00
Total credit to private sector in 2010 constant USD (in million USD)	806	1210.00	23,000.00	76,500.00
Total health expenditure in 2010 USD (in million)	905	1180.00	6220.00	11,300.00
Total education expenditure in 2010 USD (in million USD)	287	482	2070.00	4230.00
Life expectancy at birth (in years)	51.9	6.3	58.5	8.4
Trade as percentage of GDP	58.7	29.5	87.3	53.1
Gross primary school enrollment (in %)	79.6	30.7	97.2	22.9

primary school enrolment ratio as data on other measures of stock education human capital are not available from free datasets provided by the World Bank. The average gross primary school enrolment was about 79.6 and 97.2 in low and middle-income countries respectively. Flow of health human capital is measured by total health expenditure (Heshmati 2001) which averaged at about US$905 million and US$6220 million for low and middle income African countries respectively, indicating significant differences between low and middle-income countries on the African continent in terms of expenditure on health human capital as the total health expenditure in middle income countries was nearly 7 times that of low income countries. Following Knowles and Owen (1995) we also measured the stock of health human capital using life expectancy at birth, which averaged at about 52 and 59 years for low and middle-income countries respectively showing that the average life expectancy at birth was higher by about 7 years in middle income countries as compared to low income countries.

Other control variables in the growth equation are net FDI inflows; broad money as percentage of GDP; openness (measured by the ratio of exports plus imports to GDP); and gross capital formation in million USD. The average broad money as percentage of GDP was about 24.7 and 150.8 percent for low and middle-income countries respectively showing that this percentage was far higher in middle income countries as compared to low income countries. Average net FDI inflows were about US$172 million and US$618 million in low and middle-income countries respectively, with average FDI in middle income countries being 3.6 times that of low income countries. Lastly, the average gross capital formation in low and middle-income countries was about US$1080 million and US$7760 million indicating that the average gross capital formation in middle income countries was over 7 times that of low income countries. In general, the descriptive statistics indicate that low and middle income African countries significantly differed in terms of several economic indicators like income growth, inflation rate, flow and stock measures of human capital, level of their openness to the rest of the world, capacity to attract FDI, gross capital formation and level of financial deepening.

5 Estimation Results and Discussion

5.1 Economic Growth and Human Capital (Health and Education)

Before we interpret the estimated coefficients of the growth equation, it is important to conduct a number of tests: joint significance test (Wald test), Sargan test for over-identification restriction and tests for first and second order autocorrelations. Using the Wald test statistics, we rejected the claim that the variation in the dependent variable will not be explained by all regressors included in the model at less than the 1 percent level of significance. The Sargan test of over-identification restriction cannot be rejected indicating the validity of our instruments.

Table 2 gives the estimation results of the growth model for the continent and for low and middle income African countries. Specifically, the second column gives the estimation results of the growth model for all African countries while the third and fourth columns give the estimation results of the model for low income and middle-income countries respectively. The values in brackets are standard errors which measure the precision of our estimates.

In the growth equation, the estimated coefficients were interpreted for variables of interest (education and health human capital in flow and stock forms) and other control variables for all African countries and for low and middle-income countries on the African continent.

In African countries as a whole and in low and middle-income countries, flow health and education human capital which is measured by expenditure on education and healthcare, had positive and statistically significant effects on economic growth. Specifically, for all countries on the continent, a 1 percent increase in the health and education expenditure led to a 0.045 and 0.021 percent average increase in GDP respectively indicating that African countries investing in health human capital had stronger effects compared to investments in education human capital. For low income countries, when health and education expenditure increased by 1 percent on average the GDP increased by about 0.061 and 0.027 percent respectively indicating that health

Table 2 Role of human capital in economic growth (Dependent variable—log of GDP)

Independent variables	All African countries	Low income African countries	Middle income African countries
Lag of ln (GDP at constant 2010 USD)	0.717***	0.473***	0.712***
	(0.0575)	(0.0665)	(0.0460)
Inflation rate (proxied by growth rate of GDP deflator)	−0.000167	−0.000693*	0.000441**
	(0.000358)	(0.000385)	(0.000221)
Broad money as % of GDP	0.000232	−0.00233***	0.000582*
	(0.000368)	(0.000902)	(0.000329)
ln (gross capital formation)	0.0171	0.00723	0.0423***
	(0.0166)	(0.00870)	(0.0125)
ln (FDI-net inflow)	0.00467***	0.00393*	0.00329
	(0.00148)	(0.00230)	(0.00246)
ln (total domestic credit to private sector)	0.0289**	0.0408**	0.0372**
	(0.0141)	(0.0160)	(0.0150)
ln (total health expenditure)	0.0488***	0.0614***	0.0423*
	(0.0178)	(0.0204)	(0.0235)
ln (total education expenditure)	0.0208**	0.0256*	0.0345**
	(0.0101)	(0.0137)	(0.0162)
ln (life expectancy at birth)	0.0508	1.047***	−0.0731
	(0.145)	(0.261)	(0.0801)
Openness	0.000365	0.000808**	−3.42e−05
	(0.000303)	(0.000356)	(0.000230)
Gross primary school enrolment (%)	−1.23e−06	−0.000252	0.000165
	(0.000318)	(0.000408)	(0.000583)
Constant	3.783***	4.840***	3.694***
	(1.015)	(0.857)	(0.883)
Observations	267	153	114
Wald test (for joint hypothesis)	9346.68	1846.38	40940.82
	($p = 0.000$)	($p = 0.000$)	($p = 0.000$)
Sargan test (validity of instrument)	263.5 ($p = 0.360$)	144.9 ($p = 0.416$)	125.3 ($p = 0.113$)

Note Robust standard errors in parentheses. ***$p < 0.01$, **$p < 0.05$, *$p < 0.1$

expenditure had stronger effects on GDP growth in low income countries. Similarly, in middle income African countries, a 1 percent increase in health and education expenditure resulted in an average increment of about 0.042 and 0.035 percent in GDP respectively, implying that health expenditure had slightly higher effects on GDP growth in middle income countries. Our findings show that investments in health human capital have stronger effects on GDP growth in African countries as compared to investments in education human capital. In general, investments in education and health human capital are positively related to GDP growth in African countries. This finding is in line with the results of previous studies in OECD countries (Heshmati 2001); Asia (Narayan et al. 2010); Latin America (Mayer-Foulkes 2001) and African countries (Gyimah-Brempong and Wilson 2004; Sulaiman et al. 2015; Victoria 2015). However, our results contradict the findings of Eggoh et al. (2015) who found that investments in education and health human capital negatively affected economic growth in African countries.

Our study used life expectancy at birth to measure health human capital and gross primary school enrolment (in percent) as a measure for education human capital. A better measure of education human capital is average years of schooling. However, due to lack of data on average years of schooling, we used gross primary school enrolments as a majority of the residents of African countries are in primary school. In all the African countries and in low and middle-income countries, gross primary school enrolment had statistically insignificant impacts on economic growth, which is consistent with previous studies in Asia (Narayan et al. 2010). Similarly, in all the countries on the continent, life expectancy at birth was statistically insignificant in explaining economic growth. This is in line with previous findings from developed countries (Acemoglu and Johnson 2007; Hartwig 2010). In low income African countries, however, life expectancy at birth had positive and statistically significant effects on economic growth which is consistent with previous studies in other developing countries and also in studies on Africa.

A set of control variables affected economic growth both in low and middle-income countries on the African continent. Specifically, inflation negatively affected growth in low income countries due to high inflation experiences of these countries (like hyper-inflation in Zimbabwe) whereas inflation stimulated economic growth in middle income countries due to relatively low inflation rates in these nations. Net FDI inflows had positive effects on economic growth in low income countries due to their high dependency on raw materials found in these countries but it had statistically insignificant effects in middle income countries. Similarly, openness as measured by the ratio of imports plus exports to GDP had statistically significant positive effects on economic growth in low income countries due to the stimulus effects of exports and imports of basic raw materials.

In middle income countries, however, net inflows of FDI had statistically insignificant effects on economic growth although it had the right sign (positively correlated) because middle income countries export oil and import consumer goods, which has only a little impact on the economic growth of these nations. The broad money to GDP ratio, which is a measure of financial deepening, had negative effects on income growth in low income countries as more money led to inflationary pressures but it had positive and statistically significant effects on income growth in middle income African countries. In low income countries, gross capital formation had no statistically significant effects on GDP growth as these nations do not have an educated labor force to operate modern machines and their economies are agrarian, which do not need high levels of capital. In middle income countries, however, gross capital formation had statistically significant positive effects on economic growth. Domestic credit to the private sector had positive effects on economic growth both in low and middle income African countries, which implies that private sector financing could be an engine for economic prosperity in Africa.

5.2 Investments in Health Human Capital

Table 3 presents the estimated coefficients for the health human capital investment equation for both low and middle-income countries. Our findings show that investments in healthcare services were positively

Table 3 Determinants of health human capital (Dependent variable—log of health expenditure)

Independent variables	All African countries	Low income African countries	Middle income African countries
Lag of ln (total health expenditure)	0.580***	0.585***	0.536***
	(0.0533)	(0.0467)	(0.0681)
ln (GDP at constant 2010 USD price)	0.433***	0.388***	0.328***
	(0.0731)	(0.123)	(0.0715)
Inflation rate (proxied by growth rate of GDP deflator)	−0.000183**	−0.00044***	−8.61e−05***
	(8.98e−05)	(7.41e−05)	(1.82e−05)
Openness	0.00148***	0.00187***	0.00089**
	(0.000391)	(0.000204)	(0.0004)
ln (total population)	0.0737	0.159	0.272*
	(0.211)	(0.238)	(0.150)
ln (total domestic credit to private sector)	0.103***	0.0496*	0.143***
	(0.0313)	(0.0284)	(0.0497)
ln (life expectancy at birth)	−0.0221	0.163	0.144
	(0.218)	(0.309)	(0.250)
Constant	−4.559***	−4.493**	−5.975***
	(1.745)	(1.972)	(1.906)
Observations	813	407	406
Wald test (for joint hypothesis)	2773.16 ($p = 0.000$)	2644.67 ($p = 0.000$)	1457.86 ($p = 0.000$)

Note Robust standard errors in parentheses. ***$p < 0.01$, **$p < 0.05$, *$p < 0.1$

related to GDP both in low and middle-income countries in Africa. That is, when GDP increased by 1 percent on average total health expenditure increased by about 0.39 and 0.33 percent in low and middle-income countries respectively indicating that the effect of GDP on health expenditure was stronger in low income countries as the marginal contribution of GDP to health was higher in these countries. In both low and middle-income countries, inflation negatively and statistically significantly affected health expenditure with stronger effects in low income countries compared to middle income African countries implying that inflation discouraged investments in health human capital. Thus, low income countries should focus on controlling inflation as higher inflation affects both consumers and investors. International trade (imports plus exports) as percentage of GDP had positive and statistically significant effects on health expenditure both in low and middle income African countries with stronger effects in low income countries. The implication is that foreign trade promotes investments in healthcare by availing new technologies from abroad. This leads to the assertion that trade liberalization will improve healthcare investments and hence accelerate health human capital development, which is a key factor in explaining income growth across countries in Africa. Total population did not have any significant effect on health expenditure in low income countries whereas it had a statistically significant positive effect in middle income countries as these countries can afford to invest more in healthcare as their populations increase. In both low and middle-income countries, life expectancy at birth had no significant effect on health expenditure. Domestic credit to the private sector had a positive and statistically significant effect on health expenditure in both low and middle-income countries with stronger effects in middle income countries. The implication of this is that providing private sector with credit or better financing encourages better investments in the healthcare system.

5.3 Investments in Education Human Capital

Table 4 gives the GMM estimated coefficients for the education human capital equation for low and middle-income countries in Africa. According to the estimated coefficient, GDP had strong positive effects on education expenditure at less than a 1 percent level of significance. That is, an increase in GDP by 1 percent increased education expenditure by about 0.89 and 0.61 percent, on average, in low and middle-income countries respectively with stronger effects observed in low income countries. Thus, enhancing economic growth is a key factor that affects investments in the education sector across countries in Africa. However, inflation rate had a negative and statistically significant effect on education expenditure in both low and middle-income countries indicating that inflation harmed investments in the education sector. Thus, governments in African countries should follow prudent monetary and fiscal policies to control inflation which negatively affects both consumers and investors. Population positively affects investments in education as more individuals have to be educated and hence there is more education expenditure. In African countries, openness has no effect on education expenditure as education is less dependent on foreign technologies compared to healthcare. Finally, life expectancy at

Table 4 Determinants of education human capital (Dependent variable—log of education expenditure)

Independent variables	All African countries	Low income African countries	Middle income African countries
Lag of ln (total education expenditure)	0.437***	0.372***	0.462***
	(0.132)	(0.141)	(0.0911)
ln (total health expenditure)	0.211*	0.269	0.0141
	(0.125)	(0.172)	(0.0858)
ln (GDP at 2010 constant USD)	0.342	0.891***	0.606***
	(0.228)	(0.291)	(0.141)
Inflation rate (proxied by growth rate of GDP deflator)	−0.00412***	−0.00415**	−0.00380***
	(0.00124)	(0.00200)	(0.000953)
ln (total population)	0.496*	0.934*	0.0965
	(0.281)	(0.496)	(0.113)
ln (life expectancy at birth)	−0.244	−3.590***	0.677*
	(0.563)	(1.173)	(0.347)
Openness	−0.00158	−0.00206	−0.000903
	(0.00102)	(0.00171)	(0.00130)
Constant	−7.897***	−13.81***	−7.744***
	(2.112)	(4.041)	(2.028)
Observations	277	153	124
Wald test (for joint hypothesis)	503.77 ($p = 0.0000$)	292.42 ($p = 0.000$)	822.03 ($p = 0.000$)

Note Robust standard errors in parentheses. ***$p < 0.01$, **$p < 0.05$, *$p < 0.1$

birth had opposite effects in low and middle-income countries. That is, in middle income countries, higher life expectancy encouraged investments in education while it discouraged more investments in low income countries.

6 Conclusion and Policy Implications

This study examined the impact of flow and stock human capital on economic growth in low and middle-income African countries using the dynamic panel GMM estimation technique which addresses endogeneity issues that arise due to a simultaneity problem between economic growth and human capital. The study used the World Bank's WDI panel data for 52 African countries (27 low income and 25 middle income countries) over the period 1985–2015.

The results of the descriptive statistics show that low and middle income African countries significantly differed in terms of several economic indicators like income growth, inflation rate, flow and stock measures of human capital, level of their openness to the rest of the world, capacity to attract FDI, level of gross capital formation and domestic credit to the private sector.

The econometric results imply that investments in education and health human capital played a key role in enhancing economic growth in both low and middle income African countries with investments in health human capital having stronger effects on economic growth in African countries. Stock of health human capital, however, had different effects in low and middle income African countries with stock of health human capital, measured by life expectancy at birth, explaining growth across low income countries. It was, however, irreverent in explaining growth in middle income countries. Stock of education human capital had no influence on economic growth in both low and middle-income countries probably due to measurement errors in the education human capital employed in our study due to lack of data on average years of schooling. Other control variables like net FDI inflows, openness, inflation and domestic credit to the private sector affected income growth in low income countries. However, in middle income countries, FDI and openness had no effect on economic growth. The other interesting findings of our study are that investments in health and education are affected by income growth, inflation rate and domestic credit to the private sector.

The policy implications of our study are that more investments in health and education human capital will play a key role in enhancing economic growth while controlling inflationary pressures as inflation negatively affects economic growth and investments in health and education. Second, in low income countries where the stock of health human capital is low, higher income growth can be achieved by increasing the stock of human capital (at least in the long run). Third, improving financial access to the private sector also enhances economic growth and investments in health and education system. Finally, liberalizing trade could boost economic growth and healthcare investments in low income countries.

Future research directions include studying the effects of institutions on economic growth and investments in education and health human capital as our study did not address issues related to institutions due to lack of data.

References

Acemoglu, D. and S. Johnson (2007). Disease and Development: The Effect of Life Expectancy on Economic Growth. *Journal of Political Economy*, 115: 925–985.

Arellano, M. and S. Bond (1991). Some Tests of Specification for Panel Data: Monte Carlo Evidence and an Application to Employment Equations. *The Review of Economic Studies*, 58: 277–297.

Barro, R. (1991). Economic Growth in a Cross Section of Countries. *Quarterly Journal of Economics*, 106(2): 407–443.

Barro, R.J. and J.W. Lee (1996). International Measures of Schooling Years and Schooling Quality. *American Economic Review*, 86(2): 218–223.

Becker, G.S. (1962). Investment in Human Capital: A Theoretical Analysis. *Journal of Political Economy*, 70(5): 9–49, Part 2.

Benhabib, J. and M. Speigel (1994). The Role of Human Capital in Economic Development: Evidence from Aggregate Cross-Country Data. *Journal of Monetary Economics*, 34(2): 143–173.

Bhargava, A., D.T. Jamison, L.J. Lau, and C.J.L. Murray (2001). Modeling the Effects of Health on Economic Growth. *Journal of Health Economics*, 20: 423–440.

Borojo, D.G. and J. Yushi (2015). The Impact of Human Capital on Economic Growth in Ethiopia. *Journal of Economics and Sustainable Development*, 6(16): 109–118.

Colantonio, E., R. Marianacci, and N. Mattoscio (2010). On Human Capital and Economic Development: Some Results for Africa. *Procedia Social and Behavioral Sciences*, 9: 266–272.

Daghighiasli, A., T. Mohammadi, and M. Shahbaz (2014). The Survey of Human Capital Effect on Economic Growth in Oil Rich Countries. *International Review of Management and Business Research*, 3(1): 319–326.

Eggoh, J., H. Houeninvob, and G. Sossoub (2015). Education, Health and Economic Growth in African Countries. *Journal of Economic Development*, 40(93): 93–101.

Fleisher, B., H. Li, and Q. Zhao (2010). Human Capital, Economic Growth, and Regional Inequality in China. *Journal of Development Economics*, 92: 215–231.

Gebrehiwot, K.G. (2014). The Impact of Human Capital Development on Economic Growth in Ethiopia: Evidence from ARDL Approach to Co-integration. *American Journal of Trade and Policy*, 1(3): 125–134.

Gyimah-Brempong, K. and M. Wilson (2004). Health Human Capital and Economic Growth in Sub-Saharan African and OECD Countries. *Quarterly Review of Economics and Finance*, 44: 296–320.

Hartwig, J. (2010). Is Health Capital Formation Good for Long-Term Economic Growth?—Panel Granger-Causality Evidence for OECD Countries. *Journal of Macroeconomics*, 32: 314–325.

Heshmati, A. (2001). *On the Causality Between GDP and Health Care Expenditure in Augmented Solow Growth Model*. Stockholm School of Economics Working Paper in Economics and Finance No. 423.

Islam, N. (1995). Growth Empirics: A Panel Data Approach. *Quarterly Journal of Economics*, 110: 1127–1170.

Knowles, S. and D. Owen (1995). Health Capital and Cross-Country Variation in Income Per Capita in the Mankiw-Romer-Weil Model. *Economics Letters*, 48: 99–106.

Levine, R. and D. Renelt (1992). A Sensitivity Analysis of Cross-Country Growth Regressions. *American Economic Review*, 82: 942–963.

Li, H. and L. Huang (2009). Health, Education, and Economic Growth in China: Empirical Findings and Implications. *China Economic Review*, 20: 374–387.

Lucas, R. (1988). On the Mechanics of Economic Development. *Journal of Monetary Economics*, 22: 3–42.

Mankiw, N., D. Romer, and D. Weil (1992). A Contribution to the Empirics of Economic Growth. *Quarterly Journal of Economics*, 107: 407–437.

Mayer, D. (2001). The Long-term Impact of Health on Economic Growth in Latin America. *World Development*, 29(6): 1025–1033.

McDonald, S. and J. Roberts (2002). Growth and Multiple Forms of Human Capital in an Augmented Solow Model: A Panel Data Investigation. *Economics Letters*, 74: 271–276.

Narayan, S., P.K. Narayan, and S. Mishra (2010). Investigating the Relationship Between Health and Economic Growth: Empirical Evidence from a Panel of 5 Asian Countries. *Journal of Asian Economics*, 21: 404–411.

Oketch, M.O. (2006). Determinants of Human Capital Formation and Economic Growth of African Countries. *Economics of Education Review*, 25: 554–564.

Pelinescu, E. (2015). The Impact of Human Capital on Economic Growth. *Procedia Economics and Finance*, 22: 184–190.

Qadri, F.S. and A. Waheed (2014). Human Capital and Economic Growth: A Macroeconomic Model for Pakistan. *Economic Modelling*, 42: 66–76.

Romer, P.M. (1986). Increasing Returns and Long-Run Growth. *Journal of Political Economy*, 94(5): 1002–1037.

Romer, P.M. (1990). Endogenous Technological Change. *Journal of Political Economy*, 98(5): 71–102.

Sachs, J. and A. Warner (1997). Fundamental Sources of Long-Run Growth. *American Economic Review*, 87(2): 184–188.

Schultz, T.W. (1961). Investment in Human Capital. *American Economic Review*, 51(1): 1–17.

Sulaiman, C., U. Bala, A.B. Tijani, I.S. Salisu Ibrahim Waziri, and K.I. Ibrahim Kabiru Maji (2015). *Human Capital, Technology, and Economic Growth: Evidence from Nigeria*. Sage Open: http://journals.sagepub.com/doi/abs/10.1177/2158244015615166.

Victoria, J.S. (2015). Human Capital Investment and Economic Growth in Nigeria. *African Research Review: An International Multidisciplinary Journal*, 9(1): 30–46.

Zhang, C. and L. Zhuang (2011). The Composition of Human Capital and Economic Growth: Evidence from China using Dynamic Panel Data Analysis. *China Economic Review*, 22: 165–171.

9
Labour Productivity in Kenyan Manufacturing and Service Industries

Almas Heshmati and Masoomeh Rashidghalam

1 Introduction

Kenya is the largest economy in East Africa. After independence in 1964, it promoted rapid economic growth through public investments in infrastructure, by encouraging smallholder agricultural production, improving living conditions and providing incentives for private industrial investment. Its gross domestic product (GDP) grew annually by 6.6 percent between 1963 and 1973. Agricultural production grew at an average of 4.7 percent per annum during the same period. However, despite major

---

A. Heshmati (✉)
Department of Economics, Sogang University, Seoul, Korea
e-mail: heshmati@sogang.ac.kr

A. Heshmati
Jönköping International Business School, Jönköping University, Jönköping, Sweden

M. Rashidghalam
Department of Agricultural Economics, University of Tabriz, Tabriz, Iran
e-mail: m.rashidghalam@tabrizu.ac.ir

© The Author(s) 2018
A. Heshmati (ed.), *Determinants of Economic Growth in Africa*,
https://doi.org/10.1007/978-3-319-76493-1_9

efforts at achieving high growth and development objectives, economic performance during the 1980s and 1990s was far below its potential. Since its independence, Kenya had its worst economic performance in 1991–1993. GDP growth declined and agricultural production decreased at an annual rate of 3.9 percent. The economy grew by an annual average of only 1.5 percent from 1997 to 2002, which was below population growth leading to a decline in per capita incomes.

Kenya's poor economic performance between the 1980s and mid-2000s was largely due to improper agricultural, land and industrial policies which was aggravated by poor international terms of trade and governance weaknesses. Increased government intrusion into the private sector and import substitution policies made the manufacturing sector uncompetitive. Economic growth began to recover with real GDP growth of 2.8 percent in 2003, 4.3 percent in 2004, 5.8 percent in 2005, 6.1 percent in 2006 and 7.0 percent in 2007. However, the economic effects of the violence that broke out after the 27 December 2007 general elections, was compounded by drought and the global financial crisis, which decreased growth rates to less than 2.0 percent in 2008. There was moderate improvement with 2.6 percent growth in 2009 and the final 2010 growth figure was expected to be about 5.0 percent.[1] In 2012 and 2013, GDP growth was 6.9 and 5.7 respectively. GDP estimates revealed economic expansion of 5.3 and 6.5 percent in 2014 and 2015 respectively. Kenya had a GDP of $69.98 billion in 2015, which made it the 72nd largest economy in the world. Per capita GDP was estimated at $1587 (Odero et al. 2015).

Despite the fact that Kenya is industrially the most developed country in East Africa, manufacturing still contributes little to its GDP (World Bank 2015). Industrial activity, which is established around the three largest urban areas of Nairobi, Mombasa and Kisumu, is dominated by food processing industries such as grain milling, beer production, sugarcane crushing and the fabrication of consumer goods (for example, vehicles from kits). Kenya also has an oil refinery which processes imported crude petroleum into petroleum products, mostly for domestic markets. In addition, a substantial and developing informal sector engages in small-scale manufacturing of household goods, motor vehicle parts and farm

---

[1] See http://www.state.gov/outofdate/bgn/kenya/201469.htms.

instruments. Approximately half the investments in the industrial sector are foreign; the United Kingdom provides half of these. The United States' national corporations are the second largest foreign investors in Kenya.

The industry and manufacturing sectors accounted for 21.0 percent of Kenya's overall GDP in 1980 (World Bank 2015). This manufacturing GDP represented only a slight increase since Kenya's independence in 1964 after which the development of the sector has stagnated since the 1980s, hampered as it is by shortages in hydroelectric power, high energy costs, rundown transport infrastructure and the dumping of cheap imports in the absence of efficient local production. However, as a result of urbanization, the industry and manufacturing sectors have become increasingly important for the Kenyan economy. GDP per capita decreased to 19.0 percent in 1990, and in 2000 the value-added to GDP decreased again to 17.0 percent. In 2011, there was a modest increase to 19.0 percent of Keny's overall GDP.

The service sector has proven to be a major contributor to Kenya's economy. It accounted for 47.0 percent of Kenya's overall GDP in 1980. In 1990, it accounted for 51.0 percent, in 2000 it stayed constant at 51.0 percent and in 2011, the service sector contributed 58 percent to Kenya's overall GDP (World Bank 2015).

In 2006 Kenya's labour force was estimated to include about 12 million workers, of which almost 75 percent worked in agriculture. About 6 million were employed outside small-scale agriculture and pastoralism. Approximately 15 percent of the labour force was officially classified as unemployed in 2004. As Kenya became increasingly urbanized, the labour force shifted from the countryside to cities (World Bank 2015). The service sector absorbed a majority of the inflow of labour to urban areas.

Labour force participation rates for both women and men were constant between 1997 and 2010. In 1997, 65 percent of the women were employed in some type of labour market activity, while the corresponding number for men was 76 percent (World Bank 2015). Around 60 percent of the women and 70 percent of the men were in the labour force in 2005. Their shares increased in 2010, when 61 percent of the women and 72 percent of the men were a part of the labour force.

In the past 20 years, Kenyans have moved away from family farming towards jobs which pay wages or to start small businesses outside the agricultural sector. In 1989, 4.5 million Kenyans (62.0 percent), out of a total working population of 7.3 million, worked on family farms. In 2009, only 6.5 million Kenyans or 45 percent, of a total working population of 14.3 million worked on family farms. More than half the family farm workers in Kenya were women (3.8 million) as compared to men who made up 2.7 million. According to the World Bank (2012) Kenya Economic Update, "Men are much more likely than women to hold wage jobs, and women are more likely to work on family farms. Twice as many men as women hold wage jobs, and more men work principally in wage jobs than on family farms. Most Kenyans are now aiming to get modern wage jobs." In 1989, there were only 1.9 million Kenyans employed in wage work while in 2009 about 5.1 million people worked in modern, wage jobs; as expected men dominated over women in off-farm wage jobs. In 2009, 3.4 million men were employed in wage jobs, while only 1.3 million women held wage jobs (World Bank 2012).

This paper aims at analysing labour productivity in the manufacturing and service sectors in Kenya. Productivity reflects the ability of an organization or country to generate higher income or value-added. It is a ratio which shows how effectively a firm or organization turns a set of resources into products or services. However, there are various measures of productivity, some of which include capital productivity, labour productivity, profitability indices and total factor productivity. In the present study, due to lack of data we only measure labour productivity and its determinants, which is an important measure for gauging competitiveness in producing goods.

Labour productivity can simply be defined as total produced output or sales per employee at the firm level. The model is estimated using the regression analysis method by controlling for aspects of firm-specific, employment, market and public policy. The results show large variations in labour productivity across firms from the manufacturing and service sectors; these can be attributed to differences in their possible determinants.

The rest of the paper is organized as follows. Section 2 presents a literature review while Section 3 presents a data description. Method issues are discussed in Section 4. Section 5 presents the results which are followed by a summary and recommendations in Section 6.

2   Literature Review

A number of studies have attempted to analyse labour productivity and its determinants. Xiaodong et al. (2016) studied the impacts of high-temperature conditions on construction labour's productivity. Their results demonstrated that high temperature environments impose heat stress on the human body as a result of which there is a decrease in labour productivity in the construction industry. According to Baptist and Teal (2015) heterogeneity in production functions and technology is an important source of variations in firm outcomes in Africa and it is even more important than education in explaining differences in output per worker. Based on this study, there is some technological diversity within Africa with more dependence on raw materials in poor countries and higher returns to education in richer countries. Nagler and Naudé (2014) measured labour productivity in rural African enterprises and found that rural enterprises were on average less productive than those in urban areas and that female-owned enterprises were less productive than male-owned ones. They provided evidence that enterprises which operated throughout the year were more productive. According to their study, gender, education, shocks and access to finance and location mattered for labour productivity in rural Africa and that policy decisions tackling shortcomings could significantly contribute to a better business environment and increased labour productivity. Ogutu et al. (2014) assessed the impact of information and communication technology-based (ICT-based) market information services (MIS) on Kenyan smallholder farms' input use and productivity. Their study found that participation in the ICT-based MIS project had a positive and significant effect on the use of purchased seeds, fertilizers and labour and land productivity, but it had a negative and significant impact on the use of hired, family and total labour.

Heshmati and Su (2014) studied the development and the source of labour productivity in 31 Chinese provinces during 2000–2009. They identified several determinants of labour productivity and found that the share of industry output, investments in fixed asset, total volume of telecommunication investments, enterprises' profits and the average wage for labour, had positive effects on labour productivity both when productivity was measured in level and in growth rate forms. Sala and Silva (2011) have shown that vocational training is an important determinant of productivity growth. They constructed a multi-country, multi-sectoral dataset and quantified empirically to what extent vocational training had contributed to an increase in the growth rate of labour productivity in Europe between 1999 and 2005. According to this study, one extra hour of training per employee accelerated the rate of productivity growth by around 0.55 percentage points.

With reference to return to development economics, Rijkers et al. (2010) analysed the productivity of manufacturing enterprises in rural Ethiopia. The authors found that rural enterprises were less productive than urban ones, and reported an output per labour ratio for remote rural enterprises of 0.43, while it was 0.95 for enterprises in rural towns and 2.30 for enterprises in urban areas. Söderbom and Teal (2004) and Söderbom et al. (2006) found that more productive firms tended to survive longer in Africa. This however happened only in cases when these enterprises had already attained a certain firm size and scale in production that enhanced their survival.

According to Dearden et al. (2006) on-the-job training was directly associated with productivity increases. In particular, for a panel of British industries they found that a 1.0 percent increase in work-training raised the value added per hour by about 0.6 percent and the hourly wage by about 0.3 percent. Using Ghanaian enterprise level data, Frazer (2005) confirmed that more productive enterprises were more likely to survive compared to less productive ones. Wei (2000) found a positive relationship between fixed investments and real GDP per capita in China.

Some literature has also studied the performance of female-headed enterprises (Amin 2011; Kinda et al. 2011; Saliola and Seker 2011; Rijkers and Costa 2012). According to these studies female-headed enterprises were less productive than male-headed ones. Other studies include Dollar et al. (2005), Arnold et al. (2006), Eifert et al. (2008), and Dethier et al. (2010) which have found that a poor business environment reduces enterprise productivity and growth. In general, research indicates that aid support targeting female entrepreneurs is more productive in creating employment opportunities, reducing risks of defaults, increasing family welfare, reducing poverty and possibly even increasing survival of the firms.

In sum, existing literature has helped identify the key determinants of labour productivity in manufacturing and services in both developed and developing countries' environments. Among others, it suggests that environmental factors such as high-temperature conditions influence labour productivity negatively in some industries like construction and possibly even an open space working environment such as agriculture. Productivity differences can be large when rural and urban located firms are compared. This is very likely attributed to differences in education, skill, productive capital and other urban-biased development infrastructure. Gender related differences in the management and operation of firms is very likely a result of gender discrimination in the form of objectives, access to financial sources, culture, level of education, etc. Export orientation, innovative activities and training programs not only influence the survival and growth of firms but also their labour productivity positively (Kang et al. 2008; Oh et al. 2009). In Africa's case it seems that policy decisions tackling market shortcomings could significantly contribute to a better business environment and increased labour productivity. In this study we extend the set of determinants listed earlier by several factors specific to the environment in Kenyan manufacturing and service sectors. The factors are selected based on data availability and our expectation about their possible positive effects on labour productivity.

3 Methods

In economics, productivity is measured as the ratio of what is produced to what is required to produce it. Usually this ratio is in the form of an average, expressing the total output of some category of goods divided by the total inputs of, say, labour, energy, capital or raw materials. Productivity is generally defined as a measure of physical output produced from a given quantity of inputs. It is a ratio to show how effectively and efficiently a firm or organization turns a set of inputs into a product or service. It is easier to use inputs like energy and labour in the form of number of employees or hours worked and units of energy used in production. Capital stock needs to be aggregated and constructed in an index form. Due to its multi-output nature, output is the best measure in the form of an aggregate monetary measure. It has the advantage that changes in quality are reflected in prices and values (for a survey on measures of inputs and outputs in manufacturing and services see Heshmati 2003).

Researchers use various measures of productivity. Availability of data and a researcher's skills determine the approach that is used. The starting point is a production function for manufacturing:

$$Y = f(K, L, M, E) \tag{1}$$

where Y is output, K, L, M and E represent capital, labour, material and energy inputs. In recent years the set also includes information technology and public infrastructure. Labour is the dominating factor in the production of many goods and services as in general other inputs in production are proportional to the number of employees or the quantity of output. Banks, insurance companies and education and public sector services are among typical services with such characteristics. Dividing both left and right sides with L and adding technology (T) and other control variables (Z), the relation is rewritten as:

$$Y/L = f(K/L, L/L, M/L, E/L, Z, T) \tag{2}$$

where the ratio Y/L is a measure of labour productivity, and ratios K/L, M/L and E/L measure capital, material and energy intensities per employee. T captures the state of production technology and Z is a vector of control or firm-specific variables capturing the state of firm, market, policy and regulatory conditions.

Productivity in literature includes measures such as single factor capital productivity, labour productivity, energy productivity, profitability indices and total factor productivity. Productivity is estimated using a parametric approach such as estimation of production and cost functions or non-parametrically using the Divisia index of productivity. However, for single factor productivity, it is common that a simple ratio of factor productivity, namely production divided by the factor (in this case labour) is computed. In this case the objective is to maximize labour productivity for a given quantity of labour. The opposite is labour use which aims at minimizing its use for a given level of production in the manufacturing (Masso and Heshmati 2004) and service sectors (Battese et al. 2000). The labour use model is an inverted factor demand model. As such, the labour productivity method allows the use of cross-sectional data. In case of productivity growth one can use time series or panel data to compute changes over time.

In this study we only consider labour productivity, which is an important measure to gauge competitiveness in producing goods and services (Heshmati 2003; Sauiana et al. 2013). Labour is by far the most common factor of production used in measuring productivity. One reason for this is, of course, the relatively large share of labour costs in the value of most products. A second reason is that labour inputs are measured more easily than certain other inputs such as capital. It is also directly and highly related to welfare and an important measure of development and living standards. This is especially true if by measurement one means simply counting heads and neglecting differences among workers in skill levels and intensity of work. In addition, statistics on employment and labour-hours are often readily available, while information on other productive factors may be difficult to obtain and compute.

It is worth mentioning that although the ratio of output to persons engaged in production or to labour-hours is referred to as labour productivity, the term does not imply that labour is the sole factor responsible for changes in the ratio. Improvements in output per unit of labour may be due to increased quality and efficiency of the human factor as well as other factors such as capital intensity, institutions and also many other conditioning variables. Thus, there is special interest in labour productivity measures simply because they also represent welfare and development levels. GDP per capita is the corresponding measure at the aggregate national level.

The level of productivity at different levels of aggregation is determined by a number of factors including, for instance, institutions, quality of management and governance, available supplies of labour force, land, raw materials, capital and other related factors. Also included in the relation are the education and skill levels of the labour force, the level of technology and technological capabilities, organization of production, efforts of managers and workers and other social and cultural factors. Differences in environment and organizations lead to heterogeneity in outcomes including those like labour productivity.

These variables interact and mutually condition one another in determining productivity levels and their changes. Thus, in any country one expects the level of technology, the skills of the workforce, the quantity of capital and the capacity for rational economic organization to be positively correlated. A country with low productivity is likely to have deficiencies on all counts while a country with high productivity is likely to score high on all. To put it differently, the numerous productivity-determining factors behave as variables in a system of simultaneous equations, with all acting concurrently to shape the outcome. Within this system, there are no grounds for assigning causal priorities to one or a few variables. All of them interact mutually to determine labour productivity outcomes. Within certain problem frameworks, however, it may be entirely appropriate and indeed essential for explanatory purposes to emphasize certain variables over others.[2]

To estimate the labour productivity model we used a cross-sectional sample of firms, where we included data from different firms in the manufacturing and service sectors in Kenya. The model follows as:

$$\text{Labour productivity} = f(\text{output, wages, production factor intensity, control variables}) \quad (3)$$

where labour productivity is measured as value of annual production per unit of labour at the firm level. The two key variables as determinants of labour productivity are wages to compensate labour and capital intensity, namely capital per employee. Wage is measured as annual wage, while capital intensity is measured as capital per employee. Other factors that influence labour productivity include energy and material

---

[2] http://academic.eb.com/EBchecked/topic/478036/productivity.

use intensities and workers' characteristics such as age, gender, training, education and experience. The production environmental factors include specialization in production; size of firm; location of the market and industrial sectors; location and access to electricity and water utilities; and communication infrastructure, as well as various obstacles in the production and operations of firms. The model in vector form is written as:

$$\ln LABPRO_i = \beta_0 + \sum_j \beta_j \ln X_{ji}^1 + \sum_k \beta_k \ln X_{ki}^2 \\ + \sum_m \beta_m \ln X_{mi}^3 + \sum_n \beta_n \ln X_{ni}^4 + \varepsilon_i \quad (4)$$

where X^1, X^2, X^3 and X^4 are vectors of the four different categories of variables. A summary of the main factors affecting labour productivity are discussed in the next section, which identifies 21 factors divided into four categories labelled as main, labour, firm and infrastructure related. Given data availability, these factors were selected from literature reviews and are well-known common determinants of labour productivity regardless of the level of development.

The model was specified and estimated with ordinary least square with robust standard errors and is expressed as:

$$\begin{aligned}\ln(LABPRO) = &\ \beta_0 + \beta_1 \ln(CAPINT) + \beta_2 \ln(ELEINT) \\ &+ \beta_3 \ln(FUEINT) + \beta_4 \ln(WAGE) + \beta_5 EXPERI \\ &+ \beta_6 SFEM + \beta_7 TRAIN + \beta_8 FEDU \\ &+ \beta_9 PSEC + \beta_{10} AGE + \beta_{11} SIZE \\ &+ \beta_{12} SECTOR + \beta_{13} REGION + \beta_{14} WEBSI \\ &+ \beta_{15} EMAIL + \beta_{16} INSUWA + \beta_{17} WATCON \\ &+ \beta_{18} POWER + \beta_{19} LSIZE + \beta_{20} TOBSTA \\ &+ \beta_{21} EOBSTA + \varepsilon \end{aligned} \quad (5)$$

The model accounts for non-linearity by including squares of age of the enterprise and experience of the CEOs.

4   Data

The data used in this study is from the World Bank's Enterprise Survey (ES) which collects data from key manufacturing and service sectors in most developing countries. The surveys use standardized means to make the data comparable across the world's economies. The data is thus suitable for comparative country-level economic studies. Our dataset consisted of 670 firm observations in Kenya's manufacturing and service sector in 2013. The data for estimating determinants of labour productivity has dependent, independent and several characteristic variables. The dependent variable is labour productivity (LABPRO) which is defined as the annual value of sales of manufactured goods per unit of labour. For services it refers to the value of all the services provided during the year measured in per unit of labour. The independent and characteristic variables include four categories classified as main, labour related, firm related and infrastructure variables. Each category is now described.

The first category—main—comprises of capital intensity, electric intensity, fuel intensity and wages. The capital intensity (CAPINT, +) variable is measured as the sum of the annual investment on machinery, vehicles, equipment and annual investment in land, buildings and structures per labour. The '+' sign is the expected effect on labour productivity. The variable electricity intensity (ELEINT, +) is measured as the annual cost of electric energy per employee purchased from utility companies. It includes electricity received from other establishments that belong to the same firm. The fuel intensity (FEUINT, +) variable is the annual cost of all fuels per labour which are consumed for heating, power, transportation or the generation of electricity. Finally, the wage (WAGE, +) variable is the average wage per employee in a given firm and is obtained by dividing total wages by the total yearly average number of workers. It includes wages, salaries and benefits including food, transport and social security.

The second category—labour—includes six variables related to employment: the top manager's managerial experience in years (EXPERI, +), female labour share of the workforce at the firm level (SFEM, +/−), training programs for employees (TRAIN, +), average number of years of education of a typical female production worker (FEDUC, +) and the percentage of full time permanent workers who have completed secondary school (PSEC, +). The variable training program for employees is a dummy variable where 1 indicates skill upgrading for a firm's labour force.

The third category—firm—comprises of firm characterizes such as age, size and industrial sector classifications. A firm's age (AGE, +) is measured in years. For the size of the establishment (SIZE, +/−) we group firms into three size classes by the number of employees: 5–19 (small), 10–99 (medium) and over 100 (large) employees. In classifying an establishment's activities (SECTOR, +/−) we club firms into three groups of manufacture, services and others. Finally location (REGION, +/−) defines the region stratum of the establishment and includes Central, Mombasa, Nairobi and others.

The fourth category of variables labelled as infrastructure include eight variables that play an important role in the smooth operations of the studied firms. Website use (WEBSI, +) includes cases when an establishment has its own website and email (EMAIL, +) which suggests that the establishment uses emails to communicate with clients or suppliers. The utility variables include the establishment's experience of insufficient water supply (INSUWA, −) for production, waiting for a water connection (WATCON, −) and the number of power outages (POWER, −) in a typical month. The remaining variables include the size of locality (LSIZE, +), the degree to which telecommunications is seen as an obstacle by the firm (TOBSTA, −) and to what degree electricity is an obstacle (EOBSTA, −) in production.

5 Empirical Results

5.1 Model Specification and Estimation

Tables 1 and 2 provide summary statistics of the data for the input and output variables and labour, firm and market characteristics used in this study. Sales averaged at 1170 million Kenyan Shilling (KES)[3] with

---

[3]US$1 = 99.7 Kenyan Shilling (KES) on 13 March 2016.

Table 1 Summary statistics of key variables in the Kenyan manufacturing and services enterprise data (2013), N = 670

Variable	Variable definition	Mean	Std Dev	Minimum	Maximum	CV
Sale	Total sales (in Kenyan Shilling, KES)	1,170,000,000	7,650,000,000	90,000	120,000,000,000	6.54
Employment	Annual employment	98	424.80	1	8000	4.32
LABPRO	Sale per employee (labour productivity) in KES	14,400,000	90,200,000	3000	1,720,000,000	6.26
CAPINT	Annual investment per employee (capital intensity) in KES	7,806,039	35,000,000	0.16	484,000,000	4.48
EENINT	Annual cost of electric energy per labour (energy intensity) in KES	238,817	1,610,259	0.00	36,000,000	6.74
FENINT	Annual cost of all fuels per labour (fuel intensity) in KES	4,821,125	10,800,000	0.00	200,000,000	2.24
WAGE	Wage per employee in KES	1,049,785	7,095,087	1000	170,000,000	6.76

Note US$1 = 99.7 Kenyan Shilling (KES) on 13 March 2016

Table 2 Summary statistics by firm characteristics and infrastructure in Kenyan manufacturing and services enterprise data (2013), $N = 670$

Abbreviations		Variable definition	Mean	Std Dev	Minimum	Maximum
expe		Manager's experience in years	18.79	10.77	2.00	57.00
femsh		Female share of employees	0.81	1.27	0	9.50
train		Training programs for employees	0.45	0.50	0	1.00
feduc		Average number of years of education of a typical female production worker	11.66	2.95	0	25.00
psec		Percentage of full time permanent workers with completed secondary school	79.18	28.09	0	100.00
age		Enterprise age in years	24.63	18.14	2.00	108.00
size	Size0	$5 \leq \text{Small} \leq 19$	0.42	0.49	0	0.86
	Size1	$10 \leq \text{Medium} \leq 99$	0.31	0.46	0	0.67
	Size2	$\text{Large} \geq 100$	0.27	0.44	0	0.61
sector	Sec0	Manufacturing sector	0.55	0.50	0	1.10
	Sec1	Service sector	0.20	0.40	0	0.50
	Sec2	Others	0.25	0.44	0	0.57
region	Reg0	Central	0.15	0.50	0	0.30
	Reg1	Mombasa	0.19	0.40	0	0.48
	Reg2	Nairobi	0.47	0.44	0	1.07
	Reg3	Others	0.19	0.36	0	0.53
web		Does this establishment have its own website?	0.54	0.49	0.39	1.00
email		Does this establishment use email to communicate with clients or suppliers?	0.82	0.38	0	1.00
iws		Did this establishment experience insufficient water supply for production?	0.71	0.45	0	1.00
wcon		Wait for a water connection?	20.61	8.69	2.00	90.00
pout		Number of power outages in a typical month	8.86	15.56	1.00	200.00
popu		Size of locality	0.33	0.47	0	1.00

(continued)

Table 2 (continued)

Abbreviations		Variable definition	Mean	Std Dev	Minimum	Maximum
tobst		To what degree is telecommunications an obstacle?				
	Tobst0	No obstacle = 0	0.41	0.49	0	1.00
	Tobst1	Minor and moderate obstacle = 1	0.39	0.48	0	1.00
	Tobst2	Major and severe obstacle = 2	0.19	0.39	0	1.00
eobst		To what degree is electricity an obstacle?				
	Eobst0	No obstacle = 0	0.24	0.43	0	1.00
	Eobst1	Minor and moderate obstacle = 1	0.48	0.50	0	1.00
	Eobst2	Major and severe obstacle = 2	0.26	0.44	0	1.00

dispersion 6.54 times the mean.[4] The average employment in a sample firm was 98 persons. It varied in interval 1 and 8000, with a dispersion of 4.32 around the mean value. The ratio of the two variables, the amount of sales per employee, which measures labour productivity varied from 3000 to 1720 billion KES with mean and standard deviations of 14.4 million and 90.2 million KES.

The value of investment per employee shows considerable variations in the dataset. Mean wage per employee was 1.05 million KES with a large standard deviation of 7.1 million KES. It ranged in the interval of 1,000 and 170 million KES. Two other variables of energy and fuel intensity also showed large variations among the sample firms. The average capital intensity per employee was 7.8 million KES with a standard deviation of 35 million KES. One capital-intensive technology firm used 484 million KES in capital per employee. Energy use per employee also varied greatly among the firms. An average manager's experience was about 19 years, which varied between 2 and 57 years of experience. The average age of firms since their establishment was 25 years with a standard deviation of 18 years. The age of the firms varied in the interval of 2 and 108 years. On average the male labour share was 81 per cent. The firms' CEOs had about 12 years of education. Around 80 per cent of the permanently employed workers had completed secondary schooling.

In order to check for collinearity among the explanatory variables, correlation coefficients among all the 22 variables is presented in Table 3. Labour productivity, as expected, was unconditionally positively correlated with capital, energy intensities and wages. Only pairs of wages and electricity showed higher correlation than 0.50 indicating multicollinearity and possible confounded effects. The remaining pairs were low correlated with each other and did not show any signs of serious multicollinearity. The age of the firm, training for workers, secondary education of workers and firm size were positively correlated with labour productivity.

The model in Eq. (5) was estimated by ordinary least squares (OLS) with robust standard errors. Four regression models were specified and estimated using STATA. These differed by generalizations of the basic

---

[4]Measured as coefficient of variation, CV = Std Dev/Mean.

Table 3 Correlation matrix of the variables, $N = 670$

	Labpro	capi	eleci	fueli	Wagei	expe	age	femsh	Train	feduc	psec	size	sect	regi	web	email	iws	wcon	pout	popu	tobst	eobst
labpro	1																					
capi	0.45	1																				
eleci	0.65	0.51	1																			
fueli	0.23	0.04	0.09	1																		
wagei	0.84	0.48	0.87	0.13	1																	
expe	0.01	−0.08	−0.04	−0.11	−0.03	1																
age	0.03	−0.05	−0.03	−0.12	−0.02	0.32	1															
femsh	0.20	0.20	0.36	−0.03	0.33	−0.06	0.02	1														
train	0.02	−0.03	−0.05	−0.08	−0.06	0.00	0.10	−0.09	1													
feduc	−0.02	−0.10	−0.02	0.03	−0.01	0.00	−0.01	−0.12	0.00	1												
psec	0.01	0.03	0.04	0.05	0.02	0.00	−0.07	−0.16	0.13	0.25	1											
size	0.06	0.26	0.05	−0.21	0.03	0.09	0.18	−0.22	0.01	0.05	0.09	1										
sect	−0.07	0.02	−0.07	0.27	−0.06	−0.20	−0.29	−0.29	−0.05	−0.02	0.13	−0.12	1									
regi	−0.01	−0.03	0.05	0.10	0.02	0.02	−0.09	−0.19	0.01	0.38	0.17	−0.02	0.07	1								
web	−0.01	0.03	−0.05	−0.09	−0.05	0.03	0.09	−0.17	0.27	0.06	0.15	0.25	0.06	0.10	1							
email	0.01	−0.04	−0.03	−0.15	−0.03	0.20	0.02	−0.26	0.12	0.16	0.24	0.24	−0.02	0.14	0.36	1						
iws	−0.04	−0.04	−0.08	0.10	−0.08	−0.11	−0.04	−0.02	−0.04	0.25	0.03	−0.05	0.06	0.26	0.02	−0.04	1					
wcon	−0.04	−0.01	0.02	−0.03	−0.01	−0.12	0.03	0.07	−0.03	0.33	0.00	−0.03	−0.13	0.31	0.02	−0.05	0.49	1				
pout	−0.03	−0.03	−0.02	0.00	−0.03	0.02	0.08	−0.02	0.05	−0.09	0.04	−0.03	0.03	0.04	−0.02	−0.08	−0.05	−0.09	1			
popu	−0.05	−0.02	0.01	−0.02	−0.01	−0.06	0.10	0.25	0.00	−0.06	−0.16	0.00	−0.13	0.02	−0.02	−0.25	0.19	0.34	0.01	1		
tobs	0.01	−0.01	−0.03	0.02	0.00	−0.04	0.06	−0.05	0.07	0.07	0.04	−0.15	−0.13	0.02	0.05	0.02	0.05	0.07	0.00	−0.03	1	
eobst	0.03	−0.01	0.06	−0.12	0.03	0.11	0.19	0.08	0.05	−0.02	−0.02	0.11	−0.26	−0.15	0.05	0.03	−0.09	0.01	0.05	−0.06	0.33	1

model with vectors of firms, labour and market characteristic variables. They were used to study the impacts of various categories of factors on labour productivity in the manufacturing and service sectors in Kenya at the firm level. The results of Eq. (5) are presented in Table 4. Tests of functional form using F-test based on residual sum of squares suggest that the somewhat less general Model 3 was the accepted and preferred model specification with reasonable explanatory power in explaining variations in labour productivity among the sample manufacturing and service firms in Kenya.

Ideally one should estimate the labour productivity model separately for different sub-samples of manufacturing and services. However, due to relatively small sub-sample sizes and robustness of the results we estimated a pooled model, but controlled for sectors of the firms grouped into manufacturing, services and others.

5.2 Determinants of Labour Productivity

Column 1 of Table 4 displays the estimation results for our basic model (Model 1), in which labour productivity was only affected by main variables like capital intensity, electricity intensity, fuel intensity and wages. We further added labour category variables to the first model and then constructed Model 2. Model 3 was attained by adding variables from the category firm characteristics to Model 2. Finally we show the estimates for full determinants of the labour productivity in Model 4 by adding the infrastructure category variables to Model 3.

Thus, Model 1 was the most restricted and Model 4 the most generalized model specification. The models are nested and thereby allow testing for selection of appropriate model specifications. The specification test results are presented in Table 5. The test results show that the semi-general Model 3 was the accepted model specification which served as a base for the analysis. However, we also discuss the unconditional model specification. The models' performances were measured in coefficient of determinations, adjusted R^2, in explaining variations in labour productivity. Given the small and heterogeneous sample, this is relatively high, in the interval 0.28 and 0.35.

Table 4 Ordinary least squares parameter estimates (with robust standard errors) of labour productivity, N = 670

Variable	Variable definition	Model 1 Coeff.	Model 1 Robust Std error	Model 2 Coeff.	Model 2 Robust Std error	Model 3 Coeff.	Model 3 Robust Std error	Model 4 Coeff.	Model 4 Robust Std error
cons	Intercept	7.626		6.425[a]	0.682	6.483[a]	0.692	6.138[a]	0.867
CAPINT	Capital intensity	0.674[a]	0.023	0.027	0.024	0.010	0.024	0.015	0.025
ELEINT	Electricity intensity	0.007	0.022	0.040	0.023	0.029	0.023	0.027	0.023
FEUINT	Fuel intensity	0.053[b]	0.011	0.007	0.012	0.031[b]	0.015	0.032[b]	0.015
WAGE	Wage	0.002	0.050	0.510[a]	0.048	0.500[a]	0.049	0.491[a]	0.050
EXPERI	Manager's experience	0.511[a]		0.047[b]	0.020	0.042[b]	0.020	0.040[b]	0.020
EXPERI 2	Square of experience			−0.001[c]	0.000	−0.001[c]	0.000	−0.001[c]	0.000
SFEM	Female share of employees			−0.037	0.054	−0.015	0.059	0.002	0.059
TRAIN	Training of workers			0.429[a]	0.113	0.402[a]	0.113	0.328[a]	0.115
FEDUC	Female education			0.010	0.022	0.004	0.024	−0.001	0.024
PSEC	Secondary school education			0.003	0.002	0.003	0.002	0.002	0.002
AGE	Age of firm					0.014	0.009	0.014[c]	0.008
AGE 2	Square of age					<0.0001	0.000	<0.0001	0.000
SIZE 1	Size of firm—medium					−0.048	0.145	−0.059	0.144
SIZE 2	Size of firm—large					0.274[c]	0.160	0.219	0.165
SECTOR 1	Sector—service					<0.0001	0.209	0.010	0.224
SECTOR 2	Sector—others					−0.386[b]	0.184	−0.397[b]	0.194
Region 1	Region—Mombasa					0.090	0.212	0.266	0.437
Region 2	Region—Nairobi					0.170	0.172	0.178	0.359
Region 3	Region—others					−0.288	0.203	−0.258	0.207

(continued)

Table 4 (continued)

Variable	Variable definition	Model 1 Coeff.	Model 1 Robust Std error	Model 2 Coeff.	Model 2 Robust Std error	Model 3 Coeff.	Model 3 Robust Std error	Model 4 Coeff.	Model 4 Robust Std error
LSIZE	Size of locality							0.065	0.354
WEBSI	Website							0.168	0.128
EMAIL	Email							0.216	0.188
INSUWA	Insufficient water supply							0.317	0.156
WATCON	Wait for water connection							−0.005	0.010
POWER	Power outages							−0.002	0.003
TOBSTA 1	Telecommunication obstacles							0.213[c]	0.124
TOBSTA 2	Obstacle—major and severe							0.270	0.171
EOBSTA 1	Electricity obstacles							−0.050	0.140
EOBSTA 2	Electricity obstacles—major and severe							0.108	0.169
F-value		30.90		19.90		14.48		11.07	
R^2 adj		0.28		0.31		0.34		0.35	

Notes Significant at less than 1% (a) 1–5% (b) and 5–10% (c) levels of significance

Table 5 *F*-tests for alternative model specifications

Model comparison	RSS1	RSS2	F-test statistics	Critical value at 5%	Decision
Model 1 versus Model 2	1433.76	1358.76	4.53	1.96	Model 1 is rejected
Model 1 versus Model 3	1433.76	1316.11	3.87	1.74	Model 1 is rejected
Model 1 versus Model 4	1433.76	1283.92	2.98	1.54	Model 1 is rejected
Model 2 versus Model 3	1358.76	1316.11	3.00	2.03	Model 2 is rejected
Model 2 versus Model 4	1358.76	1283.92	2.19	1.64	Model 2 is rejected
Model 3 versus Model 4	1316.11	1283.92	1.60	1.85	Model 3 is accepted

Note RSS1 is restricted models' residuals sum of squares, RSS2 is unrestricted models' residual sum of squares

Labour productivity, energy intensity, capital intensity and wage variables were transformed to logarithmic form. The coefficients were elasticities and as such were directly interpretable. They reflect percentage change in labour productivity in response to percentage changes in energy and capital input intensities and wages.

In all the models wage elasticity is positive (in the range of 0.49 and 0.51) and statistically significant at less than the 1 percent level. Consistent with theory and our expectations, a higher level of wages increased labour productivity. Wages had the strongest effect on the level of labour productivity. In the simple model (Model 1) the effects of capital intensity (0.007), electricity intensity (0.053) and fuel intensity (0.002) on labour productivity were weaker than that of wages. Unexpectedly, capital intensity was not found to have effects on labour productivity. This is surprising as capital equips labour with the tools needed to make it productive. A third significant factor with effected labour productivity was fuel intensity in the third and fourth models. The electricity intensity elasticity was statistically significant in the first and second models but insignificant in the third and fourth models. Considering the accepted Model 3, wages and fuel intensity were the key determinants of labour productivity among Kenyan manufacturing and service firms.

Experience of the manager, female share of employees, training and education of workers were among the second category labour related variables expected to influence labour productivity. We allowed for non-linearity in the relationship between labour productivity and managerial experience by adding square of experience to the specification. The first and second order experience coefficients were positive and negative respectively suggesting that a higher managerial experience increased labour productivity but at a decreasing rate. An experienced manager with greater abilities can typically complete higher quality work. In addition, it is widely accepted that the training and education of labour usually increases working abilities resulting in higher labour productivity. According to Models 2 and 3, female share in labour had a negative effect on labour productivity. This finding is consistent with other studies like those by Saliola and Seker (2011) and Rijkers and Costa (2012). However, the coefficient of female share of employees was insignificant suggesting no statistical difference in labour productivity by gender. After higher wages, the training of workers was the second factor with the largest positive effect on labour productivity. The effect ranged in the interval 0.32 and 0.42 and was statistically significant at less than the 1 percent level. Education for females and completion of secondary education did not seem to affect labour productivity. Adding interactive effects between wage and managerial experience, representing higher payments to the experienced workforce will affect labour productivity positively.

The firm category consisted of age, size, sector and regional location. Like managerial experience we allowed for a non-linear relationship between labour productivity and age of the firm. The coefficients of firm age and age squared were both positive suggesting a positive relationship between labour productivity and a firm's age at an increasing rate. It indicates that labour in older firms was more productive than in young firms, which can be possibly explained by managers' experiences. However, they were statistically insignificant. The insignificant size coefficients suggest no difference in labour productivity across different age groups. The other groups of firms had lower productivity than manufacturing firms, whose productivity did not differ from that in service firms. Labour productivity did not differ by location suggesting no advantage for the capital city or a location with better productivity facilitating infrastructure. Size of locality or market had a positive but insignificant effect on labour productivity.

Next we introduced an additional infrastructure category to Model 3 and get Model 4. The category list included infrastructure variables such as use of website and email services in communication with suppliers and customers, water supply, waiting for water connections, power outages and degrees of telecommunication and electricity supply obstacles. A majority of the coefficients are of expected signs but statistically insignificant. In the fourth model we observe that having a website and email positively affected the labour's productivity in a firm. The effect of power outages and waiting for water connections were negative, as we would expect, but statistically insignificant.

6 Summary and Conclusion

Labour productivity reflects on the ability of a firm to generate higher production or values. Kenya as the largest economy in East Africa can benefit greatly from high labour productivity. Labour productivity can have strong implications for economic growth and welfare. This paper attempted to determine labour productivity and its determinants in manufacturing and service sectors in Kenya. This study provides a better understanding of the state of labour productivity in the Kenyan economy. Four regression models were used to analyse labour productivity. The results show that the third model was the best among the different nested models.

An analysis of the World Bank's Enterprise Survey database in 2013 showed that capital intensity and wages significantly and positively affected labour productivity. We also found that training of workers and education levels and managerial experience of CEOs were associated with higher labour productivity. Reliance on technologies such as emails and websites for communication purposes had insignificant positive impacts on firms' labour productivity, while various obstacles in access and use of utilities and infrastructure discouraged high labour productivity. The results indicate that when the number of power outages in one month increases, labour productivity decreases. Additionally, as expected, waiting for water connections had a negative influence on labour productivity. The findings also imply that when the female share in the labour force increases by one unit, the percentage of labour productivity decreases by 0.04 percent. In addition, this amount increases by 0.01 percent when female education increases by one year. These results are consistent with results of other studies conducted on labour productivity.

The current dataset is at firm level which helps shed light on individual firms' production and market environment conditions and performance. It is certainly positive that the sample covers both manufacturing and service sectors. It is important to acknowledge that this study has several limitations, mostly due to the nature of the data used. We had access to only one year of the Enterprise Survey data with a relatively small sample size not allowing accounting for firm effects and sector responses heterogeneity. Despite data limitations we have made a significant contribution in illustrating the usefulness of this previously not much exploited source of data and by identifying the key determinants of labour productivity as inputs, labour, firms and development infrastructure categories of variables.

This study only focused on service and manufacturing sectors. Hence, additional studies are required to analyse labour productivity and its determinants in specific sub-sectors of the Kenyan economy (for example, transportation, finance, education and health). Moreover, additional categories (for example, management and environment) should be included in future studies. Some variables such as a manager's education, payment, motivation and employees' education and skills, as well as pollution and waste and their management can be studied in management and environmental categories respectively. Hopefully, this simple and preliminary study will help initiate further research in this important field of research by using the unexploited Enterprise Survey data.

References

Amin, M. (2011). *Labour Productivity, Firm-Size and Gender: The Case of Informal Firms in Argentina and Peru*. Enterprise Note, 22. The World Bank.

Arnold, J., A. Mattoo, and G. Narciso (2006). *Services Inputs and Firm Productivity in Sub-Saharan Africa: Evidence from Firm-Level Data*. World Bank Policy Research Working Paper, No. 4048. Washington, DC: The World Bank.

Baptist, S. and F. Teal (2015). Technology and Productivity in African Manufacturing Firms. *World Development*, 64: 713–725.

Battese, G.E., A. Heshmati, and L. Hjalmarsson (2000). Efficiency of Labour Use in the Swedish Banking Industry: A Stochastic Frontier Approach. *Empirical Economics* 25(4): 623–640.

Dearden, L., H. Reed, and J.V. Reenen (2006). The Impact of Training on Productivity and Wages: Evidence from British Panel Data. *Oxford Bulletin of Economics and Statistics*, 68(4): 397–421.

Dethier, J., M. Hirn, and S. Straub (2010). Explaining Enterprise Performance in Developing Countries with Business Climate Survey Data. *World Bank Research Observer*, 26: 258–309.

Dollar, D., M. Hallword-Driemeier, and T. Mengistae (2005). Investment Climate and Firm Performance in Developing Countries. *Economic Development and Cultural Change*, 54(1): 1–31.

Eifert, B., A. Gelb, and V. Ramachandran (2008). The Cost of Doing Business in Africa: Evidence from Enterprise Survey Data. *World Development*, 36(9): 1531–1546.

Frazer, G. (2005). Which Firms Die? A Look at Manufacturing Firm Exit in Ghana. *Economic Development and Cultural Change*, 53(3): 585–617.

Heshmati, A. (2003). Productivity Growth, Efficiency and Outsourcing in Manufacturing and Services. *Journal of Economic Surveys*, 17(1): 79–112.

Heshmati, A. and B. Su (2014). Development and Sources of Labour Productivity in Chinese Provinces. *China Economic Policy Review*, 2(2): 1–30.

Kang, J.W., A. Heshmati, and G.G. Choi (2008). The Effects of Credit Guarantees on Survival and Performance of SMEs in Korea. *Small Business Economics*, 31(4): 445–462.

Kinda, T., P. Plane, and M. Veganzones-Veroudakis (2011). Firm Productivity and Investment Climate in Developing Countries: How Does the Middle East and North Africa Perform? *The Developing Economies*, 49(4): 429–469.

Masso, J. and A. Heshmati (2004). Optimality and Overuse of Labour in Estonian Manufacturing Enterprises. *Economics of Transition*, 12(4): 683–720.

Nagler, P. and W. Naudé (2014). *Labour Productivity in Rural African Enterprises: Empirical Evidence from the LSMS-ISA*. IZA Discussion Paper No. 2014: 8524.

Odero, W.O., W.A. Reeves, and N. Kipyego (2015). Kenya 2015. African Economic Outlook. http://www.africaneconomicoutlook.org/. Accessed 4 April 2016.

Ogutu, S.O., J.J. Okello, and D.J. Otieno (2014). Impact of Information and Communication Technology-Based Market Information Services on Smallholder Farm Input Use and Productivity: The Case of Kenya. *World Development*, 64: 311–321.

Oh, I., A. Heshmati, C. Baek, and J.-D. Lee (2009). Comparative Analysis of Firm Dynamics by Size: The Korean Manufacturing. *Japanese Economic Review*, 60(4): 512–538.

Rijkers, B. and R. Costa (2012). Gender and Rural Non-farm Entrepreneurship. *World Development*, 40(12): 2411–2426.

Rijkers, B., M. Söderbom, and J. Loening (2010). A Rural-Urban Comparison of Manufacturing Enterprise Performance in Ethiopia. *World Development*, 38(9): 1278–1296.

Sala, H. and J.I. Silva (2011). *Labour Productivity and Vocational Training: Evidence from Europe*. IZA Discussion Paper No. 2011: 6171.

Saliola, F. and M. Seker (2011). *Total Factor Productivity Across the Developing World*. Enterprise Note No. 23. The World Bank.

Sauiana, M.S., N. Kamarudinb, and R.M. Rani (2013). Labour Productivity of Services Sector in Malaysia: Analysis Using Input-Output Approach. *Procedia Economics and Finance*, 7: 35–41.

Söderbom, M. and F. Teal (2004). Size and Efficiency in African Manufacturing Firms: Evidence from Firm-Level Panel Data. *Journal of Development Economics*, 73(1): 369–394.

Söderbom, M., F. Teal, and A. Harding (2006). The Determinants of Survival Among African Manufacturing Firms. *Economic Development and Cultural Change*, 54(3): 533–555.

Wei, Y.H. (2000). Investment and Regional Development in Post-Mao China. *Geo Journal*, 51(3): 169–179.

World Bank (IBRD-IDA) (2015). Labour Force Participation Rate, Female (% of Female Population Ages 15+) (Modeled ILO Estimate). http://data.worldbank.org/indicator/SL.TLF.CACT.FE.ZS?page=2.

World Bank (2012). Kenya Economic Update: Kenya at Work: Energizing the Economy and Creating Jobs. Edition No. 7. http://siteresources.worldbank.org/INTAFRICA/Resources/257994-1335471959878/kenya-economic-update-December-2012.pdf.

Xiaodong, L., K.H. Chow, Y. Zhu, and L. Ying (2016). Evaluating the Impacts of High-Temperature Outdoor Working Environments on Construction Labour Productivity in China: A Case Study of Rebar Workers. *Building and Environment*, 95: 42–52.

Part III

Macroeconomic Determinants of Growth

10

Inferences on the Relationship Between Economic Growth and the Real Exchange Rate: A Meta-Analysis

Fentahun Baylie

1 Introduction

According to the purchasing power parity (PPP) theory, deviations from the equilibrium real exchange rate are temporary and hence the real exchange rate is stationary or remains fixed in the long run. Based on this argument of the purchasing power parity theory, the Balasssa hypothesis examines the interaction between the real exchange rate and relative productivity growth to explain the behavior of the real exchange rate in the long-run (Drine and Rault 2003). Several studies show that PPP does hold in many cases (Abuaf and Jorion 1990; Faria and Ledesma 2000; Hoarau 2008; Johnson 1990; Joya 2009; Steigerwald 1996). However, interest often rests on reasons why it does not hold in some cases. The Balassa hypothesis addresses one of the reasons why PPP does not hold sometimes (Ickes 2004).

F. Baylie (✉)
Department of Economics, Addis Ababa University,
Addis Ababa, Ethiopia

The Balassa hypothesis was first formulated by Harrod in 1934 and later by Balassa and Samuelson (separately) in 1964. It states that distortions from PPP are a result of international differences in relative productivity between tradable[1] and non-tradable goods' sectors. During the development process, productivity (alternatively referred to as the Balassa term) tends to improve/increase more quickly in tradable goods than in non-tradables. An increase in productivity in the tradable goods sector leads to an increase in wages in the same sector as well as in the non-tradable goods sector. This increase in wages leads to a quicker increase in relative prices in the non-tradable goods sector where productivity has not grown by the same pace. Given that prices of the tradable goods sector are set by international competition, this does not affect the domestic economy. This has the impact of raising relative prices of non-tradables (domestic goods) which may finally result in appreciation of the real exchange rate in the domestic economy (Coudert 2004; Herberger 2003; Tica and Druzic 2006).

In short, the Balassa hypothesis examines the impact of productivity growth on real exchange rate. Productivity growth in either the tradable or the non-tradable sector may lead to economic growth. The Balassa hypothesis assumes that economic growth results in the appreciation of domestic currency if economic growth is derived mainly by productivity growth in the tradable goods sector.

The Balassa hypothesis may be investigated by considering the estimated coefficient for the Balassa term (or its t-statistic) in the estimated form of the equation (Horvath et al. 2013):

$$\text{RER}_{it} = \alpha + \beta B_{it} + \gamma \chi_{it} + \delta_t + \eta_i + \varepsilon_{it} \quad (1)$$

where, for country i at time t, RER_{it} is the real exchange rate defined such that an increase in it is a real appreciation of the domestic currency; B is the Balassa term; χ_{it} is a vector of all other economic factors that explain variations in the real exchange rate; and δ_t and η_i are common time and country specific factors in each study.

---

[1]De Gregorio et al. (1994) shows a sector which exports more than 10 percent of its produce is referred to as 'tradable' otherwise 'non-tradable.'

Previous studies show mixed results regarding the impact of economic growth on the real exchange rate. While many studies (for example, Balassa 1964; Bhagwati 1984; Chuoudhri and Kahn 2004; De Gregorio et al. 1994; Guo and Hall 2008; Jabeen et al. 2011; MacDonald and Ricci 1998; Tica and Druzic 2006; Tzilianos 2006) provide empirical support in favor of the Balassa hypothesis (for example, Asea and Mendoza 1994; Chuah 2012; Canzoneri, et al. 1997; Drine and Rault 2003; Funda et al. 2007; Genius and Tzouvelekas 2008; Gubler and Sax 2008; Wilson 2010), some others present evidence against the hypothesis. Therefore, before a detailed analysis of the consequences of the hypothesis it is essential to examine the universality and strength of the impact/effect. An empirical way of examining such an effect for sample studies is referred to as meta-analysis. Therefore, the main purpose of our study is to conduct a meta-analysis of the Balassa hypothesis.

A meta-analysis is a process of using statistical methods to combine and analyze the results of previous studies. It involves a systematic, organized and structured evaluation of a problem of interest using summary statistics' information from different independent previous studies (Petitti 2000). Generally, there are two types of quantitative review procedures. One method involves combining probability values or z scores, while the second technique combines effect sizes such as Cohen's d and correlation coefficient, r (Lyons 1995). The use of the correlation coefficient as a measure of effect size is more appropriate if the dependent variable is typically presented as a continuous variable (DeCoster 2004). The dependent variable is continuous in this study and hence the correlation coefficient is used as a measure of effect size.

The major advantage of a meta-analysis is that it replaces traditional methods of testing statistical significance by a test of the strength of a magnitude (Libsey and Wilson 1999). In our study the relevance of employing meta-analysis is two-fold. First, a meta-analysis helps get a confirmation on the relevance of an effect for an emerging concept like the Balassa hypothesis from a reasonable size of previous/sample studies before further analysis. The hypothesis was proposed in the mid-1960s and empirical models for it were formulated only in the early 1990s. Second, a meta-analysis of the Balassa hypothesis is scarce and our work may contribute to narrowing filling this gap. Among studies that were easily accessible two studies were identified which are close to our study: Tica and Druzic (2006) and Egert and Halpern (2005). The first is made up of a quantitative review of studies that deal with the Balassa hypothesis but does not apply a meta-analysis. The second study employs a meta-analysis. However, its focus is not to test the Balassa hypothesis but to analyze the equilibrium real exchange rate.

Three types of meta-analyses are noted based on their goals and the nature of the information that they provide: Type A, Type B and Type C. Type A meta-analyses summarize how strong an effect is in a literature. Their main goal is to ascertain the presence and strength of an effect. Type B meta-analyses investigate what variables moderate an effect's strength. Type C meta-analyses provide new evidence related to a theory (Miller and Pollock 1994). Our paper employs a combination of Type A and Type B meta-analyses to determine the existence and strength of an effect size for the Balassa hypothesis and examines the reasons for variations in effect sizes across studies.

The quality of the findings in our study may, however, be limited because of the size of the sample of previous studies and the shortcomings of a meta-analysis itself. Like any other method of analysis, a meta-analysis too has its limitations. The quality of the findings depends on the quality of the sample of previous studies used. Any mistake by any author in any study may change the outcome. A meta-analysis of high quality can be produced by reducing these shortcomings. We made the maximum possible effort to minimize such shortcomings.

2   Measuring Effect Size

Effect size is a value which reflects the strength of a relationship between two variables. In our study, the strength of the relationship between economic growth and the real exchange rate is represented by the coefficient of the Balassa term (β in Eq. 1). β measures the strength of an effect of a per unit change in productivity growth on the real exchange rate. Two types of proxies are used for the productivity growth variable in the sample studies: total factor productivity (TFP) and average labor productivity. TFP is measured by real GDP per capita and symbolizes productivity of all factors of production. Average labor productivity is measured by value added per unit of employment and corresponds to average productivity of labor employed in different sectors (De Gregorio et al. 1994).

Effect size provides a standardized way of representing the coefficient of a dependent variable so that it is comparable across studies. Computation of the effect size index is done in such a way that it is comparable between studies in the sense that they measure the same thing. It has a technical quality and easily interpretable properties (Borenstein et al. 2009).

Effect sizes may be calculated using different statistics. The t-statistic is the most easily available and widely used measure. The t-statistic associated with the coefficients of the Balassa term after some adjustments serves as a dependent variable (effect size). The t-statistic from ith study in jth regression estimate, (t_{ij}) is converted into a common effect size known as the partial correlation coefficients (pcc_{ij}) using.[2]

$$pcc_{ij} = \sqrt{\frac{t_{ij}^2}{t_{ij}^2 + df_{ij}}} = E_{ij} \qquad (2)$$

where, E_{ij} refers to effect size and df_{ij} is the number for the degree of freedom, one less number of parameters included in the ith study's jth regression estimate (Lyons 1995). In the context of our paper, this measure represents the degree of linear association between productivity growth and the real exchange rate. Two major adjustments are made for effect sizes calculated by Eq. (2) to get an unbiased and normally distributed estimate (DeCoster 2004). The first adjustment is calculating the population correlation coefficient from the sample correlation coefficient. This improves the bias associated with the estimate. The second adjustment is the use of Fisher's r-to-z transformation to get normal

---

[2]For jointly normally distributed variables, $\frac{r\sqrt{k-1}}{\sqrt{1-r^2}} \sim t - distribution, k - 1 = df$ (Gujarati 2004).

distribution for the estimate. All statistics are estimated using these transformed scores. Yet, interpretations are made after z-scores are transformed back to correlations.

3 Methodology

3.1 Data Type and Collection Methods

Primary data was collected from statistics reported by previous empirical studies. Thus, the first step in the meta-analysis was searching for as many studies of interest as possible that were related to the topic (the list of studies used in our meta-analysis is given in Table 8). The search mainly focused on studies with models that defined the real exchange rate as a function of productivity as shown by Eq. (1). In addition, other information that described the characteristics of each study was extracted.

Almost all possible/accessible sources were searched through different means between 5 November 2015 and 20 February 2017. The main method of searching for these sources was computer based/internet. In addition, documentation centers at Addis Ababa University and Jonkoping University were also consulted. Initially, 143 studies related to the Balassa hypothesis were found of which only 61 papers were directly related to the purpose on hand and provided complete information (on standard errors and t-statistics) for a meta-analysis. Others were either indirectly related to the Balassa hypothesis or provided incomplete information.

Candidate studies were read carefully and all relevant information extracted. Mainly information on variables like the Balassa term (*PRECISION*), type of data (*DATA-TYPE*), data frequency (*DATA-FREQUENCY*), length of the study period (*PERIOD*), number of years (*YEARS*), number of countries (*COUNTRIES*), type of countries (*DEVELOPMENT*), number of parameters (*PARAMETERS*), estimation method (*METHOD*), productivity proxy (*PROXY*), type of impact measured by the dependent variable (*IMPACT*) and publication status

(*PUBLICATION*). In general, 177 observations were collected from 61 studies on five continuous and eight categorical variables.

Due to certain inconsistencies with the Balassa hypothesis such as negative results on the impact of economic growth on the real exchange rate while a positive relationship was expected, 16 studies (32 observations) were dropped by the software. Hence, 45 studies (145 observations) were included in the final analysis.

Previous literature suggests that a meta-analysis should contain enough studies to provide sufficient power for its test. For most purposes, the use of not less than 30 studies is recommended. However, the exact number depends on what analyses are being performed (DeCoster 2004). The dataset of our study met this minimum criterion.

3.2 Model Specification

There are two types of models, fixed and random-effects, which may be used to produce different types of mean effect size under different assumptions.

A fixed-effects model assumes that there is one true/common effect size which underlies all the studies in the analysis and that all the differences in the observed effects are due to sampling errors. If each study had an infinite sample size, the sampling error would be zero and the observed effect for each study would be the same as the true effect (Borenstein et al. 2009). In our case, the observed effect (E_i) for any study is given by population mean (μ) plus sampling error in that study (ε_i) defined as:

$$E_i = \mu + \varepsilon_i \quad (3)$$

While the error in any given study is random, one can estimate the sampling distribution of the errors. The width of the normal curve is based on the standard error. The smaller the sample size the higher the variance and width. The weight assigned to each study/effect size is the inverse of the variance of within studies as given by:

$$W_i = \frac{1}{V_{E_i}} = \frac{1}{SE_E^2} \quad (4)$$

A random-effects model allows the true effect to vary from study to study. There may be different effect sizes underlying different studies. The observed effect E_i for any study is given by the grand mean (μ) plus deviation of the study's true effect from the grand mean (ζ_i) and deviation of the study's observed effect from the study's true effect (ε_i) given as (Borenstein et al. 2009):

$$E_i = \mu + \zeta_i + \varepsilon_i \tag{5}$$

Therefore, to predict how far the observed effect E_i is likely to fall from μ in any given study one needs to consider both within-studies variance $\left(sigma\ squared, \sigma_\varepsilon^2\right)$ and between-studies variance $\left(known\ as\ tau\ squared, \tau^2\right)$. The weight assigned to the effect size given below is the inverse of the sum of variances of both terms:

$$W_i = \frac{1}{\text{SE}_{\bar{E}}^2 + \tau^2} \tag{6}$$

The between-studies variance (τ^2) is the variance of effect size parameters across the population of studies. Since one cannot observe the true effects, it is not possible to compute this variance directly. Instead, it is estimated from the observed effects with the estimate denoted by T^2. The most common method for estimating T^2 is the method of moments which is given by (Borenstein et al. 2009):

$$T^2 = \frac{Q - \text{df}}{C} \tag{7}$$

where $Q = \sum w_i E_i^2 - \frac{\left(\sum w_i E_i\right)^2}{\sum w_i}$ and $C = \sum w_i - \frac{\sum w_i^2}{\sum w_i}$

The difference (Q–df) represents dispersion in true effects on a standardized scale. Dividing it by a quantity (C) has the effect of putting the measure back into its original metric and of making it an average rather than a sum of squared deviations.

While the actual variance of the true effects (τ^2) can never be less than zero, the estimate of this value can be less than zero if the observed variance is less than the within-study error. That is, if Q < df, then T^2 is simply set to zero. If Q > df, then T^2 will be positive and it will be based on two factors. The first is the amount of excess variation (Q–df) and the second is the metric of the effect size index (C).

For a study which accumulates data from a series of other studies that were done by researchers operating independently, it is unlikely that all the studies are functionally equivalent. Typically, subjects or interventions in these studies will differ in ways that will have impacted on results and therefore one cannot assume a common effect size. In such a situation, the random-effects model will be more easily justifiable than a fixed-effects model (Borenstein et al. 2009). However, a test is needed to verify the type of model to be used.

3.3 Pre-Estimation Tests

3.3.1 Homogeneity Test

A homogeneity test is performed to determine if there is a common population effect size for an observed sample. The test statistic is measured as the sum of the weighted difference between the summary effect measure and the measure of effect from each study (Petitti 2000). It helps in identifying the type of model to be used and its underlying assumptions for analysis.

$$Q_T = \sum w_i (E_i - \overline{E})^2 = \sum w_i (E_i)^2 - \frac{(\sum w_i E_i)^2}{\sum w_i} \qquad (8)$$

Under the null hypothesis of homogeneity, Q_T follows a Chi-square distribution with $k-1$ degrees of freedom, where k is the number of effect sizes in the sample. Large values of Q_T indicate that observed studies likely come from multiple populations (Petitti 2000).

3.3.2 Relevance of Moderators' Test

If the test of homogeneity shows that if the random-effects model is a justifiable model for the analysis, then effect sizes significantly vary across studies and hence there are factors which explain these variations.

The reasons for the variations are explained by variables known as moderators. Several characteristics of each study are used as moderators to examine whether the variations of an effect are influenced by them (Lyons 1995).

Moderators are identified on the basis of three criteria: basic study characteristics, differences in theoretical constructs and major methodological variations. Once a moderator is identified, its relevance is evaluated with a test. Different test statistics are used for categorical and continuous moderators (DeCoster 2004).

If a moderator is a categorical variable its relevance is determined by between-studies' homogeneity statistics (Q_B). Q_T (given by Eq. 8) is split into two parts: the variability that can be explained by a moderator (Q_B) and the variability that cannot (Q_W). Q_B is calculated as (DeCoster 2004):

$$Q_B = \sum w_j (M_j - \overline{M})^2 \qquad (9)$$

where, $\overline{M}_j$ is the mean of group j moderator, the weight being the inverse of its variance. Large values of Q_B indicate that a moderator can predict a significant amount of the variability contained in an effect size. Even though the test does not tell how large is large (DeCoster 2004), a moderator is relevant if the variability it can explain is bigger than the variability that it cannot ($Q_B > Q_W$).

If a moderator is a continuous variable, the following test statistic is used to evaluate its relevance (DeCoster 2004):

$$Z = \frac{b_j}{s_{b_j}}, \text{ given; } s_{b_j} = \frac{u_{b_j}}{\sqrt{MSE}} \qquad (10)$$

where, u_{b_j} is the standard error of the slope provided by the computer software and MSE is the mean square error of the model for a moderator j. s_{b_j} is the calculated standard error. b_j is the coefficient of moderator j. The test statistic Z follows the standard normal distribution. Large values of Z indicate that there is a significant linear relationship between effect size and a moderator.

3.4 Meta Regression

A heteroskedasticity adjusted model for regression in a meta-analysis is defined as (Horvath et al. 2013):

$$\frac{\text{pcc}_{ij}}{SE_{ij}} = a_0 \frac{1}{SE_{ij}} + a_1 + \sum_{k=1}^{K} \frac{\gamma_k Z_{ijk}}{SE_{ij}} + \alpha_i + \varepsilon_{ij} \quad (11)$$

$\frac{\text{pcc}_{ij}}{SE_{ij}}$ refers to an effect size or partial correlation coefficient (pcc_{ij}) of study 'i' in the jth regression adjusted by its standard error (SE_{ij}). $\frac{1}{SE_{ij}}$ measures the precision of each study. Z represents a set of moderators which include *PERIOD, YEARS, COUNTRIES, PARAMETERS, DATA-TYPE, DATA-FREQUENCY, METHOD, PUBLICATION, PROXY, IMPACT* and *DEVELOPMENT* for k-studies. α_i is an unobserved study specific factor.

Let the ratio $\frac{\text{pcc}_{ij}}{SE_{ij}}$ be represented by upper case PCC_{ij} and $\frac{1}{SE_{ij}}$ by *PRECISION*, then:

$$PCC_{ij} = a_1 + a_0 PRECISION_{ij} + \sum_{k=1}^{K} \frac{\gamma_k Z_{ijk}}{SE_{\text{pcc}_{ij}}} + \alpha_i + \varepsilon_{ij} \quad (12)$$

PCC_{ij} refers to the partial correlation coefficient and is the dependent variable. It is measured by the t-statistic of the Balassa term adjusted for degrees of freedom. Regression of PCC_{ij} helps determine fators/moderators which explain the degree of linear association between productivity growth and the real exchange rate. This is what is referred to as the effect size in a meta-analysis.

Among the continous variables *PRECISION* refers to the inverse of standard error, *PERIOD* refers to the length of the study period, *YEARS* implies number of years in a study, *COUNTRIES* refers to the total number of countries in a study and *PARAMETERS* refers to the number of explanatory variables used in a primary study.

Among the categorical variables *DATA-TYPE* takes a value of 1 if it is panel and 0 otherwise, *DATA-FREQUENCY* takes a value of 1 if it is annual and 0 otherwise, *METHOD* takes a value of 1 if the estimation method involves a co-integration analysis and 0 otherwise, *PUBLICATION* takes a value of 1 if it is published and 0 otherwise, *PROXY* takes a value of 1 if it is total factor productivity and 0 otherwise, *IMPACT* takes a value of 1 if it is direct[3] and 0 otherwise, *DEVELOPMENT* takes a value of 1 if a country in a study is developed and 0 otherwise.

We used the comprehensive meta-analysis (CMA) version 3 for the descriptive and econometric analyses. The use of multiple estimates from the same study may cause a correlation. Mixed effects multi-level methods were employed to reduce the problem of correlation. The regression analysis was preceded by a correlation analysis to see if there was any multicollinearity among the moderators.

3.5 Post-Estimation Test: Publication Bias

Publication bias refers to a meta-analysis' problem which arises because of likely use of mainly published sources/studies. This is because studies with statistically significant results are more likely to be published than studies that report results that are not statistically significant. Even among published studies, those which are in non-English languages, are not easily accessible (costly), unfamiliar and of lower frequency of duplication and citations may not be included; these result in a publication bias (Borenstein et al. 2009). Such studies are called missing studies. The existence of a publication bias is inevitable, although possibly small. Thus, our main objective was to correct for this problem and evaluate if the change significantly affected the results.

A common step to deal with a publication bias is to start with an informal inspection for the presence of the problem using a funnel plot. In our study the effect size was plotted against precision (inverse of standard errors). Large studies with higher precision appear towards the top of the graph and generally cluster around the mean effect size.

---

[3]Direct impact refers to the external version of the Balassa hypothesis which defines the real exchange rate directly in terms of productivity. The other version is called the internal Balassa hypothesis. It defines the real exchange rate indirectly in terms of relative price as a function of productivity.

Smaller studies appear towards the bottom of the graph and tend to spread across a broad range of values. An asymmetrical plot presents a suspect for publication bias. The most powerful formal test for a publication bias is the one given by Egger's test of the intercept. It helps assess a bias by using precision (the inverse of standard error) to predict the standardized effect (effect size divided by standard error):

$$\frac{\text{pcc}_{ij}}{SE_{ij}} = a_0 \frac{1}{SE_{ij}} + a_1 + \varepsilon_{ij} \quad (13)$$

where, the size of an effect is captured by the slope of a regression line while publication bias is captured by the intercept.

Once the presence of a publication bias is indicated, the next step is to quantify it and determine whether it has a significant impact on effect size. For that, two types of tests are used. One is the classic fail-safe N test which helps determine if one needs to be concerned that the entire observed effect may be an artefact of bias. The number of missed studies that are required to nullify the effect is computed. If this number is relatively large compared to the identified studies one can be confident that an effect, while possibly inflated by the exclusion of some studies is nevertheless not nil. The second is the Duval and Tweedie's Trim and Fill test which is an iterative procedure for identifying missing studies and re-commuting an effect size (Borenstein et al. 2002). If the magnitude of the mean effect size significantly changes after inclusion of the missing studies then the mean effect size calculated earlier is doubtful.

4 Empirical Investigation

4.1 Test Results

The results of the homogeneity test for our study show that the sample followed a standard normal distribution since the number of effect sizes was greater than 100. With the degrees of freedom greater than 100 (145 in our case), the expression for Chi-square distribution $(2\chi^2 - (2k - 1) = z)$ follows a standard normal distribution where k represents the degree of freedom. The null of heterogeneity is tested for

Table 1 List of proposed moderators by different criteria (Source DeCoster 2004)

Type of variable	Study characteristics	Theoretical constructs	Methodological variations
Categorical variables	– Data type	– Type of proxy	– Estimation method
	– Data frequency	– Type of impact	
	– Publication type	– Level of development	
Continuous variables	– Sample size (precision)		
	– Length of study period		
	– Number of years		
	– Number of countries		
	– Number of parameters		

a mean effect size weighted with an inverse variance under fixed effects assumption. The results of the Q_T – statistic ($Q_T = 164.557$) with df = 144 and p-value $= 0.1156$ prove that the series are *not homogeneous*. This means variability across effect sizes does exceed what would be expected based on a sampling error. Therefore, the series and analysis are better explained/represented by the random-effects model.

A random-effects model assumes that effect sizes significantly vary across studies. Using Eq. (5), the calculated between-studies variance for the sample studies is determined to be significantly different from 0 ($T^2 = 0.024$). This implies that the weight used in the random effect model should be $W_s = \frac{1}{SE_{\bar{E}}^2 + 0.024}$ in line with Eq. (6).

Based on basic study characteristics, differences in theoretical constructs and major methodological variations criteria, the variables in Table 1 are proposed as possible moderators (both categorical and continuous) for the sample studies.

The results in Table 2 help in the selection of the best/relevant moderators among the proposed ones for the model in our study (both categorical and continuous).

The quality of the model is improved after exclusion of irrelevant moderators. The regression results including all moderators are given in Table 9.

Table 2 Test of inclusion for categorical and continuous moderators (*Source* Author's computation)

Categorical variables	Q_B-statistic	Continuous variables	z-statistic
Data type	0.61	Precision	8.24***
Data frequency	18.24***	Period	−4.96***
Method	20.95***	Years	−3.38**
Publication	0.70	Countries	7.18***
Proxy	0.01	Parameters	−3.17**
Impact	1.70		
Development	29.83***		

Note Significant at 5% (**) and 1% (***) levels of significance

Table 3 Summary statistics of sample studies (45) (*Source* Author's computation)

Variable	Obs.	Mean	Std. Dev.	Min	Max
PCC	145	0.9140	0.1411	0.1147	0.9993
PRECISION	145	6.6070	25.0823	−182.75	66.6234
PERIOD	145	49.6689	42.2866	1	142
YEARS	145	23.6551	12.4769	1	40
COUNTRIES	145	31.4138	36.5343	1	186
PARAMETERS	145	3.6552	2.2059	2	10
DATA-FREQUENCY	145	0.6621	0.4746	0	1
METHODS	145	0.6689	0.4722	0	1
DEVELOPMENT	145	0.3034	0.4613	0	1

4.2 Findings

4.2.1 Descriptive Statistics

Sample studies are symbolized by eight moderators—five continuous and three categorical. A total of 145 coefficients were called from 45 studies for the final analysis. A study may be represented by more than three coefficients on average. Summary statistics of sample studies are given in Table 3.

Since the homogeneity test implied that the sample studies were not homogeneous our study did not focus on the effect sizes of individual studies. Instead, the *mean* of effect sizes is reported.

However, we used two types of means for effect size: within-studies variance weighted mean (the fixed-effects model) and within-studies and between-studies variance weighted mean (the random-effects model). Table 4 provides final values after the z-scores were transformed back to correlation coefficients.

Table 4 Descriptive statistics of effect sizes (*Source* Author's own computation)

Statistics	Fixed effects	Random effects
Mean	0.796	0.819
Lower limit (95% confidence interval)	0.772	0.784
Upper limit (95% confidence interval)	0.818	0.849
z-test	34.025***	22.995***
Homogeneity test (Q_T) Ho: Heterogeneous studies (*p*-value)	164.557 (0.116)	
Tau-squared	0.024	

The random-effects model provides an appropriate result (shown in the last column in Table 4) given the use of non-homogeneous sample studies. However, mean effect sizes are almost the same across cases. The mean effect in the sample studies is about 0.819 under the random-effects model. A mean effect size above 0.33[4] in absolute value represents a strong relationship (Doucouliagos 2011). Even if it is over-estimated due to a publication bias, the effect is still strong since it falls in the upper limit of the criteria. Therefore, one can conclude that on average, 81.90 percent of the effect of the impact because of per unit percentage change in productivity (economic) growth is transmitted to the real exchange rate of countries in the sample studies. It is near the one-to-one correspondence as stated in the Balassa hypothesis. This shows the strength of the effect/relationship and emphasizes the necessity of doing a further analysis of the Balassa hypothesis.

4.2.2 Meta Regression Results

The results of a regression with a meta-analysis are given in Table 5. The table excludes *DATA-FREQUENCY* which is highly correlated with *PERIOD* and most of the other variables. It shows that the most common (significant) reasons for variations in effect size across studies are *PRECISION* (sample size), *PARAMETER* (number of explanatory variables) and *METHOD* (estimation method) at least at the 5 percent level

---

[4]A value between 0.33 and 0.17 represents a medium level effect and a value between 0.17 and 0.07 represents a weak effect. A value less than 0.07 is assumed to be insignificant.

Table 5 Meta-regression results (excluding irrelevant moderators) (Source Author's computation)

Explanatory variables	PCC is dependent variable		
	Coefficients	z-value	p-value
PRECISION	0.0105	4.99	0.0000
PERIOD	0.0001	0.07	0.9472
YEARS	0.0040	0.81	0.4171
COUNTRIES	0.0003	0.14	0.8867
PARAMETER	−0.0497	−2.10	0.0358
METHOD	0.3055	1.97	0.0484
DEVELOPMENT	0.3578	1.57	0.1170
Intercept	0.5118	1.53	0.1260

of significance. These moderators together explain about 63.86 percent of the variations in effect size across studies. Effect size increases with *PRECISION* and *METHOD* and decreases with *PARAMETER*, that is, the level of the impact of a change in productivity on the real exchange rate (effect size) is higher in: (a) studies with larger sample sizes (higher precision), (b) studies which use the co-integration method of estimation, and (c) studies with a smaller number of parameters in the estimated model (higher degree of freedom).

Considering only models with highly relevant moderators [*high Q_T – stat.*], increases the goodness of fit to about 73.14 percent but reduces the number of moderators that explain the variations in effect size to two: *PRECISION* and *METHOD* (Table 6). The other moderators do not matter in explaining variations in effect size across studies or are not statistically significant. The model does not lose information when less relevant moderators are excluded from the analysis.

Table 6 Meta-regression results (excluding insignificant moderators) (Source Author's computation)

Explanatory variables	PCC is dependent variable		
	Coefficients	z-value	p-value
PRECISION	0.0119	5.82	0.0000
YEARS	0.0001	0.00	0.9979
COUNTRIES	0.0008	0.46	0.6477
DATA-FREQ	−0.0218	−0.22	0.8257
METHOD	0.3141	2.17	0.0298
Intercept	0.6321	4.19	0.0000

The regression results of a model which includes all proposed moderators is given in Table 10. Moderators which do not pass the $Q_T - stat.$ test are found to be insignificant in this model. The goodness of fit of the model is less than 50 percent which means the moderators do not explain even half of the variations in effect size.

4.2.3 Post-Estimation Test

The funnel plot of the sample studies is shown by Fig. 1 in which the effect size is plotted against precision (the inverse of standard errors). Figure 1 indicates the presence of a publication bias since the funnel plot is not symmetrical to the mean and is skewed to the right at the bottom. It shows that there are more small studies on the right than on the left and some are missing from the left. There is also a high concentration of smaller studies with widely dispersed effect sizes at the bottom.

Egger's formal test of publication bias indicates the presence of a publication bias. Using Eq. (11), the estimated regression for the sample studies shows that the intercept is significant ($a_1 = 0.727$ with $Z = 13.47^{***}$) and hence there is a publication bias. But this does not

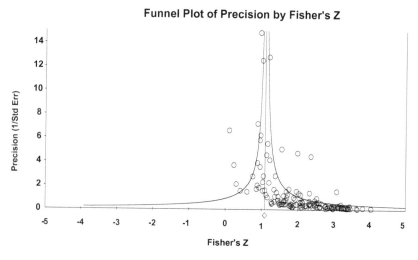

Fig. 1 Funnel plot of 45 sample studies (*Source* Author's computation)

mean that an effect does not exist. In fact, the same regression results show that the coefficient for the slope is also significant ($a_0 = 0.0124$ with $Z = 8.24$***) (see Table 11). Hence, an effect size does exist though it may be biased (over-estimated) due to the existing publication bias. This outcome also matches the results of the classic fail-safe N and Duval and Tweedie's Trim and Fill tests.

The results of the classic fail-safe N test suggest that 5849 studies were missing from the sample. Given that only 143 studies on the Balassa hypothesis were identified for the initial meta-analysis, it is unlikely that these many studies are missing. It is, therefore, most unlikely that the actual effect is zero or the impact of the identified publication bias is meaningful.

Duval and Tweedie's Trim and Fill test also conveys the same fact. Figure 2 provides an intuitive visual display of a funnel plot that includes both observed and imputed studies. The results of this test show that 68 studies (observations) are missing from the sample. Figure 2 is a funnel plot including the imputed studies (● sign) missing from Fig. 1.

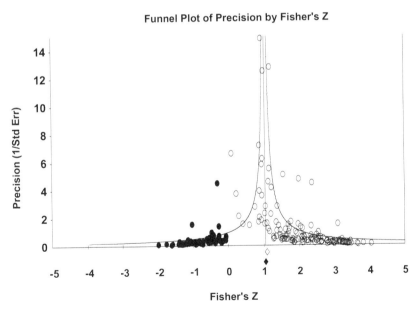

Fig. 2 Funnel plot of sample studies including missing studies (*Source* Author's computation)

The '●' signs on the lower left-hand side show the distribution of missing studies. After adjustments for publication bias, the point estimate changes from 0.819 to 0.7868 under the random-effects model.

The goal of a publication bias analysis is to classify the results of a meta-analysis into one of the following three categories: (a) where the impact of the bias is trivial, (b) where the impact is not trivial but the major findings are still valid, and (c) where the major findings might be called into question (Borenstein et al. 2009). Our meta-analysis falls within the second category. Even though there is evidence of a publication bias, there is no reason to doubt the validity of the core findings (Table 7).

Table 7 Point estimates adjusted for publication bias

Values	Observed values	Adjusted values	Q-value
Fixed effects	0.79567	0.77953	164.557
Random effects	0.81903	0.78678	227.027

5 Conclusion and Policy Recommendations

5.1 Conclusion

The results of our empirical investigation showed that the mean effect size was 0.7868. Other things remaining the same, 78.68 percent of the effect of the change in productivity growth was reflected on the level of the real exchange rate for countries in the sample. The test for publication bias showed that this level of mean effect size did exist after correcting for the problem. The magnitude was initially inflated (biased). Hence, the actual mean effect size decreased from 81.03 percent to 78.68 percent after adjustments for a publication bias.

The results of the analysis in our study match the findings of Tica and Druzic (2006) and Egert and Halpern's (2005) studies to some extent. Like the findings in our study, the variables *PARAMETER* and *METHOD* were significant in both the previous studies. However, unlike our study the variables *COUNTRIES* and *PROXY* were significant in the previous studies. In contrast to the previous studies, our study found *PRECISION* as an additional variable which explained the variations in effect size. This result may be due to differences in the use of different moderators. Previous studies with different compositions of moderators may provide different results. Moderators emanate from the characteristics of the previous studies such as methodologies, objectives and sample sizes.

Our study also shows that different outcomes (mean effect size) may be derived from the same study on the Balassa hypothesis by varying the sample size (precision), estimation method and the number of parameters in the previous studies.

In conclusion, our findings assert the relevance of doing a further analysis/study on the Balassa hypothesis. Given a reasonably significant mean effect size in our study for the relationship between productivity growth and the real exchange rate, further studies on the Balassa hypothesis are expected to add value to the stock of knowledge.

5.2 Policy Implications

The implications of our findings are that policymakers should take into account the following three main points while recommending any policies regarding the relationship between productivity growth and the real exchange rate on the basis of any given study:

- Whether the study used a relatively large sample of countries. This may actually depend on the nature of data and the purpose of the study.
- Whether the study used a reasonable size of parameters because there is a trade-off between the degree of freedom and the number of parameters.
- Whether the study employed an estimation method which involved co-integration. This is necessary to predict the long run behavior of the two variables together.

Acknowledgements I am grateful for all comments and contributions by Professor Scott Hacker, Professor Par Sjolander and Dr. Girma Estiphanos. Their comments helped improve the paper.

Appendix A

See Tables 8, 9, 10, and 11.

Table 8 Correlation coefficients of relevant moderators

VARIABLES	PERIOD	YEARS	COUNTRIES	PARAMETER	DATA-FREQ	METHOD	DEVELOPMENT	PRECISION
PERIOD	1	−0.610	−0.563	−0.263	0.925	0.263	−0.710	0.123
YEARS	−0.610	1	0.550	0.525	−0.617	−0.671	0.328	−0.011
COUNTRIES	−0.563	0.550	1	0.525	−0.535	−0.034	0.419	0.208
PARAMETERS	−0.264	0.525	0.525	1	−0.266	−0.331	0.261	−0.032
DATA-FREQ	0.925	−0.617	−0.535	−0.266	1	0.417	−0.453	0.018
METHOD	0.263	−0.671	−0.034	−0.331	0.417	1	0.078	−0.020
DEVELOPMENT	−0.710	0.328	0.419	0.260	−0.453	0.078	1	−0.313
PRECISION	0.123	−0.011	0.208	−0.031	0.018	−0.019	−0.313	1

Table 9 Regression results (including all moderators)

Covariate	Coefficient	Standard error	95% lower	95% upper	z-value	2-sided p-value
PRECISION	0.0122	0.0024	0.0075	0.0169	5.11	0
PERIOD	−0.0209	0.0058	−0.0322	−0.0096	−3.62	0.0003
YEARS	0.0242	0.0129	−0.0010	0.0495	1.88	0.0602
COUNTRIES	0.0038	0.0023	−0.0006	0.0083	1.69	0.0919
PARAMETERS	−0.0294	0.0312	−0.0905	0.0317	−0.94	0.3455
DATA-TYPE	−0.2605	0.2268	−0.7050	0.1841	−1.15	0.2508
DATA-FREQ	1.6804	0.4377	0.8226	2.5382	3.84	0.0001
METHOD	0.4533	0.2090	0.0437	0.8630	2.17	0.0301
PUBLICATION	0.1022	0.0840	−0.0623	0.2668	1.22	0.2233
PROXY	−0.0930	0.1354	−0.3584	0.1723	−0.69	0.4920
IMPACT	0.0226	0.1702	−0.3109	0.3562	0.13	0.8943
DEVELOPMENT	−0.1900	0.2781	−0.7350	0.3551	−0.68	0.4946
INTERCEPT	0.7578	0.4719	−0.1670	1.6827	1.61	0.1083

Table 10 Joint test of publication bias

Covariate	Coefficient	Standard error	95% lower	95% upper	z-value	2-sided p-value
Intercept	0.7277	0.054	0.6218	0.8335	13.47	0.0000
PRECISION	0.0124	0.0015	0.0094	0.0153	8.24	0.0000

Table 11 Tests of publication bias

Egger's regression intercept	
Intercept	0.4211
Standard error	0.0960
95% lower limit (2-tailed)	0.2312
95% upper limit (2-tailed)	0.6110
t-value	4.3834
p-value (1-tailed)	0.0000
p-value (2-tailed)	0.0000
Classic fail-safe N	
z-value for observed studies	20.5845
p-value for observed studies	0.0000
Alpha	0.0555
Tails	2.0000
z for alpha	1.9599
Number of observed studies	145

(continued)

Table 11 (continued)

Egger's regression intercept								
Number of missing studies that would brign p-value > alpha			5849					
Orwin's fail-safe N								
Correlation in observed studies			0.7956					
Criterion for a 'trival' correlation			0.0000					
Mean correlation in missing studies			0.0000					
Criterion must fail between other values								
Duval and Tweedie's trim and fill								

	Studies trimmed	Fixed effects			Random effects			Q-value
		Point estimate	Lower limit	Upper limit	Point estimate	Lower limit	Upper limit	
Observed studies		0.7957	0.7715	0.8175	0.8190	0.7839	0.8489	164.56
Adjusted studies	68	0.7795	0.7541	0.8026	0.7868	0.7503	0.8185	227.03

References

Abuaf, N. and P. Jorion (1990). Purchasing Power Parity in the Long Run. *Journal of Finance*, 45(1): 157–174.

Asea, P.K. and E.G. Mendoza (1994). *The Balassa-Samuelson Model: A General Equilibrium Appraisal*. Forthcoming Review of International Economics. Working Paper #709. USA.

Balassa, B. (1964). The Purchasing Power Parity Doctrine: A Reappraisal. *Journal of Political Economy*, 72(6): 584–596.

Bhagwati, J.N. (1984). Why Are Services Cheaper in the Poor Countries? *The Economic Journal*, 94: 279–286, 374.

Borenstein, M., L. Hedges, J. Higgins, and H. Rothstein (2002). *Comprehensive Meta-Analysis Version 3.0*. National Institutes of Health.

Borenstein, M., L.V. Hedges, J.P.T. Higgins, and H. Rothstein (2009). *Introduction to Meta-Analysis*. United Kingdom: Wiley.

Canzoneri, M.B., R.E. Cumby, and B. Diba (1997). *Relative Labour Productivity and Real Exchange Rate in Long Run: Evidence for Panel of OECD Countries*. USA.

Chuah, K.P. (2012). *How Real Exchange Rate Move in Growing Economies: Anti-Balassa Evidence in Developing Countries*. Malaysia. Unpublished, Prepared for the Central Bank of Sri Lanka 6th International Research Conference, 12 December 2013.

Chuoudhri, U.E. and M.S. Kahn (2004). *Real Exchange Rate in Developing Countries: Are Balassa-Samuelson Effect Present?* IMF Working Papers WP/04/188. Malaysia.

Coudert, V. (2004). *Measuring the Balassa-Samuelson Effect for the Countries of Central and Eastern Europe*. Banque de France Bulletin Digest #122.

DeCoster, J. (2004). *Meta-Analysis Notes*. Department of Psychology, University of Alabama.

De Gregorio, J., A. Giovannini, and H. Wolf (1994). *International Evidence on Tradables and Nontradables Inflation*. NBER Working Paper No. 4438.

Doucouliagos, H. (2011). *How large is large? Preliminary and Relative Guidelines for Interpreting Partial Correlations in Economics*, School of Accounting, Economics and Finance Working Paper SWP 2011/5. Deakin University.

Drine, I. and C. Rault (2003). *Do Panel Data Permit to Rescue the Balassa-Samuelson Hypothesis for Latin America Countries?* EUREQua. Panthéon-Sorbonne University (Paris I). Maison des Sciences de l'Economie.

Egert, B. and L. Halpern (2005). *Equilibrium Exchange Rates in Central and Eastern Europe, the CIS and Turkey: A Meta-Analysis.* Institute for Economies in Transition. BOFIT Discussion Papers No. 4. Finland: Bank of Finland.

Faria, J.R. and M.L. Ledesma (2000). *Testing the Balassa-Samuelson Effect: Implication for Growth and PPP.* USA: University of Kent.

Funda, J., G. Lukinic, and I. Ljubaj (2007). *Assessment of the Balassa-Samuelson Effect in Croatia.* Croatia: Croatian National Bank of Zagreb.

Genius, M. and V. Tzouvelekas (2008). *The Balassa-Samuelson Productivity Bias Hypothesis: Further Evidence Using Panel Data.* Greece: University of Crete.

Gubler, M. and C. Sax (2008). *The Balassa-Samuelson Effect Reversed: New Evidence from OECD Countries.* Switzerland: University of Basel.

Guo, Q. and S.G. Hall (2008). A Test of the Balassa-Samuelson Effect Applied to Chinese Regional Data. *Romanian Journal of Economic Forecasting*, 2: 57–78.

Gujarati, D.N. (2004). *Econometric Analysis.* 4th edition.

Herberger, A.C. (2003). *Economic Growth and the Real Exchange Rate: Revising the Balassa-Samuelson Effect.* Los Angeles: University of California.

Hoarau, J.F. (2008). *Long Run Purchasing Power Parity in Eastern and Southern African Countries: Evidence from Panel Data Stationary Tests with Multiple Structural Breaks. CERESUR.* France: University of La Reunion.

Horvath, R. and P. Valickova (2013). *Financial Development and Economic Growth: A Meta-Analysis.* Working Paper 5. Czech National Bank.

Jabeen, S., W.S. Malik, and A. Haider (2011). *Testing the Harrod-Balassa-Samuelson Hypothesis: The Case of Pakistan.* Islamabad: Quaid-i-Azam University.

Johnson, D.R. (1990). Cointegration, Error Correction and Purchasing Power Parity Between Canada and the US. *The Canadian Journal of Economics*, 23(4): 839–855.

Joya, J.O. (2009). *Purchasing Power Parity Breaking Trend Functions in the Real Exchange Rate.* USA: Boston University.

Libsey, M.W. and D.B. Wilson (1999). *Practical Meta-Analysis.* Florida: American Evaluation Association.

Lyons, L.C. (1995). *Meta-Analysis: Methods of Accumulating Results Across Research Domains.* Manassas, VA.

MacDonald, R. and L. Ricci (1998). *The Real Exchange Rate and the Balassa-Samuelson Effect: The Role of the Distributor Sector.* IMF Working Paper 01/38. Scotland: University of Strathclyde and IMF.

Petitti, D. (2000). *Meta-Analysis, Decision Analysis, and Cost Effectiveness Analysis: Methods for Quantitative Synthesis in Medicine.* Oxford: Oxford University Press.

Steigerwald, D.G. (1996). Purchasing Power Parity, Unit Roots and Dynamic Structure. *Journal of Empirical Finance*, 2(4): 343–357.

Tica, J. and I. Druzic (2006). *The Harrod-Balassa-Samuelson Effect: A Survey of Empirical Evidence.* University of Zagreb. Working Paper Series. Paper No. 06-7/686.

Tzilianos, E. (2006). *The Balassa-Samuelson Effect and Europe's Southern Periphery.* Dissertation Paper. New York: Fordham University.

Wilson, E. (2010). *European Real Effective Exchange Rate and Total Factor Productivity: An Empirical Study.* Wellington: Victoria University of Wellington.

List of Sample Studies

Al-Samara (2009). *The Determinants of Real Exchange Rate Volatility in the Syrian Economy.* University Paris 1—Sorbonne.

Alexandru-Chideşciuc and Codirlasu (2004). *Estimating the Harrod-Balassa-Samuelson Effect for Romania.*

Bergin, Glick, and Taylor (2004). *Productivity, Tradability, and the Long-run Price Puzzle.* NBER Working Paper 10569.

Bilyasheva and Bineau (2011). *Real Equilibrium Exchange Rate and Crawling Peg Policy: A Response to Global Instability?* France: Lille1 University.

Biswas and Dasgupta (2012). *Real Exchange Rate Response to Inward Foreign Direct Investment in Liberalized India.* India.

Brandmeier (2006). *Reasons for Real Appreciation in Central Europe.*

Caetano, M. and De Silva (2004). *Big Mac Parity, Income, and Trade.* Department of Economics. Federal University of Rio Grande Do Sul and National Council for Scientific and Technological Development, Brazil.

Camarero (2006). *The Real Exchange Rate of the Dollar for a Panel of OECD Countries: Balassa-Samuelson or Distribution Sector Effect?*

Chuah, K.P. (2012). *How Real Exchange Rate Move in Growing Economies: Anti-Balassa Evidence in Developing Countries.* Malaysia.

Chuoudhri, U.E. and M.S. Kahn (2004). *Real Exchange Rate in Developing Countries: Are Balassa-Samuelson Effect Present?* IMF Working Papers WP/04/188. Malaysia.

Combes, K. and Plane (2010). *Capital Flows and Their Impact on the Real Effective Exchange Rate.* France.

Coto-Martinez and Reboredo (2012). *The Relative Price of Non-traded Goods Under Imperfect Competition. Economics and Finance.* Working Paper Series. Working Paper No. 12–23.

De Gregorio, J. and H. Wolf (1994). *Terms of Trade, Productivity and the Real Exchange Rate.* NBER Working Paper No. 4407. Cambridge, MA and London.

Drine, I. and C. Rault (2003). *Do Panel Data Permit to Rescue the Balassa-Samuelson Hypothesis for Latin America Countries? EUREQua.* Panthéon-Sorbonne University (Paris I). Maison des Sciences de l'Economie. 106–112 boulevard de l'Hôpital. 75647 Paris Cedex 13. France.

Drine, I. and C. Rault (2004). *Does the Balassa-Samuelson Hold for Asian Countries? An Empirical Analysis Using Panel Data Cointegration Tests.* France.

Dumrongrittikul (2011). *Real Exchange Rate Movements in Developed and Developing Economies. An Interpretation of the Balassa-Samuelson's Framework.* Department of Econometrics and Business Statistics, Monash University Australia.

Eckstein and Friedman (2011). *The Equilibrium Real Exchange Rate for Israel.* Bank of Israel.

Egert, B. (2001). *Does the Balassa-Samuelson Effect Matter for Central Europe's Transition Economies During the Run-Up to EMU?* France: University of Paris.

Elbadawi, Kaltani and Schmidt-Hebbel (2006). *Post-Conflict Aid, Real Exchange Rate Adjustment, and Catch-Up Growth.* Development Economic Research Group. Washington, DC: The World Bank.

Fischer, C. (2002), *Real Currency Appreciation in Accession Countries: Balassa-Samuelson and Investment Demand.* Discussion paper 19/02. Economic Research Center of the Deutsche Bundesbank.

Frensch and Schmillen (2010). *Can We Identify Balassa-Samuelson Effects with Measures of Product Variety?* Working Papers.

Gelb, Meyer, and Ramachandran (2013). *Does Poor Mean Cheap? A Comparative Look at Africa's Industrial Labour Costs.*

Genius, M. and V. Tzouvelekas (2008). *The Balassa-Samuelson Productivity Bias Hypothesis: Further Evidence Using Panel Data*, 9(2). Greece: University of Crete.

Gubler, M. and C. Sax (2008). *The Balassa-Samuelson Effect Reversed: New Evidence from OECD Countries.* Switzerland: University of Basel.

Hassan and Holmes (2012). *Remittances and the Real Effective Exchange Rate*. Department of Economics, University of Waikato.

Hau (1999). *Real Exchange Rate Volatility and Economic Openness: Theory and Evidence*.

Ickes, B. (2004). Lecture Note on the Real Exchange Rate. Available at: https://mail.yahoo.com/d/folders/2. Accessed 15 September 2015.

Ildiko (2008). *Exploring the Correlation Between Real Exchange Rate Misalignment and Economic Growth in the CEE Countries*. Bucharest: The Academy of Economic Studies, The Faculty of Finance, Insurance, Banking and Stock Exchange.

Ito, I. and Symansky (1997). *Economic Growth and Real Exchange Rate: An Overview of the Balassa-Samuelson Hypothesis in Asia*. NBER Working Paper 5979.

Jabeen, S., W.S. Malik, and A. Haider (2011). *Testing the Harrod-Balassa-Samuelson Hypothesis: The Case of Pakistan*. Islamabad: Quaid-i-Azam University.

Jeanneney, S.G. and P. Hua (2002). *Does the Balassa-Samuelson Effect Apply to the Chinese Provinces?* CERDI-IDREC. France: CNRS-University of Auvergne.

Karadi and Koren (2008). *A Spatial Explanation for the Balassa–Samuelson Effect*. New York University.

Kohler, M. (1998). *The Balassa-Samuelson Effect and Monetary Targets*. Centre for Central Banking Studies, Bank of England.

Kravis, I.B. and R.E. Lipsey (1983). *Towards an Explanation of National Price Levels*. Princeton Studies in International Finance. No. 52. USA: Princeton University.

MacDonald, R. and C. Wojcik (2003). *Catching-Up: The Role of Demand, Supply and Regulated Price Effects on the Real Exchange Rates of Four Accession Countries*. Glasgow, Scotland: University of Strathclyde.

Miletić, M. (2011). *Estimating the Impact of the Balassa-Samuelson Effect in Central and Eastern European Countries: A Revised Analysis of Panel Data Cointegration Tests*. Serbia: National Bank of Serbia. *Panoeconomicus*. 2012. 4: 475–499. UDC 336.748:338.124.4 (4).

Miller, N. and V. Pollock (1994). 'Meta-analytic Synthesis for Theory Development', in H. Cooper, and L. Hedges (eds.), *The Handbook of Research Synthesis*. New York: Russell Sage Foundation, pp. 457–483.

Mollick and Quijano (2004). *The Mexican Peso and the Korean Won Real Exchange Rates: Evidence from Productivity Models*. ITESM-Campus Monterrey.

Montecino (2015). *Capital Controls and the Real Exchange Rate: Do Controls Promote Disequilibria?* University of Massachusetts.

Peltonen, T. and M. Sager (2009). *Productivity Shocks and Real Exchange Rates: A Reappraisal.*

Ravallion (2010). *Price Levels and Economic Growth: Making Sense of the PPP Changes Between ICP Rounds.* The World Bank Development Research Group. Policy Research Working Paper.

Rodrik, D. (2008). *The Real Exchange Rate and Economic Growth.* Harvard University.

Sallenave (2010). *Real Exchange Rate Misalignments and Economic Performance for the G20 Countries.* Économie Internationale 121.

Tintin, C. (2008). *Testing the Balassa-Samuelson Hypothesis: Evidence from 10 OECD Countries.* Department of Economics, Lund University, Sweden.

Tzilianos, E. (2006). *The Balassa-Samuelson Effect and Europe's Southern Periphery.* Dissertation Paper. New York: Fordham University.

Vieira, F. and R. MacDonald (2012). A Panel Data Investigation of Real Exchange Rate Misalignment and Growth. *Estudos Economicos* 42(3): July/September Issue.

Yan, A. and V. Kakkar (2010). *The Equilibrium Real Exchange Rate of China: A Productivity Approach.* Hong Kong: City University of Hong Kong.

11

The Balance of Trade-Economic Growth Nexus in a Panel of Member Countries of the East African Community

Ferdinand Nkikabahizi, Theogene Rizinde and Mathias Karangwa

1 Introduction

This paper examines the economic status and external position of five member countries of the East African Community (EAC). The relationship between the percentage of annual growth rate of real GDP and a balance of trade, exports, imports, exchange rate, labor force participation rate, gross capital formation and foreign direct investment (FDI) inflows

F. Nkikabahizi (✉)
School of Economics, University of Rwanda, College of Business and Economics, Butare, Rwanda

T. Rizinde
School of Economics, Department of Statistics, University of Rwanda, College of Business and Economics, Butare, Rwanda

M. Karangwa
National Bank of Rwanda, Kigali, Rwanda

© The Author(s) 2018
A. Heshmati (ed.), *Determinants of Economic Growth in Africa*,
https://doi.org/10.1007/978-3-319-76493-1_11

are control variables for the i-th country at year t as they affect the least developed countries (LDCs). The dummy variable represents the measure of regional economic integration at time t in country i for analyzing whether being a member of EAC could have an impact on GDP.

The integration of countries into the world economy is often regarded as an important determinant of the differences in income and growth across countries. Economic theory has identified the well-known channels through which trade can have an effect on growth. More specifically, trade is believed to promote the efficient allocation of resources, allow a country to realize economies of scale and scope, facilitate the diffusion of knowledge, foster technological progress and encourage competition both in domestic and international markets that leads to an optimization of the production processes and to the development of new products (Busse and Königer 2012).

Various authors have discussed the theory of economic integration and why economic integration is formed between members. Salvatore (2006) notes that the theory of economic integration can be regarded as a commercial policy of discriminatively reducing or eliminating trade barriers (technical and non-technical) only between the states joining together. Discussing the main inspiration for economic integration, Salvatore (2006) notes that the main motivation for regional integration is eliminating trade and non-trade barriers among member countries while maintaining a common tariff for non-members thus promoting intra-regional trade and sheltering domestic firms from damaging external competition.

Iyoha (2005) notes that high levels of regional economic integration result in accelerated economic growth in the end as countries commit to joining regional economic blocs to reap the benefits associated with free trade. Besides promoting intra-regional trade, free trade among member states also leads to higher economic growth. Given the features of economic integration, notably increased market size, exploitation of economies of scale, increased competition, accelerated technology transfers and increased investments, free trade among member states also leads to maximizing the benefits of pro-growth rates. Free trade in such an environment portends long-run dynamic effects on member states' economic growth thus bringing forth positive wealth effects for citizens.

However, formation of a common market is generally the lowest level of potential regional collaboration arrangements. In addition to free trade, intra-regional trade or the highest stage of economic integration also involves broader issues such as the creation of a political federation, adoption of a single currency and ensuring perfect labor and capital mobility. Except for the US, reaching the final stage of regional integration has remained a dream for many other economic blocs (Daniels et al. 2004).

While researcher and policymakers view regional integration as beneficial, its benefits require an enabling environment. For example, regional cooperation becomes easy if there is political will among member states and if the people in the region share a common history, language, culture and infrastructure. Joint investment projects like those in infrastructure pave the way for meaningful economic integration. However, the formation of a political federation remains a dream in case political differences exist among member states or if individual interests rather than overall interests of the region drive the member states. For EAC to take advantage of existing conditions like the people sharing a common history, language, culture and infrastructure (EAC 2002), member countries need to take note of their differences in political, economic and individual interests. This will facilitate successful economic integration capable of leading to, for the first time in the history of the EAC, a successful political federation.

The overall objective of our paper is to assess how openness may constitute an engine for accelerating the economy and the extent to which each macroeconomic variable promotes the economies in East African countries.

2 Literature Review

There is scare empirical literature analyzing the relationship between balance of trade and economic growth, especially in EAC member countries. Balance of trade is one of the key components of a country's gross domestic product (GDP) formula. GDP increases when the total value of goods and services that domestic producers sell to foreigners exceeds the total value of foreign goods and services that domestic consumers buy; it is otherwise known as a trade surplus. If domestic consumers spend more on foreign products than domestic producers sell to foreign consumers—a trade deficit—then GDP decreases. Very few subjects in economics have caused as much confusion and debate as balance of trade. This confusion is driven by the language involved in reporting a country's net trade in final goods; 'trade deficit' sounds bad while 'trade surplus' sounds good.

2.1 Trade, Balance of Trade (Surplus & Deficit) and Growth of the Economy

Economic literature has established a connection between trade and growth (Chatterji et al. 2013; Lee and Huang 2012; Steiner et al. 2014). Empirically, it has been difficult to establish the association between them. Though there is growing theoretical evidence of positive relationships between trade and growth in many developed nations, such relationships have not been proven empirically in developing nations, particularly among African countries (see, for example, Edwards 1993). Our paper seeks to establish the long-run empirical relationship between trade and economic growth in EAC member countries using the co-integration technique. Establishing this long run relationship is important because it allows for deviations in the short run when adjustment mechanisms for variables to their equilibrium values take place. Chatterji et al. (2013) maintain that the relationship between trade and growth does not establish a cause and effect because as economies grow, they trade more and become more open.

Some scholars relate trade to investments and the resulting growth; they argue that relaxing foreign exchange controls may increase investment opportunities as an increase in investments brings about new technologies that could improve a country's economic growth. Such investment opportunities can be facilitated by creating trading opportunities and an environment that can attract multinational companies (Marrewijk 2012; Rodriguez and Rodrik 1999). Levine and Renelt (1992) and Levine and Zervos (1993) also found a robust two chain link between trade and growth for Central and Southern African countries. Their studies show a positive robust correlation between economic growth and the share of investment in GDP. A positive and robust correlation between investment share and the ratio of trade to GDP is also evident in their studies. Similarly, Ndulu and Njuguna (1998) estimated a growth model using GDP as the dependent variable and trade and trade policy variables as explanatory variables. Their results show that trade matters to economic growth, but macroeconomic variables like the real exchange rate too have a strong influence on economic growth as they indirectly affect imports and exports. They also found that investments affected economic growth directly but investments were also affected by trade policies.

Ndulu and Njuguna's (1998) results also show that trade openness through trade liberalization is crucial for realizing a positive relationship between trade and growth in Southern Africa. Abbas (2013) notes that trade deficit has a negative effect on the economy. His study focused on the effect of trade deficit on Pakistan's economy and he states that trade deficit had a major harmful effect on the country's economy.

Empirical studies, beginning with Balassa's (1978) work and continuing throughout the 1980s, provide virtually uncontested evidence of a positive relationship between exports and economic growth in a large number of developing countries and for different periods of time. Similar arguments are given by Michaely (1977). He used simple correlation techniques; a positive correlation between exports and economic growth was inevitable since exports are a part of GDP. Undoubtedly, there is a linkage between each of the control variables and real economic growth.

2.2 Export-Growth Nexus

The relationship between export growth and economic growth has been a popular subject of debate among development economists. The relationship between economic growth and exports which form an important component of international trade has attracted the attention of many scholars. Most of the studies conclude that exports have a positive impact on economic growth (Ullah et al. 2009) and broadly speaking, export growth can promote economic growth and vice versa. Huilee and Nung-Huang (2002) emphasize the export-led-growth hypothesis to justify the benefits of regional integration. For them increased exports enable a country to get more export receipts which can be used for financing investments resulting in higher capital formation and thus higher total factor productivity. In addition, an increase in export receipts helps ease exchange rate pressures and inflation in general. Further, domestic firms need to be highly competitive to increase exports and this is often attained through the adoption of production cost-minimization strategies including the use of modern production technologies and efficient resource allocation to be able to keep pace with overseas competition. Growth in exports also helps garner enough foreign exchange needed for increased imports of capital goods, a requirement for most developing economics to spur rapid economic growth.

The export-growth hypothesis assumes that causality should only run from exports to economic growth. However, reverse causality is possible, whereby economic booms lead to an increase in exports. This is especially so for economies that attract huge sums of foreign direct investments as these often come with spillover effects in the form of advanced production technologies and capital accumulation. These may result in higher productive capacity for the country without any contemporaneous dependence on exports. An increase in domestic production in turn creates a strong base for raising exports. Another possible explanation of the growth-export nexus is the fact that for most developing countries exports depend on the level of aggregate demand in big economies. Once global aggregate demand is low, as it has been since 2015, export revenues from developing nations shrink. Although export led growth has been investigated intensively empirically, the uni- or bi-direction of causality is still under debate (see, for example, Jung and Marshall, 1985). Stolper (1947) and Tekin (2012) note that the export-led hypothesis has been one of the most studied issues and most literature shows that growth in exports positively affects economic growth through what is termed as the 'foreign trade multiplier.'

As one of the components of the country's expenditure function, an increase in export revenues leads to more spending, especially on imports. As the incremental capacity to spend increases, it positively affects the willingness to import an extra unit of a particular good/service. For economies with meager savings, export revenues are important sources of foreign exchange to finance the imports of both intermediate and capital goods to facilitate economic transformation. Export oriented economic activities induce re-allocation of scarce resources from low-productivity domestic industries to higher-productivity export industries resulting in higher economic growth. Countries with aggressive export-oriented economies tend to strive for the attainment of an efficient big market with sizable economies of scale that can help accelerate capital formation and technical change (Reppas and Christopoulos, 2005).

2.3 Import-Growth Nexus

According to Uğur (2008), quoted by Rivera-Batiz (1985), an increase in economic activity will induce an increase in imports because high real income promotes consumption. In this regard, there is a direct connection between economic growth and imports. In theory, it is widely argued that there is a two-way causal relationship between exports and economic growth. Consequently, extensive empirical literature exists on the relationship between exports and growth. Yet, relative to the empirical literature on exports and economic growth, the number of empirical studies on the relationship between imports and economic growth is quite limited because the theoretical relationship between imports and economic growth tends to be more complicated than the one between exports and economic growth. Demand for imports is determined by both economic and non-economic factors. These generally include exchange rates and/or relative prices, economic activity, domestic and external economic conditions, production and/or labor costs and political circumstances. However, relative prices and real income are the major factors that significantly affect demand for imports.

Different scholars have emphasized the importance of imports as an important channel for foreign technology and knowledge to flow into the domestic economy. The use of recent endogenous growth models shows that imports can be a channel for long-run economic growth because they provide domestic firms with access to needed intermediate and foreign technology (see, for example, Coe and Helpman 1995; Grossman and Helpman 1991; Lee 1995; Mazumdar 2000). A growth in imports can serve as a medium for the transfer of growth-enhancing foreign R&D knowledge from developed to developing countries' (Lawrence and Weinstein 1999; Mazumdar 2000). New technologies could be embodied in imports of intermediate goods such as machines and equipment and labor productivity could increase over time as workers acquire the knowledge to 'unbundle' the new embodied technologies (Thangavelu and Rajaguru 2004).

Further, it is widely recognized that imports play a central role in countries whose manufacturing base is built on export oriented industries (see, for example, Esfahani 1991; Liu et al. 1997; Riezman et al. 1996; Serletis 1992). If foreign exchange accumulation is sufficient, economic growth is promoted by importing high quality goods and services, which in turn expand production possibilities (Baharumshah and Rashid 1999).

According to Gwaindepi et al. (2014) imports are also intricately linked to economic growth even though there are two competing effects on the demand and supply sides. On the demand side, imports are seen as a leakage which constrains economic growth, but import constraints are eased with trade liberalization coupled with efficiency gains on the supply side. Gwaindepi et al. (2014) as quoted in Mishra (2012) claim that empirical evidence on the nexus between imports and economic growth is rather mixed and inconclusive. If increased GDP is always a source of finance for imports then it can constrain growth and can have a negative impact on economic growth. An increase in imports also causes the import substituting domestic market to shrink, thereby reducing investments and ultimately reducing productivity (Lim and Park 2007).

2.4 Exchange Rate-Growth Nexus

Before moving to an empirical analysis it is useful to review literature on the nexus between the real exchange rate and economic growth. The level and volatility of the exchange rate could play a role and have an impact on long run economic growth. This means that exchange rate flexibility could affect long-run economic growth if it has an impact on productivity growth. With respect to the level, Turner (2012) notes that many emerging economies continue to have growth models that are heavily reliant on exports in favor of an undervalued exchange rate for the promotion of domestic industries. Using a theoretical model Rodrik (2008) shows how an under-valuation of the exchange rate can stimulate growth if the tradable goods sector is affected disproportionately by market failures or institutional weaknesses. In addition, trend appreciations and depreciations can have negative implications for FDI through the location of industries. These considerations suggest that limiting exchange rate flexibility could matter, especially for the tradable goods sector. Most studies demonstrate that the linkage is based on the level and the exchange rate regime.

Thorbecke (2008) indicates that large and frequent changes in the exchange rate can create a volatile economic structure, particularly if financial markets are under-developed and agents have few hedging possibilities. Such a volatile economy could adversely affect prospects for investment and growth. It could also reduce international trade, especially in economies dependent on intra-regional trade because large changes in the exchange rate have compounding effects on the costs of intermediate inputs. However, greater exchange rate flexibility could also lead to a more efficient allocation of resources and higher growth. It could encourage innovations and productivity growth as domestic firms cannot rely on under-valued exchange rates and foreign exchange interventions to maintain external competitiveness. When exchange rates are flexible and financial markets are well developed, investment and production decisions can be disconnected from movements in the exchange rate. In his pessimistic survey of cross-national growth literature, Easterly (2005) agrees that large over-valuations have an adverse effect on growth (while remaining skeptical that moderate movements have determinate effects). This regularity is not always theorized explicitly but most accounts link it to macroeconomic instability (see Fischer 1993).

Over-valued exchange rates are associated with shortages of foreign currency, rent-seeking and corruption, unsustainably large current account deficits, balance-of-payments crises and stop- and-go macroeconomic cycles, all of which are damaging to economic growth.

Rodrik (2008) and other recent scholars (see Bhalla-Surjit 2007; Gala 2007; Gluzmann et al. 2007), have all made similar arguments that over-valuation hurts growth and under-valuation facilitates it. For most countries, high-growth periods are associated with under-valued currencies. In fact, there is little evidence of non-linearity in the relationship between a country's (real) exchange rate and its economic growth. An increase in under-valuation boosts economic growth just as well as a decrease in over-valuation. But this relationship holds only for developing counties; it disappears when we limit the sample to richer countries. This suggests that more than macroeconomic stability is at stake. The relative price of tradable to non-tradable (the real exchange rate) seems to play a more fundamental role in the growth process.

2.5 Labor Force Participation Rate-Growth Nexus

Duval et al. (2010) and Shahid (2014) establish that there is a strong relationship between economic growth and labor force participation rates and that a skilled labor force enhances economic growth. Even if developing countries are faced with the problem of a low level of labor force participation, they want to speed up their GDP because it plays a very important role in any economy.

A number of researchers have investigated the linkage between labor force participation rate and economic growth. They point out that a long-run relationship exists between the two and labor force participation and gross fixed capital formation have a positive relationship with economic growth. When labor force participation and gross fixed capital formation increase economic growth also increases (see Denton and Spencer 1997; Mujahid and Uz Zafar 2012).

2.6 Gross Capital Formation-Growth Nexus

It is established in economic theory that high savings coupled with high levels of capital formation are pre-requisites for long-term economic growth in any given country (Lewis 1954, 1955). Capital formation is analogous (or a pre-requisite) with an increase in the physical capital stock of a nation with investments in social and economic infrastructure. Gross fixed capital formation can be classified into gross private domestic investments and gross public domestic investments. Gross public investments include investments by government and/or public enterprises. Gross domestic investments are equal to gross fixed capital formation plus net changes in the level of inventories. Capital formation perhaps leads to production of tangible goods (plants, tools and machinery, etc.) and/or intangible goods (qualitative and high standard of education, health, scientific tradition and research) in a country (Shuaib and Evelyn-Ndidi 2015).

In their econometric evidence Ghura and Hadji-Michael (1996) and Beddies (1999) indicate that private capital formation has a stronger, more favorable effect on growth rather than government capital formation probably because private capital formation is more efficient and/or less closely associated with corruption. Capital formation has been a major bane of economic growth and development in countries. Jhingan (2006) has ascertained the existence of a relationship between them. He asserts that capital formation could not only result in investments in capital equipment that lead to an increase in production but also lead to employment opportunities. He further stresses that capital formation leads to technical progress which helps realize the economies of large-scale production and/or increases specialization and/or provides machines, tools and equipment for a growing labor force. Capital formation also leads to the expansion of markets. Jhingan (2006) further adds that capital formation helps remove market imperfections by creating economic and social overhead capital and thus breaks the vicious circle of poverty both from the demand and supply sides.

The model that captures the main objective of our study is the Harrod–Domar model which describes an economic mechanism by which more investments lead to more growth. An economic model that is relevant for our study is the Harrold-Domar model which recognizes the importance of savings in an economy. The model emphasizes that for an economy to grow economic agents must forego part of their current consumption to put aside some resources needed for financing productive investments (Shuaib and Evelyn-Ndidi, 2015). Given that their financial systems tend to remain underdeveloped and intermediation remains highly inefficient economies with low savings have undergone years of battling with economic challenges. The model also requires available savings to be efficiently channeled to productive investments for economic growth to be significantly impacted. Otherwise wastages and misallocation of resources often result in sub-optimal results that are by and large less welfare enhancing. To grow, economies must save and invest a certain proportion of their GDP. The more an economy can save and invest, the faster it can grow as growth depends on how productive the investment is.

2.7 FDI-Growth Nexus

The relationship between FDI and economic growth has motivated voluminous empirical literature focusing on both developed and developing countries. FDI and economic growth literature has long focused on the role of governments' effectiveness in attracting FDI and in establishing reasons for foreign investors and firms. FDI is said to have a huge effect on host countries in terms of economic growth and development. FDI plays an important role in the economic growth in developing countries. It influences the employment scenario, production, prices, incomes, imports, exports and general welfare in the recipient country; it also helps in the balance of payments and serves as one of the vital sources of economic growth (Ershad-Hussain and Haque

2016). FDI's contribution to economic growth is shown by several potential ways. The impact of foreign direct investment depends on the theoretical model used. A large number of neo-classical growth models consider FDI to have short-run growth effects due to the concept of diminishing returns to capital. FDI has a positive impact on economic growth in the short run but after a point the curve starts turning downwards. In new growth theories, technological changes eliminate the problem of diminishing returns to capital and thus FDI can have positive effects on economic growth both in the short- and long-run (Herzer et al., 2008). Some researchers assert that FDI is more growth enhancing as compared to domestic investments (Borensztein et al., 1998) because it gives room to tap into FDI-related technological spillovers that often enable an economy to continue on its growth trajectory in the long run thus helping it overcome the challenge of diminishing returns to capital. The relationship between FDI and growth may be positive, negative or have no significant effects (see, for example, Agrawal 2015; Ilgun et al. 2010; Tang 2015).

However, several studies have shown that FDI is only growth enhancing if it does not crowd-out investments from domestic sources, say for example through significant repatriation of profits by foreign corporations that have invested in the country. Some studies have also demonstrated that this has been the case for developing countries which despite attracting large sums of FDI over several decades remain poor. Barış-Tekin (2012) and Herzer et al., (2008) acknowledge the possibility of reverse causality, that is, from economic growth to exports. This view is premised on the process of 'cumulative causation' whereby a long-term process of economic growth based on technical progress and increased productivity helps create new economic activities, new markets and a higher demand for new consumer products thus helping attract higher FDI resulting in accelerated growth. Generally speaking, it is argued that the positive impact of FDI inflows on economic growth is conditional on a number of factors such as the level of per capita income, human capital, the degree of trade openness and the depth of the financial market.

However, in developing countries and despite these potential negative effects empirical evidence suggests that FDI has a positive impact on economic growth. Basu et al. (2003) found that there was a bi-directional causality between economic growth and FDI in 23 developing countries over the period 1978 and 1996.

FDI acts as a long term source of capital as well as a source of advanced and developed technologies. Investors also bring best global practices of management. As a large amount of capital comes in through these investments more and more industries are set up which help in increasing employment opportunities. FDI also helps in promoting international trade (Jibir and Abdu 2017).

That there are benefits of FDI in accelerating growth and developing a country has been further highlighted by many empirical studies (Eravwoke and Eshanake 2012; Jibir et al. 2015; Folorunso 2009; Okon 2011; Oyatoye et al. 2011).

3 Model, Data and Methodology

3.1 Model Specification

Our paper adopted the empirical model developed by Tsitouras and Nikas (2016). The model in our study is specified as:

$$RGDP = f(EXP, IMP, BOT, EXR, LFPR, GCF, FDI, D) \quad (1)$$

Where, RGDP refers to the real GDP of a state (country) i at year t.

EXP stands for exports, IMP: imports, BOT: the balance of payments, EXR: exchange rate, LFPR refers to the labor force participation rate, GCF: gross capital formation and FDI to foreign direct investment, all of which compose a set of the control variables., *EXP, IMP, BOT, LFPR, GCF, FDI* are all independent variables respectively, for i-th country at year t.

D_{it}: The dummy variable represents the measure of regional economic integration at time t in country i, for analyzing whether being a member of EAC could have an impact on GDP.

The primary goal of our empirical study is to find a long-run relation among real economic growth and all independent variables. Hence, the time-series econometric form of the following equation is specified as:

$$RGDP_t = \beta_0 + \beta_1 EXP_t + \beta_2 IMP_t + \beta_3 BOT_t + \beta_4 EXR_t \\ + \beta_5 LFPR_t + \beta_6 GCF_t + \beta_7 FDI_t + \beta_8 D_t + \mu \quad (2)$$

Considering that our study only employs the panel data approach, Eq. (2) can be written as:

$$RGDPit = \beta_0 + \beta_1 EXP_{it} + \beta_2 IMP_{it} + \beta_3 BOT_i \\ + \beta_4 EXR_{it} + \beta_5 LFPR_{it} + \beta_6 GCF_{it} \\ + \beta_7 FDI_{it} + \beta_8 D_{it} + \mu_{it} \quad (3)$$

where, β_0 = constant term, β_1 = regression coefficient of EXP, β_2 = regression coefficient of IMP, β_3 = regression coefficient of BOT, β_4 = regression coefficient of EXR, β_5 = regression coefficient of LFPR, β_6 = regression coefficient of GCF, β_7 = regression coefficient of FDI, β_8 = regression coefficient of D and μ_{it} = disturbance term and is independent for all time and units. The subscript $i = 1, ..., N$ stands for the country (in our study we have six countries); $t = 1, ..., T$ suggests the time period (our time frame is 1991–2015).

3.2 Data

The dataset comprises of annual measures of five EAC member countries: Rwanda, Tanzania, Uganda, Kenya and Burundi.

The variables employed in estimations are: Annual per cent of GDP growth, exports of goods and services (percent of GDP), imports of goods and services (percent of GDP), balance of trade (BOT), exchange rate, labor force participation rate, gross capital formation, foreign direct investment inflows (FDI). The dummy variable for regional integration is 1 for being a member of EAC and 0 otherwise. All data is taken from World Development Indicators' statistical database (http://www.Wdi.org). The sample period is 1991–2015 for all countries.

3.3 Methodology

In an analysis of the long-term relationship term of the panel data, we adopted the methodology under the following three steps:
In step one we examined the order of integration of our variables by applying newly established panel unit root tests, IPS, MW, Breitung and the LLC tests for panel unit root of the series in the region under study. Second, the presence of random effects was tested using the Breusch-Pagan LM and we applied the Housman test to choose between FEM and REM. The third step was estimating the long-run dynamics for Eq. (3) by applying GMM (generalized methods of moments) formalized by Hansen and Singleton (1982). The presence of random effects was tested using the Breusch-Pagan LM test (whose statistics follow the Chi-square distribution with one degree of freedom) stated as:

$$LM = \frac{NT}{2(T-1)} \left[\frac{\sum_N \left(\sum_T \varepsilon_{it}^2 \right)}{\sum_N \sum_T \varepsilon_{it}^2} \right] \qquad (4)$$

Fixed effects remove the effect of the time-invariant characteristics from the predictor variables. Therefore, researchers want to assess the predictors' net effect by the *F*-test. To choose between FEM and REM, the Hausman test (H) is often used and appears as:

$$H = \left[\hat{\beta}_{FE} - \hat{\beta}_{RE} \right] \left[Var\left(\hat{\beta}_{FE}\right) - Var\left(\hat{\beta}_{RE}\right) \right]^{-1} \left[\hat{\beta}_{FE} - \hat{\beta}_{RE} \right] \qquad (5)$$

4 Empirical Results

4.1 Panel—Stationary Test—Results

By four tests: the ADF-Fisher Chi-square test, proposed by Maddala and Wu (1999) using ADF and PP tests, Im et al. (2003), Levin et al. (2002), and Breitung (1999) panel unit root test, the panel unit root test's results are given in Table 1. As can be seen in the table, RGDP, EXR, GCF EXP, FDI, M and BOT did not contain a unit root in levels, they are all I(0) LFPR is stationary in second difference, I(2).

Table 1 Panel unit root tests

Variables	IPS-test Statistic	Prob	MW ADF Statistic	Prob	PP Statistic	Prob	Breitung Statistic	Prob	LLC Statistic	Prob	Decision At (5%)
$RGDP_{it}$	−9.3560	0.000	84.284	0.000	421.07	0.000	−6.5945	0.000	−9.5825	0.000	I(0)
EXP_{it}	−7.2431	0.000	59.440	0.000	834.463	0.000	−2.4308	0.008	−1.9514	0.025	I(0)
IMP_{it}	−5.8592	0.000	48.260	0.000	175.146	0.000	−3.8032	1E-04	−6.1975	0.000	I(0)
BOT_{it}	−23.440	0.000	275.366	0.000	30.290	0.000	−1.845	0.033	−41.199	0.000	I(0)
EXR_{it}	−9.3804	0.000	108.986	0.000	59.692	0.000	0.9417	0.827	−8.0812	0.000	I(0)
$LFPR_{it}$	−6.0480	0.000	49.577	0.000	842.073	0.000	−6.2877	0.000	−0.4424	0.329	I(2)
GCF_{it}	−5.7089	0.000	48.093	0.000	239.539	0.000	−4.4099	0.000	−4.8402	0.000	I(0)
FDI_{it}	−4.5272	0.000	37.876	0.000	392.969	0.000	−2.5573	0.005	−2.1815	0.014	I(0)

4.2 Fixed Effects Model (FEM) and the Random Effects Model (REM)

We estimated both REM and FEM and tested the null hypothesis (of no random effects and fixed effects). A further check was done using the Hausman test to determine which model—FEM or REM—was appropriate or suitable.

The Breusch-Pagan LM test for random effects accepted the null hypothesis (with Chi-square value (0.00) and a p-value (1.000) and we concluded that there were random effects. Fixed effects were also tested, the F-statistic obtained was 6.27 with a p-value of 0.000, so the null hypothesis was rejected and we concluded that there were fixed effects.

To choose between FEM and REM, we used the Hausman test and got a Chi-square value of 6.22 and a corresponding p-value of 0.5142 implying that the fixed effects model was as good as REM, therefore there were no systematic differences between FEM and REM.

4.3 Long-Run Equation Estimation and Economic Interpretation

Having confirmed that the two models are similar, we estimated the long-run model (equation). The following co-integrating equation relating RGDP, EXP, IMP, BOT, EXR, LFPR, GCF, FDI and D is estimated:

$$RGDP_{it} = 13.22 + 0.302\, EXP_{it} - 0.367\, IMP_{it} \\ - 0.786\, BOT_{it} - 5.338\, EXR_{it} + 3.716\, LFPR_{it} \quad (6) \\ + 0.532\, GCF_{it} + 0.0934\, FDI_{it} + 0.702\, D_{it}$$

The values in brackets represent the t-statistic associated with the estimated coefficient of Eq. (6). EXP, LFPR, GCF, FDI and D are positively connected with RGDP in five EAC countries, which means that an increase of 1 percent in EXP, LFPR, GCF, FDI and D leads to an increase in RGDP by 0.302, 3.716, 0.532, 0.0934 and 0.702 respectively.

Table 2 Estimation results for all models including all variables

	(OLS_POOLED) RGDP	(FEM) RGDP	(REM) RGDP
IMP	−0.388***	−0.367***	−0.388***
	(−4.65)	(−4.34)	(−4.65)
EXP	0.282**	0.302**	0.282**
	(2.25)	(1.99)	(2.25)
EXR	−1.640	−5.338**	−1.640
	(−1.09)	(−2.06)	(−1.09)
LFPR	4.654***	3.716*	4.654***
	(2.63)	(1.94)	(2.63)
BOT	1.957	−0.786	1.957
	(0.72)	(−0.26)	(0.72)
GCF	0.574***	0.532***	0.574***
	(2.88)	(2.66)	(2.88)
FDI	0.184	0.0934	0.184
	(0.45)	(0.21)	(0.45)
D	1.34	0.702	0.702
	(0.92)	(0.42)	(0.42)
_cons	12.73***	13.22***	12.73***
	(5.03)	(4.53)	(5.03)
N	125	125	125

Note t statistics in parentheses. Statistical significance: $^*p < 0.10$, $^{**}p < 0.05$, $^{***}p < 0.01$

Similarly, an increase of 1 percent in the remaining variables (IMP, BOT and EXR) which are negatively associated with RGDP leads to a decrease of 0.367, 0.786 and 5.338 respectively. R-square which is 33 percent indicates that the independent variables in our model explain only 33 percent of the variations in RGDP, 67 percent are unexplained by the model (Table 2).

4.4 Diagnostic Test

4.4.1 Cross-Sectional Dependence

Cross-sectional dependence was tested using the Pasaran CD and the Breusch–Pagan LM tests of independence respectively. The results show that there was no cross-sectional dependence between countries as

Table 3 Correlation matrix of residuals

	_e1	_e2	_e3	_e4	_e5
_e1	1.0000				
_e2	−0.0139	1.0000			
_e3	−0.2387	−0.0139	1.0000		
_e4	−0.1780	0.1333	−0.0507	1.30000	
_e5	−0.0062	−0.1008	0.1254	−0.0592	1.0000

Note Breusch-Pagan LM tests of independence: Chi2 (10) = 3.470, Pr = 0.9681, based on 25 complete observations over panel units

shown by Prob. (0.5243) and the following correlation matrix of residuals whereby prob. is (0.9681) (Table 3).

5 Concluding Comments

Our empirical study examined the relations among exports, imports, balance of trade, exchange rate, labor force participation rate, gross capital formation, inward FDI, the dummy variable and real economic growth in five EAC member countries. After conducting a panel data analysis, we found that there was a significant relationship between some independent variables and RGDP. As can be seen from our results, EXP, LFPR, GCF, FDI and D were positively connected with RGDP in these five EAC countries. This means that they are important determinants of economic growth in EAC. IMP, BOT and EXR were negatively associated with RGDP in the whole region. R-square which was low at 33 percent indicates that the independent variables in our model explain only 33 percent of the variations in RGDP, 67 percent are explained by other factors. Regional economic integration is important and our results show a positive relationship, but it is not statistically significant. Further, our study helps confirm that EXP, GCF, FDI, REI (D) and LFPR are key pillars for economic growth in EAC member countries. Finally, in the whole region appropriate monetary and fiscal policy measures should be improved and sustained in order to maintain stability in prices, reduce dependence on countries abroad (extent of imports), raise export volumes and the general macroeconomic environment.

References

Abbas, M. (2013). Effect of Trade Deficit on the Economy of Pakistan. *Interdisciplinary Journal of Contemporary Research in Business*, 4(11): 176–215.

Agrawal, G. (2015). Foreign Direct Investment and Economic Growth in BRICS Economies: A Panel Data Analysis. *Journal of Economics, Business and Management*, 3: 421–424.

Baharumshah, A.Z. and S. Rashid (1999). Exports, Imports and Economic Growth in Malaysia: Emprical Evidence Based on Multivariate Time Series. *Asian Economic Journal*, 13(4): 389–406.

Balassa, B. (1978). Exports and Economic Growth: Further Evidence. *Journal of Development Economics*, 5: 181–189.

Barış-Tekin, R. (2012). Economic Growth, Exports and Foreign Direct Investment in Least Developed Countries: A Panel Granger Causality Analysis. *Economic Modeling*, 29: 868–878.

Basu, P., C. Chakraborty, and D. Reagle (2003). Liberalization, FDI, and Growth in Developing Countries: A Panel Cointegration Approach. *Economic Inquiry*, 5: 510–516.

Beddies, C. (1999). *Investment, Capital Accumulation and Growth: Some Evidence from Gambia: 1964–1998*. IMF Working Paper 99/117.

Bhalla-Surjit, S. (2007). *Second Among Equals: The Middle Class Kingdoms of India and China*. Washington, DC: Peterson Institute of International Economics.

Borensztein, E.J., J. De Gregorio, and J.W. Lee (1998). How Does Foreign Direct Investment Affect Economic Growth? *Journal of International Economics*, 45: 115–135.

Breitung, J. (1999). *The Local Power of Some Unit Root Tests for Panel Data (No. 1999, 69)*. Discussion Papers, Interdisciplinary Research Project 373: Quantification and Simulation of Economic Processes.

Busse, M. and J. Königer (2012). *Trade and Economic Growth: A Re-examination of the Empirical Evidence*. Hamburg Institute of International Economics, Research Paper 123.

Chatterji, M., S. Mohan, and S.G. Dastidar (2013). *Relationship Between Trade Openness and Economic Growth of India: A Time Series Analysis*. SIRE Discussion Papers, Scottish Institute for Research in Economics (SIRE).

Coe, T.D. and E. Helpman (1995). International R&D Spillovers. *European Economic Review*, 39: 859–887.

Daniels, J.D., H. Radebaugh, S. Lee, and P. Daniel (2004). *International Business Environments and Operations* (10th ed.). Hoboken, NJ: Pearson Education.

Denton, F.T. and B.G. Spencer (1997). *Population, Labour Force and Long-Term Economic Growth*. Hamilton, ON: Research Institute for Quantitative Studies in Economics and Population, McMaster University.

Duval, R., M. Eris, and D. Furceri (2010). *Labour Force Participation Hysteresis in Industrial Countries: Evidence and Causes*. OECD Economics Department, OECD, Paris CEDEX, Unpublished Manuscript. https://www.oecd.org/eco/growth/46578691.pdf. Accessed 27 April 2018.

East African Community (2002). *The Treaty for the Establishment of the East African Community.* EAC Publication, No. 1, Arusha, Tanzania,

Easterly, W. (2005). 'National Policies and Economic Growth', in Philippe Aghion and Steven Durlauf (eds.). *Handbook of Economic Growth*. North Holland: Elsevier.

Edwards, S. (1993). Openness, Trade Liberalization, and Growth in Developing Countries. *Journal of Economic Literature*, XXXI: 1358–1393.

Eravwoke, K.E. and S.J. Eshanake (2012). Foreign Direct Investment Granger and Nigerian Growth. *Journal of Innovative Research in Management and Humanities*, 3(2): 132–139.

Ershad-Hussain, M. and M. Haque (2016). Foreign Direct Investment, Trade, and Economic Growth: An Empirical Analysis of Bangladesh. *Economies*, 4(7): 1–14.

Esfahani, H.S. (1991). Exports, Imports and Economic Growth in Semi-Industrialized Countries. *Journal of Development Economics*, 35: 93–116.

Fischer, S. (1993). The Role of Macroeconomic Factors in Growth. *Journal of Monetary Economics*, 32: 485–512.

Folorunso, S.A. (2009). 'Foreign Direct Investment and Economic Growth in Nigeria', in Simon Sigue (ed.). *Repositioning African Business and Development for the 21st Century*. Proceeding of the 10th Annual Conference at IAABD.

Gala, P. (2007). *Real Exchange Rate Levels and Economic Development: Theoretical Analysis and Empirical Evidence*. Sao Paulo Business Administration School, Getulio Vargas Foundation.

Ghura, D. and T. Hadji-Michael (1996). *Growth in Sub-Saharan Africa*. Staff Papers, International Monetary Fund, 43.

Gluzmann, P., L. Eduardo, and S. Federico (2007). *Exchange Rate Undervaluation and Economic Growth: Díaz Alejandro (1965) Revisited*.

Unpublished Paper, John F. Kennedy School of Government, Harvard University.

Grossman, G.M. and E. Helpman (1991). *Innovation and Growth in the Global Economy*. Cambridge: MIT Press.

Gwaindepi, C., M. Musara, and N. Dhoro (2014). Relationship Between International Trade and Economic Growth: A Cointegration Analysis for Zimbabwe. *Mediterranean Journal of Social Sciences*, 5(20): 621–627.

Hansen, L.P. and K.J. Singleton (1982). Generalized Instrumental Variables Estimation of Nonlinear Rational Expectations Models. *Econometrica*, 50: 1269–1286.

Herzer, D., S. Klasen, and F. Nowak-Lehmann (2008). In Search of FDI-Led Growth in Developing Countries: The Way Forward. *Economic Modeling*, 25: 793–810.

Huilee, C. and B. Nung-Huang (2002). The Relationship Between Exports and Economic Growth in East Asian Countries: A Multivariate Threshold Autoregressive Approach. *Journal of Economic Development*, 27(2): 45–68.

Ilgun, E.K., J. Koch, and M. Orhan (2010). How do Foreign Direct Investment and Growth Interact in Turkey? *Eurasian Journal of Business and Economics*, 3: 41–55.

Im, K.S., M. Pesaran, and Y. Shin (2003). Testing for Unit Roots in Heterogeneous Panels. *Journal of Econometrics*, 115(1): 53–74.

Iyoha, A.M. (2005). *Enhancing Africa's Trade: From Marginalization to an Export-Led Approach to Development*, African Development Bank, Economic Research Working Paper Series (77).

Jhingan, M.L. (2006). *Economic Development*. New Delhi: Vrinda Publications (P) Ltd.

Jibir, A. and M. Abdu (2017). Foreign Direct Investment—Growth Nexus: The Case of Nigeria. *European Scientific Journal*, 13(1): 304–318.

Jibir, A., I. Adamu, and H. Babayo (2015). FDI and Economic Growth Nexus: Empirical Evidence from Nigeria (1970–2012). *Journal of Economics and Sustainable Development*, 6(6): 87–89.

Jung, W. and P. Marshall (1985). Exports, Growth and Causality in Developing Countries. *Journal of Development Economics*, 18: 1–12.

Lawrence, R.Z. and D.E. Weinstein (1999). *Trade and Growth: Import-Led or Export-Led? Evidence from Japan and Korea*. NBER Working Paper, 7264.

Lee, C. and D. Huang (2012). Human Capital Distribution, Growth and Trade. *Bulletin of Economic Research and John Wiley & Sons Ltd*. 66(1): 1467–8586.

Lee, J.W. (1995). Capital Goods Imports and Long-Run Growth. *Journal of Development Economics*, 48(1): 91–110.

Levine, R. and D. Renelt (1992). A Sensitivity Analysis of Cross-Country Growth Regressions. *The American Economic Review*, 82(4): 942–963.

Levine, R. and S.J. Zervos (1993). *What We Have Learned About Policy and Growth from Cross-Country Regressions*. AEA Papers and Proceedings, 83: 426–430.

Levin, A., C.F. Lin, and C.S.J. Chu (2002). Unit Root Tests in Panel Data: Asymptotic and Finite-Sample Properties. *Journal of Econometrics*, 108: 1–24.

Lewis, W.A. (1954). Economic Development with Unlimited Supplies of Labour. *Manchester School*, 22(2): 139–191; reprint used http://www.eco.utexas.edu/facstaff/Cleaver/368lewistable.pdf.

Lewis, A.W. (1955). *Theory of Economic Growth*. London: Homewood Publications.

Lim, H. and S. Park (2007). *Could Imports Be Beneficial for Economic Growth: Some Evidence from Republic of Korea*, ERD Working Paper Series No. 103. Asian Development Bank.

Liu, X., H. Song, and P. Romilly (1997). An Empirical Investigation of the Causal Relationship Between Openness and Economic Growth in China. *Applied Economics*, 29: 1679–1686.

Maddala, G.S. and S. Wu (1999). Comparative Study of Unit Root Tests with Panel Data and a New Simple Test. *Oxford Bulletin of Economics and Statistics*, 61(1): 631–652.

Marrewijk, C. (2012). *International Economics: Theory, Application and Policy*. Oxford: Oxford University Press.

Mazumdar, J. (2000). Imported Machinery and Growth in LDCs. *Journal of Development Economics*, 65: 209–224.

Michaely, M. (1977). Exports and Growth: An Empirical Investigation. *Journal of Development Economics*, 4: 49–53.

Mishra, P.K. (2012). The Dynamics of the Relationship Between Imports and Economic Growth in India. *South Asian Journal of Macroeconomics and Public Finance*, 1(1): 57–79.

Mujahid, N. and N. Uz Zafar (2012). Economic Growth-Female Labor Force Participation Nexus: An Empirical Evidence for Pakistan. *The Pakistan Development Review*, 51(4): 565–586.

Ndulu, B.J. and N.S. Njuguna (1998). *Trade Policy and Regional Integration in Sub-Saharan Africa*. Paper Presented at the IMF, African Economic

Research Consortium Seminar on Trade Reform and Regional Integration in Africa, 1–3 December 1997.

Okon, J.U. (2011). Foreign Direct Investment and Economic Growth in Nigeria. *Current Research Journal of Economic Theory*, 4(3): 53–66.

Oyatoye, A., K.K. Arogundade, S.O. Adebisi, and E.F. Oluwakayode (2011). Foreign Direct Investment, Export and Economic Growth in Nigeria. *European Journal of Humanities and Social Sciences*, 2(1): 68–78.

Reppas, P. and D. Christopoulos (2005). The Export–Output Growth Nexus: Evidence from African and Asian Countries. *Journal of Policy Modeling*, 27: 929–940.

Riezman, G.R., C.R. Whiteman, and P.M. Summers (1996). The Engine of Growth or Its Handmaiden? A Time Series Assessment of Export-Led Growth. *Empirical Economics*, 12: 77–110.

Rivera-Batiz, F.L. (1985). *International Finance and Open Economy Macroeconomics*. New York: Macmillan.

Rodriguez, F. and D. Rodrik (1999). *Trade Policy and Economic Growth: A Skeptic's Guide to Cross-National Evidence*. NBER Working Paper No. 7081.

Rodrik, D. (2008). *The Real Exchange Rate and Economic Growth*. Brookings Papers on Economic Activity, Fall: 365–412.

Salvatore, D. (2006). *International Economics* (8th ed.). USA: Willey.

Serletis, A. (1992). Export Growth and Canadian Economic Development. *Journal of Development Economics*, 38: 135–145.

Shahid, M. (2014). Impact of Labor Force Participation on Economic Growth in Pakistan. *Journal of Economics and Sustainable Development*, 5(11): 89–93.

Shuaib, I.M. and D. Evelyn-Ndidi (2015). Capital Formation: Impact on the Economic Development of Nigeria 1960–2013. *European Journal of Business, Economics and Accountancy*, 3(3): 23–40.

Steiner, K., J. Wörz, and T. Slacík (2014). Can Trade Partners Help Better FORCEE the Future? Impact of Trade Linkages on Economic Growth Forecasts in Selected CESEE Countries. *Focus on European Economic Integration*, 1: 36–56.

Stolper, W.F. (1947). The Volume of Foreign Trade and the Level of Income. *Quarterly Journal of Economics*, 61(2): 285–310.

Tang, D. (2015). Has the Foreign Direct Investment Boosted Economic Growth in the European Union Countries? *Journal of International and Global Economic Studies*, 8: 21–50.

Tekin, R.B. (2012). Economic Growth, Exports and Foreign Direct Investment in Least Developed Countries: A Panel Granger Causality Analysis. *Economic Modeling*, 29: 868–878.

Thangavelu, S.M. and G. Rajaguru (2004). Is There an Export or Import Led Productivity Growth in Rapidly Developing Asian Countries? A Multivariate VAR Analysis. *Applied Economics*, 36(10): 1083–1094.

Thorbecke, W. (2008). The Effect of Exchange Rate Volatility on Fragmentation in East Asia: Evidence from the Electronics Industry. *Journal of the Japanese and International Economies*, 22: 535–544.

Tsitouras, A. and C. Nikas (2016). The Dynamic Links Between Exports, Foreign Direct Investment, and Economic Growth: Evidence from European Transition Economies. *Journal of East-West Business*, 22(3): 198–235.

Turner, P. (2012). *Weathering Financial Crisis: Domestic Bond Markets in EMEs*. BIS Papers, 63.

Uğur, A. (2008). Import and Economic Growth in Turkey: Evidence from Multivariate VAR Analysis. *Journal of Economics and Business*, 11(1 and 2): 54–75.

Ullah, S., B. Zaman, M. Farooq, and A. Javid (2009). Cointegration and Causality Between Exports and Economic Growth in Pakistan. *European Journal of Social Sciences*, 10: 264–272.

12

Modeling the Effect of Food Price Volatility and Transmission to Market Efficiency and Welfare in the East African Community

Jean Baptiste Habyarimana and Tharcisse Nkunzimana

1 Introduction

Food price volatility is one of the most pressing problems in ensuring food security in the East African Community (EAC). Food price volatility in EAC results from four main factors (Karanja et al. 2003; Konandreas et al. 2015; Maître d' Hôtel et al. 2013). First, population growth in EAC is high which has medium and long term effects on food demand in the community. Second, like the other parts of the world EAC too is experiencing climate change. Hence, the accumulated effects of this impact born from and/or caused by climate variability, result in crop yield and production instability. Third, global food price volatility as a result of

---

J. B. Habyarimana (✉)
Department of Economics, University of Rwanda, Kigali, Rwanda

T. Nkunzimana
Joint Research Centre (JRC/European Commission), Ispra, Italy
e-mail: Tharcisse.NKUNZIMANA@ec.europa.eu

© The Author(s) 2018
A. Heshmati (ed.), *Determinants of Economic Growth in Africa*,
https://doi.org/10.1007/978-3-319-76493-1_12

reforms in global trade policies. Fourth, food price volatility as result of spatial effects. The geographical location determines food price volatility and transmission across EAC because variations in the distance between a costal country i and a non-coastal country j or between country i neighbor/far from country j determines the cost of transport between the two countries i and j. As a result of the combined effects of all these four factors, EAC partner states have become more reliant on each other and on the world market especially in terms of demand for cereals.

This paper explores cereal price volatility and transmission among five of the six EAC member states (Burundi, Kenya, Rwanda, Uganda and Tanzania) (South Sudan is not included in the analysis). These countries were chosen based on three dimensions. First, they are in the same community which has implemented different agricultural policies to increase cereal productivity with a common import tariff. Second, they are linked by two commercial corridors (the northern and central corridors) that can facilitate easy market integration in EAC and intra-import of cereals. Third, they are different in terms of surface, population density and location which may define the differences in their level of cereal production and demand across EAC member states. The trade level with the world markets is determined by the factor that coastal countries (Kenya, Tanzania) have easy access to world markets as compared to non-coastal countries (Burundi, Rwanda and Uganda).

Given these three dimensions, this paper answers three main questions: (i) Does volatility in the market prices of cereals occur at the same degree in these five countries? (ii) Is there any inter-relationship between domestic market price volatility and transmission in these countries? (iii) If there is any price transmission, what is the speed of cereal price adjustment from price variations caused by a one unit shock in one market to cereal prices' short-run and long-run equilibrium in other markets and in that market itself?

2 Background

The statistics in Fig. 1 show that largely maize, sorghum, rice and wheat are produced in EAC and their production over time has increased but has not grown sufficiently enough. Figure 2 shows that the main reason for an increase in cereal production in EAC is related more to an increase in the area harvested over time than to the adoption of new agricultural technologies and use of improved seeds. Figure 2 also shows that the average yield of cereals in EAC is far below the world average and EAC's contribution to the total world cereal production remains insignificant. Compared to the share of other cereals in the total world production of cereals, Fig. 3 demonstrates that the share of EAC's maize production has progressively declined. This relates to the fact that maize productivity has increased in other parts of the world while its productivity in East Africa, where EAC is located, has not experienced any significant improvements. Cereals that have seen a progressive increase in their contribution to the total world production are rice and wheat. This can be related to different agricultural policies adopted in EAC especially since the 1990s to ensure food security by increasing cereal productivity (African Development Bank [AfDB] 2016). The most observable aspect in the data is a consistent increase in harvested land.

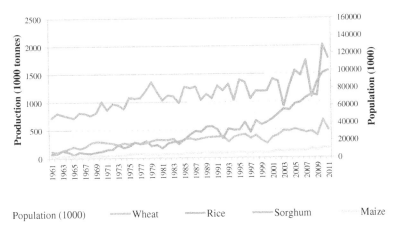

Fig. 1 Cereal production versus population (*Source* Own computation from data sourced from the FAO database)

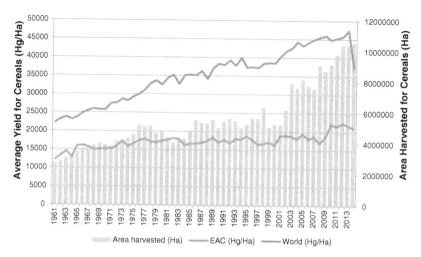

Fig. 2 Average yield and area harvested (*Source* Own computation from data sourced from the FAO database)

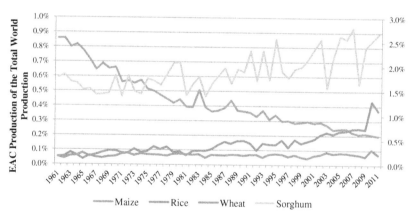

Fig. 3 EAC production of the total world (*Source* Own computation from data sourced from the FAO database)

Figure 3 also shows that the contribution of sorghum has been increasing but with high variations year after year. Figure 4 shows that since the 2000s EAC has experienced a dramatic increase in feed, waste and processing.

12 Modeling the Effect of Food Price Volatility and Transmission ...

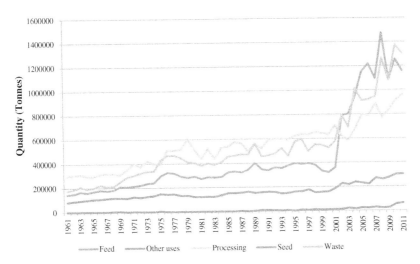

Fig. 4 Use of cereals (*Source* Own computation from data sourced from the FAO database)

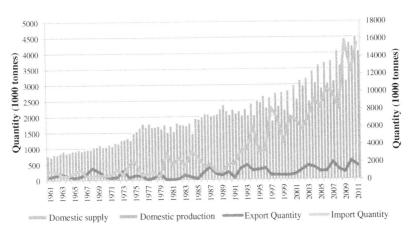

Fig. 5 Supply of cereals in EAC (*Source* Own computation from data sourced from the FAO database)

Though domestic production has increased, but it has not kept pace with population growth and demand for cereals for feed and processing. Figure 5 shows that over the last 10 and 20 years, demand for cereals in

EAC significantly increased by 44 and 108 percent respectively. Figure 5 also shows that to fill the gap between cereal demand and supply, imports of cereals in EAC have dramatically increased since the 1980s while the export of cereals has remained low and insignificant. This increase in cereal requirements has made EAC a net importer of cereals since the 1990s. Figure 6 shows that the period during which producer prices and the producer price indices for cereals in EAC increased corresponds to the period during which EAC became a bigger net importer of cereals. During this period, consumer prices also increased. This shows that in the period during which EAC became a net importer of cereals, variations in both producer and consumer prices in each EAC member state was influenced by growing EAC demand for cereals whether for human consumption, animal feed or industrial processing, intra-imports of cereals in EAC and imports of cereals from the rest of the world.

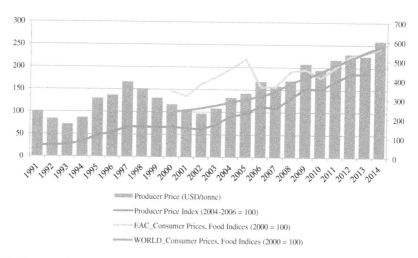

Fig. 6 Trends in food price and indices (*Source* Own computation from data sourced from the FAO database)

3   Methodology and Data

Literature shows an increasing use of PVAR and SPVAR models in measuring volatility and transmission in financial time series (Beenstock and Felsenstein 2007; Canova and Ciccarelli 2013; LeSage 1998; Mutl 2009). Our paper adopts and explains the application of PVAR and SPVAR models with multiple commodities to econometrically analyze food price volatility and transmission across EAC member countries. The application of the PVAR model with multiple commodities allows us to combine food commodities and countries to estimate price volatility and transmission. The PVAR and SPVAR models adopted in our paper are panel in the price of commodities in each market (we consider each country member of EAC as a market) Pc_{it}, where P stands for price and c for country/market and Pc_{it} is price of the ith commodity at time t in country/market c.

Hence the PVAR model of lag (2) is specified as:

$$Pc_{it} = V + \beta_1 Pc_{it-1} + \beta_2 Pc_{it-2} + u_{it} \qquad (1)$$

where, i represents different prices of cereal commodities (wheat, rice, maize and sorghum); V is the vector of cereal price effect in each market (Pb = cereal price in the Burundi market, Pk = cereal price in the Kenya market, Pr = cereal price in the Rwanda market, Pu = cereal price in the Uganda market and Pt = cereal price in the Tanzania market); β_1 and β_2 are the coefficients of variables (Pb, Pk, Pr, Pu and Pt) in lag (1) and lag (2) and u_{it} is the vector of error terms.

The SPVAR of lag (2) is specified as:

$$Pc_{it} = V + \beta_1 S_1 Pc_{it-1} + \beta_2 S_1 Pc_{it-2} + u_{it} \text{ and } u_{it} = S_2 e_{it} \qquad (2)$$

where, S_1 and S_2 are fixed matrices of spatial weights. In this SPVAR model, only the neighbors have dynamic repercussions on market c within two periods while the rest are assumed to have negligible effects. The SPVAR structure implies that a shock originating in market c can be transmitted after one/two periods to market k if market k is a neighbor of market c. However, if market k is not a neighbor of market c, the delayed effects are longer and will depend on the number of markets between market k and market c.

All the original data used in this paper is available and calculated from FAO's online database that publishes data on the prices of agricultural commodities. We used the annual average of producer prices of four cereal commodities in five markets. The sample period is 1991–2014. For incomplete series like the Uganda series, the prices were sourced from other sources and extrapolation and interpolation techniques were used to estimate the price of the incomplete series. For the purpose of analysis, the price of each i cereal commodity is expressed in US$ per kg. Apart from the actual prices of cereals, our paper also acknowledges the effect of spatial distribution of markets across EAC on price volatility and transmission. To capture the spatial effects we estimated the new prices in each market with spatial effects Pc_{it}^*.

4 Econometric Analysis and Empirical Findings

4.1 Descriptive Statistics

The statistics in Table 1 show that there are similarities among the means of prices computed without spatial effects and those computed with spatial effects; the only two exceptions are in the prices of cereals in the Rwandan and Tanzanian markets. Table 1 also shows that low cereal price variability is predictable in market prices with spatial effects in the Kenyan and Rwandan markets when compared to those without spatial effects, while high price variability is predictable in prices with spatial effects in the Burundi, Uganda and Tanzania markets when compared to those without spatial effects.

4.2 Cereal Price Correlation Among the Five Markets

Table 2 shows that there is enough evidence to conclude that there is the existence of a strong and positive linear relationship among prices without spatial effects and a very strong and positive linear relationship among prices with spatial effects. It also demonstrates that an increase

Table 1 Descriptive statistics

Variable	Without spatial effects					With spatial effects				
	Mean	p50	sd	cv	Skewness	Kurtosis	Mean	p50	sd	cv	Skewness	Kurtosis
Pb	0.324	0.314	0.115	0.355	0.934	4.359	0.342	0.325	0.157	0.459	1.050	3.586
Pk	0.296	0.257	0.169	0.573	1.368	5.440	0.295	0.275	0.113	0.383	0.908	3.816
Pr	0.421	0.362	0.236	0.560	1.063	3.263	0.304	0.299	0.105	0.345	0.629	3.101
Pu	0.327	0.289	0.141	0.430	0.965	3.552	0.326	0.298	0.151	0.464	1.183	4.414
Pt	0.262	0.263	0.098	0.373	0.797	3.882	0.342	0.311	0.145	0.425	0.907	3.480

Pb = price of wheat, rice, maize and sorghum in the Burundi market; Pk = price of wheat, rice, maize and sorghum in the Kenya market; Pr = price of wheat, rice, maize and sorghum in the Rwanda market; Pu = price of wheat, rice, maize and sorghum in the Uganda market; Pt = price of wheat, rice, maize and sorghum in the Tanzania market

Table 2 Pearson product-moment correlation coefficients

| | Without spatial effects ||||| With spatial effects |||||
	Pb	Pk	Pr	Pu	Pt	Pb	Pk	Pr	Pu	Pt
Pb	1					1				
Pk	0.473	1				0.935	1			
Pr	0.422	0.704	1			0.851	0.963	1		
Pu	0.682	0.899	0.880	1		0.968	0.966	0.88	1	
Pt	0.579	0.680	0.721	0.780	1	0.929	0.966	0.94	0.974	1

in cereal prices in any of the five markets across EAC has a tendency to also increase cereal prices in any other market across EAC. This evidence shows that this tendency increases when spatial effects are taken into account.

4.3 Unit Root Test

To infer the degree of integration and stationary properties of the respective cereal prices in each market and uncover if there are possibilities for undertaking panel co-integration tests we rely on the Pesaran (2007) CIPS test. The results in Table 3 reject the null hypothesis that all series are I(1) at 5 and 10 percent (without and with a trend) in prices without spatial effects and at 1 and 5 percent (without and with a trend) level of significance in prices with spatial effects. Therefore, cereal prices in all the five markets are I(0). The pre-condition for testing for co-integration is that all the series must be integrated of order 1 'I(1).' However, as our data is integrated of order zero 'I(0)' we proceed with PVAR and if there is no evidence of testing for co-integration we then proceed with PVECM.

Table 3 Pesaran (2007) Panel unit root test (CIPS)

| | Without spatial effects || With spatial effects ||
Variable	Without trend	With trend	Without trend	With trend
Pb	−2.339 (0.010)	−1.337 (0.091)	−3.490 (0.000)	−2.538 (0.008)
Pk	−3.558 (0.000)	−2.366 (0.009)	−3.248 (0.001)	−2.093 (0.018)
Pr	−3.373 (0.000)	−2.267 (0.012)	−2.533 (0.006)	−1.996 (0.023)
Pu	−3.197 (0.000)	−2.304 (0.011)	−3.289 (0.001)	−2.492 (0.006)
Pt	−2.796 (0.000)	−1.718 (0.043)	−3.807 (0.000)	−2.710 (0.003)

4.4 PVAR and SPVAR Models' Estimations

For the purposes of an analysis, we set the panel VAR model of lag (2) by writing (1) in matrix form as:

$$
\begin{pmatrix} Pb_{it} \\ Pk_{it} \\ Pr_{it} \\ Pu_{it} \\ Pt_{it} \end{pmatrix} = \begin{pmatrix} V_{bj} \\ V_{kj} \\ V_{rj} \\ V_{uj} \\ V_{tj} \end{pmatrix} + \begin{pmatrix} \theta_{11i1} & \theta_{12i1} & \theta_{13i1} & \theta_{14i1} & \theta_{15i1} \\ \theta_{21i1} & \theta_{22i1} & \theta_{23i1} & \theta_{24i1} & \theta_{25i1} \\ \theta_{31i1} & \theta_{32i1} & \theta_{33i1} & \theta_{34i1} & \theta_{35i1} \\ \theta_{41i1} & \theta_{42i1} & \theta_{43i1} & \theta_{44i1} & \theta_{45i1} \\ \theta_{51i1} & \theta_{52i1} & \theta_{53i1} & \theta_{54i1} & \theta_{55i1} \end{pmatrix} \begin{pmatrix} Pb_{it-1} \\ Pk_{it-1} \\ Pr_{it-1} \\ Pu_{it-1} \\ Pt_{it-1} \end{pmatrix}
$$
$$
+ \begin{pmatrix} \theta_{11i2} & \theta_{12i2} & \theta_{13i2} & \theta_{14i2} & \theta_{15i2} \\ \theta_{21i2} & \theta_{22i2} & \theta_{23i2} & \theta_{24i2} & \theta_{25i2} \\ \theta_{31i2} & \theta_{32i2} & \theta_{33i2} & \theta_{34i2} & \theta_{35i2} \\ \theta_{41i2} & \theta_{42i2} & \theta_{43i2} & \theta_{44i2} & \theta_{45i2} \\ \theta_{51i2} & \theta_{52i2} & \theta_{53i2} & \theta_{54i2} & \theta_{55i2} \end{pmatrix} \begin{pmatrix} Pb_{it-2} \\ Pk_{it-2} \\ Pr_{it-2} \\ Pu_{it-2} \\ Pt_{it-2} \end{pmatrix} + \begin{pmatrix} \mu_{1it} \\ \mu_{2it} \\ \mu_{3it} \\ \mu_{4it} \\ \mu_{5it} \end{pmatrix} \quad (3)
$$

where, i represents different prices of cereal commodities (wheat, rice, maize and sorghum); ν is the vector of cereal commodity effect in each market; and θ are the coefficient matrices of variables (Pb, Pk, Pr, Pu and Pt) in lag (1) and lag (2).

We set the SPVAR model of lag (2). In matrix form, we first estimated the W matrix reflecting first order rook's contiguity relations for the five markets which is a symmetric matrix. As we are dealing with the prices of cereal commodities in five markets in EAC (Burundi, Kenya, Rwanda, Uganda and Tanzania), W is a square matrix of 5 × 5 dimension that records neighborhoods among the markets. From the first row: the neighboring markets of the Burundi market are Rwanda and Tanzania. From the second row: the neighboring markets of the Kenyan market are Uganda and Tanzania. From the third row: the neighboring markets of the Rwandan market are Burundi, Uganda and Tanzania. From the fourth row: the neighboring markets of the Ugandan market are Kenya, Rwanda and Tanzania. From the fifth row: the neighboring markets of the Tanzanian market are Burundi, Kenya, Rwanda and Uganda. Second, we transformed the W matrix to have row-sums of unity to get a standardized first-order contiguity matrix noted as

C. Then we combined C and Pc_{it} a vector column matrix to have new prices Pc_{it} with spatial effects. For simplicity, the new price for i commodity at t time in each market is the arithmetic mean of the price of that i commodity at t time in neighboring markets c to k:

$$W = \begin{pmatrix} 0 & 0 & 1 & 0 & 1 \\ 0 & 0 & 0 & 1 & 1 \\ 1 & 0 & 0 & 1 & 1 \\ 0 & 1 & 1 & 0 & 1 \\ 1 & 1 & 1 & 1 & 0 \end{pmatrix} \text{ and } C = \begin{pmatrix} 0 & 0 & 1/2 & 0 & 1/2 \\ 0 & 0 & 0 & 1/2 & 1/2 \\ 1/3 & 0 & 0 & 1/3 & 1/3 \\ 0 & 1/3 & 1/3 & 0 & 1/3 \\ 1/4 & 1/4 & 1/4 & 1/4 & 1/4 \end{pmatrix} \quad (4)$$

$$\begin{pmatrix} Pb_{it}^* \\ Pk_{it}^* \\ Pr_{it}^* \\ Pu_{it}^* \\ Pt_{it}^* \end{pmatrix} = \begin{pmatrix} 0 & 0 & 1/2 & 0 & 1/2 \\ 0 & 0 & 0 & 1/2 & 1/2 \\ 1/3 & 0 & 0 & 1/3 & 1/3 \\ 0 & 1/3 & 1/3 & 0 & 1/3 \\ 1/4 & 1/4 & 1/4 & 1/4 & 1/4 \end{pmatrix} \begin{pmatrix} Pb_{it} \\ Pk_{it} \\ Pr_{it} \\ Pu_{it} \\ Pt_{it} \end{pmatrix}$$

$$= \begin{pmatrix} 0.5 Pr_{it} + 0.5 Pt_{it} \\ 0.5 Pu_{it} + 0.5 Pt_{it} \\ 1/3 Pb_{it} + 1/3 Pu_{it} + 1/3 Pt_{it} \\ 1/3 Pk_{it} + 1/3 Pr_{it} + 1/3 Pt_{it} \\ 1/4 Pb_{it} + 1/4 Pk_{it} + 1/4 Pr_{it} + 1/4 Pu_{it} \end{pmatrix} \quad (5)$$

Then we wrote (2) in matrix form as:

$$\begin{pmatrix} Pb_{it}^* \\ Pk_{it}^* \\ Pr_{it}^* \\ Pu_{it}^* \\ Pt_{it}^* \end{pmatrix} = \begin{pmatrix} V_{1j} \\ V_{2j} \\ V_{3j} \\ V_{4j} \\ V_{5j} \end{pmatrix} + \begin{pmatrix} \rho_{11i1} & \rho_{12i1} & \rho_{13i1} & \rho_{14i1} & \rho_{15i1} \\ \rho_{21i1} & \rho_{22i1} & \rho_{23i1} & \rho_{24i1} & \rho_{25i1} \\ \rho_{31i1} & \rho_{32i1} & \rho_{33i1} & \rho_{34i1} & \rho_{35i1} \\ \rho_{41i1} & \rho_{42i1} & \rho_{43i1} & \rho_{44i1} & \rho_{45i1} \\ \rho_{51i1} & \rho_{52i1} & \rho_{53i1} & \rho_{54i1} & \rho_{55i1} \end{pmatrix} \begin{pmatrix} Pb_{it-1}^* \\ Pk_{it-1}^* \\ Pr_{it-1}^* \\ Pu_{it-1}^* \\ Pt_{it-1}^* \end{pmatrix}$$

$$+ \begin{pmatrix} \rho_{11i2} & \rho_{12i2} & \rho_{13i2} & \rho_{14i2} & \rho_{15i2} \\ \rho_{21i2} & \rho_{22i2} & \rho_{23i2} & \rho_{24i2} & \rho_{25i2} \\ \rho_{31i2} & \rho_{32i2} & \rho_{33i2} & \rho_{34i2} & \rho_{35i2} \\ \rho_{41i2} & \rho_{42i2} & \rho_{43i2} & \rho_{44i2} & \rho_{45i2} \\ \rho_{51i2} & \rho_{52i2} & \rho_{53i2} & \rho_{54i2} & \rho_{55i2} \end{pmatrix} \begin{pmatrix} Pb_{it-2}^* \\ Pk_{it-2}^* \\ Pr_{it-2}^* \\ Pu_{it-2}^* \\ Pt_{it-2}^* \end{pmatrix} + \begin{pmatrix} \varepsilon_{it}^* \\ \varepsilon_{it}^* \\ \varepsilon_{it}^* \\ \varepsilon_{it}^* \\ \varepsilon_{it}^* \end{pmatrix} \quad (6)$$

where, i represents different prices of cereal commodities (wheat, rice, maize and sorghum); v is the vector of cereal commodity effect in each market; and ρ are the coefficient matrices of variables (Pb, Pk, Pr, Pu and Pt) with spatial effects in lag (1) and lag (2).

We estimated PVAR and SPVAR using a least squares dummy variable estimator. The estimator fits a multivariate panel regression of each dependent variable on lags of itself and on lags of all the other dependent variables. We first estimated the model's coefficients to explain the relationship among cereal prices in all the five markets. Second, we estimated impulse-response functions to draw the figures of dynamic shock responses from which we can observe the dynamic changes in cereal prices in each market under different shocks. Third, we estimated the results of variance decompositions for cereal prices in each market to evaluate the contributions of different stochastic shocks on five markets in the PVAR and SPVAR systems.

When the spatial effects are not taken into account, PVAR results in Table 4 demonstrate that, first, when the Burundi cereal market is taken as the dependent variable, a one unit shock in the Burundi market one-time back and the Uganda market two-time back increase the current cereal prices in the Burundi market to some degree (0.898 and 1.214) while a one unit shock in the Kenyan market two-time back decreases the current cereal prices in Burundi (−0.55). Second, when the Kenyan cereal market is taken as the dependent variable, a one unit shock in the Kenyan market one-time back increases the current cereal prices in Kenya to some degree (0.731). Third, when the Rwandan cereal market is taken as the dependent variable, a one unit shock in the Burundi market two-time back decreases the current cereal prices in Rwanda (−0.653). Fourth, when the Ugandan cereal market is taken as the dependent variable, a one unit shock in the Burundi market two-time back decreases the current cereal prices in Uganda (−0.461). Fifth, when the Tanzanian cereal market is taken as the dependent variable, a one unit shock in the Rwanda market one-time back decreases current cereal prices in Tanzania (−0.293).

The results in Table 4 show that when spatial effects are taken into account, first, when the Burundi cereal market is taken as the dependent variable, a one unit shock in the Burundi market two-time back

Table 4 Estimation results of PVAR and SPVAR

Independent variable		Dependent variable							
		Pb		Pk		Pr		Pu		Pt	
		Coef.	P > t	Coef.	P > t	Coef.	P > t	Coef.	P > t	Coef.	P > t
Without spatial effects	l1_Pb	0.898	0.003	0.082	0.754	0.049	0.906	0.260	0.244	0.369	0.150
	l1_Pk	0.361	0.278	0.731	0.015	−0.232	0.616	0.218	0.381	0.445	0.122
	l1_Pr	−0.026	0.892	−0.054	0.752	0.077	0.775	−0.069	0.634	0.265	0.113
	l1_Pu	−0.559	0.458	0.038	0.955	1.713	0.106	0.555	0.327	−0.696	0.285
	l1_Pt	0.062	0.698	0.183	0.200	0.114	0.609	0.023	0.847	0.335	0.017
	l2_Pb	−0.437	0.119	−0.276	0.267	−0.653	0.096	−0.461	0.030	−0.393	0.104
	l2_Pk	−0.553	0.074	−0.201	0.463	−0.266	0.535	−0.372	0.109	−0.426	0.109
	l2_Pr	−0.188	0.295	−0.119	0.453	0.386	0.124	−0.040	0.765	−0.293	0.059
	l2_Pu	1.214	0.093	0.812	0.205	−0.083	0.934	0.860	0.112	0.966	0.120
	l2_Pt	0.042	0.808	−0.165	0.285	−0.238	0.324	−0.097	0.457	0.066	0.656
	cons	0.090	0.004	0.010	0.703	0.080	0.061	0.053	0.021	0.088	0.001
With spatial effects	l1_Pb	0.130	0.769	−0.467	0.139	−0.569	0.072	−0.437	0.227	−0.576	0.085
	l1_Pk	0.599	0.776	−0.770	0.607	−1.485	0.323	0.369	0.830	0.228	0.885
	l1_Pr	−0.056	0.975	1.170	0.361	2.002	0.120	0.145	0.921	0.483	0.721
	l1_Pu	−0.364	0.849	1.221	0.371	1.499	0.273	0.589	0.707	0.325	0.821
	l1_Pt	0.910	0.482	−0.303	0.742	−0.634	0.491	0.473	0.654	0.645	0.507
	l2_Pb	0.785	0.071	0.465	0.131	0.554	0.074	0.577	0.104	0.715	0.030
	l2_Pk	1.930	0.334	2.681	0.061	2.888	0.044	2.012	0.218	2.315	0.125
	l2_Pr	−2.430	0.159	−2.424	0.049	−2.545	0.039	−2.325	0.100	−2.608	0.046
	l2_Pu	−1.899	0.297	−2.340	0.073	−2.606	0.047	−1.895	0.204	−2.281	0.098
	l2_Pt	1.148	0.366	1.524	0.093	1.672	0.066	1.337	0.199	1.650	0.086
	cons	0.084	0.008	0.071	0.002	0.077	0.001	0.059	0.021	0.058	0.014

increases the current cereal prices in Burundi (0.785). Second, when the Kenyan cereal market is taken as the dependent variable, a one unit shock in the Kenya market two-time back increases the current cereal prices in Kenya (2.681) while a one unit shock in the Rwanda and Uganda markets decreases the current cereal prices in Kenya to some degree (−2.424 and 2.340 respectively). Third, when the Rwanda cereal market is taken as the dependent variable, a one unit shock in cereal prices in the Kenya, Tanzania and Burundi markets two-time back increases the current cereal prices in Rwanda (2.89, 1.67 and 0.55), while a one unit shock in the Uganda and Rwanda markets two-time back decreases the current cereal prices in Rwanda (−2.606 and −2.545). Fourth, when the Tanzania cereal market is taken as the dependent variable, a one unit shock in the Burundi and Tanzania markets two-time back increases the current cereal prices in Tanzania (0.715 and 1.650) while a one unit shock in the Uganda and Rwanda markets two-time back decreases the current cereal prices in Tanzania (−2.281 and −2.608).

4.5 Impulse-Response Functions

In order to assess the two-way cereal price effects among the Burundi, Kenya, Rwanda, Uganda and Tanzania cereal markets, we computed the impulse-response functions of the PVAR and SPVAR models. The usefulness of the impulse-response functions is in describing the reaction of one variable to innovations in another variable of the system while holding all other shocks equal to zero. In Figs. 7, 8, 9, 10, 11, 12, 13, 14, 15, and 16, we give the impulse-response functions' plots, the response being absorbed during 30 periods ahead and their results are summarized as:

The empirical results show that in cereal prices without spatial effects, first, a one unit shock in the Burundi and Uganda markets causes positive and measurable cereal price variations in all other markets the effects of which may die out in the long term. Second, a one unit shock in the Kenya and Rwanda markets causes positive and measurable cereal price variations in all other markets and these effects may not die out in

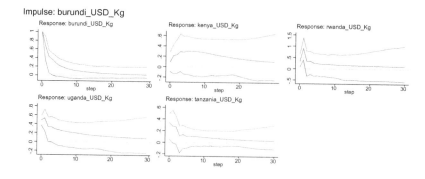

Fig. 7 Without spatial effects

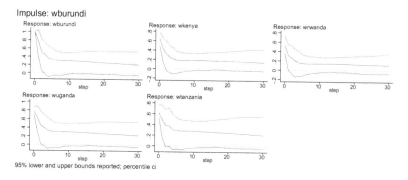

Fig. 8 With spatial effects

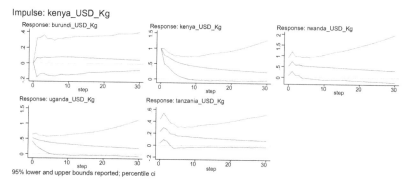

Fig. 9 Without spatial effects

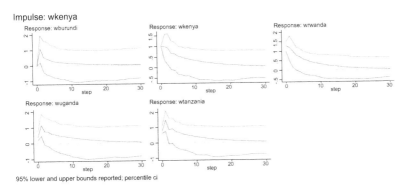

Fig. 10 With spatial effects

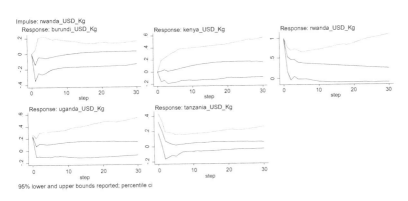

Fig. 11 Without spatial effects

the long term and may remain positive. Third, a one unit shock in the Tanzania market causes negative and measurable cereal price variations in all other markets and the effects of these variations may die out in the long term.

In cereal prices with spatial effects, the empirical results show that, first, a one unit shock in the Burundi, Uganda and Tanzania markets causes positive and considerable cereal price variations in all other

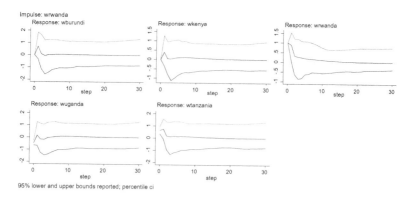

Fig. 12 With spatial effects

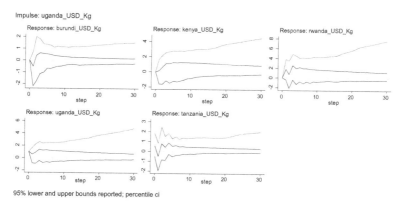

Fig. 13 Without spatial effects

markets the effects of which may not die out in the long-term and remain positive. Second, a one unit shock in the Kenya market causes positive and considerable cereal price variations in all the other four markets and the effects of the variations may totally die out in the long term. And third, a one unit shock in the Rwanda market causes positive but not considerable cereal price variations in all the other four markets and these effects may quickly and totally die out in the short term.

12 Modeling the Effect of Food Price Volatility and Transmission ...

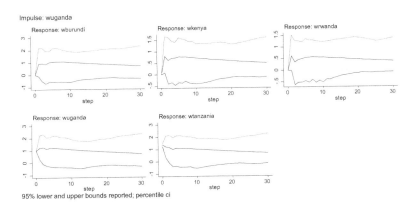

Fig. 14 With spatial effects

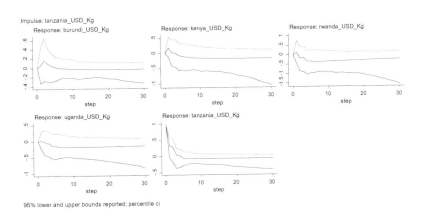

Fig. 15 Without spatial effects

4.6 Variance Decompositions

To measure the dynamic effects of different structural variations to each endogenous variable included in the model on itself and on other endogenous variables, in this section we investigate the reaction of impulse-response functions (IRFs). Variance decompositions which give information on the proportion of structural variations in each endogenous variable emanating from its own variations and variations clustering

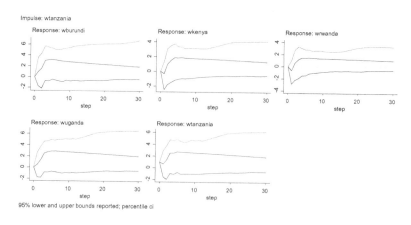

Fig. 16 With spatial effects

Table 5 Variance decomposition

		Without spatial effects					With spatial effects				
		Pb	Pk	Pr	Pu	Pt	Pb	Pk	Pr	Pu	Pt
Pb	10	0.466	0.012	0.007	0.504	0.010	0.033	0.025	0.006	0.111	0.825
Pk	10	0.047	0.263	0.002	0.681	0.009	0.028	0.136	0.006	0.144	0.686
Pr	10	0.035	0.075	0.062	0.806	0.023	0.024	0.240	0.083	0.097	0.557
Pu	10	0.071	0.108	0.011	0.800	0.010	0.025	0.053	0.004	0.182	0.736
Pt	10	0.063	0.072	0.030	0.611	0.223	0.019	0.088	0.015	0.175	0.702
Pb	20	0.402	0.021	0.006	0.561	0.010	0.022	0.013	0.003	0.113	0.848
Pk	20	0.039	0.172	0.007	0.768	0.015	0.019	0.076	0.004	0.136	0.764
Pr	20	0.024	0.072	0.051	0.824	0.029	0.018	0.145	0.048	0.111	0.679
Pu	20	0.049	0.094	0.015	0.824	0.017	0.017	0.030	0.002	0.153	0.797
Pt	20	0.054	0.074	0.026	0.675	0.171	0.014	0.050	0.008	0.151	0.776
Pb	30	0.371	0.025	0.007	0.585	0.012	0.019	0.010	0.002	0.114	0.855
Pk	30	0.033	0.147	0.011	0.790	0.019	0.017	0.056	0.003	0.132	0.793
Pr	30	0.021	0.071	0.048	0.829	0.032	0.016	0.111	0.036	0.113	0.724
Pu	30	0.041	0.089	0.018	0.831	0.021	0.015	0.022	0.002	0.144	0.817
Pt	30	0.048	0.074	0.026	0.701	0.151	0.013	0.037	0.006	0.142	0.801

from other endogenous variables are reported in Table 5. The reported variance decompositions are based on orthogonalized IRFs. To investigate how much innovations in each endogenous variable relate to variations in other endogenous variables and itself, we use 30 periods forecasts of variations in mean squared error for each endogenous variable ahead from the sample period covered in this paper.

From Table 5 we can see that, first, a shock in cereal prices in Burundi had the biggest impact on the variations of cereal prices in Burundi in both the short-run and the long-run with a gradual declining trend. With spatial effects, a shock in the Burundi, Kenya and Uganda markets had the biggest impact on variations in cereal prices in Burundi when compared to a shock in other markets. Second, a shock in cereal prices in the Kenya and Uganda markets had the biggest impact on variations in cereal prices in Kenya in both the short-run and the long-run. With spatial effects, a shock in the Kenya and Rwanda markets had the biggest impact on variations in cereal prices in Kenya as compared to a shock in other markets. Third, a shock in cereal prices in Rwanda and Tanzania had the biggest impact on variations in cereal prices in Rwanda in both the short-run and the long-run. With spatial effects, a shock in the Rwanda and Tanzania markets had the biggest impact on variations in cereal prices in Rwanda when compared to a shock in the other markets. Fourth, a shock in cereal prices in the Rwanda, Uganda, Kenya, Tanzania and Burundi markets had the biggest impact on variations in cereal prices in Uganda in both the short-run and the long-run. With spatial effects, a shock in the Uganda, Tanzania, Kenya, Burundi and Rwanda markets had the biggest impact on variations in cereal prices in Uganda both in the short-run and the long-run. And fifth, a shock in cereal prices in the Tanzania market had the biggest impact on variations in cereal prices in Tanzania in both in the short-run and the long-run. With spatial effects, a shock in the Uganda, Tanzania, Kenya, Burundi and Rwanda markets had the biggest impact on variations in cereal prices in Tanzania both in the short-run and the long-run.

In terms of 100 percent variations along 30 steps ahead from the current prices caused by a one unit shock in the prices of cereals in each market, the empirical results for cereal prices without spatial effects demonstrate that, first, from a one unit shock in the Burundi market strong variations reverberated in the prices of cereals in the Burundi and Uganda markets. Second, from a one unit shock in the Kenya market, strong variations reverberated in the prices of cereals in Uganda and also some in Kenya. Third, from a one unit shock in the Rwanda and Tanzania markets, strong variations reverberated in the prices of cereals in Uganda. And fourth, from a one unit shock in Uganda, strong variations reverberated in the prices of cereals in Uganda itself. However, the results with spatial effects demonstrate that, first, from a one unit shock in the Burundi, Kenya and Uganda markets, strong variations reverberated in the prices of cereals in Tanzania. Second, from a one unit shock in Rwanda, strong variations reverberated in the prices of cereals in Tanzania and also some in Kenya. And third, from a one unit shock in Tanzania, strong variations reverberated in the prices of cereals in Tanzania itself.

5 Discussion

When the results without spatial effects are compared with the results that account for spatial effects, it is clear that the level of a two-time back to predict variations in the current cereal prices across EAC member countries increases and the number of markets influencing the variations in the current prices of cereal in any given market among Burundi, Kenya, Rwanda, Tanzania and Uganda, also increases. Typical examples can be taken from the Kenya, Rwanda and Tanzania markets. First, the results show that it takes time for spatial effects to influence current market prices (most significant effects are those from two-time back from the current prices). Second, the results also demonstrate that the effects of price variations in one market to price variations in the other markets are high with spatial effects than those estimated without spatial effects. This suggests that price volatility and transmission are more predictable in prices with spatial effects than in those without spatial effects. If market c and market k are cereal markets in EAC in two different states, this suggest that cereal market efficiencies across EAC decline with an increment increase in the number of markets between market c and market k. Our results show that if market c and market k are neighbor and there is no other market between them and that they trade cereals with each other, their level of integration increases and price transmission between them results in low cereal price volatility and high cereal market efficiency. However, if market c and market k have to trade cereals with each other and there are n markets to connect them, their level of integration decreases with an increment increase in the number of connecting markets and the price transmission between them results in high and significant volatility and cereal market inefficiency. Price volatility and market inefficiency resulting from distance between one market and another and the related price transmission, have harmful effects on cereal market efficiency and welfare.

Cereal price volatility and transmission are linked to, first market integration and separation and second to cereal demand and supply behavior. As in our study, we are considering cereal tradability among EAC member states, if the markets to trade cereals each others are neighbors their level of integration increases and cereal price variations that may result on how those markets are trading each others are low, hence cereals market efficiency is increased at each of those markets. However, if the markets to trade cereals each others are not neighbors their level of separations increases and prices variations that may result on how those markets are trading each others are high, hence cereal market inefficiency is increased at each of those markets as the results of how markets connecting those markets to trade each other influence the price.

Nonetheless, cereal demand and supply behavior react on cereal price volatility and transmission in two ways. First, when demand for cereals is higher than their supply, cereal prices also increase. In the short-term this attracts new investors to cereal production to take advantage of the high prices. The opposite leads to low cereal prices and in the short-term, inventors leave the production of cereals and start producing other commodities whose prices are higher. However, in the long-term, cereal demand and supply adjusts as cereal prices adjust to return to their equilibrium. Therefore, cereal prices are subjected to variations between the short and the long terms till an equilibrium is attained in the long term. Second, as we also consider the effects of cereal price transmission from one market to another, when domestic cereal demand is greater than domestic cereal supply, cereal imports increase to complement the gap between domestic demand and supply. In this situation the prices of cereals that are domestically produced have to adjust to the prices of imported cereals.

When the prices of imported cereals are higher than those of the domestically produced cereals, while adjusting for this difference in the short-term, the prices of imported cereals pull the prices of domestically produced cereals higher and the prices of cereals in the long-term is set at a high level. However, when the prices of imported cereals are lower than those of domestically produced cereals, while adjusting for this difference in the short-term, the prices of imported cereals push down the prices of domestically produced cereals and the prices of cereals in the long-term is set at a low level. On the other hand, when domestic cereal demand is lower than domestic cereal supply, cereal exports increase to trade cereal surpluses. In this situation the prices of cereals that are domestically produced have to adjust to the prices of cereals in the world market.

When the prices of cereals in the world market are higher than those of domestically produced cereals, while adjusting for this difference in the short-term, the prices of cereals in the world market pull the prices of cereals in the domestic market higher and the prices of cereals in the long-term are set at a high level. And when the prices of cereals in the world market are lower than those in the domestic market, while adjusting for this difference in the short-term, the prices of cereals in the world market push down the prices of cereals in the domestic market and the prices of cereals in the long-term are set at a low level. Therefore, disequilibrium between domestic cereal demand and cereal supply in a country also results in disturbing the equilibrium among domestic cereal availability, imports and exports which lead to cereal price variations which adjust in the short-term to reach an equilibrium in the long term.

As food access plays an important role in ensuring food security and thus improved social welfare in a country, food prices in one of the most sited determinants of food access. Therefore, variations in food market prices are linked to instability in food security (Diaz-Bonilla and Ron 2010; FAO 2006, 2011; Ivanic and Martin 2008).

Our results from the impulse-response functions show that a one unit shock in one cereal market creates persistence and positive variations in cereal prices in that market and in the other markets as well. In addition, the results of the variance decomposition demonstrate that both in the short and long-term, cereal price variations caused by a shock in the prices of cereals in one market create strong variations that reverberate in the prices of cereals in the other EAC markets. As we consider each member of EAC as a market our findings show that the prices of cereals across EAC are spatially interconnected. On the one hand, high cereal prices in one market have a pull-up effect on the prices of cereals in the other markets. With the EAC market integration, an increase in cereal prices in one country leads to high cereal prices in other EAC countries throughout the intra-imports of cereals. This is because EAC member states try to trade cereals with other EAC members where they get high prices, which in the short-term results in cereal price variations across EAC. Cereal price variations continue with cereal price adjustments in all markets (Burundi, Kenya, Rwanda, Uganda and Tanzania) until a new cereal price is attained to return to an equilibrium. In this situation welfare across EAC member states is negatively affected because a surge in cereal prices will reduce households' purchasing power and households' food security will get worse. On the other hand, a sharp decline in the prices of cereals in one country has a push-down effect on the prices of cereals in the other markets. In this situation, welfare across EAC member states improves and households' food security gets better because their purchasing power increases their level of market access.

However, both the situations, with pull-up and push-down effects on cereal prices increase uncertainties in cereal prices as in all the markets cereal prices are subjected to adjustments in the short term to reach new cereal equilibrium prices in the long-term. For this, large and unexpected variations in cereal prices will risk the welfare of cereal consumers and producers in EAC. First, as the biggest proportion of food consumed by households among EAC member states is sourced from the market, unpredictable cereal price variations negatively affect the food security of a large proportion of the population. Second, when cereal price uncertainty increases, the poor and risk-averse invest less and use fewer inputs making them remain in poverty and this threatens the welfare of both cereal producers and consumers.

6 Conclusion

Our paper adopted and explained the application of PVAR and the SPVAR models to econometrically analyze food price volatility and transmission across EAC's member countries. Our main results suggest that it takes time for spatial effects to influence current cereal prices in EAC markets. We uncovered that cereal price volatility and transmission across EAC are more predictable in prices with spatial effects than in those without spatial effects. Further, the results of our paper also show that a one unit shock in one cereal market in EAC creates persistent and positive cereal price variations in that and in other markets; the only exceptions were observed when Tanzania was taken as impulse in only cereal prices without spatial effects and when the Rwandan cereal market was taken as impulse in only cereal prices with spatial effects. Moreover, our paper also shows that price variations caused by a one unit shock in the prices of cereals in one market create strong variations that reverberate in the prices of cereals both in the short and long term in the other markets across EAC.

It is important for policymakers to recognize the relationship among different prices of cereals across different countries, because they provide new thoughts for an analysis of food security. Therefore, two policy implications flow from our paper. One, since there is both a short-term and a long-term relationship among cereal prices across EAC, agricultural policies should focus on ensuring cereal yield stability and enhancing regional cereal distribution systems to stabilize cereal prices and reduce cereal market inefficiencies across EAC in particular and ensure and improve regional cereal access in general. Two, as the main results of this paper show that the spatial distribution of markets contributes to cereal price volatility and transmission across the region, trade policies should be formulated considering the gains of trading with near-neighboring markets. This may be taken into consideration in order to avoid delayed spatial effects on price volatility and transmission from which when market k is not a neighbor of market c the delayed spatial effects depend on the number of neighboring markets between market k and market c and the price prevailing in those markets.

References

African Development Bank (AfDB) (2016). *Feed Africa: Strategy for Agricultural Transformation in Africa 2016–2025*. Abidjan: African Development Bank Group.

Beenstock, M. and D. Felsenstein (2007). Spatial Vector Autoregressions. *Spatial Economic Analysis*, 2(2): 167–196.

Canova, F. and M. Ciccarelli (2013). 'Panel Vector Autoregressive Models: A Survey', in L.K. Thomas B. Fomby, and A. Murphy (eds.), *VAR Models in Macroeconomics: New Developments and Applications: Essays in Honor of Christopher A. Sims*. Bingley: Emerald Group Publishing Limited, pp. 205–246.

Diaz-Bonilla, E. and J. Ron (2010). *Food Security, Price Volatility and Trade*. ICTSD Program on Agricultural Trade and Sustainable Development, International Centre for Trade and Sustainable Development, Geneva, Switzerland.

FAO (2006). *Food Security*. Rome: Food and Agricultural Organization, United Nations.

FAO (2011). *The State of Food Insecurity in the World: How Does International Price Volatility Affect Domestic Economies and Food Security?* Rome: Food and Agricultural Organization.

Ivanic, M. and W. Martin (2008). Implications of Higher Global Food Prices for Poverty in Low-Income Countries. *Agricultural Economics*, 39: 405–416.

Karanja, M.A., A. Kuyvenhoven, and H.A.J. Moll (2003). Economic Reforms and Evolution of Producer Prices in Kenya: An ARCH-M Approach. *African Development Review*, 15(2–3): 271–296.

Konandreas, P., R. Sharma, and A. Costantino (2015). *Food Security in the East African Community: Impact of Regional Integration Under Customs Union and Common Market Policies*. IBF International Consulting.

LeSage, P.J. (1998). *Spatial Econometrics*. University of Toledo.

Maître d' Hôtel, E., T. Le Cotty, and T. Jayne (2013). Trade Policy Inconsistency and Maize Price Volatility: An ARCH Approach in Kenya. *African Development Review*, 25(4): 607–620.

Mutl, J. (2009). *Panel VAR Models with Spatial Dependence*. Vienna: Institute of Advanced Studies.

Pesaran, M.H. (2007). A Simple Panel Unit Root Test in the Presence of Cross-Section Dependence. *Journal of Applied Econometrics*, 22(2): 265–312.

Author Index

Abadi, B.M. 97
Abbas, M. 323
Abdoul, G. 64, 66
Abdu, M. 332
Abramovitz, M. 206, 209
Acemoglu, D. 1, 20, 143, 150, 162, 200, 204, 238, 240, 250
Achtenhagen, L. 3
Adamu, I. 332
Adamu, P.A. 153
Addison, T. 30
Adebisi, S.O. 332
Adenutsi, D.E. 128
Adolfo, B. 158
Adu, G. 153
Agarwal, J. 58, 60
Aghion, P. 152, 224
Agosin, M. 126
Agrawal, G. 19, 97, 103, 331
Ahmed, A. 62
Ahortor, C.R.K. 128
Aitken, B.J. 224
Akcigit, U. 224
Akinlo, A.E. 153
Alege, P. 19, 24, 97, 102
Alemayehu, G. 4, 202
Alfaro, L. 35, 155
Ali, A. 125, 127, 135
Allen, F. 152
Almfraji, M. 125
Almsafir, K.M. 125
Al-Yousif, Y.K. 155
Amin, M. 264
Ancharaz, V. 80
Anderson, J. 20
Anderson, T.W. 108, 131
Andrianova, S. 155

Author Index

Ang, J.B. 35
Annette, K. 158
Anyanwu, J. 62, 64, 65, 67
Anyanwu, J.C. 96
Apergis, N. 102
Arcand, J.L. 154
Arellano, M. 23, 44, 107, 108, 115, 131–133, 212, 239, 243
Arestis, P. 155
Arnold, J. 264
Arogundade, K.K. 332
Artelaris, P. 200
Arvanitidis, P. 200
Asiedu, E. 30, 62–66, 80, 81
Azman-Saini, W. 156

Babayo, H. 332
Bacchetta, P. 152
Baek, C. 265
Baharumshah, A.Z. 326
Baklouti, N. 103
Bala, U. 239, 240
Balassa, B. 291
Balasubramanyam, M.S. 101
Bane, J. 6
Baptist, S. 263
Baran, P. 61
Barro, R. 26, 238, 239
Barış-Tekin, R. 331
Basemera, S. 103
Basu, A. 63
Basu, P. 332
Bates, R.H. 2
Battese, G.E. 267
Bauer, P.T. 127
Baum, C. 212

Baylie, F. 8
Bbaale, E. 103
Beck, T. 150, 154, 180
Becker, G.S. 237
Beddies, C. 329
Beenstock, M. 351
Bekere, B. 4
Belshaw, D. 2
Bencivenga, V.R. 152
Bende-Nabende, A. 66
Benhabib, J. 211, 238
Benhane, K. 5, 51
Berkes, E. 154
Bersisa, M. 4
Beugelsdijk, R.S. 19, 99
Bhalla-Surjit, S. 328
Bhandari, R. 129
Bhargava, A. 238, 240
Binns, T. 2
Bitros, G.C. 218
Blalock, G. 64, 65
Blundell, R. 23, 32, 44, 47, 108, 132, 212, 213
Bolton, P. 153
Bond, S. 23, 32, 44, 47, 107, 108, 131–133, 171, 212, 213, 239, 243
Borensztein, E.J. 96, 102, 331
Borojo, D.G. 239–241
Bosworth, B.P. 205
Boujelbene, Y. 103
Bover, O. 23, 132, 133, 212
Boyd, J.H. 152
Bozoki, E. 150
Breitung, J. 334
Brixiova, Z. 68, 72
Brundin, E. 3
Buckley, P. 59, 60, 99

Author Index 375

Burnside, C. 127, 130, 131, 135
Busse, M. 320

Calderón, C. 154, 184
Canova, F. 351
Carkovic, M. 21, 35
Carletti, E. 152
Casson, M. 60, 99
Catrinescu, N. 127, 130
Caves, E.R. 224
Caves, R. 58, 59
Cecchetti, S.G. 154
Chaibi, A. 161
Chakraborti, L. 201
Chakraborty, C. 332
Chami, R. 135
Chanda, A. 35, 155
Chatterji, M. 322
Chenery, H. 127
Chika, O.G. 30
Chitonge, H. 2
Choi, G.G. 265
Chow, K.H. 263
Christian, S. 158
Christopoulos, D. 325
Christopoulos, D.K. 150, 153
Christy, R. 64, 65
Chuah, K.P. 291
Chu, C.S.J. 334
Chudik, A. 171, 172, 185
Chuoudhri, U.E. 291
Ciccarelli, M. 351
Cleeve, E. 64, 65
Coase, R. 59
Coe, T.D. 326
Cojocaru, L. 150
Colantonio, E. 239, 240

Collier, P. 71
Collins, S.M. 205
Coricelli, F. 154
Coskun, Y. 155
Costa, R. 264, 281
Costantino, A. 345
Coviello, D. 33
Curvo-Cazurra, A. 143

Daghighiasli, A. 240
Daly, S. 161
Daniel, P. 321
Daniele, V. 227
Daniels, J.D. 321
Dastidar, S.G. 322
Davis, R. 30
Dearden, L. 264
De Gregorio, J. 152, 154, 290, 291, 293
De Groote, T. 171
Degryse, H. 154, 180
Deidda, L. 154
Demelew, T.Z. 97, 117
De Mello, L.R. 20, 24, 102, 126, 224
Demetriades, P.O. 150
Denisia, V. 99
Denton, F.T. 329
Desai, S. 150
Dethier, J. 264
Devarajan, S. 206, 216, 224
Devereux, M.B. 152
Dharmendra, D. 129
Dhoro, N. 326
Diana, A. 158
Diaz-Bonilla, E. 368
Diouf, M.A. 210

Ditzen, J. 177, 179
Dixon, A. 2
Dollar, D. 32, 127, 130, 131, 135, 264
Donaubauer, J. 155
Dong, Z. 150
Dreher, A. 159
Driffield, N. 126, 128–130, 135
Drine, I. 289, 291
Ductor, L. 155
Dunning, J.H. 99
Dupasquier, C. 66
Durlauf, S. 206, 216
Duval, R. 301, 307, 312, 328

Easterly, W. 127, 137, 200, 201, 206, 215, 327
Eberhardt, M. 171
Edgerton, D.L. 165
Eduardo, L. 328
Edwards, S. 204, 322
Effiong, E. 162
Egbetunde, T. 153
Egert, B. 292, 308
Eggoh, J. 241, 250
Ehrenfeld, D. 127
Eifert, B. 264
Ekanayake, E.M. 128
Elbadawi, I. 81
Engle, R.E. 109
Engle, R.F. 168
Eravwoke, K.E. 332
Eris, M. 301, 307, 312, 328
Ershad-Hussain, M. 330
Esfahani, H.S. 326
Evelyn-Ndidi, D. 329, 330

Farooq, M. 324
Fattouh, B. 154
Fedderke, J.W. 24
Federico, S. 328
Felsenstein, D. 351
Fidrmuc, J. 150, 154
Findlay, R. 224
Fischer, S. 328
Fleisher, B. 240
Folorunso, S.A. 332
Fontaine, T. 209
Fosu, A.K. 200, 202, 205
Frazer, G. 264
Frey, B. 64, 65, 79, 81
Friedman, M. 84, 153
Fullenkamp, C. 135
Furceri, D. 328

Gaiha, R. 125, 127, 135
Gai, P. 152
Gala, P. 328
Galor, O. 152
Gebrehiwot, K.G. 239
Geda, A. 57–59, 63, 73, 76, 77
Gelb, A. 264
Genius, M. 291
Gennaioli, N. 152
Gholami, R. 30
Ghosh, S. 150, 154
Ghura, D. 218, 329
Gillman, M. 39
Giuliano, P. 127, 130, 131, 142
Gluzmann, P. 328
Goldsmith, R.W. 153
Goodwin, B. 218

Author Index

Granger, C.W.J. 109, 120, 168, 240
Grechyna, D. 155
Greenwood, J. 152
Grossman, G.M. 326
Gubler, M. 291
Gui-Diby, S.L. 126, 132
Guidotti, P.E. 154
Gunning, J.W. 200
Guo, K. 150
Gutema, G. 5
Gwaindepi, C. 326
Gyan, P. 129
Gyimah-Brempong, K. 63, 66, 238, 240, 241, 243, 250

Habyarimana, J.B. 8
Haddad, M. 35
Hadji-Michael, T. 329
Hadri, K. 109, 113
Haider, A. 291
Hailu, Y.G. 103
Halkides, M. 128
Hall, R.E. 204
Hallword-Driemeier, M. 264
Hansen, L.P. 32, 34, 37, 41, 43, 44, 107, 108, 114, 213, 217, 219–221, 223, 227, 334
Haque, M. 330
Harding, A. 264
Harris, M.N. 39
Harrison, A.E. 224
Harrison, P. 152
Hartwig, J. 240, 250
Hassan, M.K. 150, 153
Hassan, S. 102
Havranek, T. 150
Helleiner, G. 61

Helpman, E. 326
Hendry, D. 77
Hermes, N. 155
Herzer, D. 102, 126, 130, 331
Heshmati, A. 1, 3, 7, 30, 210, 238, 239, 241, 247, 250, 263, 266, 267
Hirn, M. 264
Hisali, E. 103
Hjalmarsson, L. 267
Hoffman, S.D. 150
Hook Law, S. 150
Horvath, R. 290, 299
Houeninvob, H. 241, 250
Howitt, A.P. 224
Howitt, P. 152
Hsiao, C. 108, 131
Huang, D. 322
Huang, H.C. 154, 184
Huang, L. 240
Huilee, C. 324
Hussein, K.A. 150
Hymer, S. 58, 59

Ibrahim, M.H. 156
Ibrahim Kabiru Maji, K.I. 239, 240, 250
Ilgun, E.K. 331
Im, K.S. 334
Imai, K. 125, 127, 135
Isaksson, A. 205
Islam, N. 39, 238, 239
Islam, R. 33
Ismail, N.W. 20
Itagaki, Y. 69
Ivanic, M. 368
Iyoha, A.M. 320

Jabeen, S. 291
Jafari, Y. 150
Jahjab, S. 135
Jamison, D.T. 238, 240
Jappelli, T. 153
Javid, A. 324
Jayne, T. 345
Jhingan, M.L. 329
Jibir, A. 332
Johansen, S. 76, 77, 115
Johnson, O.E.G. 2
Johnson, P. 216
Johnson, S.H. 150
Jones, C. 126, 128–130, 135
Jorgenson, D. 58
Jovanovic, B. 152
Jung, W. 324

Kahn, M.S. 291
Kahsai, M.S. 103
Kaicker, N. 125, 127, 135
Kalemi-Ozcan, S. 35, 155
Kaliappan, S.R. 20
Kamara, Y.U. 19
Kamarudinb, N. 267
Kaminsky, G.L. 154
Kang, J.W. 265
Kapadia, S. 152
Karabarbounis, L. 215
Karanja, M.A. 345
Kargbo, S.M. 153
Katsiaryna, S. 158
Khan, I. 125
Khan, M. 150
Khan, M.S. 150

Khan, S. 155
Kharroubi, E. 154
Kim, J. 156
Kim, T.Y. 1
Kinda, T. 264
Kindleberger, C. 58
King, R. 225
Kinyondo, M. 98
Kipyego, N. 260
Klasen, S. 102, 126, 331
Klenow, P.J. 206, 227
Kneer, C. 154
Knowles, S. 239, 241, 247
Koch, J. 331
Konandreas, P. 345
Königer, J. 320
Kosack, S. 129, 131
Kraay, A. 32
Krasniqi, B.A. 150
Krishna, S. 63
Krugell, H. 66
Krugman, P. 59, 62, 118, 218
Kuyvenhoven, A. 345

Lamine, K.M. 19
Lau, L.J. 238
Law, S.H. 156
Lawrence, R.Z. 326
Le Cotty, T. 345
Le, T.H. 156
Lee, C. 322
Lee, C.C. 154
Lee, J.W. 26, 96, 211, 238
Lee, J.-D. 265
Lee, M. 156
Lee, S.Y. 30

LeMay-Boucher, P. 171
Lensink, R. 155
León-Ledesma, M.A. 161
LeSage, P.J. 351
Levin, A. 334
Levine, R. 21, 35, 150, 152, 154, 215, 225, 238, 322
Levinsohn, J. 205
Lewis, A.W. 329
Li, H. 240
Li, X. 26
Lien, D. 30
Lijane, L. 201
Lim, H. 326
Lin, C.F. 334
Lin, S.C. 154
Lin, Y. 72
Liu, L. 154, 184
Liu, X. 26, 326
Livingstone, I. 2
Loayza, N. 150
Loening, J. 264
Loko, B. 210
Lu, X. 150
Lucas, R.E. 105, 126, 154
Luintel, K.B. 150
Lury, D.A. 2
Lydie, T. 62

Maasoumi, E. 1
MacDonald, R. 291
Machado, R. 126
Maddala, G.S. 165, 334
Magdoff, H. 61, 62
Maître d' Hôtel, E. 345
Malik, W.S. 291

Mankiw, N. 160, 241
Marani, U. 227
Marbuah, G. 153
Marianacci, R. 239, 240
Markowska, M. 3
Marrewijk, C. 322
Marshall, P. 324
Martin, C. 158
Martin, W. 368
Masnoon, M. 20
Masso, J. 267
Masten, A.B. 154
Masten, I. 154
Matloob, P. 127, 130
Mattoo, A. 264
Mattoscio, N. 239, 240
Mátyás, L. 39
Mauer, L. 79
Mayer, D. 240, 250
Mazumdar, J. 326
McAdam, P. 161
McDonald, S. 238, 239, 241
McKinnon, R.I. 226
McNabb, K. 171
Mendonca, M. 80
Mengistae, T. 264
Mensah, J.T. 153
Menyah, K. 150
Mhlanga, N. 64, 65
Michael, Y. 4, 6
Michaely, M. 323
Mileva, E. 47
Millard, S. 152
Miller, J.B. 150
Miller, S.M. 39, 205, 292
Mirakhor, A. 156
Mishra, P.K. 326
Mishra, S. 240, 250

Mody, A. 47, 79
Mohaddes, K. 172, 185
Mohamed, S. 64, 65
Mohammadi, T. 240
Mohan, S. 322
Moll, H.A.J. 345
Morales, R. 77
Morisset, J. 63
Morrissey, O. 130
Mujahid, N. 329
Murray, C.J.L. 238, 240
Murshid, A.P. 47
Musara, M. 326
Mutenyo, J. 103
Mutl, J. 351
Mwega, F. 81

Nachega, J.C. 209
Nagler, P. 263
Narayan, P.K. 240, 250
Narayan, S. 240, 250
Narciso, G. 264
Naudé, W. 263
Nazlioglu, S. 150
Ndambendia, H. 129
Ndikumana, L. 72
Ndudu, B.J. 2
Ndulu, B.J. 71
Neiman, B. 215
Nel, E. 2
Nelson, C.R. 167
Nelson, R.R. 206
Neumayer, E. 155
Newey, W.K. 169
Ng, A. 156
Nickell, S. 41, 47

Nikas, C. 332
Njoupouognigni, M. 129
Njuguna, N. 76
Njuguna, N.S. 323
Nkikabahizi, F. 8
Nkunzimana, T. 8, 345
Nondo, C. 103
Nonnenberg, M 80
Nowak-Lehmann, F. 102, 126, 331
Nung-Huang, B. 324
Nunnekamp, P. 64, 155
Nwaogu, U. 128, 137

Obstfeld, M. 118, 152
O'Connell, S.A. 2
Odedokun, M.O. 150, 153
Odero, W.O. 260
Ogundipe, A.A. 19, 24, 40, 97, 102
Ogundipe, O.M. 40
Oh, I. 265
Ohlin, B. 58
Ojeaga, P. 40
Okello, J.J. 263
Oketch, M.O. 240
Okon, J.U. 332
Olley, S.G. 205
Oluwakayode, E.F. 332
Omri, A. 161
Onyeiwu, S. 64–66, 110
Orhan, M. 331
Osakwe, P. 66
Osvaldo, S. 20
Otieno, D.J. 263
Owen, D. 239, 241, 247
Oyatoye, A. 332
Ozturk, I. 153

Pack, H. 206, 216, 224
Pagano, M. 153
Pake, A. 205
Panas, E.E. 218
Panizza, U. 154
Papa, N. 158
Park, S. 326
Pedroni, P. 109, 165, 168, 169, 173, 175, 178, 185
Pelinescu, E. 239
Peluso, S. 103
Perez, A. 152
Persyn, D. 169, 178
Pesaran, H. 82, 115, 116, 165, 167, 168, 171–175, 177, 179, 183, 185, 354
Petrakos, G. 200
Petrin, A. 205
Philippon, T. 153
Piketty, T. 215
Plane, P. 264
Plosser, C.R. 167
Porter, M. 61, 69, 72, 79
Prescott, E.C. 152, 203
Prichett, L. 227

Qadri, F.S. 239, 240
Quillin, B. 127, 130

Radebaugh, H. 321
Raei, F. 77
Rafindadi, A.A. 153
Rafique, N. 20
Rahman, M.M. 153, 161
Raissi, M. 172
Rajaguru, G. 326
Rajan, R.G. 224
Ramachandran, V. 201
Ramirez, M.D. 24
Ramirez-Pacillias, M. 3
Ran, B. 158
Ranciere, R. 152, 153, 180
Rani, R.M. 267
Rashid, S. 326
Rault, C. 161
Reagle, D. 332
Reed, H. 264
Reenen, J.V. 264
Reeves, W.A. 260
Reinhart, C.M. 153
Renelt, D. 238, 322
Reppas, P. 325
Richter, M. 150
Riddel, R.C. 126
Riezman, G.R. 326
Rijkers, B. 264, 281
Rivera-Batiz, F.L. 325
Rizinde, T. 8, 319
Roberts, J. 238, 239, 241
Robinson, J. 162
Robson, P. 2
Rodriguez, F. 322
Rodríguez-Clare, A. 206, 227
Rodríguez-Pose, A. 150
Rodrik, D. 162, 202, 322, 327
Rogoff, K. 152
Rojid, S. 62
Romer, P. 24, 26, 206, 237–239
Romilly, P. 326
Romm, A.T. 24
Rommerskirchen, C. 171

Author Index

Ron, J. 368
Roodman, D. 32, 47, 132, 213, 227
Root, E. 62
Rostow, W. 69
Rousseau, P.L. 153, 154
Ruiz-Arranz, M. 127, 130, 142
Ryan, M. 128, 137

Sachs, J. 238
Sahay, R. 158
Saint-Paul, G. 152
Sala, H. 19, 101, 102, 118
Sala-i-Martin, X. 1
Saliola, F. 264, 281
Salisu Ibrahim Waziri, I.S. 239
Salvatore, D. 320
Samargandi, N. 150, 154
Sanchez, B. 153
Sanchez, J.M. 152
Santomero, A.M. 153
Santos, T. 153
Saqib, N. 20
Sarmidi, T. 150
Sauiana, M.S. 267
Sax, C. 291
Sayek, S. 35
Scaperlanda, A. 79
Schaffer, M.E. 212
Scheinkman, J.A. 153
Schneider, F. 64, 65, 79, 81
Schultz, T.W. 237
Schwartz, A.J. 153
Seater, J.J. 153
Seetanah, B. 62
Seker, M. 264
Senhadji, A.S. 150
Serletis, A. 326

Seven, U. 155
Seyed, R. 158
Shah, A.M. 125
Shahbaz, M. 155, 241
Shahid, M. 328
Sharma, R. 345
Shen, C.H. 154
Shin, Y. 82
Shiu, A. 210
Shleifer, A. 152
Shrestha, H. 66, 110
Shuaib, I.M. 329
Sidiropoulos, M. 65
Silva, J.I. 264
Singh, N. 150, 154
Singleton, K.J. 334
Slacík, T. 322
Smith, B.D. 152
Smith, G.W. 152
Smith, R. 82
Smith, R.P. 165
Smith, S.C. 96
Söderbom, M. 264
Solomon, W.D. 99
Solow, R.M. 26, 105, 209
Soludo, C.C. 2
Song, H. 326
Sossoub, G. 241
Speigel, M. 238
Spencer, B.G. 329
Spiegel, M.M. 211
Ssozi, J. 218
Starr, R.M. 152
Steiner, K. 322
Stiglitz, J.E. 152
Stillman, S. 212
Stolper, W.F. 324
Stoneman, C. 20
Straub, S. 264

Strout, A. 127
Su, B. 263
Subramanian, A. 162, 224
Sukar, A. 102
Sulaiman, C. 239, 240
Suleiman, N.N. 20
Summers, P.M. 326
Sunday A. 62
Sussman, O. 152
Svirydzenka, K. 151
Sweezy, P. 61

Tahir, M. 125
Tahir, M.I. 155
Tang, D. 331
Tausch, A. 1
Teal, F. 263, 264
Tekin, R.B. 324
Temple, J. 206
Thangavelu, S.M. 326
Theodoridis, K. 150
Thorbecke, W. 327
Tijani, A.B. 239
Tobin, J. 129, 131, 132
Todaro, M.P. 96, 98
Trivin, P. 19, 101, 102, 118
Tsionas, E.G. 150
Tsitouras, A. 332
Turner, P. 327
Tzilianos, E. 291
Tzouvelekas, V. 291

Uğur, A. 325
Ullah, S. 324
Upadhyay, M.P. 39, 205

Upadhyaya, K. 129
Uz Zafar, N. 329

Valeriani, E. 103
Valickova, P. 150
Veganzones-Veroudakis, M. 264
Verick, S. 79
Vernon, R. 59, 99
Victoria, J.S. 240, 250
Vishny, R. 152

Wachtel, P. 154
Waheed, A. 239, 240
Wan, G. 1
Wang, C. 152
Wang, L. 150
Wang, M. 47
Wang, S. 150
Wang, X. 150
Warner, A.M. 201, 202, 238
Wei, S. 101
Wei, Y.H. 264
Weil, D.N. 160
Weinstein, D.E. 326
Weiss, A. 152
West, K.D. 169
Westerlund, J. 165, 169, 175, 178
Wheeler, D. 79
Whiteman, C.R. 326
Willman, A. 161
Wilson, M. 238, 240
Windmeijer, F. 132
Wolde-Rufael, Y. 150
Wolf, H. 293
Wolgin, J. 201

Wooldridge, J.M. 107
Wörz, J. 322
Wu, S. 165, 334

Xiaodong, L. 263

Yimer, A. 4
Ying, L. 263
Yuan, G. 158
Yu, J.S. 150
Yushi, J. 239, 240

Zaman, B. 324
Zeira, J. 153
Zekarias, S.M. 97, 104
Zerfu, D. 76
Zerihun, T. 161
Zervos, S. 150, 153
Zervos, S.J. 322
Zhang, C. 240
Zhang, J. 150
Zhao, Q. 240
Zhuang, L. 240
Zhu, Y. 263
Zsohar, P. 107
Zucman, G. 215
Zwinkels, R. 19, 99

Subject Index

African Development Bank 68, 347
Agricultural economics 259
Agricultural policies 9, 346, 347, 370
Agricultural technologies 347
Akaike Information Criterion 178
Alleviating poverty 3
Arellano-bond dynamic panel estimator 107
Arellano-bond test 108
Asymmetric information 152
Autocorrelation 18, 32, 41, 44, 108, 114, 115, 211, 213, 227
Autoregressive Distributed Lag 77, 78

Balanced panel data 230

Balance of payments 20, 38, 96, 110, 328, 330, 332
Balance of trade 7, 8, 319, 321, 322, 333, 338
Balassa effect 8
Balassa hypothesis 289–292, 294, 295, 300, 304, 307, 309
Balassa–samuelson effect 290
Balassa term 290, 292–294, 299
Best-practice technologies 226
Between-effects estimator 46
Bi-directional causality 332
Bi-directional relationship 239, 242
Breusch-Pagan LM test 334, 336

Capital-intensive technology 275
Capital stock 20, 23, 100, 130, 159, 163, 174–176, 206, 215, 266, 331

Subject Index

Cereal price volatility and transmission 346, 367, 370
Chi-square 84, 297, 301, 334, 336
Classical capital movement 58
Classical international trade theory 101
Cobb-Douglas production function 24, 105, 161, 206, 207, 229
Common Correlated Effects 171, 180–182, 185
Comprehensive Meta-Analysis 300
Constant Elasticity of Substitution 205, 206
Constant Returns to Scale 162, 207, 208, 229
Country Risk Guide 104
Cross-Sectional Augmented Dickey-Fuller 165, 167
Cross-sectional dependence 6, 55, 56, 68, 82, 108, 115, 116, 151, 162, 165, 166, 168, 169, 171, 173–175, 177, 179–181, 183, 185, 337

Demographic characteristics 19, 126
Dependent variable 23, 24, 28, 33, 35, 41, 50, 83, 106, 107, 110, 117, 133, 136, 138, 140, 141, 157, 164, 166, 169, 171, 172, 211, 221, 229, 243, 244, 248, 249, 252, 254, 270, 291, 293, 294, 299, 305, 323, 357–359
Developing countries 2–4, 6, 20, 21, 26, 64, 65, 95, 96, 100–103, 125–129, 135, 137, 153–155, 201, 202, 240, 250, 265, 323, 326, 328, 330, 332
Developing nations 126, 241, 322
Developing world 55, 100, 127, 201
Differenced equation 32
Differenced residuals 108
Difference-GMM estimator 131, 132
Divisia index 208, 266
Domestic investments 19, 20, 25, 38, 39, 47, 49, 50, 79, 82, 102, 126, 130, 211, 213, 329, 331
Dummy variable 24, 26, 30, 40, 271, 320, 332, 333, 338, 357
Dynamic common correlated effect 182
Dynamic cross-country growth 106
Dynamic heterogeneity 6
Dynamic model 35, 107, 227
Dynamic ordinary least squares 20
Dynamic panel data estimation 165
Dynamic panel data model 6, 44, 204, 210, 230
Dynamic panel regression model 23
Dynamic system GMM 4–7, 18, 28, 32, 66, 107, 120, 239, 254
Dynamic theory of production 68, 69

East African Community 8, 319, 321, 345
Econometric analysis 105, 352
Econometric model 165
Economic growth 1–12, 18–21, 23, 24, 26, 27, 30, 35, 38–40, 47,

49, 50, 66, 96, 97, 101–105, 107, 110–112, 117–121, 125–132, 135, 137, 142–144, 149–156, 160–162, 169, 173, 175, 177, 180, 184–186, 199–201, 204, 205, 215, 224, 225, 227, 237–242, 248–251, 253–255, 259, 260, 282, 290–292, 295, 320–333, 338
Economies of scale 79, 98, 186, 225, 320
Endogenity problem 107
Endogenous growth 24, 26, 101, 105, 126, 151, 206, 237, 326
Endogenous regressor 131, 132, 243, 244
Endogenous variable 79
Enterprise Survey 7, 270, 282, 283
Era of globalization 5, 149
Error-correction-based test 165
Error Correction Term 83, 110, 115
External trade 24

Factor driven 74, 83, 86
FDI-productivity 24, 80, 105, 199, 200, 215, 216, 220, 221, 224, 230
Female-headed enterprises 264
Female-owned enterprises 263
Financial crisis 9, 10, 18, 21, 113, 260
Financial development 4–6, 9, 24, 26, 27, 29, 39, 50, 149–164, 169, 174–177, 179–182, 184–186, 204, 210, 211, 225, 226, 228

Financial-growth 39, 50, 142, 150, 151, 154, 155, 180
First Difference Generalized Method of Moment 155
First-generation panel unit root test 165
First-order autocorrelation test 218
First-order contiguity matrix 355
First-order error autocorrelation 229
First-order serial correlation 108
Fixed Effects 33, 41, 103, 109, 110, 131, 222, 243, 302, 304, 308, 312, 334, 336
Fixed Effects Model 41, 82, 103, 295, 297, 303, 336
Food and Agriculture Organization 347–350, 352, 368
Food security 345, 347, 368–370
Foreign Direct Investment 4, 17, 25, 59, 99, 106, 107, 110, 114, 134, 136, 138, 140, 141, 149, 155, 157, 174, 176, 319, 332, 333
Fragile economies 74, 79, 85, 86

Generalized Least Square 243
Generalized Leontief 206
Generalized Method of Moments 23, 107, 108, 156
Globalization 5, 6, 102, 149–151, 153, 157, 159, 161–164, 169, 174–177, 179–182, 184–186
Gross Capital Formation 5, 6, 8, 27, 28, 34–36, 39, 42, 47, 49, 113, 130, 133–141, 143, 144, 210–213, 217–223, 228, 230,

246, 247, 249, 251, 255, 319, 329, 332, 333, 338
Gross Domestic Production 4, 8, 21–31, 33–38, 40, 42, 47, 49, 56, 80, 82, 86, 87, 106, 107, 110, 112, 113, 117, 126, 133, 134, 136–141, 143, 157, 159, 162, 164, 174, 176, 202, 205, 210–213, 217, 223, 225, 228, 229, 239–242, 244–249, 251–254, 259, 261, 267, 293, 319, 321, 323, 328, 333
Gross Fixed Capital Formation 45, 47, 106, 110, 119, 120, 211, 328, 329

Hansen-J statistic 32
Hausman test 8, 82, 188, 334, 336
Heterogeneity 2, 4, 18, 26, 27, 32, 151, 162–165, 167–169, 171, 179, 185, 263, 268, 283, 301
Heterogeneous panel co-integration analysis 165
Heteroscedasticity 44, 169
Homogeneity 162, 164–166, 297, 298, 301, 303, 304
Household survey 12
Human Capital 5–7, 9, 19, 23–26, 29, 34, 36–39, 42, 45, 47, 48, 63, 73, 101–103, 105–107, 111–113, 117, 118, 120, 126, 143, 144, 152, 157, 159, 161, 174–176, 199, 200, 204, 205, 210–212, 214, 216, 217, 219–222, 226–228, 230, 237–242, 244, 245, 247–255, 331

Income gap 105
Informal inspection 300
Informal sector 260
Information and Communication Technology 263
Information technology 231, 266
Infrastructure development 96, 97, 106, 111, 112, 117, 120
Institutional quality index 23–25, 29, 33, 34, 37, 40, 43, 45, 158, 159, 174, 176, 210, 211, 214, 216, 217, 219–221, 227, 228, 230
Inter-economy relationships 164
International capital flows 23
International Monetary Fund 151, 157, 160
Intra-Africa investments 57
Investment driven 82, 83, 85

J-test 32, 213

Labor factor productivity 6
Lagged dependent variables 23, 41, 185
Lagrange-Multiplier 84, 334
Lagrange Multiplier test 109, 113
Large-scale production 329
Least Developed Countries 320
Linear dynamic panel data models 41
Literacy rate 238, 239
LLC tests 334

Logarithmic form 26, 47, 280
Log-linearization 229
Long-run economic growth 6, 185, 326, 327
Long-term economic growth 225, 329
Long-term relationship 48, 98, 334, 370
Lower-middle-income 5, 150, 160, 175, 182, 184
Low-income 5, 7, 142, 150, 154, 155, 160, 164, 174, 175, 178, 182, 184, 186, 245

MacDougal model 58
Macro-econometrics 5, 185
Macroeconomic stability 6, 19, 24, 25, 67, 68, 85, 112, 126, 149, 211, 216, 218, 328
Macro-panel data 49
Manufactured exports 87
Manufactured goods 270
Marginal product 130, 205
Marginal value 35, 229, 252
Market efficiency 7, 8, 366, 367
Market Information Services 263
Mean Squared Error 364
Meta-analyses 292
Meta-regression 305
Methodological variations 298, 302
Middle East and North America 103
Middle-income countries 5, 7, 127, 129, 133, 137–139, 142, 154, 239, 245, 247, 248, 250–255
Migrant remittances 125, 129, 133
Multi-level methods 300

Multinational Corporations 20
Multinational Enterprises 21, 100
Multi-output nature 266
Multi-sectoral dataset 264
Multivariate regression 64, 65

Natural resource endowments 24, 28, 30, 63, 67, 80, 86, 149, 203
Near-neighboring markets 9, 370
Neo-classical growth models 331
Neoclassical growth theory 126
Neo-classical production function 206
Nickell bias 41
Non-agricultural 74, 87
Non-economic factors 325
Non-Governmental Organization 11
Non-stationary process 76
Non-stationary variables 168
Non-tradable goods 290
Non-tradable sector 290
Null-hypothesis 31, 227

Off-farm wage 262
Official development assistance 24, 25, 29, 125, 133, 140, 141, 212
On-job training 111
Openness to international trade 80
Ordinary Least Squares 101, 166, 177, 275, 278
Organization for Economic Co-operation and

Development 57, 75, 96, 98, 240, 250
Over-identification 32, 108, 133, 213, 227, 248
Over-valued exchange rates 328

Pairwise granger causality test 120
Panel-based vector error correction 109
Panel cointegration 4, 109
Panel Co-integration Test 168–170, 173, 175, 185, 354
Panel Granger causality test 109
Panel-level effects 41
Panel-mean-group model 165, 171
Panel model 23, 164, 171, 199
Panel stationary 334
Panel unit root test 108, 109, 113, 114, 175, 176, 334, 354
Panel Vector Autoregressive 351, 354, 355, 357–359, 369
Parametric approach 266
Parametric estimation 205
Pasaran CD and Breusch-Pagan LM tests 337
Perfect competition 58, 207
Petroleum products 39, 260
Physical capital/Physical capital formation 6, 161, 162, 200, 207, 211, 241, 242, 244, 329
Physical output 265
PMG estimator with a Common Correlated Effects Correction 165
Politically-motivated violence 158
Pooled Mean Group 165, 179, 181

Population density 346
Population growth 5, 133, 134, 137, 139, 202, 203, 240, 260, 345, 349
Poverty reduction 3, 127
Pre-crisis levels 21
Pre-estimation diagnostic tests 82
Price volatility 7–9, 345, 346, 351, 352, 366, 367, 369, 370
Principal Component Analysis 204
Probability values 291
Problematic statistical inferences 32
Product cycle 59
Productivity-determining factors 268
Productivity growth 2, 3, 6, 8, 162, 200, 201, 204, 209–211, 224, 264, 267, 290, 292, 293, 299, 308, 309, 327
Pull-up effect 369
Purchasing Power Parity 289
Push-down effect 369

Quality-augmented labor 244

Random-effects estimator 46
Random-effects model 8, 296, 297, 302–304, 308
Real exchange rate 7–9, 81, 83, 224, 289–295, 299, 300, 304, 305, 308, 309, 323, 327, 328
Research and Development 101, 237
Resource-poor 28, 30, 31, 49
Resource-rich 28, 30, 31, 40, 49

Subject Index

Sargan test 44, 114, 133, 136, 248, 249
Second-generation co-integration tests 169
Second-generation panel co-integration 169
Second-generation panel unit root 165, 167, 173, 185
Semi-elasticity parameters 164
Skilled labor force 328
Skilled workers 153
Small-scale agriculture 261
Small-scale manufacturing socioeconomic development 96, 260
Socioeconomic factors 18
Solow-Swan aggregate production 105
Solow-Swan model 209
Southern Africa Custom Union 20
Spatial Panel Vector Autoregressive 351, 355, 357–359, 369
Spillover effects 18, 20, 49, 97, 126, 155, 215, 216, 230, 237
Stable macroeconomic environment 4
Standardized effect standardized first-order 301
Standardized indicators 238
Standardized survey instruments steady-state growth 270
Steady-state income 209
Steady-state linear relationship 168
Sub-optimal low savings 153
Sub-Saharan African countries 5, 6, 66, 97, 102, 103
Sustainable Development Goal 18

Tax treatment 38
Technical efficiency 215
Three Stage Least Squares 244
Time-invariant 4, 18, 27, 32, 163, 334
Total Factor Productivity 6, 24, 39, 130, 152, 166, 199, 203, 204, 206, 207, 209, 210, 216, 262, 266, 292, 300, 324
Trade openness 19, 23, 102, 112, 118, 126, 139, 143, 144, 156, 204, 210, 228, 323, 331
Transcendental logarithmic (translog) 205
Two-Stage Least Square 131
Two-step system-GMM 213

Unbalanced growth 324
Unbalanced panel data 133
Under-developed areas 61
Under-developed financial systems under-valued currencies 216
Under-valued exchange rates 327
Undeveloped financial systems 226
Unequal variance 31
United Nations Development Program 226
Unit root test 354
Unobserved common factor 171
Unobserved factors 165
Unobserved panel-level effects 41
Upper-middle-income 5, 150, 151, 160, 164, 173, 175, 182, 184–186

Urban-biased development infrastructure 265

Vector Error Correction Model 115
Vernon's product cycle theory 59

Wald-chi-square test 46
Wald test 248, 249, 252, 254
Welfare 7, 8, 10, 12, 58, 111, 204, 265, 267, 282, 330, 367–369
Well-being 3
Well-developed financial sector 38
Well-developed financial system 27, 152
Well-established infrastructure 111
Well-functioning financial institutions 226
Well-functioning financial system 155
World Development Indicator 104, 157

CPSIA information can be obtained
at www.ICGtesting.com
Printed in the USA
LVHW04*2119200518
577859LV00012B/673/P